Politics in Mexico

Politics in Mexico

Democratic Consolidation or Decline?

Sixth Edition

RODERIC AI CAMP
Claremont McKenna College

New York   Oxford
OXFORD UNIVERSITY PRESS

Oxford University Press is a department of the University of Oxford.
It furthers the University's objective of excellence in research,
scholarship, and education by publishing worldwide.

Oxford   New York
Auckland   Cape Town   Dar es Salaam   Hong Kong   Karachi
Kuala Lumpur   Madrid   Melbourne   Mexico City   Nairobi
New Delhi   Shanghai   Taipei   Toronto

With offices in
Argentina   Austria   Brazil   Chile   Czech Republic   France   Greece
Guatemala   Hungary   Italy   Japan   Poland   Portugal   Singapore
South Korea   Switzerland   Thailand   Turkey   Ukraine   Vietnam

For titles covered by Section 112 of the US Higher Education
Opportunity Act, please visit www.oup.com/us/he for the
latest information about pricing and alternate formats.

Published by Oxford University Press
198 Madison Avenue, New York, New York 10016
http://www.oup.com

Oxford is a registered trademark of Oxford University Press

Library of Congress Cataloging-in-Publication Data

Camp, Roderic A.
  Politics in Mexico : democratic consolidation or decline? / Roderic Ai Camp,
Claremont-McKenna College. — Sixth edition.
    pages cm
  Includes bibliographical references and index.
  ISBN 978-0-19-984397-8
  1. Mexico—Politics and government.   I. Title.
JL1281.C35   2013
324.0972—dc23

2013003844

Printing number: 9 8 7 6 5 4 3 2 1

Printed in the United States of America
on acid-free paper

To Don and Elsie Maxam, Special Friends and Role Models for the Next Generation

Brief Contents

Contents

Preface

Since publishing the fifth edition of *Politics in Mexico* in October 2006, three major changes have taken place in Mexico that deserve emphasis in this new edition. First, the broad effort of Mexico to consolidate its democracy is evaluated and extensively analyzed. Indeed, the thematic focus of the 6th edition, subtitled *Democratic Consolidation or Decline?*, is on the failures and accomplishments of achieving a consolidated political system since 2000. Mexico has not been as successful as its citizens had hoped in moving beyond electoral democracy. Under President Calderón, governance has floundered, as was the case under Vicente Fox, due in part to intensive partisan divisions in the legislative branch and partisan divisions in society. In evaluating the country's efforts, I place as much emphasis on informal as well as formal structures and institutions.

I have also assessed the changing values of ordinary Mexicans and leaderships, using comprehensive, comparative surveys of the region from Vanderbilt University's Latin American Public Opinion Project (LAPOP). In each chapter's conclusion, the relevance of those findings to the goal of democratic consolidation are analyzed. I also emphasize the importance of various actors and institutions and their influence, or attempts to influence, policy outcomes. I have expanded emphasis on various groups, but especially on the impact of social movements. I believe that drug trafficking organizations have become so influential socially, politically, and economically that they deserve their own original analysis in this context. I also discuss the consequences of the 2006 election on political legitimacy and the importance of the 2009 election for understanding what took place in the 2012 presidential race, which witnessed the remarkable comeback of the Institutional Revolutionary Party. It remains to be seen how well Mexico's new president, Enrique Peña Nieto, meets his predecessors' challenges.

Second, Calderón introduced an entirely new component into Mexico's political situation by pursuing an aggressive strategy against drug cartels. This proactive strategy has serious implications for Mexico's political sovereignty at the local and regional level, its relationship with the United States, the real and perceived sense of security amongst its population, as well as social and economic implications for growth and development. Each of these is explored in great depth, both independently and in relation to other consequences. The use of numerous new tables to document citizen attitudes toward the drug-related homicides, the government's anti-drug strategy, and the degree to which the United States should be involved in Mexican efforts to destroy the cartels, are incorporated throughout the text. I have incorporated my own research on the armed forces' role against drug trafficking in Mexico, as well as the work of dozens of other authors, to evaluate all aspects of drug trafficking organizations in Mexico.

Third, the global recession introduced by the United States in 2008 has affected Mexico more significantly than any other country in the region due to the economic dependence of their trading partnership. The recession's negative impact on economic growth has hindered Mexico's ability to reduce poverty, an issue that has been addressed by the last three administrations, achieving some success toward the end of the Fox administration and into the first year of the Calderón administration. I have incorporated numerous new international statistics from the World Bank and the OECD, as well as from Mexican government agencies, which have attempted to measure Mexican levels of poverty in more sophisticated and useful ways. I have strongly emphasized this issue as a central policy concern because it is critical to informing Mexican attitudes toward democracy, social justice, and the elimination of drug cartel violence.

Finally, the findings from some two hundred studies by national and international scholars have been incorporated in this new edition. Original research from my own recent books on democratic leadership (*The Metamorphosis of Leadership in a Democratic Mexico*), on the most important cultural, economic, historical and political themes and questions (*Mexico, What Everyone Needs to Know*), and the views of thirty-two leading scholars on all aspects of Mexican development and their impact on democratic consolidation (*The Oxford Handbook of Mexican Politics*), all published by Oxford University Press since 2010. At the suggestion of several reviewers, for the first time, I have incorporated a number of personal anecdotes, experiences, and observations from more than four decades of traveling and studying in Mexico, which shed light on numerous aspects of Mexican politics. The reviewers are: James Bowen, Saint Louis University; Kenneth Greene, University of Texas at Austin; Victor J. Hinojosa, Baylor University; Claudio A. Holzner, University of Utah; Adrian P. Hull, State University of New York at Cortland; Mark A. Martinez, California State University at Bakersfield; Dag Mossige, Davidson College; and Pamela K. Starr, University of Southern California.

Acknowledgments

Anyone who has been in the business of teaching eventually writes a mental textbook, constantly revised and presented orally in a series of lectures. As teachers, however, we often dream of writing just the right book for our special interest or course. Such a book naturally incorporates our own biases and objectives. It also builds on the knowledge and experiences of dozens of other teachers. While still a teenager, I thought of being a teacher and, perhaps unusually, a college professor. Teachers throughout my life, at all levels of my education, influenced this choice. They also affected the way in which I teach, my interpersonal relationship with students, and my philosophy of learning and life. To these varied influences, I offer heartfelt thanks and hope that this work, in some small way, repays their contributions to me personally and professionally and to generations of other students.

Among those special teachers, I want to mention Thelma Roberts and Helen Weishaupt, who devoted their lives to the betterment of young children, instilling worthy values and beliefs and setting admirable personal examples, and to Mrs. Lloyd, for numerous afternoon conversations at Cambridge School. I wish to thank Ralph Corder and Don Fallis, who encouraged my natural interest in history toward a more specific interest in social studies. Sharon Williams and Richard W. Gully, my toughest high school teachers, introduced me to serious research and to the joys of investigating intellectual issues; and Inez Fallis, through four years of Spanish, prompted my continued interest in Mexico. Robert V. Edwards and Katharine Blair stressed the importance of communication, orally and in writing, helping me understand essential ingredients in the process of instruction. My most challenging professor, Dr. Bergel, during a high school program at Chapman College, opened my eyes to Western civilization and to the intellectual feast that broad interdisciplinary teaching could offer.

For his humanity, advice, and skill with the English language, I remain indebted to George Landon. As a mentor in the classroom and a model researcher, Mario Rodríguez led me to the Library of Congress and to the joys of archival research. On my arrival in Arizona, Paul Kelso took me under his wing, contributing vastly to my knowledge of Mexico and the out-of-doors, sharing a rewarding social life with his wife, Ruth. I learned more about Latin America and teaching in the demanding classrooms of George A. Brubaker and Edward J. Williams. Both convinced me of the importance of clarity, teaching writing as well as substance. Finally, Charles O. Jones and Clifton Wilson set examples in their seminars of what I hoped to achieve as an instructor.

Indirectly, I owe thanks to hundreds of students who have graced my classrooms and responded enthusiastically, sometimes less so, to my interpretations of Mexican politics. I am equally indebted to Bill Beezley, David Dent, Oscar Martínez, Steve Mumme, Kenneth Greene, Peter Ward, and Edward J. Williams, devoted teachers and scholars, who offered many helpful suggestions for this book.

Politics in Mexico

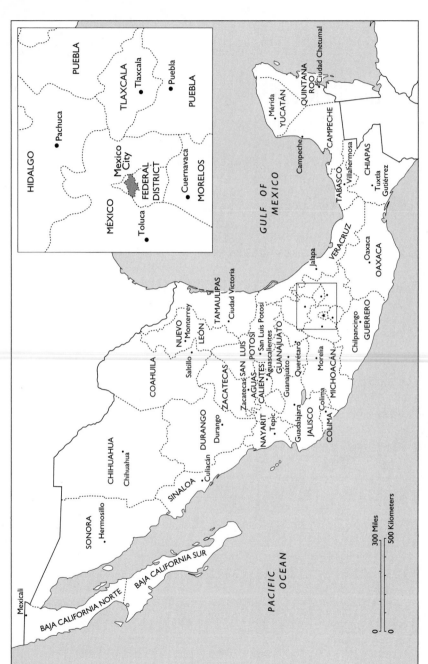

Mexico General Political Map, States and Capitals

1

Mexico in Comparative Context

At the same time, the pattern of democratization in Mexico has acquired, or produced, a series of defining features. The Mexican transition resulted from a steady, step-by-step process, one that focused essentially on national elections. As a result, there remains a good deal of unfinished business—including the quality of local (and statewide) local elections, the redefinition of civil-military relations, the impartial application of the rule of law, and the strengthening of the judiciary. The problem is not that Mexico has struggled mightily if unsuccessfully to bring about productive reforms in these areas; it is that these issues never found their way onto the transitional agenda.

PETER H. SMITH, *"Mexican Democracy in Comparative Perspective"*

An exploration of a society's politics is, by nature, all-encompassing. Political behavior and political processes are a reflection of a country's evolution, involving history, geography, values, ethnicity, religion, internal and external relationships, and much more. As social scientists, we often pursue topics of current political interest, ignoring the medley of influences from the past.

Naturally, each person tends to examine another culture's characteristics, political or otherwise, from his or her own society's perspective. This is not only a product of ethnocentrism, thinking of one's society as superior to the next person's, for which we Americans are often criticized, but also a question of familiarity. Although we often are woefully ignorant of our own society's political processes and institutions, being more familiar with the mythology than actual practice, we become accustomed to our way of doing things in our own country.[1]

I will attempt to explain Mexican politics, building on this natural proclivity to relate most comfortably to our own political customs, by drawing on implied as well as explicit comparisons with the United States. Specifically, the book will focus on Mexico's recent transformation from a

1

semiauthoritarian to a democratic electoral political model, analyzing the democratic transition in the 1990s and the democratic consolidation in the 2000s and 2010s. This comparison is further enhanced by the fact that Mexico and the United States have been joined together in a free-trade agreement since January 1994. Moreover, since 2006, the two countries have increased their collaboration on bilateral national security issues, most specifically focused on drug trafficking organizations. We also are products of a more comprehensive Western European civilization, into which other traditions are gradually making significant inroads, including those from Hispanic cultures. Some critics suggest that we have relied too exclusively on Western traditions in our education; nevertheless they are unquestionably the primary source of our political values. Thus our familiarity with political processes, if it extends at all beyond United States boundaries, is typically that of the Western European nations and England.[2] For recent immigrants, of course, that heritage is different. Again, where possible, comparisons will be made with some of these political systems, including Latin America, in order to place the Mexican experience in a larger context. Finally, Mexico is a Third World country, a category into which most countries fall, and hence its characteristics deserve to be compared with characteristics we might encounter elsewhere in the Third World.

WHY COMPARE POLITICAL SYSTEMS?

The comparison of political systems is an exciting enterprise. One reason that the study of politics in different societies and time periods has intrigued inquiring minds for generations is the central question: Which political system is best? Identifying the "best" political system, by attributes other than its merely being the one with which you are most familiar and consequently comfortable, is, of course, a subjective task. It depends largely on what you want out of your political system. One way to measure a political system's effectiveness is to observe the demands made on it and assess its ability to respond efficiently and appropriately to them.

Throughout the twentieth century, perhaps the major issue attracting the social scientist, the statesperson, and the average, educated citizen is which political system contributes most positively to economic growth and societal development. From an ideological perspective, much of international politics since World War II has focused primarily on that issue.

The two political systems most heavily analyzed since 1945 have been democratic capitalism and Soviet-style socialism. Each has its pluses and minuses, depending on individual values and perspectives. Given events in Eastern Europe and the breakup of the Soviet state, socialism is in decline. Nevertheless, socialism as a model is far from dead, nor is it likely to be in the future. Indeed, the fastest growing major economy in the world is that of China, which represents the striking hybrid model of political authoritarianism based on a collective leadership combined with rampant capitalism. Some scholars even have attempted interesting comparisons between Mexico and China.[3] It is human nature to want alternative choices in every facet of life. Politics is just one facet, even if somewhat all-encompassing. The history of humankind reveals a continual competition between alternative political models.

In short, whether one chooses democratic capitalism, authoritarian capitalism, or some other hybrid ideological alternative, societies and citizens will continue to search for the most viable political processes to bring about economic and social benefits. Because most of the earth's peoples are economically underprivileged, they want immediate results. Often, politicians from less fortunate nations seek a solution through emulating wealthier (First World) nations. Mexico's leaders and its populace are no exception to this general pattern.

One of the major issues facing Mexico's leaders is the nature of its capitalist model, and the degree to which Mexico should pursue a strategy of economic development patterned after that of the United States. Since 1988 they have sought to alter many traditional relationships between government and the private sector, increasing the influence of the private sector in an attempt to reverse Mexico's economic crisis and stimulate economic growth. In fact, Mexico received international notice in the 1990s for the level and pace of change under President Carlos Salinas de Gortari.[4] He advocated economic liberalization, which he defined as increased control of the economy by the private sector, more extensive foreign investment, and internationalization of the Mexican economy through expanded trade and formal commercial relationships with the United States and Canada. Simultaneously, Salinas advocated political liberalization, which he defined as including more citizen participation in elections, greater electoral competition, and integrity in the voting process, but in reality, he did little to implement democratic change, preferring instead to retain power in the hands of the presidency.

Salinas's successor, Ernesto Zedillo, who took office on December 1, 1994, inherited a political system in transition and an economic situation that shortly turned into a major financial and political crisis. Zedillo continued to pursue an economic liberalization strategy and increased the pace of political reforms compared to his predecessor. Strong doubts about neoliberal economic policies remained from various quarters, however, generating some nationalistic, anti–United States sentiments. Nevertheless, when he left office in 2000, President Zedillo transferred a healthy economy to his successor, the first president in decades to do so. More importantly, he succeeded in creating a competitive electoral arena, administered by autonomous institutional actors, which witnessed the landmark election of Vicente Fox, the first opposition party candidate to defeat the Institutional Revolutionary Party (PRI) in a presidential race.

Vicente Fox, a former businessman and representative of the National Action Party (PAN), formed a bipartisan cabinet and aggressively pursued a neoliberal economic model, including closer trade ties with the United States. His actions as president legitimized democratic practices and the rule of law. Mexicans voted for Fox because he represented change, and most importantly, they wanted increased improvement in their standard of living and personal security from crime.[5] Fox, building on antipoverty programs introduced under Zedillo, was able, for the first time in decades, to achieve a decline in the percentage of Mexicans living in poverty.

In 2006, Mexico experienced its most ambitious and intensive presidential campaign, testing the newly established democratic institutions. The two leading candidates in the campaign, Andrés Manuel López Obrador of the Democratic Revolutionary Party (PRD), and Felipe Calderón of the incumbent PAN, fought to a photo finish. Calderón won with less than a half percent of the vote in what became the most controversial election since 1988. The candidates represented strongly differing views on Mexico's path to economic development, with López Obrador emphasizing the failures of government economic policies to solve the level of poverty, suggesting that a larger state role was essential to combat and alleviate poverty, in contrast to Calderón's view that Mexico's economic growth, building on his predecessor's foundation, should continue to emphasize the neoliberal economic strategy and the global influences institutionalized through NAFTA.[6] Politically, the closeness of the outcome of the election, and the impact of alleged fraud in determining the vote, left a large minority of Mexicans with doubts about the integrity of the democratic electoral process. Economically, Mexico's increased linkages to the United States under Calderón, after the U.S. recession in 2008, led to a dramatic downturn in Mexico's economic growth. The level of unemployment in Mexico, combined with the government's strategy against drug cartels, led to unprecedented levels of violence throughout Calderón's administration, raising serious doubts about the level of legitimacy of public institutions and the ability of those institutions to maintain political sovereignty.

In 2012, during a much shorter presidential campaign, the three major parties offered their nominees. The presidential race of 2012, once again, focused largely on economic issues, given the high rates of unemployment and the effects of the global recession, but highlighted the issue of personal security, the single most important issue identified by Mexican citizens, at a time when the drug-related violence had produced more than 50,000 homicides. But this election tested electoral democracy in a different way in that the PRI's candidate, Enrique Peña Nieto, who led all the potential party candidates since 2009, sustained a 10 to 15 point lead over his two opponents, Josefina Vázquez Mota of the PAN, the first female presidential candidate from a major party, and Andrés Manuel López Obrador of the PRD, in his second bid for the presidency, for nearly all of the campaign. Peña Nieto's victory, by a smaller margin, not only meant a return of the PRI to power, raising potential implications for democratic consolidation, but for only the second time since the 1920s, produced a change in control from the incumbent party.

Naturally, the combined political and economic challenges that confronted Calderón from 2006 to 2012, raises questions about Mexico's incipient democracy to resolve the underlying issues. This question has been raised generally in comparative politics, and specifically about Latin American countries, and is linked to what citizens in developing economies most value.

If the average Mexican is asked to choose between more political influence or greater economic growth, as it affects him or her personally, the typical choice is the latter. This is true in other Third World countries too. People with inadequate incomes are much more likely to worry about bread-and-butter issues than about more political freedom. For example, half of all Mexicans considered a high level of economic growth as the most important goal in 1995, 2000, and 2006. In contrast, only a quarter of all respondents chose giving citizens a greater voice in government decisions as Mexico's most important priority.[7] A country's political model becomes paramount, however, when its citizens draw a connection between economic growth (as related to improving their own standard of living) and the political system. If they believe the political system, and not just the leadership itself, is largely responsible for economic development, it will have important repercussions on their political attitudes and their political behavior. If Mexicans draw such a connection, it will change the nature of their demands on the political leadership and the system, and the level and intensity of their participation.

It appears, based on careful analysis of the 2006 presidential race, that many Mexicans began to link these issues together. The economy has mattered in every election since 1988, but it did so in different ways in 2006. Essentially, the two leading candidates, Calderón and López Obrador, attracted two different sets of voters. Those voters, many of whom identified themselves as independents, who viewed the economy as improving, voted for the candidate they thought most capable of keeping the economy growing, and that candidate was Calderón. Those voters, on the other hand, who wanted a leader who could best cope with poverty, were more likely to have voted for López Obrador.[8]

The comparative study of societies provides a framework by which we can measure the advantages and disadvantages of political models as they affect economic growth. Of course, economic growth itself is not the only differentiating consequence. Some political leaders are equally concerned, in some cases more concerned, with **social justice** (*a concept focusing on each citizen's quality of life and the equal treatment of all citizens*). Social justice may be interpreted in numerous ways. One way is to think of it as a means of redistributing wealth. For example, we often assume that economic growth— the percentage by which a society's economic productivity expands in a given time period—automatically conveys equal benefits to each member of the society. More attention is paid to the level of growth than to its beneficiaries. It is frequently the case that the lowest-income groups benefit least from economic growth. This has been true in the United States, but is even more noticeable in Third World and Latin American countries. Of the twenty-five countries with the worst income ratio between the poorest 10 percent versus the wealthiest 10 percent, seventeen were from Latin America in 2009.[9] There are periods, of course, when economic growth produces greater equality in income distribution.[10] Per capita income figures (national income divided by total population) can be deceiving because they are averages. In Mexico, for example, even during the remarkable sustained growth of the 1950s and 1960s, the real purchasing power (ability to buy goods and services) of the working classes actually declined.[11] Although the percentage of Mexicans who are not poor remained at approximately 57 percent of the population from 1984 to 1999, the number of Mexicans who have fallen into the category of absolute poverty (living on one dollar or less daily) nearly doubled, from 16 percent in 1992 to 28 percent in 1999.[12] Midway through the Fox administration, Mexico's antipoverty programs (which received greater attention under President Zedillo and were expanded under his successor), combined with economic growth, began to reduce poverty and absolute poverty. Even though Calderón increased the social budget for antipoverty programs, and Mexico's *Oportunidades* antipoverty strategy became a model used by the World Bank in other Third World settings, the severe impact of the 2008 recession in the United States on Mexico's growth, combined with the reduction in economic remittances from migrants north of the border, eliminated most of those improvements in poverty levels. In 2009, just a year after the recession, Mexico had the lowest level of economic growth in the hemisphere (−6.5), below that of Haiti, and 40 percent of Mexican households from 2008 to 2010 had lost a job.[13]

Another way of interpreting social justice is on the basis of social equality. This does not mean that all people are equal in ability but that each person should be treated equally under the law. Social justice also implies a leveling of differences in opportunities to succeed, giving each person equal access to society's resources. Accordingly, its allocation of resources can be a measure of a political system.

The degree to which a political system protects the rights of all citizens is another criterion by which political models can be compared. In Mexico, where human rights abuses are a serious problem, the evidence is unequivocal that the poor are much more likely to be the victims than are members of the middle and upper classes. Mexicans express little confidence in their justice system. In 2011, four-fifths disagreed that justice was prompt, complete, and impartial, as specified in their constitution. Only 14 percent of Mexicans believed honesty and justice characterized their courts.[14] The same can be said about many societies, but there are sharp differences in degree between highly industrialized nations and Third World nations.[15]

From a comparative perspective, then, we may want to test the abilities of political systems to reduce both economic and social inequalities. It is logical to believe that among the political models in which the population has a significant voice in making decisions, that people across the board obtain a larger share of the societal resources. On the other hand, it is possible to argue that in the last two decades, China serves as an extraordinary example of a collective, authoritarian leadership that has brought about unprecedented growth altering the economic condition of millions of its citizens through careful economic choices and global capitalism.

Leaders also are concerned with the distribution of wealth and resources *among* nations, not just within an individual nation, when considering social justice and its relationship to various political models. The choice of a political model, therefore, often involves international considerations. Such considerations are particularly important to countries that achieved independence in the twentieth century, especially after 1945. These countries want to achieve not only economic but also political and cultural independence. Mexico, like most of Latin America, achieved political independence in the early nineteenth century, but it found itself in the shadow of an extremely powerful neighbor. Its proximity to the United States eventually led to its losing half of its territory and many natural resources.

A third means to compare political models is to look at their ability to remake a citizenry, to alter political, social, and economic attitudes. A problem faced by most nations, especially in their infancy, is building a sense of nationalism. A sense of nationalism is difficult to erase, even after years of domination by another power, as in the case of the Soviet Union and the

Baltic republics, but it is equally difficult to establish, especially in societies incorporating diverse cultural, ethnic, and religious landscapes.[16] The political process can be used to mold citizens, to bring about a strong sense of national unity, while lessening or dampening local and regional loyalties. The acceptability of a political model, its very legitimacy among the citizenry, is a measure of its effectiveness in developing national sensibilities. Mexico, which had an abiding sense of regionalism, struggled for many decades to achieve a strong sense of national unity and pride.[17] In fact, a recent analysis by the Inter-American Development Bank argues that while Latin America ranks low in an index of ethnolinguistic fragmentation (level of ethnic and linguistic differences) compared with Africa, East Asia, and Asia, it is geographically (based on ecozones) the most fragmented region in the world. As the bank argues, culture usually differs widely in different ecozones, and therefore geographic fragmentation is an important dimension of social conflict.[18] On the other hand, Mexico did not have sharp religious and ethnic differences, characteristic of other cultures such as India, to overcome.

Many scholars have suggested that the single most important issue governing relationships among nations in the twenty-first century will be that of the haves versus the have-nots.[19] In fact, Mexico's linkage to the United States and Canada in a free-trade agreement highlights this point. One of the arguments against such an agreement was the impossibility of eliminating trade barriers between a nation whose per capita wage was one-seventh of the per capita wage of the other nation.[20] One of the arguments for such an agreement was that it could temper this disparity. More importantly, it might reduce the increasing numbers of Mexicans seeking work in the United States, which is why President Fox proposed a guest worker program to address the controversial issue of immigration reform, a proposal that was never acted on by Presidents Calderón and Obama.

Another reason that examining political systems from a comparative perspective is useful is personal. As a student of other cultures you can learn more about your own political system by reexamining attitudes and practices long taken for granted. In the same way a student of foreign languages comes to appreciate more clearly the syntax and structure of his or her native tongue and the incursions of other languages into its constructions and meanings, so too does the student of political systems. Comparisons not only enhance your knowledge of the political system in which you live, but are likely to increase your appreciation of particular features.

Examining a culture's politics implicitly delves into its values and attitudes. As we move quickly into an increasingly interdependent world, knowledge of other cultures is essential to being well educated. We have witnessed the extraordinary impact of the Internet, and Facebook specifically, on political change in

North Africa and the Middle East. In Mexico, only 40 percent of citizens were using the Internet at the beginning of 2012, and 90 percent of users boasted Facebook accounts.[21] Nevertheless, it played an important role in the 2006 presidential race, and nearly did so in the 2012 race since both the PAN and PRI candidates, by the third week of the campaign, had over a million and a half followers on Facebook.[22]

Comparative knowledge, however, allows us to test our values against those of other cultures. How do ours measure up? Do other sets of beliefs have applicability in our society? Are they more or less appropriate to our society? Why? For example, one of the reasons for the considerable misunderstanding between the United States and Mexico is a differing view of the meaning of political democracy. Many Mexicans attach features to the word *democracy* that are not attached to its definition in the United States.[23] I spent many years as a student of Mexico believing that was the case, but my evidence of these differences were based on dozens of conversations with Mexicans and observations of group interactions. In 2000, I was given an opportunity by the Hewlett Foundation to simultaneously survey Americans and Mexicans. Most Americans conceptualize democracy as liberty. Mexicans, however, reflect no consensus, giving equal weight to equality and, to a somewhat lesser extent, progress and respect. Problems arise when people do not realize they are using a different vocabulary when discussing the same issue.

Another reason for comparing political cultures is to dispel the notion that Western industrialized nations have all the solutions. It is natural to think of the exchange of ideas favoring the most technologically developed nations, including Japan, the European Union, and the United States. But solutions do not rely on technologies alone; in fact, most rely on human skills. In other words, how do people do things? This is true whether we are analyzing politics or increasing sales in the marketplace. Technologies can improve the efficiency, quality, and output of goods and services, yet their application raises critical questions revolving around values, attitudes, and interpersonal relationships. The broader the scope of human understanding, the greater the potential for identifying and solving diverse, human-made problems.

Finally, as a student new to the study of other societies, you may be least interested in the long-term contributions such knowledge can make for its own sake. Yet your ability to explain differences and similarities between and among political systems and, more important, their consequences, is essential to the growth of political knowledge. Although not always the case, it is generally true that the more you know about something and the more you understand its behavior, the more you can explain its behavior. This type of knowledge allows social scientists to create new theories of politics and political behavior, some of which can be applied to their own political system as well as to other cultures. It also allows—keeping in mind the limitations of human behavior—some level of prediction. In other words, given certain types of institutions and specific political conditions, social scientists can predict that political behavior is likely to follow certain patterns.

SOME INTERPRETATIONS OF THE MEXICAN SYSTEM

We suggested earlier that social scientists set for themselves the task of formulating some broad questions about the nature of a political system and its political processes. A variety of acceptable approaches can be used to examine political systems individually or comparatively. Some approaches focus on relationships among political institutions and the functions each institution performs. Other approaches give greater weight to societal values and attitudes and the consequences these have for political behavior and the institutional features characterizing a political system. Still other approaches, especially in the last third of the twentieth century, place greater emphasis on economic relationships and the influence of social or income groups on political decisions. Taking this last approach a step further, many analysts of Third World countries, including Mexico, concentrate on international economic influences and their effect on domestic political structures.

Choosing any one approach to explain the nature of political behavior has advantages in describing a political system. In my own experience, however, I have never become convinced that one approach offers an adequate explanation. I believe that an examination of political processes or functions entails the fewest prejudices and that by pursuing how and where these functions occur, one uncovers the contributions of other approaches.[24] An eclectic approach to politics, incorporating culture, history, structures, geography, and external relations, provides the most adequate and accurate vision of contemporary political behavior. Such an eclectic approach, combining the advantages of each, will be used in this book.

Currently, the study of Mexican politics focuses on analyzing Mexico as an example of democratic and neoliberal, capitalist transformation. The fundamental political questions in this new era are: To what degree has Mexico actually achieved a democratic political system? Has it gone beyond an electoral democracy? Has it shed many of its semi-authoritarian features? Has it improved the distribution of economic and social benefits? Is Mexico a **consolidated democracy** (*a democratic political system which has gone well beyond democratic elections, and may be characterized by other features described by democratic theorists, including accountability, transparency,* *division of powers, federalism, human rights, rule of law, and subordination of the armed forces to civil control*)? And perhaps most important of all, are democratic beliefs and practices sufficiently entrenched that Mexico will remain a democracy in the future?[25]

Mexico can be fairly labeled a democracy, if democracy is defined narrowly as a competitive political system in which two or more parties compete in an open and fair electoral process and exchange control over national political leadership. Mexico dramatically achieved this form of democracy with the electoral victory of Vicente Fox in July 2000. Mexico has moved toward a more difficult and influential stage in this process since 2001, one deeply embedded in institutional and structural conditions inherited from the past. For example, President Fox introduced a transparency law in 2003, designed to make all federal agencies more accountable to citizens and the media. The law definitely improved transparency, but instead of building on those first steps, both federal and state agencies since 2006 have become more rather than less resistant to promptly replying to queries.[26] In 2010, President Calderón initiated a legal reform that would alter the Mexican military's internal legal system. Again, it was a step forward in eliminating a remaining enclave of military autonomy from civil institutions, but the reforms only made some incremental changes, allowing the armed forces to continue to receive special legal protections.

Mexico presently is in the throes of a wholesale upheaval in its traditional political practices. Thus, if we are highlighting its most important features, these features, by necessity, are also in transition. In the recent past, Mexico featured a unique, semiauthoritarian system, unique because it allowed for much greater access to the decision-making process and, more important, its decision makers changed more frequently, than typically was the case elsewhere. Under this system, its leadership remained largely in the hands of the executive branch, especially the president, who was limited to a six-year term. The presidency retains this important structural limitation today; an individual can serve only one term in the presidency.

The strength of the presidency specifically, and the executive branch generally, continued well into the 1990s, resulting in a weak legislative and ineffectual judicial branch. Increasing electoral competition at the national level brought opposition party influence into the legislative branch, and by 1997, the Chamber of Deputies, Mexico's lower house, was in the hands of opposition parties. Yet a decade later, 46 percent of Mexicans, just behind citizens of Ecuador, Colombia, and Chile, supported the view that the executive should govern alone if the legislature hinders the governmental process.[27] Thus, the presidency remains the dominant political institution in Mexico, symbolically and practically.

As Mexico moves into the twenty-first century, **federalism** (*a political concept that describes rights and obligations shared by national versus state and local governments*) and decentralization replace semiauthoritarianism as a dominant feature of the political landscape.[28] Beginning under President Zedillo, the presidency experienced a gradual reduction of its power, both intentionally and unintentionally. President Fox accentuated that pattern during his administration, stressing the importance of other national institutions, notably the Supreme Court.[29] By 2010, 55 percent of Mexicans expressed confidence in their Supreme Court, above that of Americans (53 percent) and only slightly below Uruguayans and Canadians, leaders in the hemisphere.[30]

Decentralization has affected Mexico in two ways. First, although the federal government still is responsible for collecting the vast majority of revenues, it has increased the amount of funds assigned directly to state chief executives. According to George Grayson, Congress has been "extremely generous in allocating money to the states," giving governors significant leeway to expend those monies as they see fit.[31] Many governors have used these funds to promote their own political ambitions, suggesting why many of the leading contenders for the presidential nomination of their respective parties in 2012 were governors. Similar consequences also have occurred at the local level. As Andrew Selee discovered from extensive field research, "Mexico's process of democratization drove a significant expansion in the role that municipalities play in policymaking today in Mexico, which is far different from the limited role they played three decades ago. However, structural weaknesses, lack of accountability, and real differences in capacity have limited municipalities from playing a larger role in the country's policymaking process."[32]

Decentralization has another, even more complex face. As Mexico takes on participatory structural features in the political arena, it has generated alterations within institutions and organizations. For example, because of its loss of the presidency in 2000, various factions within the PRI were struggling for control over the party during the Fox and Calderón administrations. These factions represent different visions of the party's platform and internal structure. The National Action Party (PAN) was not immune to these same changes, largely because President Fox was viewed as an outsider who did not represent the interests of the PAN's traditional leadership. The selection of Felipe Calderón in 2006 represented a rejection of the PAN outsider, and his replacement by a representative of traditional party leadership, and Josefina Vazquez Mota's campaign in 2012 was marred by divisions between her, Calderón, and other PAN figures.

A second structural feature of a democratic Mexico is the rise of new political actors, or the altered influence of previously important actors.

Established institutions, such as the Catholic Church and the armed forces, are expanding their roles and filling a vacuum in the political space created by the departure of the PRI from the presidency and by the democratic transition of the 1990s and the efforts at consolidation in the 2000s.[33] Their new relationship to the state is complemented by the dramatic rise of civic and human rights organizations, some of which are likely to fill the role traditionally played by interest groups in other democratic societies.

The growing importance of nongovernmental organizations, autonomous interest groups, and independent institutions, such as the Catholic Church, has altered but not yet eliminated another traditional feature of Mexican politics prior to 2000, **corporatism** (*the process through which organizations channel their demands to the government*). Corporatism in the Mexican political context refers to how groups in society relate to the government or, more broadly, the state; and how the government responds to their demands.[34] Perhaps no characteristic of the Mexican political model has undergone more change in the 2000s than corporatism. In the United States, any introductory course in U.S. politics devotes some time to interest groups and how they present their demands to the political system. Mexico instituted in the 1930s a corporate relationship between the state and various important interest or social groups. This means that the government took the initiative to strengthen various groups, creating umbrella organizations to house them and through which their demands could be presented. The government placed itself in an advantageous position by representing various interest groups, especially those most likely to support opposing points of view. The state succeeded over a period of decades in acting as the official arbiter of these interests. It generally managed to make various groups loyal to it in return for representing their interests.

The essence of the corporatist relationship is political reciprocity. In return for official recognition and official association with the government or government-controlled organizations, these groups can expect some consideration of their interests on the part of the state. They can also expect the state to protect them from their natural political enemies. For example, labor unions hope the state will favor their interests over the interests of powerful businesses.[35]

The political victory of the National Action Party in the presidential race of 2000, however, broke down some of the linkages that made corporatism possible. The most important of these relationships was the ability of the Institutional Revolutionary Party to use the state to provide economic rewards to favored individuals and groups, especially by appointing them to political posts. During the PRI's long reign, essentially no separation existed between the state and the political party.[36] President Zedillo himself altered this pattern somewhat in the last few years of his administration, and Fox's and Calderón's administrations provided clearer evidence of the separation. As study after study reveal, however, corporatist linkages and practices remained at the end of the Calderón administration, especially in those states and municipalities where the PRI retained control, but also where the PRD governed, thus providing at the state and local level a similar continuity once guaranteed at the national level.[37]

The final structural feature of the Mexican model is the presence and level of influence exercised by international capital and, since the 1980s, international financial agencies. As was the case among so many of its fellow Latin American nations, the impact of foreign investment on macroeconomic policy, and on the lives of ordinary Mexican citizens, became paramount in the 1980s, and again to an even greater degree in 1995, when Mexico suffered its worst recession since the worldwide depression of the 1930s. The dependence of Mexico on outside capital and on foreign trade has exercised an important effect on policymaking, if not to the same degree on how decisions are taken.[38] It has even been clearly demonstrated that links between international financial agencies and Mexican governmental institutions contributed importantly to the dramatic, economic ideological shift in the 1980s and 1990s.[39] Fox committed his government to increased economic ties with the United States and Canada, and appointed a chief cabinet officer with two decades of experience at the World Bank. Calderón followed in his predecessor's footsteps, while renegotiating some of the NAFTA side agreements. Mexico also specifically increased its trade ties with the United States, and in 2011, Mexico edged out China, once again becoming the second most important U.S. trading partner (Canada remained first) making it even more sensitive to the vagaries of the U.S. economy. The global recession, initiated by the financial and housing crisis in the United States from 2008 to 2012, directly produced more negative economic consequences on Mexico than on any other significant trading partner. Such influences raise significant issues of national sovereignty and autonomy.

The structural features of Mexico's political model—electoral democracy, incipient federalism, the rise of autonomous actors, and the influence of international capital—are complemented by a dual political heritage incorporated into the political culture. The political culture is dominated by democratic attitudes, but strong strains of authoritarian beliefs remain ingrained among many Mexicans. It is contradictory: modern and traditional. It bears the burden of many historical experiences, precolonial, colonial, independence, and revolutionary. These experiences produced a political culture that admires essential democratic values, such as citizen participation, yet many remain attracted to an authoritarian model. By 2010, for example, on a 100 point scale, Mexicans ranked 67 in their support for democracy (see Table 1-1), significantly below such countries as Uruguay, Costa Rica, Argentina, Chile, and the United States, and essentially equal to Haiti, a country that has little experience with democratic governance. Indeed, only 47 percent of Mexicans expressed satisfaction with democracy (that is, were satisfied with its performance), the lowest in the Western Hemisphere except for Guyana and Haiti.[40]

Place and historical experience also have contributed to another feature of mass political culture: a psychology of dependence.[41] The proximity of the United States, which shares a border with Mexico nearly two thousand miles long, and the extreme disparities between the two in economic wealth and size, tend to foster an inferiority complex in many Mexicans, whether they operate in the worlds of business, academia, technology, or politics. The economic, cultural, and artistic penetration of the United States into Mexico carries with it other values foreign to its domestic political heritage. Psychologically and culturally, Mexicans must cope with these influences, most of which are indirect, often invisible. A strong sense of Mexican nationalism, especially in relation to its political model, is expressed in part as a defensive mechanism against

Table 1-1 Support for Democracy in Comparative Perspective

Uruguay	86.2
Costa Rica	80.4
Argentina	79.6
United States	77.5
Chile	76.1
Panama	75.5
Venezuela	74.0
Brazil	73.7
Canada	73.5
Colombia	72.3
Nicaragua	71.3
Bolivia	70.3
Ecuador	68.4
Mexico	**66.8**
Haiti	65.8
El Salvador	64.1
Paraguay	63.3
Guatemala	62.8
Honduras	62.6
Peru	60.1

0	20	40	60	80	100

Note: Responses were recoded on a 100 point scale; the higher the numbers, the greater the support for the statement: "Democracy may have some problems, but it is better than any other form of government."
Source: AmericasBarometer, *Political Culture of Democracy, 2010,* "Democratic Consolidation in Hard Times," Latin American Public Opinion Project, December 2010, 102.

United States influences. Indeed, it is astonishing that a fifth of Mexicans mistakenly believe they achieved their independence from the United States.[42] Underlying this defensive mechanism, however, are fundamental beliefs about many issues, in addition to democracy, which are distinctly Mexican.

MEXICO'S SIGNIFICANCE IN A COMPARATIVE CONTEXT

From a comparative perspective, Mexico provides many valuable insights into politics and political behavior. The feature of Mexico that has most intrigued students of comparative politics in the past is the stability of its political system.[43] Although challenged seriously by military and civilian factions in 1923, 1927, and 1929, its political structure and leadership prevailed for most of this century, at least since 1930—an accomplishment unmatched by any other Third World country. Even among industrialized nations like Italy, Germany, and Japan, such longevity is remarkable. The phenomenon leads to such questions as: What enabled the stability? What made the Mexican model unique? Was it the structure of the model? Was it the political culture? Did it have something to do with the country's proximity to another leader of political continuity? Did it result from the values and behavior of the people?

We know from other studies of political stability that a degree of political legitimacy accompanies even a modicum of support for a political model. Social scientists are interested in political legitimacy and political stability each for its own sake, but they assume, with considerable evidence, that some relationship exists between economic development and political stability. It is misleading to think that the characteristics of one system can be successfully transferred to another; still, it is useful to ascertain which may be more or less relevant to accomplishing specific, political goals.

Mexico also has attracted considerable international interest because it was a one party–dominant system encountering only limited opposition from 1929 through 1988, the year in which a splinter group from the official party, supported by long-standing parties and groups on the left, ran a highly successful campaign. Mexico's system is unusual in that the antecedent of the PRI, the National Revolutionary Party (Partido Nacional Revolucionario, the PNR), did not bring the political leadership to power. Rather, the leadership established the party as a vehicle to *remain* in power; the PRI was founded and controlled by the government bureaucracy. This had long-term effects on the nature of the party itself, and on its importance to policymaking.[44] In this sense, the PRI was unlike the Communist Party in the Soviet Union, whose death in 1991 spelled the end of Communist leadership in the successor states. The PRI, because it did not produce Mexico's leadership, as do the Democratic and Republican parties in the United States, was much more tangential to political power. In fact, under Lázaro Cárdenas, a former head of the party and the first president to serve a full term after its founding, only one-fifth of the prominent politicians who held posts during his administration were party militants, the lowest figure in the twentieth century. As the Mexican model continued to evolve along democratic lines, the party's function, and consequently its importance, grew significantly.[45] Although it lost its first presidential race in 2000, and again in 2006, and suffered sharp divisions among its leadership, the party continued to thrive at the local level, winning back state governorships and municipalities from the PAN and the Democratic Revolutionary Party (PRD).

A third reason that Mexico's political system intrigues outside observers has been its ability to subordinate military authorities to civilian control. Mexico, like most other Latin American countries, endured a century when violence became an accepted tool of the political game. Such acceptance makes it extremely difficult, if not impossible, to eliminate the military's large and often decisive political role. Witness many Latin American countries; one has only to look at Argentina and Chile during the 1970s and 1980s. No country south of Mexico, excepting Costa Rica, has achieved extended *civilian* supremacy beyond three decades. This is precisely why theorists of Latin American democracy have included civilian supremacy over the armed forces as a component of a functional democracy. Nevertheless, many Latin American countries where civilian leadership is once again in ascendancy have begun making important changes in the institutional relationships between civil and military authorities.[46]

Mexico, therefore, is a unique case study in Third World civil-military relations. What produced civilian supremacy there? Is the condition found elsewhere? A confluence of circumstances and policies gradually succeeded in putting civilian control incrementally in place. Some involved the special characteristics of the system itself, including the creation of a national political party. Some are historical, the most important of which is the Mexican Revolution of 1910, which led to the development of a popular army whose generals governed Mexico in the 1920s and 1930s, and who themselves initiated the concept of civilian control.[47] As pluralization increases, many of the features that sustained the relationship prior to 2000 are disappearing. Furthermore, the intensive use of the armed forces in pursuit of drug cartels since 2006, and the dramatic increase in drug-related homicides and allegations of human rights violations by the army, have intensified criticisms of remaining pockets of military autonomy from civilian oversight.[48] It remains to be seen whether those changes will alter the traditional pattern and how.

A fourth reason for studying Mexico is the singular relationship it has developed with the dominant religious institution, the Roman Catholic Church. Throughout much of Latin America, the Catholic Church has been one of the important corporate actors. For significant historical reasons in the nineteenth and twentieth centuries Mexico's leadership suppressed and then isolated itself from the Catholic hierarchy and even in some cases the Catholic religion.[49] The Catholic Church often has played a political role in Latin American societies and currently has the potential to exercise considerable political and social influence, as it did in the 1994 and 2000 presidential elections. A study of church-state relations in Mexico offers a unique perspective on how the church was removed from the corporatist structure and the implications of this autonomy for a politically influential institution. It is readily apparent that the church performed a significant task in bringing electoral democracy to Mexico. It is equally apparent that it has become a vocal critic of selected government policies in the last two administrations.[50]

A fifth reason for examining Mexico in a comparative political context is the opportunity to view the impact of the United States, a First World country, on a Third World country. No comparable geographic relationship exists anywhere else in the world: two countries that share a long border exhibit great disparities in wealth. Mexico provides not only a test case for those who view Latin America as dependent on external economic forces but also an unparalleled opportunity to look at the possible *political* and *cultural* influences and consequences of a major power.[51] A recent survey of citizens in Mexico and the United States, which explored a series of political and social attitudes, suggests the importance of cross-national influences along the border.[52]

The relationship is not one-way, but instead is asymmetrical. The United States exercises or can exercise more influence over Mexico than vice versa. This does not mean that Mexico is the passive partner. It, too, exercises influence, and in many respects its influence is growing. Because of European civilization's influence on our culture, we have long studied the political models of England and the Continent. Our obsession with the Soviet Union exaggerated our focus on Europe. As Latino and other immigrant cohorts in the United States grow larger, our knowledge of the Mexican culture will become far more relevant to understanding *contemporary political behavior* in the United States than anything we might learn from contemporary Europe. The political impact of Latinos on the United States presidential election in 2012 reinforces their significance.

A sixth reason to explore the Mexican political model is its experiences since 1989 with economic liberalization. One of the issues that has fascinated social scientists for many years, but especially since China's rapid economic expansion, is the linkage between economic and political liberalization. What does the Mexican case suggest about its earlier strategy of concentrating on opening its markets, which then may create conditions favorable to political development? Indeed, is there a causal linkage between economic and political liberalization? If so, what lessons can be offered by the Mexican transition?[53]

A seventh reason Mexico may offer some useful comparisons is the transition taking place between national and local political authorities. Long dominated by a national executive branch in both the decision-making process and the allocation of resources, Mexico has witnessed, since the first opposition-party victory at the state level in 1989, an increasing pattern of decentralization and deconcentration of political control at the state and local level, as the PAN and the PRD won more elections.[54] Now that Mexico has evolved into a three-party system on the national level, and the National Action Party controlled the executive branch from 2000 to 2012, how did it respond to PRI- and PRD-controlled local and state governments? How are these patterns affecting the process of governance, as distinct from electoral competition? The potential implications of such change from the bottom up offer many insights into structural political relationships in Mexico and the rise of federalism. It also sheds light on the extent to which Mexican democracy has become consolidated.[55]

Finally, most scholars believe that Mexico's path along a political transition to democracy differed from many other countries in the 1980s and 1990s. For example, Steve Morris has argued that Mexico's democratic reforms occurred over a lengthy period. The incumbent party permitted, indeed sometimes initiated, institutional changes in the electoral process. These processes in turn encouraged opposition parties to mobilize their supporters. Second, political parties played a crucial role in the Mexican transformation. These parties operated within the electoral context created by a one-party monopoly. Although that electoral system generated peculiar characteristics within the opposition parties' structures, making them less flexible than would be the case in a typical competitive electoral arena, the parties were able to survive and successfully initiate and accomplish system reforms, allowing them ultimately to defeat the governing party. Third, Mexico's transformation occurred from the bottom up, in which state and local forces provided a firm grassroots base for national political change. The growth of opposition-party control at the municipal level trained a new generation of leadership, altered voter behavior and partisan support, and increased demands for the decentralization of power.[56]

Mexico presently is shifting from a transition to democracy to a complex process of consolidation or deepening of democratic patterns of behavior, including fresh institutional relationships among the branches of government. This consolidation process raises questions about the accountability of leadership, the legitimacy of democracy in meeting citizen expectations, and their respect for opposing parties and actors. These and other features of a consolidated democracy are being seriously challenged by the inability of the Mexican state to reduce criminal violence and bring drug trafficking organizations under governmental control.

Definitions of consolidation and democratic deepening abound. In the Mexican context, the clearest presentation of these two terms has been offered by Steven Barracca, who suggests that consolidation refers exclusively to "a low probability of democratic breakdown. More specifically, I suggest that a democratic regime can be considered consolidated when a political system is free of factors that can be demonstrated to *clearly* and *directly* lead to a return to non-democratic rule."[57] Most definitions of this term are much broader and more ambiguous. Widely offered criteria for testing the broader definitions of democratic consolidation include such variables as the level of socioeconomic equality; the behavior, structure, and role of institutions; the routine practice of democratic politics; and the citizenry's view of the democracy as legitimate. Many of these characteristics have been criticized by students of recently democratically transformed societies, including Russia, as being far too demanding.[58]

The deepening of democracy in Mexico involves numerous tasks. These include establishment of the rule of law, strengthening of the federal judiciary, campaign finance reform, expansion of other actors, decentralization of decision-making, and increased accountability across institutions. The degree to which Mexico has implemented these changes, and the difficulties it has encountered, can be compared with the experiences of other countries engaged in similar reforms.

CONCLUSION

To summarize, then, approaching politics from a comparative perspective offers many rewards. It allows us to test political models against one another; it enables us to learn more about ourselves and our own political system and culture; it offers a means for examining the relationship between political and economic development and the distribution of wealth; and it identifies the common interests of rich and poor nations and what they do to solve their problems.

Scholars have interpreted Mexico's political system in different ways. This book argues that the system is democratic, but is in consolidation; is dominated by a declining presidency, with legislative and judicial branches growing in influence; is built on a contradictory political culture that includes liberal and authoritarian qualities; is characterized by international economic features embedded in its domestic structures; is affected psychologically and politically by its proximity to the United States; and reflects the growing significance of new actors, including NGOs, state and local governments, and drug trafficking organizations. Mexico offers unique opportunities for comparative study because of its political continuity and stability, historic one party–dominant system, civil-military relations, unique separation of church and state, peaceful democratic transition, and nearness to a powerful, wealthy neighbor.

NOTES

1. Gabriel Almond and Sidney Verba, *The Civic Culture* (Boston: Little, Brown, 1965), 59.
2. Compare, for example, the number of academic course offerings and textbooks available on Europe and European countries with those representing other, especially Third World, regions and societies.
3. He Li, *From Revolution to Reform: A Comparative Study of China and Mexico* (Lanham, MD: University Press of America, 2003.)
4. See for example, the glowing statement in the *Washington Post*, that Salinas "has proved to be as radical in his own way as the revolutionaries who galloped over Mexico at the beginning of the century." Edward Cody, "Salinas Revolution Attacking Mexican Attitudes," May 17, 1991.
5. Roderic Ai Camp, "Citizen Attitudes Toward Democracy and Vicente Fox's Victory in 2000," in *Mexico's Pivotal Democratic Election*, eds. Chappell Lawson and Jorge Domínguez (Stanford, CA: Stanford University Press, 2004), 25–46.
6. Jorge I. Domínguez, Chappell Lawson, and Alejandro Moreno, eds., *Consolidating Mexico's Democracy: The 2006 Presidential Campaign in Comparative Perspective* (Baltimore, MD: Johns Hopkins University Press, 2009).
7. Jorge I. Domínguez, "Conclusion: The Choices of Voters during the 2006 Presidential Election in Mexico," in *Consolidating Mexico's Democracy*, 297–98.
8. Ibid., 298.
9. United Nations, *Human Development Report 2009* (New York: United Nations Development Program, 2009), 195–98.
10. It has been argued, as a general rule, that as countries achieve advanced industrial economies, greater economic equality will be achieved. See Samuel P. Huntington, *Political Order in Changing Societies* (New Haven, CT: Yale University Press, 1968), 57.
11. Roger D. Hansen, *The Politics of Mexican Development* (Baltimore, MD: Johns Hopkins University Press, 1971), especially "Trends in Mexican Income Distribution," 72ff.
12. "Población, pobreza y marginación," *Este País* (April 1999), 15.
13. Mitchell A. Seligson and Amy Erica Smith, eds., *Political Culture of Democracy, 2010: Democratic Consolidation in the Americas during Hard Times: Report on the Americas*, Executive Summary, December 2010, 1–3.

14. "Presunta justicia?," 400 respondents nationally, 4.9% margin of error, February 12–16, 2011, www.parametria.com.mx.

15. Of course, this is true worldwide. Unfortunately, the problems *seem* less severe when these groups are the primary victims. Human Rights Watch, *Uniform Impunity: Mexico's Misuse of Military Justice to Prosecute Abuses in Counternarcotics and Public Security Operations* (New York: Human Rights Watch, 2009).

16. Irakli Chkonia, "Timeless Identity versus Another Final Modernity, Identity Master Myth and Social Change in Georgia," in Lawrence E. Harrison and Peter L. Berger, eds. *Developing Cultures: Case Studies* (New York: Routledge, 2006), 349–68.

17. Frederick Turner, *The Dynamics of Mexican Nationalism* (Chapel Hill: University of North Carolina Press, 1968).

18. Within the region, Mexico ranks about in the middle. "The Dangers of Diversity," *Latin American Economic Policies* 10 (First Quarter 2000): 6.

19. The classic argument for this was presented by Barbara Ward, *The Rich Nations and the Poor Nations* (London: Hamilton, 1962).

20. Jeff Faux, "No: The Biggest Export Will Be U.S. Jobs," *Washington Post Weekly Edition*, May 13–19, 1991, 8.

21. Asociación Mexicana de Internet, "Hábitos de los usarios de Internet en México," May 17, 2012. The association asserts that 90 percent access it daily. YouTube and Twitter follow in importance.

22. See Luis César Torres Nabel "Disceminación de creencias conspirativas en la blogasfera, la elección presidencial de 2006," *Estudios sobre Estado y Sociedad* 18, no. 50 (Enero–Abril, 2011): 141–82. López Obrador made use of Twitter (as did the other two candidates), as well as YouTube, but had less than 250,000 "likes" during that same period.

23. These findings are reinforced empirically in Roderic Ai Camp, ed., *Citizen Views of Democracy in Latin America* (Pittsburgh, PA: University of Pittsburgh Press, 2001).

24. Some of these issues have been examined by Diane E. Davis, *Urban Leviathan: Mexico City in the Twentieth Century* (Philadelphia: Temple University Press, 1994).

25. Chappell Lawson, "Mexico's Unfinished Transition: Democratization and Authoritarian Enclaves in Mexico," *Mexican Studies* 16 (Summer 2000): 267–87.

26. Mariclaire Acosta, "NGOs and Human Rights," in Roderic Ai Camp, ed., *Oxford Handbook of Mexican Politics* (New York: Oxford University Press, 2012), 423–45.

27. Diana Orces, "Popular Support for a Government without Legislatures," *AmericasBarometer Insights: 2009*, no. 25, 1.

28. Emily Edmonds-Poli, "Decentralization under Fox: Progress or Stagnation?" *Mexican Studies* 22, no. 2 (Summer 2006): 387–416; and Alain De Remes, "Democratization and Dispersion of Power: New Scenarios in Mexican Federalism," *Mexican Studies* 22, no. 1 (Winter 2006): 175–204.

29. Julio Ríos-Figueroa, "Fragmentation of Power and the Emergence of an Effective Judiciary in Mexico, 1994–2002," *Latin American Politics and Society* 49 (April 2007): 31–57.

30. Arturo Maldonado, "What Determines Trust in the Supreme Court in Latin America and the Caribbean," *AmericasBarometer Insights: 2011*, no. 54, 1.

31. George Grayson, "Mexican Governors: The Nation's New Feudal Lords," Mexico Under Calderón Task Force, University of Miami Center for Hemispheric Policy, November 10, 2010, 7.

32. Andrew Selee, *Decentralization, Democratization, and Informal Power in Mexico* (University Park: Penn State University Press, 2011).

33. See, for example, Raúl Benitez Manaut, "Reforming Civil-Military Relations during Democratization," in *Mexico's Democratic Challenges: Politics, Government and Society*, eds. Andrew Selee and Jacqueline Peschard (Washington, DC: Woodrow Wilson Center, 2010), 162–86; and from the same book, Roberto Blancarte, "Churches, Believers, and Democracy," 281–95.

34. Ruth Spalding, "State Power and its Limits: Corporatism in Mexico," *Comparative Political Studies* 14 (July 1981): 139–61.

35. Ruth Berins Collier, *The Contradictory Alliance: State-Labor Relations and Regime Change in Mexico* (Berkeley: University of California International and Area Studies, 1992).

36. James G. Samsted, "Corporatism and Democratic Transition: State and Labor During the Salinas and Zedillo Administrations," *Latin American Politics and Society* 44, no. 4 (2002): 1–28.

37. Tina Hilgers, "Causes and Consequences of Political Clientelism: Mexico's PRD in Comparative Perspective," *Latin American Politics and Society* 50 (Winter 2008): 123–53; and Daniel M. Sabet's monograph, *Nonprofits and Their Networks: Cleaning the Waters along Mexico's Northern Border* (Tucson: University of Arizona Press, 2008).

38. For reactions to the intervention of the International Monetary Fund, see Rick Wills, "The IMF's Economic Role Causes Controversy," *El Financiero International Edition*, October 6, 1997, 8. Fifty-six percent of Mexicans believed that U.S. influence over Mexico was excessive.

39. Roderic Ai Camp, *Mexico's Mandarins: Crafting a Power Elite for the Twenty-First Century* (Berkeley: University of California Press, 2002).

40. Mitchell A. Seligson and Amy Erica Smith, eds., *Political Culture of Democracy, 2010, Democratic Consolidation in the Americas during Hard Times*, Latin American Public Opinion Project (Washington, DC: AID, 2010), 105.

41. See Octavio Paz's classic, *The Labyrinth of Solitude: Life and Thought in Mexico* (New York: Grove Press, 1961).

42. "Bicentenario: identitdad, conocimiento y celebración," Parametría, national sample, 1,200 respondents, 2.8% margin of error, April 7–11, 2010, www.parametria .com.mx. A fourth of Mexicans did not know from which country they achieved their independence.

43. For an overview of these issues, see Francisco E. González, *Dual Transitions from Authoritarian Rule, Institutionalized Regimes in Chile and Mexico, 1970–2000* (Baltimore, MD: Johns Hopkins University Press, 2008).

44. John J. Bailey, *Governing Mexico: The Statecraft of Crisis Management* (New York: St. Martin's Press, 1988).

45. Roderic Ai Camp, *The Metamorphosis of Leadership in a Democratic Mexico* (New York: Oxford University Press, 2010), 66.

46. Anthony Pereira, "Virtual Legality: Authoritarian Legacies and the Reform of Military Justice in Brazil, the Southern Cone, and Mexico," *Comparative Political Studies* 34 (June 2001): 556–73; and Rut Diamint, "The Military," in Jorge Domínguez and Michael Shifter, *Constructing Democratic Governance in Latin America* (Baltimore, MD: Johns Hopkins University Press, 2003), 43–73.

47. For greater detail about the causes, see Roderic Ai Camp, *Mexico's Military on the Democratic Stage* (New York: Praeger, 2005).

48. Roderic Ai Camp, "Armed Forces and Drugs: Public Perceptions and Institutional Challenges," in *Shared Responsibility: U.S.-Mexico Policy Options for Confronting Organized Crime*, eds. Eric L. Olson, David A. Shirk, and Andrew Selee (Washington, DC: Woodrow Wilson International Center for Scholars, 2010), 291–326.

49. Karl Schmitt, "Church and State in Mexico: A Corporatist Relationship," *Americas* 40 (January 1984): 349–76.

50. Vikram K. Chand, *Mexico's Political Awakening* (Notre Dame, IN: University of Notre Dame Press, 2001); and Roderic Ai Camp, *Crossing Swords: Politics and Religion in Mexico* (New York: Oxford University Press, 1997).

51. For some examples of noneconomic variables, see Andrew Selee, Christopher Wilson, and Katie Putnam, *The United States and Mexico: More Than Neighbors* (Washington, DC: Woodrow Wilson International Center for Scholars, 2010).

52. "Encuesta CIDAC-ZOGBY México y Estados Unidos Cómo Miramos al Vecino," 2006, www.cide.edu, 2011.

53. Francisco E. González, *Dual Transitions from Authoritarian Rule: Institutionalized Regimes in Chile and Mexico, 1970–2000* (Baltimore, MD: Johns Hopkins University Press, 2010).

54. See especially "The Politics of Public Administration," in *Opposition Government in Mexico*, ed. Victoria Rodríguez and Peter M. Ward (Albuquerque: University of New Mexico Press, 1995). The editors also provide an excellent case study in their *Policymaking, Politics, and Urban Governance in Chihuahua* (Austin: University of Texas LBJ School of Public Affairs, 1992).

55. Steven Barracca, "Devolution and the Deepening of Democracy: Explaining Outcomes of Municipal Reform in Mexico," *Journal of Latin American Studies* 37, no. 1 (2005): 2.

56. Stephen D. Morris, "Mexico's Long Awaited Surprise," *Latin American Research Review* 40 (2005): 418–21.

57. Steven Barracca, "Is Democracy Consolidated?," *Third World Quarterly* 25, no. 8 (2004): 1469–85.

58. See, for example, Stephen E. Hanson, "Defining Democratic Consolidation," in *Postcommunism and the Theory of Democracy*, ed. Richard D. Anderson, Jr., et al. (Princeton, NJ: Princeton University Press, 2001), 126–51.

2

Political-Historical Roots:
The Impact of Time and Place

The Constitution of 1812, the most radical charter of the nineteenth century, abolished seigniorial institutions, the Inquisition, Indian tribute, and forced labor and asserted the state's control of the church. It created a unitary state with equal laws for all parts of the Spanish monarchy, substantially restricted the authority of the king, and entrusted the legislature with decisive power. The Charter of 1812 also dramatically increased the scope of political activity by establishing representative government at three levels: the city or town with a thousand or more inhabitants (constitutional *ayuntamiento*), the province (provincial deputation), and the monarchy (Cortes). Political power was thus transferred from the center to localities, as large numbers of people were incorporated into the political process for the first time. When it enfranchised all adult men, except those of African ancestry, without requiring either literacy or property qualifications, the constitution of 1812 surpassed all existing representative governments, such as Great Britain, the United States, and France, in providing political rights to the vast majority of the male population. An analysis of the 1813 election census in Mexico City, for example, concludes that 93 percent of the adult male population of the capital possessed the right to vote.

JAIME E. RODRÍGUEZ O. *"Democracy from Independence*
to Revolution"

Understanding politics is not just knowing who gets what, where, when, and how, as Harold D. Lasswell declared in a classic statement years ago, but also understanding the origins of why people behave the way they do. Each culture is a product of its own heritage, traditions emerging from historical experiences. Many aspects of the U.S. political system can be traced to our English colonial experiences, our independence movement, our Western frontier expansion, and our immigrant origins. Mexico has had a somewhat similar set of experiences, but the sources of the experiences and their specific characteristics were quite different.

THE SPANISH HERITAGE

Mexico's political heritage, unlike that of the United States, draws on two important cultural foundations: European and indigenous. Although large numbers of Indians were never absorbed into the conquering culture in New Spain (the colonial Spanish viceroyalty that extended from Central America to what is now the United States Midwest and Pacific Northwest), a vast integration process took place in most of central Mexico. Conversely, British settlers encountered numerous Native Americans in their colonization of North America, but they rarely intermarried with them and thus the two cultures never blended. Racially, African blacks played an important role in some regions; politically, this was a limited role because of the small numbers brought to New Spain.

Mexico's racial heritage, unlike that of the United States, has a mixed or *mestizo* quality. In the initial absence of Spanish women, the original Spanish conquerors sought native mistresses or wives. In fact, cohabiting with female royalty from the various indigenous cultures was seen as an effective means of joining the two sets of leaders, firmly establishing Spanish ascendancy throughout the colony. The Indian-Spanish offspring of these unions at first were considered socially inferior to Spaniards fresh from Spain and the Spanish born in the New World. Frank Tannenbaum describes the complex social ladder in his major work:

> With the mixture of races in Mexico added to by the bringing in of Negroes in sufficient numbers to leave their mark upon the population in certain parts of the country, we have the basis of the social structure that characterized Mexico throughout the colonial period and in some degree continues to this day. The Spaniard—that is, the born European—was at the top in politics, in the church, and in prestige. The *criollo*, his American-born child, stood at a lower level. He inherited most of the wealth, but was denied any important role in political administration. The *mestizo* and the dozen different *castas* that resulted from the mixtures of European, Indian, and Negro in their various degrees and kinds were still lower.[1]

In the late nineteenth century, mestizos reached a new level of social ascendancy through their numbers and control over the political system.

Early Mexican political history involved social conflicts based on racial heritage. Moreover, large indigenous groups were suppressed, exploited, and politically ignored. The prejudice with which indigenous people were treated by the Spanish and mestizo populations, and the mistreatment of the mestizo by the Spanish, contributed further to the sharp class distinctions that have plagued Mexico.[2] Social prejudice was transferred to economic status as well, with those lowest on the racial scale ending up at the bottom of the economic scale. The degree of social inequality ultimately contributed to the independence movement, as the New World–born Spanish (*criollos*) came to resent their second-class status relative to the Old World–born Spanish (*peninsulares*). It contributed even more significantly to the Mexican Revolution of 1910, in which thousands of downtrodden mestizo peasants and workers and some Indians joined a broad social movement for greater social justice.

All societies have some type of social structure. Most large societies develop hierarchical social groups, but from one society to another the level of deference exacted or given varies. In the United States, where political rhetoric, beginning with independence, focused on greater social equality, class distinctions were fewer and less distinct.[3] In Mexico, in spite of its revolution, the distinctions remain much sharper, affecting various aspects of cultural and political behavior. For example, a major study of U.S. intellectuals found that 40 percent of the younger generations were from working-class backgrounds. By contrast, in Mexico, fewer than 5 percent fell into this social category.[4] In the political and economic realms, lower-income groups are rarely represented in influential, leadership roles. Only among Catholic clergy and the military do such individuals exist in larger numbers.[5] In addition, lower-income groups have limited protection from abuses by governmental authorities and rarely receive equal treatment under the law. In the United States differences exist in the legal treatment of rich and poor, but they are fewer, and the gap between them is much smaller than in Mexico.

The Spanish also left Mexico with a significant religious heritage: Catholicism. Religion played a critical role in the pre-Conquest Mexican indigenous culture and was very much integrated into the native political processes. In both the Aztec and Maya empires, for example, religion was integral to political leadership. The Spanish were no less religious. Beginning with the Conquest itself, the pope reached some agreements with the Spanish crown. In these agreements, known collectively as the *patronato real* (royal patronate), the Catholic Church gave up certain rights it exercised in Europe for a privileged role in the Conquest generally and in New Spain specifically. In return for being allowed to send two priests or friars with every land or sea expedition, and being given the *sole* opportunity to proselytize millions of Indians, the church gave up its control over the building of facilities in the New World, the appointing of higher clergy, the collecting of tithes, and other activities. In other words, Catholicism obtained a monopoly in the Spanish New World.[6]

The contractual relationship between the Catholic Church and the Spanish authorities in the colonial period established two fundamental principles: the concept of an official religion, that is, only one religion recognized and permitted by civil authorities, and the *integration* of church and state. In the United States, of course, a fundamental principle of our political evolution is the *separation* of church and state. Moreover, many of the settlers who came to the English colonies came in search of religious freedom, not religious monopoly. As Samuel Ramos suggested,

> It was our [Mexico's] fate to be conquered by a Catholic theocracy which was struggling to isolate its people from the current of modern ideas that emanated from the Renaissance. Scarcely had the American colonies been organized when they were isolated against all possible heresy. Ports were closed and trade with all countries except Spain was disapproved. The only civilizing agent of the New World was the Catholic Church, which by virtue of its pedagogical monopoly shaped the American societies in a medieval pattern of life. Education, and the direction of social life as well, were placed in the hands of the church, whose power was similar to that of a state within a state.[7]

The consequences of Mexico's religious heritage have been numerous. It is important to remember that Catholicism was not just a religion in the spiritual sense of the word, but extended deeply into the political culture, given the influence of the church over education and social organizations, such as hospitals and charitable foundations, and its lack of religious competition.

One of the consequences is structural. In the first chapter, corporatism was identified as one of the traditional features of the political system. Corporatism extends back to the colonial period, when certain groups obtained special privileges from civil authorities, giving them preferred relationships with the state. Among these groups were clergy, military officers, and merchants. The most notable privileges received by the clergy were special legal *fueros*, or legal rights, allowing them to try their members in separate courts, where they were not subject to civil laws.[8] The Spanish established the precedent for favored treatment of specific groups. Once groups are thus singled out, they will fight very hard to retain their advantages. Much of nineteenth-century politics in Mexico became a battle between the church and its conservative allies on just this issue.

The monopoly of the church in New Spain was very jealously protected. No immigrants professing other beliefs were allowed in before

Mexican independence. The church also took on another task for the state: ferreting out religious and political dissenters by establishing the Inquisition in the New World. The primary function of this institution was to identify and punish religious heretics, those persons who threatened religious beliefs as taught by church authorities, but in practice the Inquisition controlled publishing, assembled a book index that censored intellectual ideas from abroad, and fielded special customs inspectors.[9] These activities were not entirely successful, but in general the church and the civil authorities were intolerant of any other religious and secular thought. The Inquisition has been described in this fashion:

> The belief that heretics were traitors and traitors were heretics led to the conviction that dissenters were social revolutionaries trying to subvert the political and religious stability of the community. These tenets were not later developments in the history of the Spanish Inquisition; they were inherent in the rationale of the institution from the fifteenth century onward and were apparent in the Holy Office's dealings with Jews, Protestants, and other heretics during the sixteenth century. The use of the Inquisition by the later eighteenth-century Bourbon kings of Spain as an instrument of regalism was not a departure from tradition. Particularly in the viceroyalty of New Spain during the late eighteenth century the Inquisition trials show how the Crown sought to promote political and religious orthodoxy.[10]

The heritage of intolerance plagued Mexico during much of its post-independence political history. It has been argued that because culturally there had been little experience with other points of view and in promoting respect for them, accommodation was not perceived as desirable. Some analysts suggest that the Catholic religion's continuation as a dominant presence in spite of religious freedom and the existence of other faiths encourages the persistence of intolerance. The applicability of that view in recent years requires reexamination in light of the church's proactive posture on democratization. Furthermore, the level of tolerance is particularly relevant to democratic consolidation since recent studies have determined that it is a critical variable in creating support for stable democracy.[11]

To carry out the conquest of New Spain, the Spanish relied on armed expeditions and missionaries. Typically, once an area was made "safe" by an exploratory expedition, a permanent settlement around a mission and a *presidio*, or fort, was established. Some of the settlements were sited along a route known as the *camino real* (king's highway), which today is the old California Highway 1. The original mission towns are now among the most important cities in the Southwest: San Francisco (Saint Francis), San Diego (Saint James), Santa Barbara (Saint Barbara), Albuquerque, Tucson, and Santa Fe.

Originally, the authorities used Spanish armed forces; in the colonial period, American-born Spaniards began filling officer ranks as the government came to rely more heavily on the colonial militia. The armed forces were called on from time to time to protect the coast from French and British attacks, but the army was used primarily to suppress Indian rebellions and to keep internal order. It patrolled the highways to keep them free of bandits. Basically, then, it functioned as police, not as defenders against external enemies.

The military, like the clergy, received special *fueros* in New Spain. It too had its own courts for civil and criminal cases, but unlike the clergy, military officers were immune to civil prosecution.[12] Importantly, this issue has become significant during the Calderón administration, as the dramatic increase in human rights allegations against the army as a consequence of its confrontations with drug cartels has provoked increased criticism of its continued legal autonomy from the civil justice system. Their favored status historically inevitably led to legal conflicts. Some historians have argued that one of the reasons for the disintegration of civil authority at the time of independence was declining respect caused by its inability to control military cases.

As in the case of the church, granting the military special privileges—which were passed on to the colonial militia before independence—created another powerful interest group. Their professional heirs in the nineteenth century wanted to retain the privileges. Furthermore, the close ties between military and civil authorities and the unclear lines of subordination led to the blurring of distinctions in civil-military relations.[13]

In the nineteenth and early twentieth centuries, these patterns in civil-military relations and civil-church relations had a great impact on Mexico's political development. They complemented the corporatist heritage by establishing groups that saw their own interests, not those of society, as primary. These groups competed for political ascendancy, reinforcing the already-present social inequality by creating a hierarchy of interests and prestige.

To the legacies of corporatism, social inequality, special interests, and intolerance can be added the Spanish bureaucratic tradition. Critics tend to focus on the inefficiencies of the Spanish bureaucracy and the differences between legal theory and the application of administrative criteria.[14] In part, problems can be attributed to the distance between the mother country and the colonies, as well as to the distance between Mexico City, the seat of the viceroyalty of New Spain, established in 1535, and its far-flung settlements in Yucatán, Chiapas, and what is today the southwestern United States. A more important feature of Spanish religious and civil structures was their strongly hierarchical nature and centralization. Low-level bureaucrats lacked authority. Decisions were made only at the top of the hierarchy, with delay, inefficiency, and corruption as the outcome.[15]

The hierarchical structure of the Spanish state in the New World is no better illustrated than through the viceroy himself. The viceroy (*virrey*) was in effect the vice-king, a personal appointee of and substitute for the king of Spain. He had two sources of power: He was the supreme civil authority and also the commander in chief of the military. In addition, he was the vice-patron of the Catholic Church, responsible for the mission policies in the colonization process. Remember, this individual, along with a second viceroy in Lima, Peru, governed all of Spanish-speaking Latin America and the southwestern United States.

Upon its independence, the viceregal structure left Mexico with two political tendencies. First, the individual viceroys became extremely important, some serving for many years, completely at the whim of the crown. This shifted considerable political legitimacy away from Spanish institutions to a single person. The personalization of power tended to devalue the institutionalization of political structures, thereby enhancing the importance of political personalities. It also left Mexico with an integrated civil and religious/cultural tradition, complemented by an equally blended, hierarchical indigenous tradition of executive authority. Justo Sierra, a Mexican historian, described the viceroy's power and the church-state relationship:

> The viceroy was the king. His business was to hold the land—that is, to conserve the king's dominion, New Spain, at all costs. The way to conserve it was to pacify it; hence the close collaboration with the church. In view of the privileges granted by the pope to the Spanish king in America, it could be said that the church in America was under the Spanish king: this was called the royal patronate. But the ascendancy that the church had acquired in Spanish America, because it consolidated, through conversions, the work of the Conquest, made it actually a partner in the government.[16]

Spanish political authority was top-heavy, placing most of the power in the hands of an executive institution. The viceroy's decision-making authority had few restrictions. In many respects, the viceroy's self-developed political aura was equivalent to the *presidencialismo* described earlier. A wonderful illustration of this influence on political elite culture in the late twentieth century was revealed to me in an interview. When cabinet members met with President Echeverría, who was widely known for his loquaciousness and lengthy meetings, no one wanted to excuse themselves to use the bathroom, instead waiting for hours for the president to be the first to do so. No doubt this may have happened to some of the viceroy's advisers.

The Spanish did create an *audiencia*, a sort of quasi-legislative-judicial body that acted as a board of appeals for grievances against the viceroy and could channel complaints directly to the crown, bypassing the viceroy. Also, the crown appointed its own inspectors, often secret, who traveled to New Spain to hear charges against a viceroy's abuse of authority. These *visitadores* were empowered to conduct thorough investigations and report to the crown.

The minor restrictions on viceregal powers did not mean there was a separation of powers, an independent judiciary, a legislative body, or decentralization. Some participation at the local level existed, but Mexico had no legislative heritage comparable to that found in the British colonies' colonial assemblies until 1808, when the French invaded Spain and the monarchy collapsed. As Jaime Rodríguez O. has argued in his path-breaking contributions providing evidence of the colonies' liberal, political heritage, after Spanish patriots established a legislative body at Cádiz in 1810:

> The liberal tradition that emerged in Cádiz formed the basis of later Mexican political, economic, and institutional development. The constitution of 1812 established representative government at three levels: the cities and towns (the constitutional ayuntamiento), the provinces (the provincial deputations), and the monarchy (the Cortes). When it allowed cities and towns with one thousand inhabitants or more to form *ayuntamientos*, it transferred political power from the center to the periphery and incorporated a great number of persons in the political process.[17]

Rodríguez goes on to suggest that "the scope of political participation was extraordinary. Hundreds of thousands of citizens, possibly more than a million, or about a sixth of New Spain's population, including Indians, mestizos, castas, and blacks, who were legally prohibited from voting, participated in elections and in government at the local, provincial, and monarchy-wide levels."[18] Thus, it is not surprising that Mexico quickly established a legislative body after independence, but it functioned effectively for only brief periods in the 1860s and 1870s and again in the 1920s, remaining ineffectual and subordinate throughout most of the twentieth century to executive authority until the 1990s. As one scholar concluded from years of archival research, it is fair to say that colonialism and Catholicism left Mexico with ambiguous political practices and ideas, including both liberalism and authoritarianism.[19]

Finally, another important Spanish political heritage is the role of the state in society. The strong authoritarian institutions in New Spain and the size of the Spanish colonial bureaucracy established the state as the pre-eminent institution.[20] The only other institution whose influence came close was the Catholic Church. Educated male Spaniards born in the New World essentially had three career choices: the colonial bureaucracy, the clergy (which appealed to only a minority), and the military. New Spain's private sector was weak, underdeveloped, and closed. The crown permitted little commercial activity among the colonies or with other countries. The mono-polistic relationship between Spain and the colonies kept the latter from developing their full economic potential. Michael Meyer and William Sherman characterized Spain's policies as:

> protectionist in the extreme, which meant that the economy in New Spain was very much restricted by limitations imposed by the imperial system. Thus the natural growth of industry and commerce was significantly impeded, because manufacturers and merchants in Spain were protected from the competition of those in the colony. In accord with the classic pattern, the Spanish Indies were to supply Spain with raw products, which could be made into finished goods in the mother country and sold back to the colonists at a profit.[21]

A long-term political consequence of a strong state and a weak private sector was the overarching prestige of the state, to the disadvantage of the private sector. Economically, then, the state was in the driver's seat, not because it controlled most economic resources, but because it provided the most important positions available in the colonial world. The same mentality developed in the twentieth century in other colonial settings. For example, Indians came to believe that the British civil service was the preeminent institution in India and that government employment would grant them great prestige.[22] In the same way, positions in the Mexican state bureau-cracy were seen by many educated Mexicans as the ultimate employment, and so the competition for places was keen. One cultural theorist, Glen Dealy, argues that "public power like economic wealth is rooted in rational accumulation. Capitalism measures excellence in terms of accumulated wealth; *caudillaje* [Latin American culture] measures one's virtue in terms of accumulated public power."[23] This way of life did not end with the decline of the Spanish empire and Spain's departure from Mexico. Figures from the last third of the nineteenth century demonstrate that the govern-ment employed a large percentage of educated, professional men, suggesting again the limited opportunities in the private sector.

The Mexican state's importance can be explained by not only eco-nomic underdevelopment, but also by the status of the state in the New World. In other words, it was natural for Mexicans to expect the state to play an influential role. Not liking state intervention in their lives, similar to the feeling of most people in the United States.[24] Mexicans nevertheless came to depend on the state as a problem solver, in part because there was no well-developed, institutional infrastructure at the local level contributing to self-reliant thinking.

Spain bequeathed to Mexico an individualistic cultural mind-set. North Americans, although characterized by self-initiative and independence, exhibited a strong sense of community. That is, throughout the western expansion, U.S. settlers saw surviving together as in the interest of the group as well as in the interest of its members. Mexicans, on the other hand, exhibited a strong sense of self. This, combined with the sharper social-class divisions and social inequality, led to a preeminence of individual or familial preservation, unassociated with the protection of larger groups. The lack of communal ties reinforced the primacy of personal ties. It was a familiar phenomenon elsewhere in Latin America as well. In the political realm, it generally translates into *whom* you know rather than *what* you know. This statement is an almost universal truism, but whom you know gains in importance where access to authority is limited.[25]

Finally, the structural arrangements of the Spanish colonial empire and the distances between the colonies and the mother country and between the colonies themselves made for considerable dissatisfaction with the rules imposed. The Spanish settlers, and later their mestizo descendants, increasingly disobeyed orders from overseas. Sometimes they could justifiably assert that a law no longer applied to the situation at hand. At other times they would flout a law they found inconvenient. The inefficiencies inherent in the transatlantic management of possessions in two continents, built-in social inequalities, and the gap between Old World theory and New World reality meant the marginalization of Spain's laws in the Western Hemisphere. A lack of respect for the law and the importance of personal and familial interests were fundamental factors in Mexico's political evolution from the 1830s through the beginning of the twenty-first century. Current, contradictory views of the culture of law in Mexico are especially relevant to success in consolidating democracy.

NINETEENTH-CENTURY POLITICAL HERITAGE

Shortly after its independence Mexico experimented briefly with a monarchical system, but the rapid demise of the three-hundred-year-old colonial structure left a political void. The only legitimate authority, the crown, and its colonial representative, the viceroy, disappeared. Intense political conflict ensured as various groups sought to legitimize their political philosophies. The battle for political supremacy affected the goals of the antagonists and influenced the process by which Mexicans settled political disputes. By the 1840s, Mexico had fluctuated between a political model advocating federalism, the decentralization of power similar to that practiced in the United States, and centralism, the allocation of more decision-making authority to the national government.

As was true of many Latin American countries, Mexico was caught between the idea of rejecting its centralized, authoritarian Spanish heritage and the idea of adopting the reformist U.S. model. The obstinacy of their proponents kept political affairs in constant flux. Violence was a frequent means for settling political disagreements, which enhanced the presence and importance of the army as an arbiter of political conflicts, and consumed much of the government budget that might otherwise have been spent more productively.

By the mid-nineteenth century two mainstreams of political thought confronted Mexicans: conservatism and liberalism. Mexican liberalism was a mixture of borrowed and native ideas that largely rejected Spanish authoritarianism and tradition and instead drew on Enlightenment ideas from France, England, and the United States. Some of its elements included such basic U.S. tenets as guarantees of political liberty and the sovereignty of the general will, in combination with nineteenth-century laissez-faire economic principles. Among its principles were greater citizen participation in government, free-speech guarantees, and a strong legislative branch. Liberals complemented these principles with a concept known as Jeffersonian agrarian democracy. Jefferson had advocated encouraging large numbers of small landholders in the United States. His rationale was that people with property constitute a stable citizenry; having something to lose, they would vigorously defend the democratic political process. The liberals also believed in classic economic liberalism, the philosophy pervading England and the United States during the same period. Economic liberalism of this period referred to the encouragement of individual initiative and the protection of individual property rights.[26]

Mexican conservatives held to an alternative set of political principles. Whereas an examination of liberal ideas reveals that most of them were borrowed from leading thinkers and political systems foreign to Mexico's experience, the conservatives praised the reform-minded Bourbon administration of the Spanish colonies prior to independence and emphasized a strong central executive. They argued for a strong executive because it would follow naturally after centuries of authoritarian colonial rule, and because the postindependence violence in the 1830s, 1840s, and 1850s seemed to be part of a larger struggle between anarchy and civilization in Latin America. Without forceful leadership, Mexico would succumb to disorder and remain underdeveloped economically.[27]

The conservatives favored policies promoting industrialization, stressing light manufacturing rather than expansion of the small-landholder class.

Mexico desperately needed capital, much of which had fled after independence and during the chaotic political period that followed. Both conservatives and liberals looked approvingly on foreign investment and encouraged policies that would attract outside capital, particularly to mining and struggling industries such as textiles.[28]

Neither the conservatives nor the liberals gave much attention to the plight of indigenous Mexicans. Because the thinkers in both camps generally were *criollos* of middle- and upper-middle-class background, their primary concerns were the maintenance of social order and the interests of their classes. Although the conservatives essentially ignored the Indians, the liberals sought to apply their philosophy of economic individualism to the indigenous system of communal property holding, believing it to be an obstacle to development.

Liberals and conservatives clashed most violently on the role of the Catholic Church. The liberals believed, and correctly so, that the church, as an integral ally of the Spanish state, conveyed support for the hierarchical, authoritarian, political structure.[29] Essentially, it was the church's control of education and nearly all aspects of cultural life that permitted its influence. The conservatives, on the other hand, saw the church as an important force and worked toward an alliance with it.

Because the liberals viewed the church as a staunch opponent and as the conservatives' political and economic supporter, they wanted to reduce or eliminate altogether its influence. They introduced the Ley Lerdo (Lerdo law) on June 1, 1856, essentially forcing the church to sell off its large landholdings, which at that time accounted for a sizable portion of all Mexican real estate. But the law did not have its intended consequences. The church traded land for capital, thereby preserving a source of economic influence and at the same time enlarging the already substantial estates of the buyers.[30] The liberals also attacked the church's special privileges, which had been left inviolate by the 1824 constitution immediately after independence. They eliminated its legal *fueros* and placed cemeteries under the jurisdiction of public authorities.[31]

From this brief overview, we can see that each side had something useful to offer. Yet their unwillingness to compromise and the intensity with which they held their opinions led to a polity in constant disarray. The battles between conservatives and liberals culminated in the War of the Reform (1858–1861), in which the victorious liberals imposed, by force, their political views on the defeated conservatives. These views are well represented in the constitution of 1857, a landmark political document that influenced its revolutionary successor, the constitution of 1917.

The issue of church versus state, or the supremacy of state over church, was a crucial element of the conservative-liberal battles and a focus of nineteenth-century politics. The leading liberals of the day saw the classroom as the chief means of social transformation, and the church's control in that arena as undesirable, and so decided to establish secular institutions. To implement this concept, President Benito Juárez appointed in 1867 a committee under Gabino Barreda, an educator who set down some basic principles for public education in the last third of the nineteenth century. The liberals hoped to replace church-controlled schools with free, mandatory public education, but their program was never fully implemented. Most important, they introduced a preparatory educational program, a sort of advanced high school to train future leaders in secular and liberal ideas.

By 1869 the liberals succeeded in defeating the conservatives' forces. Their unwillingness to compromise and their introduction of even more radical reforms—particularly those associated with suppressing the Catholic Church, and incorporated into the 1857 constitution—impelled the conservatives and their church allies to take the unusual step of seeking help from abroad. This ultimately led to the French intervention of 1862 to 1867, and an attempt to enthrone a foreign monarch, Austrian archduke Ferdinand Maximilian. The liberals were nearly defeated during this interlude, but under Benito Juárez's leadership they ultimately won and executed the archduke.

The liberals reigned from 1867 to 1876. This brief period is important because it gave Mexicans a taste of a functioning, liberal political model. The legislative branch of government exercised some actual power. The successors to Benito Juárez lacked the political skills and authority to sustain the government, and their experiment came to an end with the successful revolt of Porfirio Díaz in 1876, a leading military figure in the liberal battles against the French.[32]

Díaz's ambition and his overthrow of Juárez's collaborators introduced a new generation of liberals to leadership positions. These men, most of whom were combat veterans of the liberal-conservative conflicts and the French intervention, were *moderate* liberals, distinct from the radical orthodox liberals of the Juárez generation. Díaz and the moderate liberals paved the way for the introduction of a new political philosophy into Mexico: positivism. As described by historian Charles A. Hale,

> Scientific or positive politics involved the argument that the country's problems should be approached and its policies formed scientifically. Its principal characteristics were an attack on doctrinaire [radical] liberalism, or "metaphysical politics," an apology for strong government to counter

endemic revolutions and anarchy, and a call for constitutional reform. It drew upon a current of European, particularly French, theories dating back to Henri de Saint-Simon and Auguste Comte in the 1820s, theories that under the name of positivism had become quite generalized in European thought by 1878. Apart from the theoretical origins of their doctrine, the exponents of scientific politics in Mexico found inspiration in the concrete experience of the contemporary conservative republics of France and Spain and in their leaders.[33]

The motto for many positivists in Mexico and elsewhere in Latin America was liberty and progress through peace and order. The key to Mexican positivism, as it was implemented by successive administrations under Porfirio Díaz, who ruled Mexico from 1877 to 1880 and 1884 to 1911, was order. After years of political instability, violence, and civil war, these men saw peace as a critical necessity for progress. Their explanation for the disruptive preceding decades centered on the notion that too much of Mexico's political thinking had been based on irrational or "unscientific" ideas influenced by the spiritual teachings of the church and that alternative political ideas were counterproductive. As Díaz himself suggested, "all citizens of a republic should receive the same training, so that their ideas and methods may be harmonized and the national identity intensified."[34]

Building on the philosophy of their orthodox liberal predecessors, the Díaz administrations came to believe that the most effective means for conveying rational positivist thought, or this new form of moderate liberalism, was public education. Education therefore became the essential instrument for homogenizing Mexican political values. It would turn out a new generation of political, intellectual, and economic leaders who would guide Mexico along the path of material progress and political development. Preeminent among the public institutions was the National Preparatory School in Mexico City, which enrolled children of regional and national notables. Its matriculation lists read like a roll of future national leaders.[35]

The acceptance of positivist ideas by the moderate liberals ultimately led to the dominance of order over liberty and progress. Indeed, it can be argued that after decades of civil conflict, positivism became a vehicle for reintroducing conservative ideas among Mexico's liberal leadership. Díaz increasingly used the state's power to maintain political order, allowing economic development to occur without government interference. His government encouraged the expansion of mining and made generous concessions to foreigners to obtain investment.

The Porfiriato, as the period of Díaz's rule is known in Mexico, had significant consequences that led to the country's major social upheaval of the twentieth century, the Mexico Revolution of 1910, and numerous political and social legacies. Díaz attacked two important social issues: the relationship between church and state and the role of indigenous Mexicans in the society.

Ironically, the Catholic Church regained considerable influence during the liberal era. Even Benito Juárez realized after Maximilian's defeat that pursuit of radical antichurch policies would only generate further resistance and disorder. Díaz pursued a pragmatic policy of reconciliation in the 1870s, separating church and state, but permitting the church to strengthen its religious role as long as it remained aloof from secular and political affairs.[36] Thus, the two parties achieved a modus vivendi, although the state remained in the stronger position, and the 1857 constitution retained repressive, antichurch provisions.

Díaz's attitude toward the Indians was also significant because it reflected a broader attitude toward social inequality. He and his collaborators, as did the original liberals, saw the Indians as obstacles to Mexican development. They applied the provisions of the law forcing the sale of church property to the communal property held by Indian villages, accelerating the pace of sales begun by the orthodox liberals in the 1860s. But the positivists were not satisfied with this economic measure. Many of them accepted the notion, popular throughout Latin America at the time, that Indians were a cultural and social burden and were racially inferior.[37] To overcome this racial barrier, they proposed introducing European immigration, in the hope of wiping out the indigenous culture and providing a superior economic example for the mestizo farmer.

To ensure that immigration would take place, the Mexican government passed a series of colonization laws in the 1880s that granted generous concessions to foreigners who would survey public lands. By 1889 foreigners had surveyed almost eighty million acres and had acquired large portions of the surveyed acreage at bargain-basement prices. For the most part, however, these people were not typical settlers; rather, they, like the Mexicans who purchased church and Indian lands, were large-landholders. Two million acres of communal Indian lands went to them and to corporations. Hence, the colonization laws not only increased the concentration of land in the hands of wealthy Mexicans and foreigners, but antagonized small mestizo and Indian farmers, who became a force during the Mexican Revolution.

Díaz implemented policies that improved the country economically, but the primary beneficiaries were the wealthy at home and abroad. The laboring classes, generally mestizo in origin, benefited little from the politics of peace. Díaz focused on a small group of supporters and ignored the plight of most of his compatriots. Even middle-class mestizos, who rose to the top of the ladder politically by 1900, were limited in their abilities to share in the economic goods of the Díaz era. As two recent historians of Mexico suggested,

> The structure of Mexican society during the Porfiriato consisted of a number of levels that must be noted in order to understand the social dynamics of the era. Large holders of commercialized agriculture land constituted the top of the pyramid. Land provided the economic core as well as status. From this base large landholders diversified into manufacturing, mining, or other profitable activities. An elite, allied with national and regional political groups, with business and personal connections to foreign capitalists and investors, formed an interlocking socioeconomic and political directorate. They used their political, economic, and social influence to reinforce their position. Economic concessions, contracts, and other forms of political patronage fell to this group. They negotiated among themselves for a share of the political power and economic fruits of modernization.[38]

To understand Mexican politics in the twentieth century, in the post-revolutionary era, it is even more important to explore the political heritage left by Díaz and his cronies. In the first place, although church and state were separate and the lines were more firmly drawn between secular and religious activities, Díaz maintained fuzzier relationships between the state and two other important actors, the army and the private sector.

In effect, Díaz established the pattern for civil-military relations that characterized Mexico until the 1940s. Because he himself was a veteran of so many civil conflicts, it was only natural that he recruited many of his important collaborators, on both the national and state level, from among fellow officers.[39] Military men occupied many prominent positions. Although the presence of career officers in the top echelon declined across Díaz's tenure as they were replaced by younger civilian lawyers, no clear relationship of subordination between civil and military authorities was established. Díaz left a legacy of shared power and interlocking leadership.[40]

The unclear lines between military and civilian political power were duplicated between politicians and the business elite. It is the nature of a capitalist system to have an exchange of leaders between the economic and political spheres, as in the United States, but such linkages in an authoritarian political structure, where access to power and decision-making is closed, can produce potentially significant consequences. Díaz, who had control over most of the important national political offices, used appointments to reward supporters or as a means to co-opt opponents. At no time since 1884 has any administration had stronger elite economic representation in political office than under Díaz. Approximately a fifth of all national politicians from 1884 to 1911, with the peak in 1897, were businessmen. For most of the twentieth century they made up fewer than 5 percent of Mexico's public figures.[41] This pattern did not change until Vicente Fox and Felipe Calderón were presidents, during which time (2000–2012), businessmen went from 5 percent in the pre-democratic era to 12 percent after 2000, a dramatic 120 percent increase. Among cabinet members alone, a fifth boasted successful business careers.[42] Giving these positions, especially at the provincial level, to members of prominent families during the Porfiriato, further closed paths of upward social mobility to less-favored groups, especially the mestizo middle class.[43]

By the time Díaz began his third term as president in 1888, he had succeeded in controlling national elections, although he had not created a national electoral machine similar to that of the Partido Nacional Revolucionario (PNR), established in 1929, and its successors. He continued to hold elections to renew the loyalty of the people to his leadership and to allow him to reward his faithful supporters with sinecures as federal deputies (congressmen) and senators. His control was so extensive that occasionally he chose the same person for more than one elective office.

Building on the original conservative philosophy and the colonial heritage, Díaz reversed the tenuous decentralization trend begun under President Juárez. It should be noted, however, that Juárez had no intention of giving up executive power, repeatedly seeking the presidency, only to die in office. Indeed, as Jaime Rodríguez O. points out, when Porfirio Díaz initially revolted against Juárez in 1871, which failed, he "issued the Plan of La Noria, which challenged Juárez's reelection [for the fourth time], opposed a 'lifetime president' and called for 'effective suffrage and no reelection'."[44] Díaz accomplished his centralization strategy structurally by decreasing the powers of the legislative and judicial branches, making them subordinate to the executive branch and to the presidency specifically. He also strengthened the presidency as distinct from the executive branch. Although the legislative branch was subordinated to the executive, recent research clearly demonstrates that many members of Congress expressed independent opinions. As Armando Razo has demonstrated, "Two years after Díaz seized control more than two-thirds of the votes recorded opposition."[45] While opposing votes in Congress continued throughout his administration, they declined significantly by the 1890s.

Díaz went beyond aggrandizement of political authority in the executive branch and the presidency by strengthening the federal government or state generally. He did this by expanding the federal bureaucracy. Between 1876 and 1910 the government payroll grew some 900 percent. In 1876 only 16 percent of the middle class worked for the government; by 1910 the figure was 70 percent.[46] As in the colonial period, the private sector was not incorporating new generations of educated Mexicans; rather, their careers were being pursued within the public sector, notably the federal executive. Díaz provided the twentieth century with a dominant state, an apparatus that most successful Mexicans would want to control because it was essential to their economic future.

Because Díaz held the presidency for some thirty years, a personality cult developed around his leadership. His collaborators conveyed the message that progress, as they defined it, was guaranteed by his presence. His indispensability enhanced his political maneuverability. On the other hand, Díaz put in place a political system that was underdeveloped institutionally. In concentrating on his personality, political institutions failed to acquire legitimacy. Even the stability of the political system itself was at stake because continuity was not guaranteed by the acceptability of its institutions, but by an individual person, Díaz.

The Porfiriato also reinforced the paternalism handed down from the political and social culture of the precolonial and colonial periods. Díaz's concessions to favored people, providing them with substantial economic rewards, encouraged dependence on his personal largesse and the government generally.[47] This technique, which he used generously to pacify opponents and reward friends, produced corruption at all levels of political life. It encouraged the belief that political office was a reward to be taken advantage of by the officeholder rather than a public responsibility. The political cultures of many other countries are similarly characterized to a greater or lesser degree.

Against his most recalcitrant foes, Díaz was willing to use less ingratiating techniques. Toward the end of his regime, press censorship became widespread. As a whole, he favored a controlled, complimentary press to counter criticism from independent sources. If threats or imprisonment were not sufficient to deter his opponents, he resorted to more severe measures. Typically, lower social groups were the victims of violent suppression. A notorious example of this policy was the treatment of the Yaqui Indians in northwestern Mexico, who rebelled after influential members of the Díaz administration began seizing their lands. The Yaquis were subjected to brutalities and were forced into what were in effect concentration camps, and many were deported to Yucatán, where most perished in forced labor on the henequen plantations in the hot tropical climate.[48]

As Mexico emerged from the first decade of the twentieth century, it acquired a political model that drew on Spanish authoritarian and paternal heritages. Like the viceroys before him, but without reporting to any other authority, Díaz exercised extraordinary power. He built up a larger state apparatus as a means of retaining power, and although he strengthened the role of the state in society, he did not legitimize its institutions. While he did succeed in building some economic infrastructure in Mexico, he failed to meet social needs and maltreated certain groups, thereby continuing and intensifying the social inequalities existing under his colonial predecessors. His favoritism toward foreigners caused resentment and contributed to the rise of nationalism after 1911. The lack of separation between civilian and military leadership left Mexicans unclear about the principle of civilian supremacy and autonomy, an issue that would confront his successors. Finally, although the moderate liberals/converted positivists replaced orthodox liberals and, in many cases, substituted conservative principles for their original political ideas, the excluded liberal followers who remained faithful to the cause of political liberty and democratic elections rose up once again after 1910.[49] Today, revisionist historians believe that many Mexicans throughout the nineteenth century believed in the principles of popular sovereignty, local rights, and civilian, representative, constitutional government, and that these beliefs, providing a foundation for democratic political development, have been undervalued in our analysis and understanding of significant political themes leading up to the 1910 Revolution.[50] As one historian has deftly argued, the defense of *Libertad* "meant one thing for elites and another for popular classes. Porfirian elites sought the centralization of a fragmented nation, while popular classes fought for more meaningful local autonomy."[51]

THE REVOLUTIONARY HERITAGE:
SOCIAL VIOLENCE AND REFORM

It can never be forgotten that contemporary Mexico is the product of a violent revolution that lasted, on and off, from 1910 through 1920. The decimation of its population—more than a million people during the decade—alone would have left an indelible stamp on Mexican life, and those figures can be calculated at even higher numbers.[52] The revolution touched all social classes, and although it did not affect all locales with the same intensity, it brought together the residents of villages and cities to a degree never achieved before or since. In the same way that World War II altered life in the United States, the revolution brought profound changes to Mexican society.

The causes of the revolution have been thoroughly examined by historians. They are numerous, and their roots can be found in the failures of the Porfiriato. Among the most important to have been singled out are foreign economic penetration, class struggle, land ownership, economic depression, local autonomy, the clash between modernity and tradition, the breakdown of the Porfirian system, the weakness of the transition process, the lack of opportunity for upward political and social mobility, and the aging of the leadership.[53] Historians do not agree on the primary causes or on whether the 1910 revolution was a "real" revolution, that is, whether it radically changed the social structure.[54]

In my own view, the revolution introduced significant changes, although it did not alter social structures to the degree one expects of a major social revolution on a par with the Cuban, Soviet, or Chinese revolutions.[55] For example, recent research comparing the impact of violent change versus peaceful change on the composition of national political leadership in Mexico suggests that peaceful change through the electoral process produced equally significant alterations in leadership characteristics (see Table 2-1). Nevertheless, to understand Mexican political developments in the twentieth century, it is necessary to explore the ideology of the revolution and the political structures that emerged in the immediate postrevolutionary era.

Ideologically, one of the best ways to understand the diverse social forces for change is to trace the constitutional provisions of 1917 to the precursors and revolutionary figures. Among the most important precursors, Ricardo Flores Magón and his brothers offered ideas leading up to the revolution and revived the legitimacy of orthodox liberalism by establishing liberal clubs throughout Mexico.[56] This provided a basis for middle-class participation in and support for revolutionary principles. Flores Magón and his adherents published a newspaper in exile in the United States, *La Regeneración*, banned in Mexico. Many prominent political figures in the revolution, including General Alvaro Obregón, cited its influence on their

Table 2-1 Career Experiences of Revolutionary and Democratic Politicians

Generation	Type of Experience (%)			
	Local[a]	Governor	Military	Business
Revolutionary	43	38	47	6
Change %	48+	3+	15+	−71
Pre-revolutionary	29	37	41	21
Democratic	46	8	4	12
Change %	170+	−68	−67	140+
Pre-democratic	17	25	12	5

Source: Mexican Political Biographies Project, 2009 and Mexican Political Biographies Project, 1995.
Pre-revolutionary refers to the 1885 to 1911 administrations; **pre-democratic** refers to the 1935 to 1988 administrations.
[a]Local refers to mayor, local deputy and syndic for the revolutionary and pre-revolutionary generations, but only to mayor and local deputy for the democratic/pre-democratic generations.

attitudes, as did younger politicians who dominated Mexican politics in the 1940s and 1950s.[57] Perhaps more than in any other area, Flores Magón offered arguments in support of workers' rights, establishing such principles as minimum wage and maximum hours in strike documents and Liberal Party platforms.[58] He also advocated the distribution of land, the return of communal (*ejido*) properties to the Indians, and the requirement that agricultural land be productive.

Politically, the most prominent figure in the pre-revolutionary and revolutionary eras was Francisco I. Madero, son of wealthy Coahuilan landowners in northern Mexico, who believed in mild social reforms and the basic principles of political liberty. He founded the Anti-Reelectionist Party to oppose Porfirio Díaz. A product of his class, he did not believe in structural change but did believe in equal opportunity for all.[59] His *Presidential Succession of 1910*, the Anti-Reelectionist Party platform, and his revolutionary 1910 Plan of San Luis Potosí advocated three important political items: no reelection, electoral reform (effective suffrage), and revision of the constitution of 1857. The most important of Madero's social and economic ideas concerned public education; he believed, as did the orthodox liberals, that education was the key to a modern Mexico.

More radical social ideas were offered by such revolutionaries as Pascual Orozco, who later turned against Madero, Francisco Villa, and Emiliano Zapata. Orozco, who expressed many popular social and economic views, some complementary to those of Flores Magón, also called for municipal autonomy from federal control in response to Díaz's centralization of political authority. Villa, from the northern state of Chihuahua, did not offer a true ideology or program, but the policies he implemented in the regions under his control reflected his radical social philosophy. In Chihuahua, for example, he nationalized large-landholders' properties outright and, because of his own illiteracy (he learned to read only late in life), instituted a widespread primary school program. Zapata, who came from the rugged state of Morelos just south of Mexico City, fought largely over the issue of land. His ideology, expressed by his collaborators, appeared in his famous Plan de Ayala.[60]

With the exception of Madero, these men offered few specific political principles. Consequently, the political ideology of the revolution, with the possible exception of effective suffrage and no reelection, emerged piecemeal, either in the constitutional debates at Querétaro, before the writing of the 1917 constitution, or from actual experience.[61]

One of the most important of these themes was Mexicanization, a broad form of nationalism. It is a revolutionary principle stressing the importance of Mexicans and Mexico, enhancing their influence and prestige.

Simply stated, Mexico comes first, outsiders second. In the economic realm, it can be seen in placing Mexicans instead of foreigners in management positions, even if the investment is foreign in origin. An even more important expression of economic nationalism occurred in regard to resources: the formalization of Mexican control. With few exceptions, at least 51 percent of any enterprise had to be in the hands of Mexicans. But after 1988, desperate for foreign investment, the government eliminated many restrictions in most economic sectors.[62]

Mexicanization spread to cultural and psychological realms. On a cultural level, the revolution gave birth to extraordinary productivity in art, music, and literature, in which methodology was often as important as the content. In the visual fields, Mexicans revived the mural, an art form that could be viewed by large numbers of Mexicans rather than remain on the walls of private residences or inaccessible museums.[63] Political cartoons, during and after the revolution, blossomed. In literature, the social protest novel—the novel of the revolution—came to the fore. Often cynical or highly critical, these works castigated not only the failures of the Porfiriato, but the apparent failures of the revolutionaries too.[64] Musicians paid attention to the indigenous heritage, even composing the classical *Indian Symphony*, whose roots lie in the native culture. Ballads and popular songs flourished throughout Mexico as each region made its contributions.[65]

Mexicanization also affected a line of intellectual thought known as *lo mexicano*, which was concerned with national or cultural identity, and pride in Mexican heritage. Henry Schmidt, one of the most insightful students of the Mexican cultural rebirth, assessed its impact: "The 1910 revolution generated an unprecedented expansion of knowledge in Mexico. At the same time as it lessened the tensions of an unresponsive political system, it ushered in a new age of creation. If the post-revolutionary political development cannot always be viewed favorably, the efforts to reorient thought toward a greater awareness of national conditions at least merit commendation. Thus the 1920s is known as the period of 'reconstruction' and 'renaissance,' when the country, having undergone its most profound dislocation since the Conquest, attempted to consolidate the gains its people had struggled for since the waning of the Porfiriato."[66]

Another important theme of the revolution was social justice. Economically, although not expressed specifically in the constitution, this included a fairer distribution of national income. Socially, and called for by nearly all revolutionary and intellectual thinkers, it involved expanded public education. Madero wanted to improve access. Many others promoted education as an indirect means to enhance economic opportunity, particularly for the Indians, whose integration into the mainstream mestizo culture could thereby be accomplished. A leading intellectual, José Vasconcelos, who made significant contributions to Mexican education, praised a coming "cosmic race," suggesting that a racial mix would produce a superior, not inferior, culture.[67]

The revolution did not react adversely to a strong state. Instead, building on the administrative infrastructure created under the Porfiriato, postrevolutionary regimes contributed to its continued expansion. Yet unlike Díaz, the revolution heralded a *larger state role*, giving the state responsibilities not expected of a government before 1910. According to Héctor Aguilar Camín and Lorenzo Meyer, the construction of a new state incorporated "the first bold attempts at developing the state as an instrument of economic, educational, and cultural action and regulation."[68] For example, as a consequence of Mexicanization, the state gained control over subsoil resources and eventually became the administrator of extractive enterprises. The phenomenal growth in the value of the nation's oil in the 1970s cast the state in an even more important role. When the state nationalized foreign petroleum companies in 1938, it established national and international precedents elsewhere.[69] In later periods, the state came to control such industries as fertilizers, telephones, electricity, airlines, steel, and copper. In the mid-1980s the trend gradually began to be reversed.

The revolution stimulated the political liberalism that had lain dormant under the ideology of positivism during the last twenty years of the Porfiriato. Freedom of the press was revived during the revolution. The media underwent a regression in the 1920s, and although censorship continued to raise its head, the conditions under which the media operated were much improved. The most important principle of political liberalism—increased participation in governance expressed through effective suffrage—was given substance in Madero's election in 1911, probably Mexico's freest, but never returned to that level until 1997.[70]

The political mythology of the revolution, "Effective Suffrage, No Reelection," was stamped on all official government correspondence I received until the 1970s. Effective suffrage is close to being achieved in practice, even though many Mexicans still do not believe elections are honest or fair.[71] On the other hand, no reelection, with but a few exceptions in the 1920s and 1930s, has become the rule. When General Alvaro Obregón tried to circumvent it in 1928 by forcing the Congress to amend the constitution to allow him to run again after a four-year hiatus, he was elected but then assassinated before taking office. No president since has tried this maneuver. No elected executive, including mayors and governors, repeats officeholding, consecutively or otherwise.[72] Legislators may repeat terms, but not consecutively, a concept introduced in the 1930s.

The revolution also produced an extraordinary influence on Mexico's political leadership after 1920. Half the national political leaders born between 1870 and 1900 participated in this violent event. Among those who held national office for the first time, 47 percent fought on the side of the revolutionaries, 9 percent in opposition to these forces, and 2 percent on both sides. Presidents Alvaro Obregón (1920–1924) and Plutarco Elías Calles (1924–1928), as well as Díaz, recruited many of their wartime cronies. Through 1940, the presidents who succeeded them were, with one exception, generals who fought in these battles, often under these two predecessors. Veterans continued to dominate Mexican administrations from 1914 through 1934. As might be expected, the 1910 revolution introduced a different type of politician as well, one whose social origins were quite distinct from those of his noncombatant contemporary. In effect, the revolution reintroduced the importance of working-class origins among Mexico's leadership, since 72 percent of the public figures who were combat veterans were from working-class families, compared with only 34 percent who came from middle- and upper-class backgrounds.[73]

Another revolutionary outcome was the changed relationship between church and state. Once again, the seeds of orthodox liberalism appeared in the constitutional debates. Many of the revolutionaries eyed the church with severe distrust and reinstituted many of the most restrictive provisions advocated by the early liberals. Until 1992 these provisions could be found, unchanged, in the constitution. They include removing religion from primary education (Article 3), taking away the church's right to own real property (Article 27), and secularizing certain religious activities and restricting the clergy's potential political actions (Article 130). No clergy of any faith were permitted in their capacity as ministers to criticize Mexican laws or even to vote. In spite of the 1992 reforms, some restrictions on clergy remain in the constitution.

The breakup of large landholdings is also a primary economic and social product of revolutionary ideology. As part of the redistribution of land in Mexico after 1915, the government made the Indian *ejido* concept (village-owned lands) its own, distributing land to thousands of rural villages to be held in common for legal residents, who obtained use rights, not legal title, to it.[74] In effect, the government institutionalized the indigenous land system that the liberals and positivists had attempted to destroy. This structure remained unchanged until 1992.

The revolution also introduced a change in attitude toward labor. For the first time, strikes were legalized, and the right to collective bargaining was sanctioned. Provisions regarding hours and wages, at least for organized labor, were introduced. The 1917 constitution was the first to mention the concept of social security, although it was not implemented until 1943. Organized labor helped General Obregón defeat president Venustiano Carranza in the last armed confrontation of the revolutionary decade.

Finally, although this list is incomplete, the revolution gave greater emphasis to a sense of constitutionalism. In a political sense, constitutionalism provides legitimacy for a set of ideas expressed formally in the national document. It is not only a reference point for the goals of Mexican society after 1920, as a consequence of the revolution, but it also identifies the basic outline of political concepts and processes. The constitution of 1917 itself took on a certain level of prestige. Many of its more radical social, economic, and political provisions are observed more in abeyance than reality, but its contents and its prestige together influenced the values of successive generations.[75] In 2010, during the centennial celebrations of the Mexican Revolution, half of Mexicans believed the Mexican Revolution helped Mexico a lot, and an additional four out of ten Mexicans believed it helped the country some.[76]

THE POLITICS OF PLACE: INTERFACE WITH
THE UNITED STATES

The proximity of the United States has exercised an enormous influence on Mexico. As I argue, "The United States constitutes a crucial variable in the very definition of Mexico's modern political culture."[77] Beginning with independence, the political leaders who sought solutions emphasizing federalism, and later the decentralizing principles of liberalism, borrowed many of their concepts from U.S. political thinkers and documents. In fact, the intellectual ideas provoked by U.S. independence from England provided a fertile literature from which independence precursors could also borrow.

The destiny of the two countries became intertwined politically in more direct ways as a consequence of the annexation of Texas, a northern province of New Spain. Immediately after Mexico won independence, large numbers of Americans began to settle in Texas, quickly outnumbering the Mexicans there. The differences within Texas between Mexicans and Americans and between Texas and the Mexican government led to armed conflict. The Mexican army under General Antonio López de Santa Anna lay siege to the Alamo in February 1836, but was routed from Texas later that year. Texas remained independent of Mexico until 1845, when the United States, by a joint congressional resolution, annexed it. This provoked another conflict, one with even more serious repercussions.[78]

Desirous of more territory, President James Polk used several incidents as a pretext for war. In 1846, U.S. troops drove deep into Mexico's heartland and, in addition to occupying outlying regions of the former Spanish empire in New Mexico and California, seized the port of Veracruz and Mexico City. In the Treaty of Guadalupe Hidalgo, signed on February 2, 1848, Mexico ceded more than half its territory to the United States. Seven years later, the Mexican government, again under Santa Anna, sold the United States a strip of land (in what is now southern Arizona and southern New Mexico), known as the Gadsen Purchase, although this time it was not done under duress.

The war left a justifiably bitter taste in the mouths of many Mexicans. As has been suggested, "The terms of the Treaty of Guadalupe Hidalgo are among the harshest imposed by a winner upon a loser in the history of the world."[79] More than any single issue, the terms established a relationship of distrust between the two nations. Physical incursion from the north took place twice more. Voices in the United States always seemed to call for annexations. Even as late as the first decade of the twentieth century, California legislators publicly advocated acquiring Baja California.

During the Mexican Revolution the United States repeatedly and directly or indirectly intervened in Mexican affairs. The intense personal prejudices or interests of its emissaries often determined U.S. foreign policy decisions. Henry Lane Wilson, ambassador during the Madero administration (1911–1913), played a role in its overthrow and in the failure to ensure the safety of Madero and his vice-president, who were murdered by counter revolutionaries led by Felix Díaz and Victoriano Huerta. Huerta established himself in power, and the violent phase of the revolution began in earnest. President Woodrow Wilson removed the U.S. ambassador and sent personal emissaries to evaluate Huerta. He decided to channel funds to the Constitutionalists, revolutionaries who had remained loyal to Madero and to constitutional government. But after a minor incident involving U.S. sailors in the port of Tampico, Wilson used it as a pretext to order the occupation of the port of Veracruz, resulting in the deaths of numerous Mexicans.[80]

Wilson's high-handedness produced a widespread nationalistic response in Mexico that nearly brought Wilson's intention—to oust Huerta from the presidency—to naught. Based on my own conversations with Mexicans alive at the time of the occupation, they recall discontinuing classes in English, switching back to Mexican cigarettes, and throwing away their Texas-style hats in symbolic protest. Young men as far away as Guadalajara, in western Mexico, readily joined volunteer companies to go fight the Americans.[81] But Huerta fell, and the North Americans did not invade and, indeed, soon left Veracruz.

After the Constitutionalists' victory under Carranza, rebel chieftains began to bicker among themselves. They divided into two major camps: one led by Francisco Villa and Emiliano Zapata and the other by Álvaro Obregón and Carranza. After several major battles, Obregón defeated Villa's forces. In March 1916, after remnants of Villa's forces moved north and attacked Columbus, New Mexico, Wilson ordered a punitive expedition under General John "Black Jack" Pershing against Villa. The U.S. forces battled the Constitutionalists, never caught Villa, and remained in Mexico until 1917.[82]

From this necessarily brief selection of historical examples, it is clear that Mexicans have reason to distrust the United States and to have created an extremely strong sense of nationalism, and as suggested in the previous chapter especially directed toward its northern neighbor, supported to the extent that one-fifth of all Mexicans in 2010 mistakenly believed Mexico obtained its independence from the United States, not Spain![83] The economic, political, and cultural exchanges between the two countries since the 1920s have given rise to issues common to Mexico's relations in all parts of the world, as well as others peculiar to relations between Mexico and the United States. The geographic proximity of two such culturally and economically different societies has generated numerous consequences for domestic politics and their respective national security agendas. These issues will be examined in a broader perspective in a later chapter. For now, I just want to emphasize that Mexico's nearness to the United States has noticeably affected its political and economic history and development.

CONCLUSION

Throughout its recent history, Mexico, as both a colony and an independent nation, established patterns that have contributed heavily to the development of its political model. Some of the more important remnants from the Spanish colonial period are the conflicts of social class, exacerbated by sharp social divisions. Catholicism, introduced as the official religion of the Spanish conquerors, has been equally significant. Its monopoly encouraged a cultural intolerance of other ideas or values and enabled a symbiotic, profitable relationship between the state and the church. The Spanish also fostered a strong sense of special interests, granting privileges to other selected groups, including the military, and ultimately contributing to a particularized civil-military relationship. These elements led to corporatism, an official relationship between important occupational groups or institutions and the state. The Spanish, through their own political structure, particularly the viceroy, imposed three hundred years of authoritarian, centralized administration. Great powers accrued to the executive, to the neglect of other government branches. Nevertheless, shortly before independence, Spanish patriots on the peninsula and Hispanic and Mexican citizens interested in representing the New World established an influential heritage of participation and representation. Furthermore, restrictive economic policies discouraged the growth of a strong colonial economy, thus shoring up the role of the state versus that of an incipient private sector. The state's power and prestige attracted New Spain's most ambitious citizens.

Many features of the colonial period were further enhanced after independence. The conflicts between the liberals and conservatives, driven by an intolerance of counterviews, produced ongoing civil war and anarchy. Although Mexico experimented briefly with a more decentralized form of government, authoritarian qualities were back in the saddle by the end of the nineteenth century. The presidency replaced the viceroyalty in wielding power, and President Díaz expanded the size and importance of the executive branch, thereby continuing to enhance the state's image. Díaz introduced political stability and some economic development, yet he perpetuated the social inequalities inherited from the Spanish period. He also made sure that the military would maintain a large voice in the political system, leaving unresolved the matter of military subordination to civilian authority. The Spanish paternal traditions remained.

The revolution reactively introduced changes, but in many respects retained some of the basic features from the previous two periods. One important innovation was Mexicanization, an outgrowth largely of Mexico's exploitation by foreigners and especially its proximity to the United States. Mexicanization strengthened Mexican values and culture as well as political nationalism. The revolution altered Mexicans' political rhetoric and social goals of legitimizing the needs and interests of lower-income groups and Indians. Yet instead of reducing the role of the state, it made the state into an even more comprehensive institution. The revolution also revived important principles of orthodox liberalism, including political liberties, suppression of the church's secular role, and decentralization of authority, but a decade of civil violence and the need for effective leadership in the face of successive rebellions in the 1920s discouraged implementation of a federal, democratic system. Instead, the revolution left Mexico with a heritage of strong, authoritarian leadership, and military supremacy, even though pockets of democratic participation occurred in various locales for much of the twentieth century, providing a basis for grassroots electoral democracy, which exploded across the republic in the last decade of the twentieth century. Even so, the revolution established the importance of constitutionalism, even if many of the constitution's liberal provisions were never enforced. The legitimacy of its concepts provided the basis for political liberalization under Presidents Salinas and Zedillo (1988–2000).

Finally, Mexico's long, troublesome relationship with the United States produced implications for its political evolution and the functioning of its model. The level of the United States' economic influence in Mexico, and the United States' seizure of more than half of Mexico's national territory, prompted Mexican nationalism and anti-Americanism. And yet, we can witness dramatic shifts in ordinary citizens' nationalistic responses to the United States in the last decade, especially as it relates to their personal security. When asked in 2010 if they would be in favor of organizations from other countries, such as the FBI or the UN, intervening in their country if the government lacked the ability to reduce the level of criminality and violence, an extraordinary 57 percent of Mexicans favored such a response, compared to a only a third who were opposed.[84] Nevertheless, for many decades Mexico has had to labor under the shadow of its internationally powerful neighbor, a psychological, as well as a practical, political burden. Historical experience and geographic proximity influenced many domestic policy decisions and perhaps subtly encouraged a strong, even authoritarian regime prior to 2000 that could prevent the kind of instability and political squabbling that had left Mexico open in the past to territorial depredation.

NOTES

1. Frank Tannenbam, *Mexico: The Struggle for Peace and Bread* (New York: Knopf, 1964), 36.

2. Magnus Mörner's classic study, *Race Mixture in the History of Latin America* (Boston: Little, Brown, 1967).

3. Interestingly, this is even true when comparing the United States with its colonizer, England. See Richard Rose, *Politics in England*, 5th ed. (Boston: Little, Brown, 1989), 69.

4. Charles Kadushin, *American Intellectual Elite* (Boston: Little, Brown, 1974), 26.

5. Roderic Ai Camp, *Mexico's Mandarins: Crafting a Power Elite for the Twenty-First Century* (Berkeley: University of California Press, 2002).

6. For background, see Robert Ricard, *The Spiritual Conquest of Mexico: An Essay on the Apostolate and the Evangelizing Methods of the Mendicant Orders in New Spain, 1523–1572* (Berkeley and Los Angeles: University of California Press, 1966).

7. Samuel Ramos, *Profile of Man and Culture in Mexico* (Austin: University of Texas Press, 1962), 27.

8. Nancy Farriss, *Crown and Clergy in Colonial Mexico, 1759–1821* (London: University of London Press, 1968).

9. Irving A. Leonard, *Books of the Brave: Being an Account of Books and of Men in the Spanish Conquest and Settlement of the Sixteenth-Century New World* (Cambridge, MA: Harvard University Press, 1949).

10. Richard Greenleaf, "Historiography of the Mexican Inquisition," in *Cultural Encounters: The Impact of the Inquisition in Spain and the New World*, ed. Mary Elizabeth Perry and Anne J. Cruz (Berkeley and Los Angeles: University of California Press, 1991), 256–57.

11. Mitchell A. Seligson and Amy Erica Smith, eds., *Political Culture of Democracy, 2010, Democratic Consolidation in the Americas during Hard Times*, Latin American Public Opinion Project (Washington, DC: AID, 2010), 93–97.

12. Lyle McAlister, *The "Fuero Militar" in New Spain, 1764–1800* (Gainesville: University of Florida Press, 1967).

13. Edwin Lieuwen, *Mexican Militarism: The Political Rise and Fall of the Revolutionary Army, 1910–1940* (Albuquerque: University of New Mexico Press, 1968).

14. Henry Bamford Parkes, *A History of Mexico* (Boston: Houghton Mifflin, 1969), 87; Colin M. MacLachlan, *Spain's Empire in the New World* (Berkeley and Los Angeles: University of California Press, 1991), 34ff.

15. For background, see Stafford Poole, *Juan de Ovando: Governing the Spanish Empire in the Reign of Philip II* (Norman: University of Oklahoma Press, 2004), and Charles Gibson, *Spain in America* (New York: Harper & Row, 1967).

16. *The Political Evolution of the Mexican People* (Austin: University of Texas Press, 1969), 107.

17. "Introduction: The Origins of Constitutionalism and Liberalism in Mexico," in Jaime E. Rodríguez O., *The Divine Charter, Constitutionalism and Liberalism in Nineteenth-Century Mexico* (Lanham, MD: Rowman & Littlefield, 2005), 13.

18. Jaime E. Rodríguez O.,"Democracy from Independence to Revolution," in *The Oxford Handbook of Mexican Politics*, ed. Roderic Ai Camp (New York: Oxford University Press, 2012), 34.

19. Matthew D. O'Hara, *A Flock Divided: Race, Religion, and Politics in Mexico, 1749–1857* (Durham, NC: Duke University Press, 2010), 238.

20. *La formación del estado mexicano* (Mexico City: Porrúa, 1984); Juan Felipe Leal, "El estado y el bloque en el poder en México," *Revista Mexicana de Ciencias Políticas y Sociales* 35 (October-December 1989): 12ff.

21. Michael C. Meyer, William L. Sherman, and Susan Deeds, *The Course of Mexican History* (New York: Oxford University Press, 2011), 128.

22. Edward A. Shils, *The Intellectual Between Tradition and Modernity: The Indian Situation* (The Hague: Mouton, 1961).

23. Glen Dealy, *The Public Man: An Interpretation of Latin American and Other Catholic Cultures* (Amherst: University of Massachusetts Press, 1977), 8.

24. In his examination of the heartland, William Least Heat Moon reported that rural Kansas still strongly opposes any project representing federal government intervention. See his *PrairyErth* (New York: Houghton Mifflin, 1991).

25. Larissa Lomnitz, "Horizontal and Vertical Relations and the Social Structure of Urban Mexico," *Latin American Research Review* 17 (1982): 52.

26. For the views of a leading theoretician, and the larger context of liberalism in Mexico, see Charles A. Hale's *Mexican Liberalism in the Age of Mora, 1821–1853* (New Haven, CT: Yale University Press, 1968).

27. John H. Coatsworth and Alicia Torres, "Los orígenes del autoritarismo moderno en México," *Foro Internacional* 16, no. 2 (October–December 1975): 205–32; and Lorenzo Meyer, "The Origins of Mexico's Authoritarian State: Political Control in the Old and New Regimes," in *Authoritarianism in Mexico*, eds. Luis Reyna and Richard Weinert (Philadelphia: ISHI, 1977), 3–22.

28. For examples, see David M. Pletcher, *Rails, Mines, and Progress: Seven American Promoters in Mexico, 1867–1911* (Ithaca, NY: Cornell University Press, 1958).

29. For the long-term consequences of this relationship, see Karl Schmitt, "Church and State in Mexico: A Corporatist Relationship," *Americas* 40, no. 3 (January 1984): 349–76.

30. Robert J. Knowlton, "Some Practical Effects of Clerical Opposition to the Mexican Reform," *Hispanic American Historical Review* 45, no. 2 (May 1965): 246–56, provides concrete examples.

31. Jan Bazant, *Alienation of Church Wealth in Mexico: Social and Economic Aspects of the Liberal Revolution, 1856–1857* (Cambridge, UK: Cambridge University Press, 1971).

32. The conflicts and ideologies are described insightfully by Paul Vanderwood, "Betterment for Whom? The Reform Period: 1855–1875," in *The Oxford History of Mexico*, eds. William H. Beezley and Michael C. Meyer (New York: Oxford University Press, 2010), 349–72.

33. Charles A. Hale, *The Transformation of Liberalism in Late-Nineteenth-Century Mexico* (Princeton, NJ: Princeton University Press, 1989), 27.

34. Robert M. Buffington and William E. French, "The Culture of Modernity," in *The Oxford History of Mexico*, eds. William Beezley and Michael C. Meyer (New York: Oxford University Press, 2010), 377.

35. *Inscripciones*, Universidad Nacional Autónomo de Mexico, Escuela Nacional Preparatoria, official registration records.

36. Karl Schmitt, "The Díaz Conciliation Policy on State and Local Levels, 1867–1911," *Hispanic American Historical Review* 40 (1960): 513–32.

37. Martin S. Stabb, "Indigenism and Racism in Mexican Thought, 1857–1911," *Journal of Inter-American Studies and World Affairs* 1, no. 4 (1959): 405–23.

38. Colin M. MacLachlan and William H. Beezley, *El Gran Pueblo: A History of Greater Mexico* (Englewood Cliffs, NJ: Prentice Hall, 1994), 131.

39. For evidence of this, see the officer promotion lists from various battles in the published records of the Secretaría de Guerra y Marina, *Escalafón general del*

ejército (Mexico City, 1902, 1911, 1914). For his collaborators, see Roderic Ai Camp, *Mexican Political Biographies, 1884–1934* (Austin: University of Texas Press, 1994).

40. For background and the long-term consequences of this relationship, see Roderic Ai Camp, *Generals in the Palacio: The Military in Modern Mexico* (New York: Oxford University Press, 1992).

41. Roderic Ai Camp, *Political Recruitment across Two Centuries: Mexico 1884–1991* (Austin: University of Texas Press, 1995), 132.

42. Roderic Ai Camp, *The Metamorphosis of Leadership in a Democratic Mexico* (New York: Oxford University Press, 2010), 217, 237.

43. For an excellent case study of these interlocking economic-political families, see Mark Wasserman, *Persistent Oligarchs: Elites and Politics in Chihuahua, Mexico, 1910–1940* (Durham, NC: Duke University Press, 1993).

44. Rodríguez O., "Democracy from Independence to Revolution," 26.

45. Armando Razo, *Social Foundations of Limited Dictatorship, Networks and Private Protection During Mexico's Early Industrialization* (Stanford, CA: Stanford University Press, 2008), 69–71.

46. See Francisco Bulnes, *El verdadero Díaz y la Revolución* (Mexico City: Editorial Hispano-Mexicana, 1920), 42. This latter figure is probably exaggerated but indicates the bureaucracy's importance.

47. For details about this favored group of entrepreneurs, see Armando Razo, *Social Foundations of Limited Dictatorship*, 131ff.

48. See John Kenneth Turner's muckraking, autobiographical account in *Barbarous Mexico: An Indictment of a Cruel and Corrupt System* (Austin: University of Texas Press, 1969); or Evelyn Hu-Dehart, "Development and Rural Rebellion: Pacification of the Yaquis in the Late Porfiriato," *Hispanic American Historical Review* 54, no. 1 (February 1974): 72–93.

49. Aldo Flores-Quiroga, "Legitimacy, Sequencing, and Credibility," in *The Divine Charter: Constitutionalism and Liberalism in Nineteenth-Century Mexico*, ed. Jaime E. Rodríguez O. (Lanham, MD: Rowman & Littlefield, 2005), 339–50.

50. Rodríguez O., "Democracy from Independence to Revolution," 34.

51. Patrick J. McNamara, *Sons of the Sierra: Juárez, Díaz, & the People of Ixtlán, Oaxaca, 1855–1920* (Chapel Hill: University of North Carolina Press, 2007), 201.

52. Robert McCaa, argues that deaths, lost births, and emigrants, which totaled two million Mexicans or 13 percent of the population, should all be calculated to understand the impact of this decade of violence. See his "Missing Millions: The Demographic Costs of the Mexican Revolution," *Mexican Studies/Estudios Mexicanos* 19, no. 2 (Summer 2003): 367–400.

53. I am suggesting that *intra-generational* mobility, measured by access to political office for the first time, may be far more significant in explaining political stability and instability than *generational* access to power, measured by age cohort alone. Camp, *Political Recruitment Across Two Centuries*, 45.

54. Paul J. Vanderwood, "Explaining the Mexican Revolution," in *The Revolutionary Process in Mexico: Essays on Political and Social Change, 1880–1940*,

ed. Jaime E. Rodríguez O. (Los Angeles: UCLA Latin American Center, 1990), 97–114.

55. John Womack Jr., "The Mexican Revolution, 1910–1920," in vol. 5 of *The Cambridge History of Latin America*, ed. Leslie Bethell (Cambridge: Cambridge University Press, 1986), 74–153.

56. For background on Flores Magón and other precursors, see James Cockcroft's excellent *Intellectual Precursors of the Mexican Revolution, 1900–1913* (Austin: University of Texas Press, 1968).

57. See the comment of Antonio Armendáriz in my *The Making of a Government: Political Leaders in Modern Mexico* (Tucson: University of Arizona Press, 1984), 79.

58. These can be found in Jesús Silva Herzog, *Breve historia de la revolución mexicana, los antecedentes y la etapa maderista* (Mexico City: Fondo de Cultura Económica, 1960), annexes.

59. Stanley R. Ross, *Francisco I. Madero: Apostle of Mexican Democracy* (New York: Columbia University Press, 1955).

60. See John Womack Jr., *Zapata and the Mexican Revolution* (New York: Knopf, 1968); Michael Meyer, *Mexican Rebel: Pascual Orozco and the Mexican Revolution, 1910–1915* (Lincoln: University of Nebraska Press, 1967).

61. John Mason Hart, "The Mexican Revolution, 1910–20," in Beezley and Meyer, eds., *The Oxford History of Mexico*, 409–37.

62. Randal Sheppard, "Nationalism, Economic Crisis and 'Realistic Revolution' in 1980s Mexico," *Nations and Nationalism* 17, no. 3 (2011): 500–519.

63. Jean Charlot, *The Mexican Mural Renaissance, 1920–1925* (New Haven, CT: Yale University Press, 1967), provides an overview of this movement. For its influence on United States culture, see Helen Delpar, *The Enormous Vogue of Things Mexican: Cultural Relations Between the United States and Mexico, 1920–1935* (Tuscaloosa: University of Alabama Press, 1992).

64. See John Brushwood's, *Mexico in Its Novel: A Nation's Search for Identity* (Austin: University of Texas Press, 1966), 173ff.

65. For wonderfully revealing examples of popular appraisals of various revolutionary figures, see Merle E. Simmons, *The Mexican Corrido as a Source for Interpretive Study of Modern Mexico, 1879–1950* (Bloomington: Indiana University Press, 1957).

66. Henry C. Schmidt, *The Roots of Lo Mexicano: Self and Society in Mexican Thought, 1900–1934* (Austin: University of Texas Press, 1978), 97.

67. José Vasconcelos, *La raza cósmica: Misión de la raza iberoamericana* (Paris: Agencia Mundial de Librerías, 1925).

68. Héctor Aguilar Camín and Lorenzo Meyer, *In the Shadow of the Mexican Revolution: Contemporary Mexican History, 1910–1989* (Austin: University of Texas Press, 1993), 78.

69. Paul Sigmund, *Multinationals in Latin America: The Politics of Nationalization* (Madison: University of Wisconsin Press, 1980), 81.

70. The August 1994 presidential elections could be said to have been the most successful in the level of participation and the degree of integrity on election

day until the July 2000 contest. However, the larger electoral setting in which these elections occurred left much to be desired, especially since the conditions were favorable to the government party.

71. A survey taken before the 2012 presidential election revealed that two-fifths of likely voters believe they are not fair or clean. See "La desconfianza en las elecciones," www.parametria.com.mx, March 30, 2011.

72. I discovered in state and local records that there have been a few cases of governors and more so for mayors of individuals repeating in these positions.

73. Camp, *Political Recruitment across Two Centuries*, 72.

74. Paul Lamartine Yates, *Mexico's Agricultural Dilemma* (Tucson: University of Arizona Press, 1981).

75. The best discussion of this consequence can be found in Frank Brandenburg, *The Making of Modern Mexico* (Englewood Cliffs, NJ: Prentice-Hall, 1964), 10–11. For the state's role in evolving a revolutionary myth, see Thomas Benjamin, *La Revolución: Mexico's Great Revolution as Memory, Myth and History* (Austin: University of Texas Press, 2000).

76. Banamex, *Encuesta nacional de valores: Lo que une y lo que divide Mexicanos* (Mexico, 2010), 13.

77. John H. Coatsworth and Carlos Rico, eds., *Images of Mexico in the United States* (La Jolla, CA: Center for U.S.-Mexican Studies, UCSD, 1989), 10.

78. For background, see Karl M. Schmitt, *Mexico and the United States, 1821–1973: Conflict and Coexistence* (New York: Wiley, 1974), 51ff.

79. Josefina Zoraida Vázquez and Lorenzo Meyer, *The United States and Mexico* (Chicago: University of Chicago Press, 1985), 49.

80. Robert E. Quirk, *An Affair of Honor: Woodrow Wilson and the Occupation of Veracruz* (New York: Norton, 1962), 95ff.

81. Interview with Ernesto Robles Levi, Mexico City, May 21, 1985.

82. For a firsthand account of this experience by a U.S. officer on the expedition, see Colonel Frank Tompkins, *Chasing Villa* (Harrisburg, PA: Military Service Publishing Company, 1934).

83. Parametria, "Bicentenario: Identitdad, conocimiento y celebración, primera parte" national sample, 1,200 respondents, 2.8% margin of error, April 7–11, 2010.

84. Parametria, "Ejército, FBI, o Cascos Azules: a quién le importa la soberanía," national sample, 400 respondents, 4.0% margin of error, March 10, 2010.

3

Contemporary Political Culture: What Mexicans Believe and Their Consequences for Democracy

What is problematic about the content of the emerging world culture is its political character. Although the movement toward technology and rationality of organization appears with great uniformity throughout the world, the direction of political change is less clear. But one aspect of this new world political culture is discernible: *It will be a political culture of participation* [italics added]. If there is a political revolution going on throughout the world, it is what might be called the participation explosion. In all the new nations of the world the belief that the ordinary man is politically relevant—that he ought to be an involved participant in the political system—is widespread. Large groups of people who have been outside of politics are demanding entrance into the political system. And the political elites are rare who do not profess commitment to this goal.

GABRIEL ALMOND AND SIDNEY VERBA, *The Civic Culture*

The political culture of any society is partially a product of its general culture. Culture incorporates all the influences—historical, religious, ethnic, political—that affect a society's values and attitudes. The political culture is a microcosm of the larger culture, focusing specifically on those values and attitudes having to do with a person's *political* views and behavior.[1]

In the Mexican society, as in many societies, the intensity with which someone holds certain beliefs is related to religion, level of education, income, age, gender, place of residence, and other variables. Their consequences will be examined in the following chapter and are important to understand. Equally important for comparative purposes is to evaluate the beliefs that may influence Mexico's politics and Mexican attitudes toward the changing political and economic system, and specifically its ability to consolidate a democratic political model.

LEGITIMACY: SUPPORT FOR A DEMOCRATIC POLITICAL SYSTEM

One of the most significant explanations for a political system's stability is its legitimacy in the eyes of the society. Of course, any political model consists of a variety of institutions, some of which have been accorded greater respect than others. Level of respect permits a comparison of citizen trust toward political and other types of institutions.

When Mexicans evaluate their institutions, it is apparent that those most closely associated with the state are held in lowest regard (see Table 3-1). Only three institutions are widely esteemed: family, church, and schools.[2] The selection of family is not surprising because a culture with strong values generally ranks family and tradition highly. However, if loyalty to family is excessive, it makes transferring loyalty to governmental institutions difficult. It could be argued that this might be the case in Mexico, since Mexicans express some serious reservations about the trustworthiness of *governmental* institutions and institutions as a whole. The same pattern is found in Japan, where the level of trust in institutions is lower than in Mexico.[3] A more persuasive explanation might be that Mexicans became disenchanted with their governmental institutions during the decades of a one-party system, which failed to meet their expectations in recent decades prior to 2000.

The figures in Table 3-1 permit us to view the evolution of Mexican attitudes toward institutions over the last two decades, beginning in 1988, which marks the initiation of significant, national, electoral competition, and an increase in the pace of democratic transition. What is remarkable about these figures is that for the most part they remain stable, even after the Fox victory in July 2000. For example, one might have expected increased citizen confidence in political parties and in the legal system, given the fact that each contributed to some degree to the fair presidential election in 2000, and the beginnings of democratic consolidation. Instead, most governmental institutions, including the courts, Congress, and police, generate little enthusiasm or trust among citizens. The only governmental institution in Table 3-1 that is viewed positively by Mexicans is the army. The lack of trust in such institutions, as will be argued in this chapter, poses a serious obstacle to increasing support for democracy.

Table 3-1 Legitimacy of the State in the United States and Mexico: Confidence of Citizens in Institutions

	Percentage of Respondents Giving Positive Evaluation								
	United States			Mexico					Latin America
Institution	1990	2000	2010	1988	1998	2000	2005	2011	2010
Family	—	99	—	84	92	92	—	—	—
Church	85	86	78	62	77	75	54	76	63
Schools	82	—	73	60	64	—	—	—	—
Television[a]	—	58	63	37	36	38	31	—	—
Law/courts	—	80	79	32	31	22	27	37	49
Army	86	90	94	32	45	49	54	77	62
Newspaper/ media	69	53	66	25	29	24	44	65	59
Business	84	—	61	22	52	41	41	49	—
Congress	83	—	48	16	28	21	4	30	45
Unions	52	—	61	14	24	25	25		—
Political parties	—	56	—	—	29	20	20	33	35
Police	88	87	86	12	33	23	22	36	—

Sources: Este País, August 1991, 5; Laurence Parisot, "Attitudes About the Media: A Five-Country Comparison," *Public Opinion* 10 (1988): Table 1; Marta Lagos, "Atitudes económicas y democracia en Latinoamérica," *Este País* (January 1997): Table 16; "Democracy Through Latin American Lenses," Grant, Hewlett Foundation, Principal investigator, Roderic Ai Camp, June, 1998; "Democracy Through U.S. and Mexican Lenses," Grant, Hewlett Foundation, principal investigator, Roderic Ai Camp, September, 2000; World Values Survey, 2000; "So It Begins," Opinion Report, No. 13, MUND, October 21, 2005; Mitchell A. Seligson and Amy Erica Smith, eds., *Political Culture of Democracy, 2010: Democratic Consolidation in Hard Times,* Latin American Public Opinion Project, December, 2010, 101; Gallop, Institutions in American Society series, July, 2010; and "Encuesta Ciudanía, Democracia, y Narcoviolencia," Cidena, 2011.
[a]For the United States in 1990, included under newspapers.

An important exception to the legitimacy of governmental institutions included in Table 3-1 can be found in the level of trust Mexicans express in the Federal Electoral Institute (IFE), the body, in its current form, which has been responsible for the 2000, 2006, and 2012 elections. Mexicans express a high level of confidence in this institution compared to all other governmental institutions. In 2008, after the controversial 2006 presidential elections, the average level of trust for this agency in Mexico was 62 on a 100-point scale, the fourth highest in Latin America, after Uruguay, Costa Rica, and the Dominican Republic.[4] During April and May of 2012, as the presidential race began, 55 to 73 percent of Mexicans approved of the job IFE was doing, continuing its high positive response.[5]

The confidence Mexicans have in the church, media, and schools, on the other hand, is significant. In the first place, as suggested in the previous chapter, both the liberal tradition and the revolution encouraged anti-church sentiment. Nevertheless, although we will discover that Mexicans developed sentiments supporting the separation of church and state, secular criticism has not done away with respect or sympathies for the Catholic Church, particularly in a society in which at least 83 percent of the members are Catholic. Regard for the church as an institution may be a partial reaction to state suppression, especially before the 1992 constitutional reforms.

The fact that support for the church has increased from 1988 to the late 1990s suggests, however, that it has earned Mexicans' respect. Although the church no longer earns confidence figures comparable to this earlier period, it still ranks first, along with the army, as the most trustworthy institution in Mexico and Latin America. On a political and social level, the church has been the most proactive, traditional autonomous actor in favor of democracy. It openly favored free and fair elections, it maintained a constant barrage of criticism against fraud, and it encouraged its parishioners to vote, arguing that it was a Christian responsibility. It is noteworthy that Americans also give high marks to their churches as institutions, indicating both their respect and, implicitly, the importance of religion and religious beliefs in the U.S. culture.

The most interesting shift in public opinion with regard to institutional trust is that of the media. Ordinary Mexicans failed to see the role the media was playing during the 1990s, but with increased professionalization and investigative journalism, newspapers and the media were viewed much more positively toward the end of the Fox administration, and again at the end of the Calderón regime, having played a significant role in increasing accountability and exposing governmental corruption. Interestingly, the media is viewed quite positively in Latin America as well.

Mexican attitudes toward education, borne out in survey after survey, are usually quite positive. The significance of this for the legitimacy of the political system is perhaps more important for Mexico than for the United States, where schools are also viewed positively. The school system in Mexico is largely public, although Catholic schools do play an important role. Unlike in the United States, however, public schools until the 1990s were operated by the federal government, and so the teachers were its employees. Today, financial control is in the hands of state governments. Schools may not be perceived as doing so, but they could serve as a positive, indirect means of reinforcing the state's legitimacy—especially because texts in elementary schools are selected by the government. Most important, Mexicans' satisfaction with the school system has been one of the few consistent pluses for the government. In 2009, however, many Mexicans increased their criticism of inadequacies in the public school system.[6]

In comparing Mexican figures with those from the United States, several patterns immediately stand out. Americans gave equally high marks to family, church, and schools, suggesting their importance across cultures. Americans also gave extremely high marks to governmental institutions, or agencies representing national and local governments, including the courts, the armed forces, and the police. Mexicans' confidence in other institutions is low. What one notices immediately when comparing it with those of Americans from 1990 to 2010 are the generally significantly lower levels of support. The weaker positive responses are not necessarily an indication of extreme frustration with the Mexican system; rather, Mexicans are likely to have lower expectations of their institutions, given their institutions' past performances, than Americans have. Nevertheless, the fact that police, political parties, the courts, and Congress tail off in the rankings indicates a lack of confidence in as well as alienation from these institutions. For Americans, this is only true of Congress, where support has declined dramatically for this institution, making it the lowest ranked institution among all institutions, nongovernmental and governmental, surveyed by Gallop since the 1970s.

Attitudes toward the police are an important indication of basic trust in government. On the local level, police are the most likely representatives of government to come in contact with the citizenry. Therefore, a good opinion of the police is generally seen as an important grassroots indicator of trust in government. A sense of personal security is often a significant variable in one's evaluation of government performance. In the United States among formal institutions, the police achieved the highest level of confidence in 1990, and second highest in 2000 and 2010; in state and local surveys throughout Mexico, the police consistently rank lowest. Explanations usually include the perception that they are dishonest, often involved in criminal activities, and abuse their authority, especially among lower-income and rural groups. For example, 6 percent of Mexicans reported being abused by police in the last twelve months in 2010.[7] Given the rapid increase in crime in the 1990s, 2000s and 2010s, the widespread involvement of police as criminals, and the inability of the police to reduce or control extraordinary levels of drug-related violence, confidence remains low. In 2008, 54 percent of Mexicans viewed police as involved in crime, among the highest percentage in Latin America. Such perceptions produce a direct effect on attitudes toward democratic consolidation. A recent study found that "the more people see the police involved in crime, the less they think democracy is better than any other form of government." Furthermore, the "prospects for a supportive population toward democracy are significantly lower."[8]

As early as 2002, 47 percent of Mexicans asserted that they lived in an unsafe state.[9] In 2004, 14 percent of all Mexican households reported a family member was a victim of crime, a figure that jumped dramatically under the Calderón administration, reaching 44 percent in 2010.[10] Twenty-six percent of Mexicans reported personally being a victim of crime in that year alone, placing them among those Latin Americans reporting the highest levels of victimization, including Argentina, Venezuela, and Bolivia. In the same survey, 16 percent of Americans reported being victims.[11] The level of personal security is one of the most significant variables in generating support for political institutions generally, and democracy specifically.

Despite the widespread differences in support for specific institutions between Americans and Mexicans, a recent survey which interviewed both groups of citizens simultaneously, and asked a broader set of questions providing insights into their support for the political system, demonstrates that both groups share much more in common in attitudes about political processes, citizenship, and institutions (see Table 3-2) In fact, two-thirds of Mexicans, slightly more than Americans, had confidence in their political system in 2010, which was good news for the democratic model. Yet, by the end of 2011, satisfaction with democracy had declined dramatically, with only a fourth of Mexicans expressing satisfaction with that form of government. Citizens from both countries generally have more confidence in their political system than they do for all of the institutions that collectively make up that system. What might surprise most Americans in this survey is that half of Mexicans have some or more trust in the legislative branch compared to only one-fifth of Americans. The survey also demonstrates that Mexicans in 2010 expressed greater confidence in national and local governments, and the presidency, than did Americans.[12] Both countries share similar opinions about their modest support for the Supreme Court as well as the justice system, as well as little support for political parties. And again, as was the case in Table 3-1, both countries express the highest trust in the army. Compared to Americans, who have little confidence in the media (which is at its lowest level of support in decades), Mexicans are much more likely to view television and radio positively. Finally, Mexicans indicate strong pride in being citizens. Of the 95 percent who responded positively to this question, four-fifths were in the highest possible category compared to only half of the Americans.

Mexican attitudes toward institutions may be explained in part by the unpredictable economic, political, and social conditions of Mexican life in the 1980s, 1990s, and 2000s. Mexicans faced a number of political crises in the last year of the Salinas administration, beginning with the uprising of indigenous groups in Chiapas in January 1994, followed by the assassination of

Table 3-2 Comparison of U.S. and Mexican Political Attitudes

Support for or Confidence in	Percentage of Respondents with Positive a Response[a]	
	Mexicans	Americans
Political system	68	63
Justice system	41	45
Elections	45	—
Federal Electoral Court	53	—
Political parties	25	19
Congress	49	20
Executive Branch	57	43
Supreme Court	51	47
Army	79	76
National Police	26	55
Catholic Church	69	—
Evangelical/Protestant Church	24	—
Media	56	25
Pride in being a citizen	95	84

Source: Latin American Opinion Project, December, 2010, from raw data made available courtesy of Pablo Parás.
[a]The original question asked respondents to rank their response on a 7-point scale, 7 being a lot and 1 being none. The percentages in the table are from collapsing the responses for 5, 6 and 7.

the PRI's presidential candidate, Luis Donaldo Colosio, in March. The assassination of Colosio, an unprecedented event in recent Mexican politics, began to initiate some doubts about both their personal economic future and their governmental institutions. Then, a few months after Ernesto Zedillo took office in December 1994, their confidence as a whole began to erode dramatically with the economic devaluation and harsh austerity policies—combined with an untested cabinet and president.

By the time Zedillo left office in November 2000, he had been able to restore considerable confidence in the presidency and in the government.[13] For the first time in recent history, he was able to provide for a presidential transition without a devaluation and economic crisis. Although his party lost the presidency, Zedillo was able to give his successor a stable economic situation on which to build citizen trust in institutions. Fox's personal popularity ratings remained high throughout his presidency. His performance ratings, however, declined by his second year in office and remained disappointing until the end of his term. Similar to Zedillo, however, Fox also was able to pass on an economic situation that had improved during his administration. Unfortunately, just two years into his presidency, Calderón faced an extraordinary economic decline in growth rates, linked to the global recession caused by its major trade partner, the United States. Combined with a severe loss of jobs, the return of migrants from the United States to

Mexico, and a dramatic decline in personal security unmatched since the revolution, little has happened to alter Mexican confidence in private or public institutions.

Mexicans long have expressed a much more favorable opinion of civil society in general than of specific governmental institutions, indicating a much higher level of trust in societal responses to problems. Scholars cite the 1985 earthquake in Mexico City as a notable example.[14] Criticism abounded of ineffective government efforts to save persons trapped in the rubble; in contrast, neighborhood volunteers' efforts were looked upon as exemplary. My own personal experience confirms this view. I visited an editor at the Fondo de Cultura Económica several weeks after the earthquake. As a publicly funded institution, they were asked to donate one day's pay for earthquake relief. The editor indicated that all employees agreed to do so, but insisted that they would make such a contribution only on the condition that they be allowed to donate the monies directly to the Catholic Church or other charities providing direct assistance to the victims. The government's inadequacies after the quake produced a groundswell of popular movements that together pressed demands on the government.

During the last two decades, there has been a remarkable change in Mexican attitudes toward fellow citizens, rather than toward institutions. In 1981, only 18 percent of Mexicans expressed confidence in their fellow citizens. By 1990, that figure grew dramatically to 33 percent of respondents sharing positive views of other Mexicans. By the end of the decade, it declined once again to 1981 levels. Even after the Fox election, citizen confidence in other Mexicans remained low. By 2003, it reached an all-time low of only 10 percent. The fluctuations in confidence levels suggest that citizen responses to such questions, even in the United States, are sometimes determined by immediate conditions, and not necessarily by long-term impressions. In the Mexican case, personal insecurity may have played a significant role, since unemployment rates were found to have a significant impact on crime, and Mexicans faced a major economic crisis from 1995 to 1998. Personal insecurity has become pronounced since 2000. On an individual level Mexico appears to have produced a consistent pattern since 2003; approximately one-fifth of the population expresses confidence in the trustworthiness of fellow citizens. The same can be said for Americans, but at a level closer to one-third. Another way in which differences in Mexican and American levels of interpersonal trust can be presented is that 40 percent of Mexicans have little or no trust in others compared to only 15 percent of Americans.[15]

In terms of political behavior, trust in people is an important measure of the potential for democratic political institutions. Mexicans have demonstrated their interest in democratizing their political institutions, sharing in the wave of democratization occurring elsewhere. To survive, the general view has been that democratic institutions rely on the high levels of personal trust necessary to effect compromise and operate within the rules of the political game. However, a recent study argues that while trust in institutions remains an important variable in evaluating support for democracy, interpersonal trust has been overvalued, and that citizen skepticism about politicians and fellow citizens is to be expected.[16]

PARTICIPATION: ACTIVATING THE ELECTORATE

One of the most important variables that might explain citizen attitudes toward politics and their trust in institutions and fellow citizens is their level of political interest and participation. At least since the early 1960s, interest in political affairs in urban Mexico has been much lower than in the United States and England. In the early 1990s, a survey of forty-three countries revealed that only 52 percent expressed some or much interest in politics. In 1995, shortly after the presidential election with the highest voter turnout ever, only 32 percent expressed a similar interest, well below the world average.

Mexicans' lack of interest in politics continued well into the 2000 presidential race. In February 2000, only 28 percent expressed some or much interest in politics and less than a month before the election, only 44 percent of Mexicans expressed an interest in politics. Two months after Vicente Fox's electoral victory, marking the most radical change in Mexican politics since the 1920s, only 38 percent continued that same degree of interest. Citizen interest in politics is linked to broader democratic participation. As I have argued elsewhere, that pattern did not change as the 2006 presidential race heated up. By February 2006, well into the race, 54 percent indicated little or no interest in the campaign, and nearly two-thirds rarely or never discussed the candidates.[17] Similarly, after the election, in spite of the major controversy about the outcome, 54 percent expressed a lack of interest in politics and 51 percent in the presidential campaign![18] And well into the 2012 presidential race, with the strong possibility of returning the PRI to national power, only 49 percent expressed an interest in politics.[19]

These figures demonstrate that ordinarily, most Mexicans share little interest in politics. Their interest does increase temporarily when the stakes are higher and they have an opportunity to affect the outcome of a major national election. Accomplishing such a result does not, as these data suggest, sustain citizen interest in politics. Interestingly, the 2010 Latin America Public Opinion Project found that among eleven Latin American countries, the mean interest of citizens in politics had increased in a "statistically significant fashion" from 2006 to 2010.[20] Interest in politics among Americans is well above any other group of citizens in Latin America. Uruguayans expressed the most interest. Mexico, however, does not appear to be part of this shift in the region. More importantly, the advent of democracy and twelve years of democratic consolidation have not achieved any measureable change in political interest.

Why has Mexican interest remained so low, despite the dramatic changes in the political system since 2000? It has been shown that certain characteristics can accentuate citizen interest in politics. Among these are increased education, gender, higher income, and "post-materialist beliefs," which are attitudes emphasizing self-expression and quality of life. Such attitudes are not only critical in explaining stronger levels of interest in politics, but in much higher levels of support for democracy.[21]

People generally move from an interest in politics to political activism when they believe they can affect outcomes in the system. One way to test peoples' attitudes toward outcomes is to examine *political efficacy*. This measures the degree to which a person believes he or she can participate in politics and the responsiveness of the system to their involvement. In 2010, the AmericasBarometer survey included two questions on political efficacy, one that asked if an individual believed that those who govern were interested in what he or she thought (external political efficacy), and a second question that asked if the individual understood the most important political issues in his or her country (internal political efficacy). In a comparison among all Latin American countries and Canada and the United States, Mexico ranked near the bottom for both forms of efficacy. On a scale of 1 to 100, Mexico's level was 46 and the United States was 67. Thirty-seven percent of Mexicans agreed strongly that they understood the major problems, and 34 percent agreed strongly that those who govern do not care about what they think.[22] An analysis of some of these data concluded that political knowledge and political participation, including attending local meetings and participating in demonstrations, influenced Latin American and Mexican levels of political efficacy.[23] An examination of citizen participation in two municipal decision-making processes discovered that "the way politicians perceive citizen engagement in governance and how they behave inside and outside the formal institutions of participation seem to be important factors to consider when assessing the performance of participatory mechanisms in improving the quality of democracy at the local level," rather than the mere existence of such participatory organizations.[24]

Most citizens in political systems where elections occur become involved through voting. Therefore, their ability to affect the outcome of government policy is influenced by their perception of the integrity of the voting process.[25] Mexico has had a long history of voter fraud in the twentieth century. Shortly before the 1988 election, more than half of all Mexicans believed their votes would not be counted honestly (see Table 3-3). By the spring of 1994, after several political crises had led to a number of structural reforms in the electoral process, including the presence of international observers, a third of Mexicans believed the elections would be fair. By 2000, shortly before the presidential election, 30 percent of Mexicans believed their vote would not be counted honestly. On the other hand, a huge decline occurred among those citizens with no opinion, producing a dramatic increase among those Mexicans who believed the election would be honest.

Citizen efficacy can be altered significantly if citizens view the consequences of participation as accurately reflecting their involvement. The Vicente Fox electoral victory produced such a dramatic change. The percentage of Mexicans who thought the elections were clean after Fox's victory increased to 75 percent. However, those Mexicans who were most convinced of the election's integrity were supporters of the National Action Party, Fox's party.[26] Those Mexicans who were least persuaded by a large margin were, not surprisingly, supporters of the PRI, the incumbent party that lost the election. These figures are important for another reason. They indicate the fragility of beliefs among some Mexicans toward the integrity of electoral structures and institutions, determined not just by their actual performance, but by the success of their specific candidate. Such beliefs affect the successful implementation of democratic consolidation, which relies heavily on citizen confidence in a fair and competitive electoral process. The pattern that occurred after the 2000 presidential election

Table 3-3 Mexicans' Views of Elections

Will Your Vote Be Respected in Elections	Percentage of Respondents				
	1988	1994	2000	2005	2010
Yes	23	37	67	75	45
No	53	34	30	23	55
Don't know	24	29	3	2	—

Source: Este País, August 1991, 6; *Este País,* weekly poll, urban voters only, May 25, 1994. "The Mexico 2000 Panel Survey," NSF Grant, Principal investigator, Chappell Lawson, *Reforma,* 1,515 respondents, November 2005. The question in the 2005 survey was: In our country, can people vote freely? Latin American Public Opinion Project, 2010, www.Lapopsurveys.org. The question in the 2010 survey was: "How much confidence do you have in elections? Some or much/little or none."

continued through the 2006 presidential election, which was even more controversial than the 2000 results. In a poll taken in 2008, 33 percent of the respondents still viewed that election as fraudulent, a percentage nearly equal to the voters who had cast their ballots for Andrés Manuel López Obrador, who narrowly lost the election to Felipe Calderón.[27]

People's proclivity to participate in the electoral process is affected to some extent not only by confidence in their political efficacy or by the integrity of the institutions and the process itself, but also by their level of activism in general. Mexicans' involvement in organizations was not high in 2000 (see Table 3-4). Among the most important organizations were religious and sports organizations followed by parent-teacher groups. Mexicans who belong to organizations typically belong to voluntary groups.

One of the important changes taking place in Mexico is the increased number of Mexicans who are actually participating in social and professional organizations. In the 2010 LAPOP surveys, the percentage of Mexicans active in some organizations now equals or in many cases, exceeds that of Americans. The level of membership in various organizations is a dramatic reversal from 2000. For example, the numbers of Mexican women who are involved in women's associations exceeds that of Americans. More significantly, Mexicans were more than three times as active in parents' organizations as Americans and exceeded the activity level of Americans belonging to religious organizations. Both countries' citizens were equally likely to be active in political, neighborhood organizations, or professional and business groups.[28]

Table 3-4 Organizational Membership in Mexico and the United States

| | Percentage of Respondents | | | |
| | Mexico | | United States | |
	2000	2010	2000	2010[a]
Religious	36	46	71	36
Sports	25	—	43	—
Parent/teacher	16	29	40	8
Union	10	—	28	—
Neighborhood	10	10	51	10
Political	7	6	27	7
Women	—	11	—	8
Professional/business	—	8	—	8

Source: "Democracy Through U.S. and Mexican Lenses," Grant, Hewlett Foundation, September 2000; Latin American Public Opinion Project, Mexico, Political Culture of Democracy, 2010, Free On-Line Data Analysis, www.Lapopsurveys.org, 2011.
[a]The question in the 2010 survey was "How often do you attend meetings of ...?" The percentages reported in Table 3-4 refer to those individuals who attend at least several times a month or more.

Since 2000, compared to other leading economies in Latin America such as Chile, Mexicans have been less involved in voluntary organizations, and have far fewer organizations with which they can associate. Nevertheless, a recent study suggests that greater numbers of Mexicans actually are involved in voluntary activities, and they debunk prevailing myths about citizen participation in such activities, while not formally belonging to organized service groups (see Table 3-5).

Only two percent of Mexicans in the late 1980s belonged to political parties or political organizations, suggesting a relatively low level of interest in politics when the democratic transformation began.[29] By 2010, 8 percent of Mexicans compared to 14 percent of Americans had worked for a political party or a candidate. Nevertheless, the small absolute numbers of Mexicans politically involved has increased threefold since 1989, suggesting that a democratic opening has increased such participation and, in return, their participation has encouraged electoral competition. These figures suggest that while democratic consolidation has not significantly increased the level of interest in politics among all Mexicans, it has increased the level of involvement of a higher percentage of Mexicans who do express an interest in politics.

Recent studies clearly demonstrate that increased involvement in community organizations, attendance at town meetings, identification with a political party, or participation in party meetings, all increase the likelihood that those individuals will campaign for their party or candidate in a presidential election. Yet, in a comparative study of Latin American countries in 2010, when asked if they worked for a party or candidate in the most recent presidential election in their country, Mexicans ranked at the bottom, above only Chile and Peru, with 8 percent having worked for their party or candidate in the highly contentious 2006 presidential race.[30] One of the likely explanations for why Mexicans rank so

Table 3-5 Major Findings about Volunteering in Mexico

- 66 percent of Mexicans had participated in at least one voluntary activity
- 40 percent were involved in such an activity at the time of the survey
- 33 percent had been involved for ten years or more in an activity
- 32 percent were involved at least one time a week
- 76 percent do not belong to any organized group
- 29 percent volunteer through an organized group
- 21 percent volunteer by themselves
- 13 percent volunteer with neighbors or friends
- 36 percent of Mexicans have received assistance from a group

---

Source: Miguel Basáñez and Jacqueline Butcher, "Trabajo voluntario en México: Mitos y realidades," *Este País*, November 2007: 46–51.

low in active political participation can be attributed to their general lack of interest in politics as well as a widespread belief that elections remain unfair.

Most Mexicans, as do most Americans, however, participate politically through voting. Most Mexicans, on the other hand, have not supported a political party. In fact, approximately two-fifths of all Mexicans in the 1990s were what Americans label independent or uncommitted. In the United States in 2000, only 12 percent of all Americans considered themselves independent or uncommitted; 52 percent, Democrats; and 32 percent, Republicans. The higher percentage of Americans affiliated with a party is a consequence of a higher level of knowledge about the two major parties, which have operated during the entire century, and the fact that both parties have controlled both branches of government.[31] Among Mexicans, 44 percent sympathized with specific parties in 1991, 57 percent did in 1994, 72 percent did in 2000, 49 percent did in 2006, 33 percent in 2008, and in 2010, only 29 percent identified with any political party. Party identification increased dramatically in Mexico in the 1990s as its importance became apparent to the Mexican voter. Parties other than the PRI not only were winning state and local offices, but took control of the national legislative branch in 1997. Vicente Fox's victory in July 2000, as the candidate of the PAN, reinforced the importance of partisan support. But as the period of democratic consolidation extended beyond the first opposition government, the percentage of citizens who considered themselves independents once again increased significantly. During the 2012 election, they composed the largest single voting bloc, at times equal to partisan supporters of all three parties combined.

DEMOCRACY: WHAT DOES IT MEAN FOR MEXICANS?

We have explored Mexican attitudes toward legitimacy and participation, attitudes that may affect their political behavior and their views of democracy. Mexico formally achieved an electoral democracy on December 1, 2000, when Vicente Fox took office. But what is the extent of Mexican beliefs in democracy? How do Mexicans conceptualize democracy? Are Mexicans deeply committed to attitudes that will sustain democracy in the next decades? Do these attitudes affect their achievement of a consolidated democracy? These and other questions have attracted significant attention from students of Latin American politics. Some observers remain skeptical about Mexican support for democracy either because democratic practices are not the norm within other settings, including interpersonal relationships, social and economic organizations, and even the family.[32]

Recent research does make clear that Latin Americans generally, and Mexicans specifically, conceptualize democracy differently from each other, and from Americans (see Table 3-6). Their differing interpretations of the meaning of democracy also have dramatic consequences for what citizens expect from democracy. Americans, not surprisingly, define democracy primarily in terms of liberty. Costa Ricans, who typically are viewed by analysts of the region as from the most democratic country, also define democracy in similar terms. Moreover, they have experienced a continuous, electoral, democratic model longer than any other country in Latin America. What is also distinctive about the American and Costa Rican responses to defining democracy is that both countries' citizens share a high level of consensus on its meaning.

Mexicans, similar to Chileans, who have only recently restored an electoral democracy, share more disparate views about democracy. In the first place, an equal number of Mexicans, about one-fifth of the respondents, give equality and liberty the same importance in defining democracy. Mexicans' views of democracy include four additional interpretations, each receiving about the same level of support: voting/elections, form of government, welfare/progress, and respect/rule of law. The fact that Mexicans define democracy in numerous ways suggests a lack of consensus about democracy. This lack of consensus potentially creates problems in developing

Table 3-6 Citizen Views of Democracy in Latin America and the United States

		(Figures in Percentages)				
	Chile	Costa Rica	Mexico		United States	
How Defined	1998	1998	1998	2000	1999	2000
Liberty/freedom	25	54	21	25	68	64
Equality	18	6	21	26	5	8
Voting/elections	10	3	12	11	2	4
Form of government	12	6	14	9	2	2
Well-being/progress	8	7	14	7	1	1
Respect/lawfulness	10	3	13	8	1	4
Don't know/No answer	8	13	3	—	12	—
Other	8	7	2	14	9	12

Source: "Democracy through Latin American Lenses," Grant, Hewlett Foundation, June 1998; *Wall Street Journal,* Hewlett Foundation Poll, April 1999. "Democracy through U.S. and Mexican Lenses," Grant, Hewlett Foundation, September 2000.

Question: In one word, could you tell me what democracy means to you?

citizen unity about the legitimacy of a political model and in agreeing on the rules of political behavior.

The preferences that Mexican citizens give to equality and liberty are inherently interesting. In fact, when Mexicans were asked to choose between equality and liberty in defining democracy, more than two-fifths chose equality compared to one-third who chose liberty. The American response was the reverse. Half of all Americans chose liberty followed by a third who believed democracy had more to do with equality. These differences in defining democracy are not surprising given the comparatively higher levels of social and economic inequality in Mexico compared with the United States. Mexicans consequently view democracy as a political model that should ameliorate the levels of inequality.

Five years into electoral democracy in 2005, the World Values Survey asked which concepts Mexicans considered to be essential characteristics of democracy. Four ranked at the top of their list: Women have the same rights as men (80 percent agreed), people choose their leaders through free elections (73 percent), civil rights protect people's liberty against oppression (62 percent) and the economy prospers (61 percent). Support for these components of democracy suggest a continued combination of social, economic, and political definitions as important to citizen definitions of Mexican democracy.[33]

The manner in which Mexicans conceptualize democracy affects their expectations about governmental performance. In spite of the fact that sufficient democratic practices exist in Mexico to have permitted the election of Vicente Fox, who represented a political alternative symbolizing change, Mexicans are not satisfied with the level of democracy in their country. When citizens were asked: How democratic would you say this country is? The majority described it as having little or no democracy. Only 46 percent of Mexicans considered Mexico to be somewhat or very democratic. Nearly double that number in the United States, 85 percent, described their country in these democratic terms. In 2005, only 59 percent of Mexicans rated democracy as preferable to other kinds of government, and only a fourth were satisfied with democracy. After the presidential election of 2006, only 59 percent claimed Mexico was a democracy in contrast to 28 percent who denied that was the case. Those Mexicans who were most skeptical about Mexico being a democracy were politically independent and in the top income bracket. Those Mexicans who were most convinced that it was a democracy were in the middle income category and were PAN supporters. In fact, 75 percent of the "Panistas" interviewed in the survey agreed that Mexico was a democracy.[34]

One insightful explanation for why Mexicans view democracy in problematic terms, as suggested above, is how they link a competitive electoral model to their own partisan perspective. Luis Rubio recently argued that:

> Mexicans have been unable to agree on the basic definition of the current political reality. For example, the members of [the] PRI believe that Mexico was always a democracy. For PAN members, democracy surfaced only in 2000, which was, coincidently, when they won the presidency by defeating the PRI. The members of the Party of the Democratic Revolution (PRD) largely believe that democracy will arrive only when they win a presidential election. Thus, according to one party or another, all elections to date have been corrupt and illegitimate. When a country's key politicians cannot even agree on the nature of the foundation on which they are standing—or even on the era in which they are living—it is impossible to negotiate specific bills. Everything is viewed through a prism that has nothing to do with development, progress or accomplishment, but much to do with the destruction of an enemy. Within this context, a reform of political power becomes both critical and difficult.[35]

Finally, it has also been argued that a primary explanation for the difficulties Mexico faces in achieving a functioning, consolidated democracy can be attributed to the elimination of old practices before new institutions and practices have been created to take their place. In other words, the disappearance of informal institutions that once helped guarantee political stability has exposed weak formal institutions.[36]

CONCLUSION

Attitudes and beliefs play a significant role in the evolution of a political system and the behavior of its citizens, as do other institutional and structural factors. Political attitudes, as a component of general cultural beliefs and values, are most important. In particular, two sets of beliefs, legitimacy and participation, are central to the interrelationship between societal values and political behavior.

Mexicans have high levels of respect for and trust in certain institutions, especially churches and schools, but Mexicans have very low levels of respect for most political institutions and the persons associated with them, such as bureaucrats, politicians and police. Their appraisals reflect a general lack of trust in government. This may be explained by their belief that most government agencies, and their representatives, are corrupt. Indeed, they believe corruption is the single most important obstacle to achieving democracy in Mexico. Social scientists in a recent empirical study provide some support for this interpretation: "The lack of trust bred by corruption can potentially undermine citizens' willingness to actively work with others or the government to seek solutions to the problem of corruption. This tendency severely undermines societal and governmental efforts to fight corruption and may even weaken democracy in the process."[37]

Mexican citizens also believe it is the single most important explanation for the government's inability to reduce the dramatic levels of drug-related violence characterizing the country since 2006. Illustrative of the breadth of corruption in Mexico is that citizens are even victimized by the public health system. For example, in 2008, only 2 percent of Americans claimed that they had to pay a bribe to receive hospital or clinic care at a public institution. In contrast, 11 percent of Mexicans reported such bribes, placing them among the highest level of victims of health care corruption in the region, following Haiti, Jamaica, and Belize.[38] Mexicans are unusual, compared with Americans, for the low levels of respect they give to most societal institutions. This is likely to change as their own involvement in and respect for civic and social organizations grow, if post-democratic governments fulfill some of their expectations.

Although some governmental institutions receive lower levels of support, and therefore have less legitimacy in Mexico than in the United States, the universal decline in governmental legitimacy in most nations during the 1980s was less sharp in Mexico. It is likely that Mexicans reached an even lower level of support for institutions in the mid-1980s and, through the efforts of President Salinas, who personally achieved high levels of popularity in the early 1990s, recovered from that level, thus considerably reducing the overall decline in government legitimacy before 1994. Serious political and economic events throughout 1994 and the first half of 1995 reversed this pattern, destroying gains in legitimacy and bringing perceptions of the presidency and governmental institutions to new lows. Since 1998, however, the pattern remains contradictory. The police and Congress improved their levels of trust since the late 1980s, but they remain among those institutions with the lowest rankings. What is surprising is that as of 2005, although the percentages changed between 2005 and 2010, there are low levels of respect for political parties and courts, two institutions that will be crucial to democracy's success.

Mexicans traditionally expressed less trust than did Americans or Canadians in their fellow human beings. Their confidence in others rose dramatically during the 1980s, but was still substantially below that found in the United States in the 1990s. Since 2003, however, Mexicans' levels of trust in one another have begun to rise significantly, although surprisingly interpersonal trust "is not a strong predictor of political participation in Latin America."[39] The fact that as of 2010 it has again achieved levels occurring in the late 1990s may suggest that a democratic context for at least a decade may have produced a positive effect on interpersonal attitudes. Whether or not this pattern continues to hold remains to be seen.

Other changes also have taken place in how Mexicans view their political efficacy. Many remain cynical about the election process and consequently their ability to influence government policy or leadership, but a considerable shift occurred between 1988 and 1994 in the number of Mexicans who see the integrity of the process positively. More Mexicans view the election process as an accurate measure of their demands, and the principal reason for not participating relates to lack of interest or knowledge.

Many Mexicans have become highly active in voluntary social organizations since 2000, even though far fewer are involved in political parties or organizations. In fact, only 15 percent reported membership in any kind of organized group as late as 2001. Most of those who are politically involved are members of party organizations. What is notable in the last decade is that active membership in a range of organizations has increased dramatically among Mexicans, while decreasing among Americans. Mexicans as of 2010 are more or equally involved than Americans in various organizations, suggesting that the process of democratic consolidation has led to legitimizing this form of activity. Furthermore, of some surprise is Mexicans' increasing tolerance of informal channels of political participation. They favored, to a much greater degree than in the 1980s and 1990s, direct political actions on par with the level of support found in the United States for selective, peaceful activities. While they are equally likely to attend lawful demonstrations as Americans in 2010, they are far less likely to sign petitions or join a boycott.

The average Mexican, however, is not in favor of radical social and economic change but prefers a peaceful, incremental approach. For example, poll after poll demonstrated public sympathy for the goals of the Zapatista National Liberation Army (EZLN), which initiated a guerrilla movement in Chiapas in 1994, but few agreed with its original methods, specifically violence. In a 1996 poll in the newspaper *Reforma*, two-thirds of urban Mexicans surveyed did not favor the use of violence to achieve political change.[40] In fact, most Mexicans consider themselves moderate or conservative ideologically.

Table 3-7 Support for Democratic and Nondemocratic Government

	Percent Agreeing			
	Strong Leader	Military Government	Support for Democracies	Democracies Are Indecisive
Advanced democracies	22	6	86	47
Africa	34	22	72	41
East Asia	27	9	77	36
Latin America	35	20	84	57
Mexico	41	25	65	46
Post-Communist	37	10	70	48
South Asia	52	26	78	44
Mexico 1997	39	23	65	44
Mexico 2000	44	27	65	48

Source: Alejandro Moreno and Patricia Méndez, "Attitudes Toward Democracy: Mexico in Comparative Perspective," *International Journal of Comparative Sociology* 43 no. 3–5 (October 2002): 357.
Questions: (a) Having a strong leader who does not have to bother with parliament and elections is good or very good; (b) Having a military government is good or very good; (c) Democracy is the best system; (d) Democracies are indecisive and have too much quibbling.

An important obstacle to expanding support for democracy can be found in the shared values of Mexicans toward support for nondemocratic governments. A comprehensive analysis of the crucial years in the democratic transition from 1997 to 2000, when comparing Mexico with other regions (Table 3-7), reveals significant support for such attitudes that strengthen citizen receptivity to authoritarian leadership or governments. For example, Mexico ranked second only to South Asia in its acceptance of a strong leader who ignores democratic principles and believes a military government would be good or very good. Its support for democracy reached nearly two-thirds of the citizens, but placed it at the bottom of all other regions.

Nevertheless, most Mexicans favor a democratic political model. The majority of citizens believe that they have a functioning democracy, but are not yet satisfied with its performance. By 2010, Mexican citizens and elites ranked in the middle of Latin American countries when expressing satisfaction with democracy. Costa Ricans and Uruguayans were most satisfied.[41] By the end of 2011, however, they expressed the least satisfaction in the region. Many Mexicans hope that democracy will improve their economic and social situation. The crucial question for the second decade of the twenty-first century remains, however, whether a fledgling democracy can fulfill citizen expectations, increase confidence in governmental or political institutions, encourage participation in civic and social organizations, and consolidate democratic values, behavior, and institutions, while solving serious economic and social problems, the most widespread of which is poverty.

NOTES

1. For a more comprehensive definition, see Walter A. Rosenbaum, *Political Culture* (New York: Praeger, 1975), 3–11.

2. Ronald Inglehart, Neil Nevitte, and Miguel Basáñez found that Mexico demonstrated greater levels of "strong" confidence in *nongovernmental* institutions. See *Convergencia en Norteaméric: Comercio, política y cultura* (Mexico City: Siglo XXI, 1994), Figure 4-3.

3. Ibid., Figure 4-2.

4. Daniel Montalvo, "Trust in Electoral Commissions," *AmericasBarometer Insights 2009*, No. 23, Latin American Public Opinion Project, 1.

5. Sixty-two percent expressed confidence in 2010, 1000 respondents nationally, 3.1% margin of error, July–August 2010, www.parametria.com.mx. For data from 2007 through May 2012, See Carta Paramétrica, "Confianza en instituciones," www.parametria.com.mx, May 2012.

6. Mexicans' positive views of teachers were adversely affected in 2009 because large numbers of teachers failed a teacher competency test that received widespread publicity in the media. Favorable views of teachers went from 66 percent in 2007 to 57 percent in September 2009. They may well have recovered from that decline since 2010. "Pierden credibilidad los maestros en México," www.parametria .com.mx, 2009.

7. José Miguel Cruz, "Police Abuse in Latin America," *AmericasBarometer Insights 2009*, No. 11, 1.

8. José Miguel Cruz, "Police Misconduct and Democracy in Latin America," *AmericasBarometer Insights 2010*, No. 33, 3, 4.

9. Isabel Vázquez, "Socio-Political Indicators: Public Insecurity," *Review of the Economic Situation of Mexico*, February 2003, 82.

10. "La violencia en México," *Consulta Mitofsky*, 2005; Mary Anastasia O'Grady, "Mexicans Vent Their Anger over Rampant Crime," *Wall Street Journal*, July 2, 2004, A1; Elisabeth Malkin, "Tens of Thousands March in Mexico City," *New York Times*, May 8, 2011.

11. Mitchell A. Seligson and Amy Erica Smith, eds., *Political Culture of Democracy, 2010: Democratic Consolidation in Hard Times*, Latin American Opinion Project, December 2010, 61, 66.

12. Mexicans and Americans expressed about equal satisfaction with municipal services in the Latin American Public Opinion Project poll in 2008, placing them in the middle of all countries polled. Daniel Montalvo, "Citizen Satisfaction with Municipal Services," *AmericasBarometer Insights 2009*, No. 18. Montalvo went on to analyze these patterns further in "Understanding Trust in Municipal Governments," *AmericasBarometer Insights 2010*, No. 35.

13. Roderic Ai Camp, ed., *Citizen Views of Democracy in Latin America* (Pittsburgh, PA: University of Pittsburgh Press, 2001), CD-ROM, national survey of 1,200 Mexicans, +/–3.0 percent margin of error, June 1998.

14. Carlos B. Gil, *Hope and Frustration: Interviews with Leaders of Mexico's Political Opposition* (Wilmington, DE: Scholarly Resources, 1992), 48–57.

15. Latin American Public Opinion Project, "Mexico: Political Culture of Democracy, 2010," Free On-Line Data Analysis, www.Lapopsurveys.org, 2011.

16. Matthew Cleary and Susan Stokes, *Democracy and the Culture of Skepticism: Political Trust in Argentina and Mexico* (New York: Russell Sage Foundation, 2006), 185.

17. "Divide su voto 1 de cada 5," *Reforma*, February 20, 2006, 6, 565 respondents nationwide, with a 2.5 percent margin of error, February 11–12, 2006.

18. Roderic Ai Camp, "Democracy Redux? Mexico's Voters and the 2006 Presidential Race," in *Consolidating Mexico's Democracy: The 2006 Presidential Campaign in Comparative Perspective*, eds. Jorge I. Domínguez, Chappell Lawson, Alejandro Moreno (Baltimore, MD: Johns Hopkins University Press, 2009), 30.

19. "2012: La Elección, Preferencias Ciudadanas," Consulta Mitofsky, April 29, 2012.

20. Seligson and Smith, eds., *The Political Culture of Democracy*, 125.

21. Alejandro Moreno, "Democracy and Mass Belief Systems in Latin America," in *Citizen Views of Democracy in Latin America*, ed. Roderic Ai Camp (Pittsburgh, PA: University of Pittsburgh Press, 2001), 37.

22. Free On-Line Data Analysis, http://www.vanderbilt.edu/lapop/surveydata.php, 2011.

23. Heather Borowski, et al., "Political Efficacy in the Americas," *Americas-Baromenter Insights: 2011*. No. 65, 5.

24. "Overcoming Clientelism Through Local Participatory Institutions in Mexico: What Type of Participation?," *Latin American Politics and Society* 53, no. 1 (2011): 117.

25. James McCann and Jorge Domínguez, "Mexicans React to Electoral Fraud and Political Corruption: An Assessment of Public Opinion and Voting Behavior," *Electoral Studies* 17, no. 4 (1998): 499.

26. "Socio-Political Pulse of the Population," national sample of 2,400 Mexicans, +/−4 percent margin of error, September 2000, *Review of the Economic Situation of Mexico* (October 2000): 429.

27. Latin American Public Opinion Project, Mexico, *Political Culture of Democracy, 2010*, Free On-Line Data Analysis, www.Lapopsurveys.org.

28. The Latin American Public Opinion Project did not use percentages in its question, but instead had respondents rank their level of activity on a scale.

29. Alberto Alvarez Gutiérrez, "Cómo se sienten los mexicanos?" in *Cómo somos los mexicanos*, eds. Alberto Hernández Medina, and Luis Narro Rodríguez (Mexico City: CREA, 1987), 81, 87.

30. Erica Graff, Maranda Orrell, and Alex Rigl, "Riches Don't Explain Campaign Participation in the Americas, but Community Involvement Does," *AmericansBarometer Insights 2012*, No. 82, 1–4.

31. William H. Flanigan and Nancy H. Zingale, *Political Behavior of the American Electorate* 10th edit (Washington, DC: CQ Press, 2002), 52.

32. Luis Rubio, "Economic Reform and Political Liberalization," in *The Politics of Economic Liberalization in Mexico*, ed. Riordan Roett (Boulder, CO: Lynne Rienner, 1993), 19–20.

33. Alejandro Moreno, "Concepto y valoración de la democracia: Hallazgos de la Encuesta Mundial de Valores 2005 en Mexico," *Este País*, April 2006, 67.

34. Carta Parametría, "Democracia mexicana aprobada de panzazo," July 22–25, 1,000 respondents, +/–3.1% margin of error, www.parametria.com.mx; and *Excélsior*, August 18, 2006.

35. "The Conundrum of Mexican Politics," Mexico under Calderón Task Force, Center for Hemispheric Policy, University of Miami, May 20, 2010, 5.

36. Stephen Morris, "Continuity and Change in Mexican Politics: The Legacies of the Mexican Revolution," *The Latin Americanist* 54, no. 4 (2010): 191–92.

37. Stephen D. Morris and Joseph L. Klesner, "Corruption and Trust: Theoretical Considerations and Evidence From Mexico," *Comparative Political Studies* 43 (2010): 1276.

38. Diana Orces, "Corruption Victimization in the Public Health Care Sector," *AmericasBarometer Insights 2009*, No. 30, 1.

39. Joseph Klesner, "Who Participates Politically in Mexico? Socioeconomic Resources, Political Attitudes, and Social Capital as Determinants of Political Participation," *Latin American Politics and Society* 51, no. 2 (2009): 59–90.

40. *The Dallas Morning News*, September 8, 1996, 1A.

41. Margarita Corral, "The State of Democracy in Latin America: A Comparative Analysis of the Attitudes of Elites and Citizens," *Boletín PNUD & Instituto de Iberoamérica* (January 2011), 4.

4

Political Attitudes and Their Origins: Interest, Knowledge, and Partisanship

> Support for democracy is seen as a cultural matter. . . . support for democracy is also a matter of information, cognition, and belief systems. The way people think about democracy is based on cognitive and informational skills and resources. The concept of democracy varies depending on society's belief systems, and mass belief systems depend on individual characteristics such as education, informational background, cognitive skills, degrees of political "sophistication," and so on.
>
> ALEJANDRO MORENO, *"Democracy and Mass Belief Systems in Latin America"*

Many experiences have a bearing on the formation of beliefs in general and political beliefs specifically. Attitudes are general orientations toward basic aspects of life, abstract principles that guide behavior.[1] Children, for example, are affected by the attitudes and values of their parents, and most children carry the consequences with them for years.[2] Other persons have reported the influence of education and the specific role of teachers and professors.[3] Some individuals, generally as young adults, consciously or unconsciously take on the attitudes of their peers in their working environment. Experiences other than those within the family, the workplace, and in school contribute to the formative years of many citizens, especially when the experiences are broad and deep, permeating the environment of an entire nation. The Great Depression, for example, tremendously affected Americans, their political and social values, and their voting behavior.[4] Undoubtedly, although we have no surveys to prove it empirically, the revolution exerted a similar influence in Mexico.[5] A small exploratory study of workers in three cities in 1978 revealed surprisingly strong memories of the revolution among third-generation Mexicans. The size of the sample makes it impossible to generalize about the data, nevertheless 45 percent reported family participation in the event, and 25 percent reported lost property or injury of a family member. Family involvement was associated with fears of renewed violence and has helped discourage political protests in recent decades.[6] Even in the mid-1990s, Mexicans identified liberty and justice most strongly with the revolution.[7]

Surprisingly (in the last three decades), excluding religious influences, social scientists have largely ignored how citizens learn their political attitudes, a truly critical process in a country undergoing a political transformation to democracy.[8] In Mexico, for example, no broad studies of this phenomenon exist. Fortunately, the Hewlett Foundation survey in September 2000 for the first time explored this issue in considerable detail. However, no follow-up studies have been published. In the previous chapter we noted that Mexicans and Americans both expressed considerable confidence and trust in religion, school, and the family. Therefore, one might expect these institutions to play significant roles in influencing citizen beliefs generally, and political attitudes specifically.

Interestingly, when citizens from both countries were asked to identify which sources influenced the formation of their political attitudes, a correlation did not necessarily emerge between institutions receiving strong levels of trust and their perceived impact on individual beliefs (see Table 4-1). For example, among Americans, religion is a significant source of political attitudes. Mexicans, who ranked religion at the very top of trusted institutions, rank it at the bottom of sources of political beliefs. In fact, nearly half of all Mexicans considered religion to play no role whatsoever in molding their political attitudes. On one hand, this is not a surprising finding, given the fact that the role of Catholicism outside of its narrow spiritual

Table 4-1 Sources of Political Socialization in Mexico and the United States

Source of Political Socialization	Group (percentages)	
	Americans	Mexicans
Religion	69	26
Family	77	48
School	78	40
Television	59	40
Friends	71	28
Work	58	32

Source: "Democracy Through U.S. and Mexican Lenses," Grant, Hewlett Foundation, September 2000.
Question: "For each of the following . . . please tell me how strongly each one has influenced your way of thinking with respect to politics."

boundaries was denigrated for decades by post-revolutionary governments. On the other hand, since the Catholic Church was a vocal and proactive actor in laying the groundwork for electoral democracy since the late 1980s, it is surprising how few Mexicans attributed any influence to that institution in 2000.

Another highly ranked institution among Americans and Mexicans both is school. The general literature always has considered schools a primary source of attitudes and values. Again, as Table 4-1 reveals, schools are the number one source of American political values. Although not as important to Mexicans comparatively speaking, schools tie for second as an important source of political beliefs.

The third and the single most revered institution among both Mexicans and Americans is the family. Family produces the strongest correlation between trust and socialization, ranking at the top as the source of Mexican political attitudes and essentially tied with schools as Americans' primary source of political attitudes. What is remarkable, however, is that given the importance of family in the Mexican culture, only half of all Mexicans attribute their political beliefs to that institution. In fact, a third of all Mexicans say family plays no role in determining their political attitudes. A strong explanation for this divergence might be that only half as many Mexican compared with American families actually discuss politics at home.[9]

Studies from other countries suggest a number of variables that affect the political attitudes and values of ordinary citizens. They typically include race, ethnicity, socioeconomic background, level of education, occupation, region, and religion. Mexico has an indigenous population, but Indians account for only approximately 8 percent of the population, depending on the definition of *Indian*. Indians, however, are a minor political and economic presence and hence have not been treated as a separate group in most national political surveys. The typical Mexican thinks of himself or herself as, and is, mestizo, thereby minimizing race or ethnicity as a significant variable in voting behavior. Some evidence now exists to suggest that ethnicity in Mexico does affect political beliefs, including Mexicans' receptivity to democracy.[10] In fact, a recent study using data from the Latin American Public Opinion Project demonstrated empirically that when comparing a poor indigenous woman with an average white woman, an average white man, or a wealthy and educated man, the indigenous woman had the lowest probability of preferring democracy, primarily because poor indigenous Mexicans have the least knowledge about their country's politics.[11] In the most comprehensive survey of indigenous groups in Mexico to date, Todd Eisenstadt found that while ethnicity was indeed linked to the respondents' political attitudes, other circumstances were more important, including their historical development, economic conditions, state politics, land tenure institutions, and isolation.[12] It is also interesting to point out that in 2010, 42 percent of indigenous Mexicans, compared to 44 percent of mestizos, disagreed with the statement that "those who govern are interested in what people like you think." In contrast, only 14 percent of those Mexicans who classified themselves as white gave a similar response. Moreover, 53 percent of Mexicans agreed that race mixture is good for their country.[13]

As elections become more competitive and, more important, if indigenous groups in certain states or regions were to organize themselves politically, ethnicity could become a more significant variable. The consequences of this on a national level can be seen as a result of an indigenous-led guerrilla movement in the southern state of Chiapas. Calling themselves the Zapatista National Liberation Army (EZLN), this uprising occurred in January 1994, affecting the larger political context during two presidential elections, 1994–1995, and again in 2000–2001. This is particularly the case because the EZLN demanded indigenous autonomy in its negotiations with the Mexican government, ultimately rejecting a government bill in 2001. Nevertheless, other regions characterized by high concentrations of indigenous groups, such as the state of Oaxaca, introduced traditional, indigenous governance practices in the past decade, differentiating their villages from the predominant mestizo communities. Such practices are now widely referred to as *tradiciones y costumbres*, traditions and customs.

Because of sharp social-class divisions, Mexican values are likely to be influenced by income level. Furthermore, the origins of Mexico's leaders, particularly political and economic, set them apart from the ordinary citizen. Widespread differences exist between Mexican and other Latin America citizens and elites from 2008 to 2010 in the level of trust they express towards various institutions including electoral courts, political parties, branches of government, as well as their preference for democracy.[14] Consequently, it is important to ascertain differences between mass and elite political opinion. And because political knowledge has much to do with education, and disparities in schooling are substantial in Mexico, education is a means of distinguishing one Mexican from another and is strongly related to social class and occupation.[15]

Historically, as suggested in Chapter 2, regionalism played an important role in national politics. It declined in prominence by the 1960s, yet it continues to exert an influence over some values, in the same way that it does in the United States. As different political movements strengthen their representation at the local and state levels, dominating specific regions politically, and as regional-ethnic groups such as the Zapatistas focus on local social and economic issues, geography has reasserted its influence Comparative studies also reveal that the degree of regionalization in Mexican presidential elections for the winning candidate in 2000 exceeded that found in Brazil in 2002 and in 2006, and that of the United States in 2000. As suggested earlier, Mexico ranks high among geographically fragmented countries in the world, and those divisions have been found to have cultural consequences. This revival of geography clearly inserted itself into the 2006 and again in the 2012 presidential races, in which regionalism exerted an unusually influential impact on partisanship and voting behavior, more so than in the recent past.[16] A careful analysis of such voting patterns also discovered that local, regional settings significantly influence political discussions and consequently voting behavior.[17]

Religion is often still another determinant of political behavior, and in many societies, plays a role in the formation of social and political values, especially when religious diversity is present. In Mexico, however, the predominance of Catholicism has obviated sharp religious differences. Most of the disharmony historically related to religion can be described as a battle between secularism and religion, not among religions. Nonetheless, the rise of evangelical Protestantism throughout Latin America since the 1960s, although not as greatly felt in Mexico, and the presence of a small proportion of nonbelievers and atheists, render religious beliefs deserving of consideration, too.

INCOME AND POLITICS

The confidence people have in a political system and in their ability to influence the outcome of political decisions—level of political efficacy—depends on many things. One is income level. People who have achieved economic success not only perceive the system as fairer and more beneficial to their own interests but also believe they can change aspects of it that they dislike. In 1989, in a national survey, half of Mexican respondents with high incomes believed they could do something about electoral fraud. By contrast, only one in four low-income respondents agreed with that statement.[18] During this same period, over half of all Americans thought they could affect government policies.[19] In 2000, after President Fox was elected, Mexican responses to a different question measuring political efficacy reflect a dramatic increase. When asked if their vote would make a difference in improving conditions in the future, two-thirds believed that was true. As democratic influences affected the outcome of elections, and parties other than the PRI began winning state and local elections and congressional seats in large numbers in the late 1990s, Mexicans became convinced that their votes could affect governmental leadership and, therefore, policy outcomes. Yet by 2006, after the completion of the Fox administration, two-thirds of all respondents, when asked if "people like me do not have any influence over what the government does," agreed with that statement, suggesting that their experience with a democratic polity had not reinforced their efficacy and that their confidence in their ability to influence government had declined drastically.[20]

Another explanation for why Mexicans increased their political efficacy in the 1980s and 1990s is related to their increased participation in civic organizations. Even low-income people who become active in non-governmental organizations and make demands on the system collectively develop a stronger sense of efficacy.[21] The growing numbers of such groups and their greater involvement has raised the level of participation.[22] Over time, an increase in middle- and higher-income groups would also contribute to an increased level of political efficacy, but a redistribution of the population among income groups in Mexico was not significant in the 1990s. By the second decade of the twentieth century, in spite of the global economic downturn, more Mexicans had joined the middle-income categories. We cannot compare the precise changes in political efficacy from 2000 to the present because this question has not been repeated in recent surveys. However, different questions that focus on support for democracy as well as involving oneself with government officials to resolve problems suggest fewer distinctions among the three broad income groups. For example, when given the statement, "Democracy may have problems but it is better than any other form of government," 38 and 39 percent of low and middle income Mexicans agreed strongly with this statement in 2010, compared to 35 percent of citizens in the highest income categories. In the same year, when asked, "In order to solve your problems have you ever requested help or cooperation from a member of Congress?," 11 percent from the lower and middle income brackets responded affirmatively compared to 6 percent from the highest income categories.[23]

Income levels also affect partisan support. Analysts of Americans' voting behavior always have been attentive to variables affecting political sympathies for the Republicans and Democrats. Their studies suggest that among the most important of these variables is personal income. This was also true in the case of Mexicans. Over the last decade, some dramatic changes in partisan sympathy have taken place on the basis of income. Traditionally, the PRI obtained its strongest support among higher income groups, illustrated in the data for 1989 in Table 4-2. In fact, 44 percent of

Table 4-2 Mexicans' Partisan Sympathies, by Socioeconomic Status, 1989–2010

| | Income Level | | | | | | | | | | | |
| Sympathy for Party | Low (%) | | | Middle (%) | | | High (%) | | | All Respondents (%) | | |
	1989	2000	2010	1989	2000	2010	1989	2000	2010	1989	2000	2010
PAN	12	28	7	13	40	5	21	35	12	13	31	8
PRI	26	32	16	38	21	14	44	19	15	31	29	15
PRD	17	9	3	16	10	4	5	15	4	16	10	4
Other	3	0	1	3	1	1	3	3	1	3	1	1
None	32	27	73	23	25	76	21	25	70	28	27	72
Don't know/ No answer	10	4	—	7	3	—	6	3	—	9	2	—

Source: Los Angeles Times poll, August 1989; "Democracy Through U.S. and Mexican Lenses," September 2000; Free Online Data Analysis, Mexico 2010, www.Lapopsurveys.org, 2011.

Mexicans in the upper income brackets expressed a preference for the PRI in 1989. By 2000, however, that figure had changed, falling by more than half to only 19 percent of adult citizens. Among middle-income groups, the same pattern, with almost the same percentage of change, took place. Only among lower-income groups did the PRI retain considerable support during the 1990s. The PAN, which won the presidency in 2000, attracted most of those middle- and upper-income voters who abandoned the PRI. For example, middle-income voters increased their support for the PAN in just eleven years by more than 200 percent. The PAN also was able to more than double its support among lower-income groups. The PRD, which was the second-strongest party in 1989, lost more than a third of its partisan supporters by 2000. The only party that increased its partisan support from 1989 to 2000 was the PAN. However, many voters only temporarily altered their partisan preferences to oust the PRI from the presidency, thus such partisan patterns did not persist.[24]

The longitudinal data in Table 4-2 illustrate several significant patterns in the relationship between income and partisanship. The most important difference in the data between 2000 and 2010 is the dramatic increase of Mexicans from all income groups who express no partisan sympathies. These figures also suggest only small differences in the numbers of Mexicans who are nonpartisan. What is most interesting to note, however, is the shift in partisan support among middle-income Mexicans from the PAN in 2000 back to the PRI in 2010, strongly suggesting that the PRI is recapturing many former supporters lost to Vicente Fox in the benchmark 2000 presidential race. The PAN appealed to twice as many middle income citizens as the PRI in 2000 compared to the PRI capturing the sympathies of nearly three times as many of those same Mexicans by 2010, creating a broad foundation of support for the party in 2012.

EDUCATION AND POLITICS

A variable closely related to income in determining political preferences is education. Access to education, especially in a country like Mexico where opportunities are fewer than in the United States, is strongly related to parental income; the higher the income, the more likely a person will attend and *complete* higher education. For example, of the students at the National University in the early 1990s, more than 90 percent were from families with incomes in the upper 15 percent.[25] Many Mexicans attend public universities, which charge minimal fees, but most low-income students do not complete their degree requirements. Students with higher education obtain the necessary credentials to pursue the most prestigious professions, just as they do elsewhere and thus on the whole earn more.

With education come knowledge, social prestige, economic success, and greater self-confidence. Consequently, when Mexicans were asked whether they could change conditions by voting, 75 percent of those with higher education believed they could during 2000. In contrast, only slightly more than half who had received a primary education believed they could alter political conditions. In the United States, education affects responses in the same direction, although anyone with a secondary education or higher believes in the efficacy of voting.[26] If efficacy is taken to the next logical step, participation measured in terms of voting, a strong relationship exists between higher education and actual voter turnout. This larger turnout among educated voters helped Vicente Fox in 2000, especially since voters with a preparatory and university education were stronger supporters of the PAN compared to the PRD and especially to the PRI.[27] In the United States, education as a single variable does not have a dramatic effect,[28] but because Mexico also is characterized by sharper class divisions, the relationship is stronger. Even in the United States, citizens with only a sixth grade education differ from the rest of the population on measures of political efficacy and risk-taking.

Educational achievement also played an important role in determining partisan preferences in Mexico during the last two decades. The evolution of this pattern is clearly illustrated in the data comparing partisan responses in 1989, shortly after the benchmark Mexican election, in which viable national options became a reality, and in 2000, following Vicente Fox's victory. The comparative data between 1989 and 2000 support several significant trends. The PRI, which traditionally did well among less-educated voters, retained its appeal among that group. The PAN, which has done poorly among such voters, increased its support dramatically, by 150 percent.

The PRD, which relied heavily on these voters in the 1988 election, lost their support. Six years later, in the 2006 presidential election, voters frustrated with the failures of the Fox administration to pass and implement major reforms who were sympathetic to the PAN in 2000 began to shift their support back to the the PRD. Whereas Felipe Calderón, the PAN candidate in 2006, continued to dominate among high school- and college-educated voters, the PAN's margin over the PRD declined rapidly, to a 2 percent margin of preparatory educated voters and only a 5 percent margin in the case university educated voters. Among secondary students, Calderón led López Obrador by a slim 1 percent margin.[29]

By 2012, the PRI still maintained a strong appeal in the presidential election to Mexicans who only finished elementary school, nearly more than half again as many of those who voted for the PRD, which ironically emphasized an antipoverty economic strategy. This group was crucial because they accounted for half of all voters, and half of that group voted for the PRI. The PRD, on the other hand, whose candidate came in second place, performed best among college- and secondary-educated Mexicans of the three leading parties. Nevertheless, the PRI attracted a third of Mexicans with secondary educations, and nearly that same percentage of college-educated voters, with the PAN attracting nearly similar support from these educational categories.

RELIGION AND POLITICS

Students of the Catholic heritage in Mexico identify it as an important contributor to values within the family and within the culture generally. When ranking the role of God in their lives, Mexicans and Americans give it equal importance; in contrast, only one in four Canadians consider God important.[30] By 2006, 59 percent of Mexicans considered religion to be "very important in their lives," an increase of 25 percentage points since 1990. Americans, by contrast, have long maintained the importance of religion in their lives, with 54 percent agreeing with that statement in 1990, remaining essentially the same at 56 percent in 2006.[31] Religion's potential for influencing the formation of societal norms is enhanced by the fact that most Mexicans consider themselves religious, with 83 percent identifying themselves as Catholic, 7 percent as Protestant, and only 3 percent as nonbelievers.[32] Moreover, 85 percent declare they received a religious education in their homes.[33] It is true that the number of Mexicans who attend church services has fallen since the turn of the century, but the number who attend regularly is higher than is typically believed. Throughout the 1990s, 44 percent of all Catholics went to church weekly or more often, and 20 percent monthly.[34] This pattern has continued and increased in the last decade. Nearly two thirds of Mexicans reported attending church at least once a month, and nearly half, once a week or more, in 2006.[35] At the end of 2007, more than seven out of ten Mexicans were attending church at least once a month. Nine percent of Mexicans attended church two or more times a week, but among non-Catholics (largely evangelical Protestants, that figure was an astonishing 30 percent. Eight percent of Mexicans report attending their chosen religious institution daily.[36]

Given the overwhelming dominance of Catholicism, it would be useful to measure its effect on political attitudes according to the intensity of belief. For example, when Gabriel Almond and Sidney Verba completed their classic study, they discovered that the more religious a person was, regardless of faith, the more intolerant of others' political beliefs he or she would be.[37] The 2006 World Values Survey asked Americans and Mexicans if they would not like having people of a different religion as neighbors. Only 3 percent of Americans agreed with this statement compared to 14 percent of Mexicans, a much higher response than was recorded in Argentina, Brazil, and Chile, but comparable to Italy and Portugal. Many Mexicans continue to express more negative than positive views of evangelicals, orthodox Jews, Jehovah's Witnesses, and Protestants.[38] In recent years, as a result of the rise of drug cartels and drug-related violence, many Mexicans involved in drug trafficking criminal activity also have identified themselves with the nontraditional La Santa Muerte or Holy Death.[39]

The contribution of religion to Mexican attitudes is embedded in the general culture. Scholars have argued that the Catholic Church might function as an *indirect* agent of socialization (even though most Mexicans suggested earlier that the church is not an important source of their political beliefs). In fact, a recent examination of the relationship between political knowledge and religion in Latin America suggests that only in the case of mainline Protestants, a tiny group in Mexico, does religious involvement convey some political information.[40] A more sophisticated argument by the same author, however, suggests that Latin Americans with religious beliefs can be influenced on such religiously unrelated issues as free trade compared to those Latin Americans who profess no religious beliefs.[41] Mexicans today are not advocating that their religion express a formal voice in the political arena, either as ministers or priests pursuing political careers or as advocates of partisan political support. As the data in Table 4-3 suggest, a large minority of Mexicans believe that elementary school children should receive some religious education, and Mexicans are overwhelmingly

Table 4-3 Mexican Attitudes toward Religious Practices

	Classes for Elementary Students		Run as Candidates for Office		Encourage Voting for Parties	
Region	Approve	Disapprove	Approve	Disapprove	Approve	Disapprove
North	32	65	13	82	8	88
Bajío	39	58	28	71	11	88
Center	19	79	7	90	3	95
Southeast	22	66	14	76	12	76
National	26	69	13	81	8	87

Source: Consulta Mitoksky "Encuesta: La cercanía con la religión," 1000 respondents, +/− 3.5% margin of error, December 7–12, 2007, www.consulta.com.mx.

opposed to religious leaders running for office or advocating that parishioners vote for specific political parties. The responses in Table 4-3 are revealing in the degree that they also highlight regional differences, suggesting once again how regionalism exerts considerable influence on a variety of attitudes and beliefs. For example, the north and especially the Bajío (Guanajuato and parts of Michoacán and Querétaro where the heart of the Cristero rebellion occurred) are the most Catholic regions in Mexico. Therefore their citizens are above the national norm in advocating the teaching of religion in elementary schools. The Federal District, which accounts for a large percentage of residents in central Mexico, whose citizens are the least orthodox in their religious beliefs and consist of a larger percentage of nonbelievers, explains the overwhelming disapproval rate for all three proposals. In contrast, the most radical of these proposals, in direct violation of the constitution and the Catholic Church's own internal regulations, having a priest run for public office, receives approval among three out of ten Bajío residents.

While the Catholic Church does not advocate influencing partisan votes or running for office, it has been explicit in recent years in identifying voting behavior it considers sinful. In a publication written by the bishop of Cuernavaca, sinful behavior included such sins as not voting, voting without knowing the party or a candidate, selling, buying or stealing votes, advocating fear voting, and voting for those who do not respect religious liberty.[42]

Analysts also have suggested that Catholicism may have encouraged deference, obedience, and respect for hierarchy in laity interactions with secular authorities because those are the norms it has conveyed in its own interactions.[43] As late as 2005, two-thirds of Mexicans viewed the church as representing order, solidarity, respect for human rights, discipline, and integrity.[44] Such patterns are obviously changing, and whatever impact the Church may have exercised in the past, its openly critical posture implicitly in favor of political change in the 1990s also was reflected among practicing Catholics.

What has most intrigued students of Mexican politics and religion is an assumed relationship between Catholicism and party affiliation. The reason for this assumption is that the National Action Party adopted many of the ideas of the European and Latin American Christian Democratic movements. Moreover, prominent early leaders of the party were known to be active Catholics.[45] Contrary to a common belief, being Catholic has had little or nothing to do with party sympathy in Mexico. In fact, as I pointed out in a more comprehensive examination of the issue, all the survey data from the 1980s and 1990s indicate that the only relationship between the PAN and Catholicism is between the party and a tiny group of Catholics, 3.4 percent, who attended church daily (see Table 4-4). This group does differ from the rest of the population in its intensity of support for the PAN. Because they are so small in number, they exerted little influence on partisanship and electoral outcomes. But in the razor thin margin of victory in the 2006 presidential race, intensely religious Mexicans could have made the difference in Felipe Calderón's victory. As I argued elsewhere, "These intensely religious individuals surprisingly accounted for 11 percent of voters in 2006, which translated into 4,472,000 of the valid votes cast. The PAN partisans obtained 44 percent more support from those selective, highly religious voters than did the PRD partisans. Considering that such voters were 47 percent less likely to support the PRD than the PAN, they alone could have determined the outcome of this election since Calderón beat López Obrador by only 233,831 votes."[46] In their analysis of this election, Alejandro Moreno and Alejandro Díaz Domínguez argue that increased electoral competition is contributing to the rising importance of religion on partisan preferences, and that this relationship is extremely likely to continue into the 2010s.[47]

Table 4-4 Religious Intensity and Partisanship in Mexico

Which Party You Sympathize With	Mexicans Who Attend Church More Than Once a Week (Intense)			
	Mexicans Who Attend Church Weekly or Monthly (Moderate)			
	Catholics 1990		All Beliefs 2008	
	Intense	Moderate	Intense	Moderate
National Action Party	18	10	40	26
Democratic Revolutionary Party	2	7	8	13
Institutional Revolutionary Party	9	25	53	59

Source: Miguel Basáñez, *Encuesta nacional de opinión pública, iglesia-estado*, 1990; Free Online Data Analysis, Mexico 2008, www.Lapopsurveys.org, 2011.

Religious and party preferences are revealing, even if a significant tie between the PAN and Catholicism does not exist.[48] Indeed, it is the Protestants and the nonreligious who deviate from the norm. In 1989 and 2008 Protestants gave the least support to the PAN, followed by the PRD in 2008. In fact, although the PAN increased its support among Protestants in the 1990s, largely because Protestants hoped the PAN would win and introduced electoral democracy to Mexicans, a change which many Protestants viewed as beneficial to its minority status among all religions, the PAN lost ground among this group in the last decade. Nearly a third of all Mexicans preferred the PAN by 2000, but that was the case among only one out of ten Protestants. On the other hand, among Catholics, the PRI regained a slight edge over the PAN by 2008. The PRI improved its support among Protestants in the 1990s, the group most likely to support that party on the basis of their religious beliefs for the last two decades, but the percentage difference in support among Protestants between the PRI and the PAN declined dramatically by 2008. This significant preference among Protestants in 2000 is also explained by the fact that most of their adherents live in rural communities, until the 2006 election, the strongest regional supporters of PRI. The most interesting group, religiously speaking, based on partisan preferences, is nonbelievers. They always have shown a higher level of support for the PRD, a pattern continuing into the twenty-first century. But in 2000, the nonreligious also was the group most likely to express no party preference, thus making up a larger percentage of independent voters. These findings for Mexico are confirmed in a recent study for Latin America, in which the author concluded that, "In general, religious factors are positively related to partisanship. These factors include *belonging*, measured using three main religious groups; *believing*, measured using the importance of religion; and *behaving*, measured using attendance of religious groups." The author found that "attendance" and "importance" among both Protestants and Catholics increased party identification.[49]

Protestants illustrate differing political sympathies, indicating they may be a more heterogeneous group in terms of background characteristics. Protestants are much more diverse, however, in religious composition. From 1992 to 1994, the Secretariat of Government registered 2,010 religious associations in response to newly introduced constitutional reforms. Of those, only 21 percent were Catholic, and 77 percent were evangelical Protestant. The evangelicals could be subdivided as follows: independent groups, 48 percent; Baptists, 29 percent; Pentecostals, 21 percent; and traditional Protestants (such as Methodists), 2 percent.[50] This level of diversity is important to differences in partisanship, because as research from the United States reveals, churches do have distinctive political orientations, and the extent of theological traditionalism prevailing in a congregation moves individual members toward more conservative positions on social issues and makes them more likely to identify themselves as political conservatives.[51] In short, substantial differences in religious-political orientations, if they exist, are most likely to occur within each individual religious community. It is also likely that the intensity of church involvement is not only a personal preference, but is reinforced by one's local religious community. In other words, if a particular church or parish emphasizes regular church attendance, then an individual is more likely to increase his or her own attendance in conformity with the community norm. This characteristic probably is one of the conditions that explains Joseph Klesner's empirical finding that residence in a specific community, in combination with religious beliefs, is politically significant.

As I stated elsewhere, and recent survey data confirm, many Mexicans are interested in redefining the church's role in society. Their redefinition has serious, long-term implications for the role of the church as both an institution and a religion in Mexicans' political life. Fewer than half of all Mexicans define the church's task as religious, whereas more than half viewed its primary activities as political, social, moral, economic, or something else. This suggests that large numbers of Mexicans do not view church activities in a narrow and traditional sense, and this same group is most critical of the church's response to social and economic needs.[52] Individually, many Mexicans toward the end of first decade of the twenty-first century have admitted being influenced by Catholic priests on specific issues.[53]

GENDER AND POLITICS

One of the influences on values about which we have the least understanding is the role of gender in Mexico. A number of studies of Latin America examine political behavior from a female viewpoint. Research on the political behavior of women in the United States has rarely discovered sharp differences with men, but they typically note that women are not as interested in politics, have less knowledge of politics, and are somewhat more alienated from the political system than are men. In fact, one study concludes that a high level of alienation was associated with the rise of feminism and the recognition of their exclusionary treatment by the system.[54]

Differences in political attitudes and behavior attributable to gender can be explained by roles assigned to Mexican women.[55] Although many women today obtain advanced education and a large percentage are in the workforce, opportunities for women remain fewer than for men. In part this is due to education, since women over the age of fifteen accounted for 63 percent of illiterate Mexicans.[56] Women who do enter the workforce have educational achievements that, on the whole, are equivalent to that of men. It is the nearly two-thirds of women who do not participate in the economically active workforce (38 percent were women in 2010) who have fewer educational attainments. We now know for a fact that women who remain at home and who have larger families engage in different levels of political participation than men.[57] Attitudes favoring men in the workplace continue relatively unchanged in Mexico, as suggested by a fourth of Mexicans agreeing with the statement in 1990 and again in 2006 that "men should have more right to a job than women when jobs are scarce."[58] Nevertheless, the 2010 census demonstrates that women are fast closing the educational gap in Mexico. In percentage terms, the greatest gaps between men and women are among Mexicans with no formal education and those with college degrees. What is important to note, however, is that women for the first time have exceeded the percentage of men completing elementary school, suggesting that they are likely to overtake men in all the remaining educational categories. Indeed, women already have achieved equality with men among those Mexicans completing academic high school (preparatory).

Increasing educational achievements among women are likely to decrease differences between men's and women's levels of political knowledge. In a recent survey about Mexican's political history, men were 22 percent more likely than women to know Mexico's first president (29 percent of all Mexicans knew), 11 percent more likely to know when the independence movement began (49 percent of all Mexicans knew), 25 percent more likely to know the beginning of the Mexican Revolution (40 percent of all Mexicans knew), and 25 percent more likely to know the date of the nationalization of petroleum (only 14 percent of all Mexicans knew).[59] Most important of all, in a recent study by Roy Campos and Regina Campos, they found that women for nearly a decade are voting in greater numbers than men. In fact, in 2009, women accounted for 56 percent of the registered voters who participated in the national elections. Even more striking was the fact that women in rural areas exceeded male voters by 7 percent. The authors attribute the impact of women receiving the right to vote in 1953 as an essential determinant of reversing the roles of men and women at the ballot box, noting that all age groups of women under sixty-four outvoted men, and that the percentage difference increased as their age decreased between sixty-four and thirty.[60] Midway through the 2012 presidential race, 20 percent more women expressed a preference for the PAN presidential candidate, Josefina Vázquez Mota, suggesting for the first time in a presidential election that women's partisan preferences were *significantly* different from men's.[61] However, she did not maintain that percentage of support through election day, and preliminary data suggest women accounted for only 51 percent of the electorate in the 2012 presidential election.

Given these and other conditions that have restricted women's roles in society and hence in politics, it is natural that they might feel more powerless to change the political system. However, a remarkable change in gender-based political efficacy occurred since the 1960s. When Richard Fagen and William Tuohy carried out a study of Jalapa, Veracruz, in the 1970s, they found extreme differences between men and women, regardless of social class. Typically, only half as many women as men reported high levels of political efficacy.[62] By 1989 almost no statistical difference existed between men and women on this issue, a pattern persisting to the present. This finding is similar to recent U.S. data on women and men.[63] In 2010, although not as clear an expression of efficacy, women, more so than men, believed the Mexican government was interested in what they thought.[64]

As Mexicans make the transition from a more authoritarian political culture to one characterized by democratic characteristics, it is desirable to understand women's potential role. Given the traditional literature on women, it might be expected that more women than men would be unwilling to risk political change. The data on the issue of risk-taking identify a more definitive difference between men and women in Mexico, and bear out gender-related tendencies found elsewhere. Twenty-five percent more women than men were inclined to stick with the status quo than to risk change in 2000. This also explains, in part, another more significant pattern. Where women differ most from men politically in Mexico is on political activism. Few Mexicans have actually participated in some type of political protest, but only half as many women as men have done so.[65]

These data could convey the false impression that women are not politically active. In fact, recent research shows that women in urban areas are the backbone of the social and civic organizations that have flourished in Mexico in recent years, contributing significantly to the democratic transition and to the democratic consolidation after 2000. It is important to repeat the information from Table 3-4 that 11 percent of Mexican women compared to only 8 percent of American women belonged to women's organizations in 2010. It is interesting to report that based on data from the World Values Survey, Mexicans' strong confidence in the women's movement in the country rose from only 44 percent in 1995 to 65 percent in 2006, a dramatic 48 percent increase. As one researcher commented, "Independent organizations are giving women a political experience which is

profoundly affecting their lives, leading them to question the power relations which limit them at a societal level, as well as within their personal,
familial relations."[66]

This active feminist presence emerged in earnest in the 1970s, especially in Mexico City. By the 1980s, a network of women's organizations
existed throughout Mexico, linking together NGOs, unions, and urban poor
and middle-class organizations. As was true elsewhere in the region, socioeconomic differences among women created tensions in generating
a common agenda.[67] The expansion of women into different employment
opportunities, and the changing political landscape in the 1990s, encouraged the growth of women's organizations and increased the breadth and
influence of a feminine political agenda. Sex crimes became the most
important issue contributing to unification of a feminist agenda.

In 2000, a leading feminist, Patricia Mercado, launched a political
party, México Posible (Mexico Possible), which analysts described as
having feminist demands at its core. It was short-lived and did not have a
significant political impact.[68] Six years later, Patricia Mercado co-founded
another party, and became a presidential candidate in the 2006 election,
where she attracted considerable media attention and support from voters.
Despite the fact that two women have run for the presidency on the tickets
of smaller parties in Mexico, a general bias against women as political leaders continues into the period of democratic consolidation. When Mexicans
were asked if "men made better political leaders than women," 56 percent
in 1995, 61 percent in 2000, 72 percent in 2006, and 69 percent in 2011
disagreed with that statement.[69] In 2011, two-thirds of Mexicans believed a
female president would improve Mexico's general image.[70] The general decrease in support of men over women in public life suggests a significant,
positive change in attitude toward future female leadership. In a practical
sense, this was reflected, for the first time in Mexican political history, in
the fact that two of the strongest candidates throughout 2011 for the presidential nomination of both the PRI and the PAN were women, Beatriz
Paredes and Josefina Vázquez Mota, and that by 2012, Josefina Vázquez
Mota won the PAN nomination.

As the democratic transition in electoral politics became a reality,
women fought successfully for affirmative action quotas among party candidates for political office. Members of the PRD were the first to achieve
this goal, persuading the party to require 20 percent of its candidates to be
women in 1990. A year later they increased that level of representation to
30 percent of the party's candidates, and the same percentage among the
party's national executive committee. The PAN refused to pass such a mandate, but the PRI accepted the same percentage levels among its national

congressional candidates in 1996.[71] In the fall, 2001, however, the PRI increased the percentage of female candidates to 40 percent, the highest level of any party. Some state party committees also began replicating these patterns for legislative candidates. More importantly, in 2002, the Mexican Congress passed its own quota law requiring that no more than 70 percent of the candidates for single-member districts (accounting for three hundred of the five hundred seats in the lower house of congress) can be of the same gender. According to Lisa Baldez, who examined this issue in detail, the Federal Electoral Institute imposed strict compliance requirements, and the Supreme Court confirmed its legality. It went into effect in the 2003 congressional elections, and as a result, women members of Congress rose from 16 to 23 percent.[72] From 2009 to 2012, women accounted for 25 percent of the Chamber of Deputies, and 22 percent of the senate. However, serious concerns have risen about the quota system, which was widely abused in the 2009 congressional elections, when eleven of the victorious female candidates resigned their posts so that their boyfriends, political mentors, husbands, and others who were their elected alternates could automatically replace them. They became known in the press as *diputadas Juanitas*, and as pointed out by Victoria Rodríguez, included plurinominal deputies (representing votes for the parties by regions not individual districts) from both the PRI and the PAN.[73] Interestingly, however, gender quotas do not exert a significant impact on mass participation by women.[74]

A new study demonstrates that there are some significant differences in political attitudes between men and women, and these cross-national boundaries, including Mexicans, Mexican-Americans, and Americans. One of the most interesting differences is that women and men have different expectations from democracy. Among Mexicans, men were more likely than women to see democracy as liberty, voting/elections, and type of government. These conceptualizations incorporate the three most traditional definitions of democracy, two of which, voting/elections and type of government, can be viewed as a *procedural* conceptualization, that is, defining democracy by its process. Mexican women, on the other hand, are more likely than men to view democracy as improving one's quality of life and standard of living, viewing government in productive economic and social terms. Gender does make a difference in the specific way in which a person defines expectations from democracy. Women in general are more likely than men to view democracy as a means of achieving equality, as improving the culture of law, and as producing progress.[75] It is also not unreasonable to draw the conclusion that because "44 percent of women over the age of fifteen have been the victims of some form of intrafamily violence, and 60 percent of women between the ages of fifteen and thirty-four reported such abuse" in Mexico, that women's personal experiences would contribute to their emphasis on these democratic goals.[76]

REGION AND POLITICS

Many years ago Lesley Byrd Simpson wrote the classic, *Many Mexicos.* "Many" in the title referred in large part to regionalism's influence on Mexican values. As Mexico developed and communications improved, regional differences declined, but they did not disappear. Economically speaking, the north is highly developed. It is characterized by heavy in-migration, dynamic change, industrialization, and of course, its proximity to and economic and cultural linkages with the United States. The south, on the other hand, is the least developed economically. It is rural; has a large indigenous population, mainly in Oaxaca and Chiapas; and is the most isolated from the cultural mainstream. The center, which includes the Federal District, has been the traditional source of political leadership, religious infrastructure, industrialization, and intellectual activity.[77] Today, Mexicans continue to identify strongly with their region, indeed, nearly as strongly as they identify themselves as Mexicans. Nationally, 87 percent of Mexicans strongly or somewhat identify themselves with their city, and 83 percent with their region. Even in the Federal District, given its size and density, 79 percent and 75 percent respectively identify with these same geographic designations.[78]

Regional differences can be translated into political behavior. In the first place, interest in politics varies among individual citizens on the basis of many variables, and region is prominent among them. In general, however, twenty years of data suggest no increased interest in politics despite a major transformation to participatory democracy! Northern and Mexico City residents are most interested in politics, measured by its importance to their daily lives. Furthermore, their level of sophistication produces an interest in politics that leads to greater political competition. As the data in Table 4-5 show, a majority of Mexicans, typically three out of four, actually discuss politics. But among those who *discuss it frequently*, nearly twice as many do so in the north and in Mexico City as in the south. Although the questions are different in 1990 compared to 2006 and 2010, little change has occurred during the democratic consolidation. The only pattern that is apparent in the newer data is that interest does increase somewhat during a presidential election year. On the other hand, for residents of the south, even controversial presidential

Table 4-5 Mexicans' Interest in Politics, by Region

Response to Statement	North (%) 1990	2006	2010	Center (%) 1990	2006	2010	South (%) 1990	2006	2010	Mexico City (%) 1990
Frequently or a lot (2006/2010)	19	12	7	13	11	9	11	8	8	18
Occasionally some or little (2006/2010)	53	68	62	58	69	63	63	69	68	54
Never	25	20	30	26	20	26	24	23	24	27

Source: World Values Surveys. World Value Survey, 1990 data, courtesy of Miguel Basáñez.
Question: 1990 Survey, "How often politics are discussed?"
Question: 2006 and 2010 Surveys, "How much interest do you have in politics?"

elections do not spur greater interest. It is impossible to determine whether Mexicans' interest in politics has increased electoral competitiveness in both regions, or whether electoral competitiveness has exaggerated their interest. It is fair to conclude, however, that interest and activity are interrelated.[79]

Regional patterns also exist when measuring citizen political efficacy. Survey data suggest a complex pattern, not easily explained, but the regional differences are sharp. Three-quarters of Mexicans from the center, which in terms of population would be dominated by the Federal District and the state of México, compared to all Mexicans, believe going to the polls has actually changed conditions for the better. This idea may be due to citizen satisfaction with three consecutive elected governors from the PRD since 1997. What is interesting about the responses to political efficacy from the west and the north is that both regions have witnessed selective PAN victories at the state and local levels, yet two-fifths of their residents remain cynical about voting producing change. It may be that while some Mexicans in these regions brought the PAN into power as an alternative to the PRI, their level of expectation toward change was not actually met, which clearly had become the case by 2006 and again in 2012. Non-PRI parties will have to govern in other states in the region before clearer and more pronounced patterns of regional efficacy can be determined.

Place of residence can also affect other attitudes, including religious beliefs, which in turn, as was shown earlier, may have some effect on political preferences. Regional differences do not affect all politically related attitudes equally. In many circumstances, region is not an influential variable.

The most significant consequence of region as one of the variables analyzed in this section is partisan political preferences. Traditionally, the opposition before 2000, primarily the PAN, did well in Mexico's most dynamic regions—those showing the highest levels of economic growth. The PAN's greatest number of sympathizers until 2000, based on those economic figures, have been the north and the Federal District, including the Mexico City metropolitan area, which is found in the center region. The PAN always has done poorly in the south, Mexico's least developed and most indigenous region; consequently, the lack of partisan supporters there is not surprising. The PRI, on the other hand, historically has relied heavily on the south and the west for support. Of the three leading parties, its partisans are the most evenly distributed by region. Their significant weakness, regionally, was in the Federal District and state of México, the country's most populous entities, and the most industrialized. The PRI's regional weakness in the center is explained by the PRD's strength.[80] The PRD, in 1989, counted numerous adherents in Mexico City and in several central states, notably Morelos and Michoacán. It demonstrated its strength again in these states in 1997, and decisively won control of Mexico City in the capital's first mayoralty race in seventy years, repeating that victory in 2000, 2006, and 2012.

Some dramatic shifts in regional partisan support took place six years later during the campaign and election of 2006. The PAN not only retained its dominance among voters residing in the north, but increased support in that region, reflected by the fact that half of all residents voted for Felipe Calderón. The PRI, which retained strong support in the north as late as the beginning of the presidential campaign, due to the presence of many PRI governors in those states, lost its influence in the north, which shifted to both the PAN and the PRD. Even more astonishing, the PAN's weakest support had come from the south, a former PRI stronghold, and it was able to increase its influence there and also in the west. The other pattern that is readily apparent is the overwhelming strength of the PRD in Mexico City in 2006. Equally significant is the fact that the PRD dominated the south, further decimating the PRI's influence in that region.

The PRI's dramatic recovery in the eyes of potential voters in 2012 completely alters, once again, the regional distributions of partisan preferences. Regional influences not only are more complex but are equally fluid, making it difficult to predict their influence on electoral outcomes beyond any single national election. The PRI made substantial gains in all regions, the least in the center, which included the Federal District. The PAN's regional gains in the south have been devastated since 2006, having declined by 42 percent. Except for the center-west, the PAN's long-time stronghold, the PRI by 2012 had captured the partisan sympathies of nearly two-fifths of all Mexicans and essentially was able to maintain nearly that same level of support, distributed evenly across all regions, with a slightly higher level of support in the center-west, throughout 2012. The PRD experienced a dramatic decline in support in the north and center-west, while receiving strong partisan support in the center and south. The PAN declined in all regions, but continued to be strongest in the north.

Higher levels of political interest, activism, and sophistication are associated with higher levels of economic development, education, and urbanization. In turn, these qualities are most likely to promote the development of alternative political views, sympathy for political parties not in power, and opposition to closed decision-making. One of the most strongly held beliefs among all Mexicans is that decision-making is inaccessible and that local and state policymaking should be more autonomous and less under the thumb of the national authorities. Increasing federalism, giving greater decision-making authority and fiscal resources to state and local governments, is likely to reinforce rather than moderate regional differences. Whether the changing allocations in power will affect attitudes on specific, local issues, or whether it will influence broader political attitudes, remain to be seen.

AGE AND POLITICS

Age often determines important variations in values and, more important, indicates changes in the offing as generations reach political maturity.[81] In their significant comprehensive study, Ronald Inglehart, Neil Nevitte, and Miguel Basáñez found that thirty-four issues had been characterized by intergenerational change in the 1990s, the decade of democratic transition.[82] Inglehart and others had discovered in earlier studies that economic conditions during a person's preadult years were the most significant determinant of adult values. Changing economic conditions, then, are likely to alter values from one generation to the next. For example, in the first World Values Survey, Inglehart learned that attitudes toward authoritarian values changed for each age cohort, moving in the direction of greater freedom and autonomy. The pattern peaked in all countries in the cohort aged twenty-five to thirty-four years old and began to reverse among the next generation.

Another consequence of generational change appears in party identification. As Inglehart reported, studies of Western Europe and in the United States demonstrate that older citizens identified more strongly with political parties but that in recent decades younger voters are less likely to identify with a specific party. Although better educated than their elders and more interested in politics, younger Mexicans, like citizens elsewhere, no longer exhibit strong party loyalty. For example, in 2010, 29 percent of Mexicans reported partisan attachments to political parties, compared to 61 percent in the United States.[83] As the presidential race began to heat up at the end of 2011, 46 percent claimed to identify strongly with a political party (23 percent PRI, 11 percent PAN, and 7 percent PRD, 5 percent other).[84] This phenomenon makes it difficult to predict future partisan sympathies and gives the independent or uncommitted voter considerable power to determine electoral outcomes. More than two-thirds of citizens in non–presidential election years express no sympathy for any party. These voters determined the outcome of Fox's, Calderón's, and Peña Nieto's victories.

There is no question that younger Mexicans under the age of thirty-nine, who have witnessed the dramatic changes in Mexico since 1988 as young adults, determined the outcome of the 2000 presidential race. One of the reasons why their partisan preferences favored the PAN, and why they were translated into actual votes for Fox, is the attitude of younger Mexicans toward risk-taking. As one might expect, this group, seven out of ten Mexicans, most favored a change. Over half of all Mexicans over 60 opposed change, and those older Mexicans were the PRI's strongest partisans among any age group. Twice as many older Mexicans sympathized with the PRI compared with the PAN in the 2000 election.

Younger voters persisted in similar patterns in 2006, providing a significant portion of Fox's and Calderón's supporters. After Fox won the election, 31 percent of Mexicans claimed to be partisan sympathizers of the PAN. But among those individuals from age eighteen to twenty-four, 39 percent expressed a preference for the PAN. In contrast, the PRI, which had nearly the same percentage of sympathizers nationally, obtained support from only 20 percent of this age cohort, half of that received by the PAN. The next age cohort, twenty-five to thirty-nine, follows a similar pattern favoring the PAN, but the differences are not as dramatic. In 2006, Calderón received 38 percent support from voters from eighteen to twenty-nine, compared to only 21 percent and 34 percent for the PRI and PRD candidates, the age group which gave both of these parties their lowest levels of support.[85] Most importantly, the supporters for the PRI through 2006 increased in age. By 2012, the PRI presidential candidate, for most of the race, appealed to all age groups, whereas Andrés Manuel López Obrador did well among older voters and Josefina Vázquez Mota performed better among middle age voters, the largest demographic block. On election day, however, Peña Nieto and López Obrador essentially tied for the eighteen-to-twenty-nine group at 36 to 37 percent, and Peña Nieto dominated the thirty-to-forty-nine and fifty-or-older age groups with 41 and 40 percent, respectively, of their votes.[86] López Obrador's significant comeback in the final days of the campaign can be attributed in large part to direct college student involvement, again reinforcing the importance of younger generations.

CONCLUSION

The foregoing brief analysis of just a few variables in the making of political attitudes and their partisan consequences demonstrates their complexities. Many Mexicans have gained confidence in their ability to change the political system since the 2000 presidential election, but large numbers, nearly a third, believe themselves powerless. Those expressing the least confidence in their ability are the uneducated, the poor, and minorities. Nevertheless, the civic attention focused on the 1994 presidential elections and the unprecedented turnout of nearly four-fifths of Mexican voters indicate that numerous citizens took their responsibilities seriously and that even many first-time voters believed that they might make a difference. Perhaps because the PRI once again was victorious in 1994, turnout was lower in the 2000 elections, but voters further strengthened opposition representation nationally, and first-time voters played a crucial role in the PAN victory. In 2006, voter sympathy shifted strongly to a third party, the PRD, which nearly defeated the incumbent PAN. In 2012, the PRI posted a remarkable recovery from its disastrous performance in 2006, suggesting the fluidity of partisan loyalty and the pragmatism of Mexico voters.

Mexican political attitudes are undergoing change, and support for change itself is strong among them. Younger people are contributing most to this alteration, as are those who are more highly educated, who come from affluent backgrounds, and who live in the most dynamic regions. Mexicans are religious, but their Catholicism per se does not impinge on their political behavior, their support for change, or their partisanship. The intensity of their religious beliefs, or the lack of them, does translate into important partisan differences. Many of the trends in political attitudes, as well as attitudes in general, that are apparent in Mexico appear in other countries as well, including the United States.

One of the most important variables that drives personal political behavior is one's level of political knowledge. The level of political knowledge is affected by many traditional demographic variables, including income, education, and gender, and is distributed differently across regions. The percentage of Mexicans and Americans responding to questions about their political knowledge are similar in the levels of correct responses on surveys. A Mexican's level of knowledge plays a significant role in the extent to which citizens will participate in a democracy, a critical ingredient in evolving a more sophisticated and consolidated form of democratic governance. For example, a comprehensive examination of the relationship between level of political knowledge and political participation, given the evidence of the linkage between interest and knowledge, demonstrates clearly that whether one was registered to vote, actually voted, tried to convince others to vote, or worked for a party or candidate in a presidential race, the response was greater in all of these activities among Mexicans whose knowledge was the highest. Differences between those with the lowest level of knowledge compared to those with the highest level of knowledge are substantial. The same pattern can be found among some forms of participation in local, community affairs. For example, only 20 percent of Mexicans with the lowest scores on political knowledge have contributed to solving a community problem compared to 39 percent having the highest political knowledge, and 47 versus 56 percent respectively had attended community meetings.[87]

Equally important in the evolution of Mexican democratic practices is the relationship between political knowledge and political tolerance. As the government's own cultural survey in 2006 concluded, "The advance of political pluralism has not been accompanied by a culture of acceptance and respect for ideological and cultural differences."[88] The level of tolerance is illustrated in the response citizens gave to the question, "Would you agree or disagree with permitting a person to appear on television who was going to say something opposed to your own views?" Only 34 percent agreed completely with this statement, followed by 19 percent who accepted it in part. When asked, "Who should participate in politics and who should not?" Only 42 percent accepted artists, 56 percent homosexuals, 60 percent college professors, and 63 percent journalists. Eight out of ten Mexicans thought indigenous citizens, women, and young people should participate.[89] In 2010, Mexicans were compared with other Latin Americans and Americans about their willingness to extend the right to vote to critics of their respective governments. Mexico ranked in the lower half of countries on a tolerance scale, while the United States, Argentina, and Costa Rica were at the top.[90] Although it has been shown that statistically the relationship between political knowledge and tolerance is modest, it does affect citizen perceptions.

Finally, political knowledge has been shown to have a critical influence on how citizens view democratic governance. Political knowledge influences non-Mexicans' and Mexicans' awareness of democratic values and reinforces their acceptance, critical elements in achieving democratic consolidation. As María Fernanda Boidi clearly demonstrates in her study, not only did the most politically aware Mexicans prefer democracy to any other form of government, but were 76 percent more likely to express such a preference than their least knowledgeable counterparts. At the same time, the least informed Mexicans were 30 percent more likely to believe that under certain circumstances an authoritarian government might be preferable to a democracy.[91]

NOTES

1. Joseph A. Kahl, *The Measurement of Modernism: A Study of Values in Brazil and Mexico* (Austin: University of Texas Press, 1974), 8.

2. K. L. Tedin, "The Influence of Parents on the Political Attitudes of Adolescents," *American Political Science Review* 68, no. 4 (December 1974): 1592.

3. Alex Edelstein, "Since Bennington: Evidence of Change in Student Political Behavior," in *Learning about Politics*, ed. Roberta Sigel (New York: Random House, 1970), 397.

4. Richard Centers, "Children of the New Deal: Social Stratification and Adolescent Attitudes," in *Class, Status and Power*, ed. Reinhard Bendix and Seymour Martin Lipset (New York: Free Press, 1953), 361.

5. For example, see such memoirs as Ramón Beteta, *Jarano* (Austin: University of Texas Press, 1970); and Andrés Iduarte, *Niño, Child of the Mexican Revolution* (New York: Praeger, 1971).

6. See Linda Stevenson and Mitchell Seligson, "Fading Memories of the Revolution: Is Stability Eroding in Mexico?" in *Polling for Democracy: Public Opinion and Political Liberalization in Mexico*, ed. Roderic Ai Camp (Wilmington, DE: Scholarly Resources, 1996), 61–80.

7. Ulises Beltrán, *Los mexicanos de los noventa* (Mexico: UNAM, 1996), 137.

8. Harry Eckstein, "Culture as a Foundation Concept for the Social Sciences," *Journal of Theoretical Politics* 8, no. 4 (October 1966), 485.

9. Roderic Ai Camp, "Learning Democracy in Mexico and the United States," *Mexican Studies* 19, no. 1 (Winter 2003): 3–28.

10. Miguel Basáñez and Pablo Páras, "Color and Democracy in Latin America," in *Citizen Views of Democracy in Latin America*, ed. Roderic Ai Camp (Pittsburgh, PA: University of Pittsburgh Press, 2001), 151.

11. María Fernanda Boidi, "Political Knowledge and Political Attitudes and Behaviors in Mexico," Paper presented at the Midwest Political Science Association, Chicago, April 12–15, 2007, 28.

12. Todd A. Eisenstadt, *Politics, Identity, and Mexico's Indigenous Rights Movements* (Cambridge: Cambridge University Press, 2011), 169.

13. Free online analysis, Mexico 2010, www.vanderbilt.edu/lapop, 2011.

14. "The State of Democracy in Latin America: A Comparative Analysis of the Attitudes of Elites and Citizens," *Boletin PNUD & Instituto de Iberoamérica*, January 2011.

15. The most important variable determining the level of education that a child obtains in Mexico is the socioeconomic status of the father, according to Kahl, *The Measurement of Modernism*, 71.

16. See Joseph Klesner, "A Sociological Analysis of the 2006 Election," in *Consolidating Mexico's Democracy: The 2006 Presidential Campaign in Comparative Perspective*, eds. Jorge I. Domínguez, Chappell Lawson, and Alejandro Moreno (Baltimore: John Hopkins University Press, 2009), 65–70.

17. Andy Baker, "Regionalized Voting Behavior and Political Discussion in Mexico," in Dominguez et al., eds., *Consolidating Mexico's Democracy*, 73–75.

18. *Los Angeles Times* poll, August 1989.

19. Michael M. Gant and Norman R. Luttberg, *American Electoral Behavior, 1952–1988* (Itasca, NY: Peacock Publishers, 1991), 140.

20. Alejandro Moreno, "Citizens' Values and Beliefs toward Politics: Is Democracy Growing Attitudinal Roots?," in *Mexico's Democratic Challenges: Politics, Government, and Society*, ed. Andrew Selee and Jacqueline Peschard (Washington, DC: Woodrow Wilson Center Press, 2010), Table 2.5, 45.

21. Ann Craig and Wayne Cornelius, "Political Culture in Mexico, Continuities and Revisionist Interpretations," in *The Civic Culture Revisited*, ed. Gabriel Almond and Sidney Verba (Boston: Little, Brown, 1980), 369.

22. For evidence of these ongoing changes and their linkage to politics, see Joe Foweraker and Ann L. Craig, eds., *Popular Movements and Political Change in Mexico* (Boulder, CO: Lynne Rienner, 1990).

23. Free Online Data Analysis, Mexico 2010, www.vanderbilt.edu.LAPOP.

24. For another way of viewing this pattern of partisan support, see Irina Alberro, "Political Competition and Empowerment of the Poor," paper presented at the Midwest Political Science Association Meeting, Chicago, Illinois, Spring 2004.

25. Ramon Eduardo Ruiz, *Triumphs and Tragedy: A History of the Mexican People* (New York: Norton, 1992), 469.

26. Michael Gant and Norman R. Luttbeg, *American Electoral Behavior: 1952–1988* (Itasca, IL: Peacock, 1991), 141.

27. Joseph L. Klesner, "The Structure of the Mexican Electorate: Social, Attitudinal, and Partisan Bases of Vicente Fox's Victory," in *Mexico's Pivotal Democratic Election: Candidates, Voters, and the Presidential Campaign of 2000*, ed. Jorge Domínguez and Chappell Lawson (Stanford, CA: Stanford University Press, 2004), 108.

28. William Flanigan and Nancy Zingale, *Political Behavior of the American Electorate*, 7th ed. (Washington, DC: Congressional Quarterly Press, 1991), 68.

29. Joseph L. Klesner, "A Sociological Analysis of the 2006 Elections," 52–53. It is important to point out, based on a recent study, that while education is a key explanatory variable in support for the PRD, when it is also accompanied by higher income levels, support shifts in favor of the PAN. See Manuel Suárez and Irina Alberro, "Analyzing Partisanship in Central Mexico: A Geographical Approach," *Electoral Studies* 30, no. 1 (2011), 146.

30. Ronald Inglehart, Neil Nevitte, and Miguel Basáñez, *Convergencia en Norte América: Comercio, política y cultura* (Mexico City: Siglo XXI, 1994), Figure 3-20.

31. World Values Survey, 2006.

32. 2010 Mexican Census, www.ingei.org.mx, 2011.

33. World Values Survey, 1990.

34. Miguel Basáñez, "Encuesta nacional de opinión pública, iglesia y estado (1990)," 14; "Democracy Through U.S. and Mexican Lenses," September 2000.

35. Panel Survey 2006, First Wave, October 2006.

36. Consulta Mitoksky's "Encuesta: La cercanía con la religión," 1,000 respondents, +/−3.5% margin of error, December 7–12, 2007, www.consulta.com.mx.

37. Gabriel Almond and Sidney Verba, *The Civic Culture: Political Attitudes and Democracy in Five Nations* (Boston: Little, Brown, 1965), 101.

38. Consulta Mitoksky's "Encuesta: La cercanía con la religión," 8.

39. Alma Guillermoprieto, "Troubled Spirits," *National Geographic* (May 2010), http://ngm.nationalgeographic.com.

40. Alejandro Díaz-Domínguez, "Political Knowledge and Religious Channels of Socialization in Latin America," *AmericasBaromenter Insights: 2011*, No. 5, 5.

41. Alejandro Díaz-Domínguez, "The Influence of Religion on Support for Free Trade in Latin America," *AmericasBarometer Insights: 2010*, No. 40, 4.

42. www.elvigia.net, July 29, 2007.

43. Charles L. Davis, "Religion and Partisan Loyalty: The Case of Catholic Workers in Mexico," *Western Political Quarterly* 45, no. 1 (March 1992): 227.

44. "Imágen de la iglesia católica," Ipsos-Bimsa, one thousand respondents, +/- 3.5% margin of error, November 25–December 5, 2005.

45. See Donald Mabry, *Mexico's Acción Nacional: A Catholic Alternative to Revolution* (Syracuse, NY: Syracuse University Press, 1973), for the well-documented ideological influence.

46. Roderic Ai Camp, "Exercising Political Influence, Religion, Democracy, and the Mexican 2006 Presidential Race," *Journal of Church and State* 50, no. 1 (Winter, 2008): 101–122. Data are from the Tribunal Electoral del Poder Judicial de la Federación, *Dictamen relative ala cómputo final de la elección de Presidente de los Estado Unidos Mexicanos, declaración de validez de la elección y de presidente electo*, September 5 2006. www.te.org.mx. Calderón received 14,916,927 valid votes to 14,683,096 for López Obrador and 9,237,000 for Roberto Madrazo. Fifty-eight percent of registered voters participated.

47. Alejandro Moreno and Alejandro Díaz Domínguez, "The Religious Vote in Mexico: Is a Religious Cleavage (Re) Emerging in Mexico's New Party System?," paper presented at the Midwest Political Science Association, Chicago, April 2007, 20.

48. See Roderic A. Camp, "The Cross in the Polling Booth: Religion, Politics, and the Laity in Mexico," *Latin American Research Review* 29 (1994): 89–90.

49. Alejandro Díaz-Domínguez, "The Impact of Religion on Party Identification in the Americas," *AmericasBarometer Insights: 2010*, No. 51, 3–4.

50. Rubén Ruíz Guerra, "Las verdades de las cifras," *Este País*, May 1994, 17.

51. Kenneth D. Wald, Dennis E. Owen, and Samuel D. Hill Jr., "Churches as Political Communities," *American Political Science Review* 82, no. 2 (June 1988): 543–44.

52. Camp, "The Cross in the Polling Booth," 92–93.

53. "Imágen de la iglesia Cátolica," Ipsos Bimsa, 1,000 respondents, +/−3.8% margin of error, November 25–December 4, 2005, 9.

54. Robert S. Gilmour and Robert B. Lamp, *Political Alienation in Contemporary America* (New York: St. Martin's Press, 1975), 55.

55. Almond and Verba, *Civic Culture*, 327.

56. Alicia Inés Martínez, "Políticas hacia la mujer en el México moderno," paper presented at the Latin American Studies Association, Atlanta, March 1994, 36.

57. Federico Batista Pereira, "Gender and Community Participation in Latin America and the Caribbean," *AmericasBarometer Insights: 2012*, No. 78, 5.

58. World Values Survey, 2006.

59. "Conocimiento históricos," August 2007, www.consulta.com.mx, 2007.

60. "Una verdad: las mujeres votan más que los hombres," October 4–6, 2011, www.consulta.com.mx, 2011.

61. "Preferencia para president por segmentos," 2012: La elección, April, 2012, www.mitofsky.com.mx, 2012.

62. Richard Fagen and William Tuohy, *Politics and Privilege in a Mexican City* (Stanford, CA: Stanford University Press, 1972), 117.

63. Gant and Luttberg, *American Electoral Behavior*, 141.

64. Free online analysis, Mexico 2010, www.vanderbilt.edu/lapop, 2011.

65. World Values Survey, 1990, courtesy of Miguel Basáñez.

66. Nikki Craske, "Women's Political Participation in Colonias Populares in Guadalajara, Mexico," in *Viva: Women and Popular Protest in Latin America*, eds. Sarah A. Radcliffe and Sallie Westwood (London: Routledge, 1993), 112.

67. Marta Lamas et al., "Building Bridges: The Growth of Popular Feminism in Mexico," in *The Challenge of Local Feminisms: Women's Movements in Global Perspective*, eds. Amrita Basu (Boulder, CO: Westview, 1995), 340–41.

68. Adriana Ortiz-Ortega and Mercedes Barquet, "Gendering Transition to Democracy in Mexico," *Latin American Research Review* 45, Special Issue, (2010): 129.

69. World Values Survey, 2010.

70. "Mujeres en la política, el género la la Presidencia," www.parametria.com.mx, 2011.

71. Linda Stevenson, "Gender Politics in the Mexican Democratization Process: Sex Crimes, Affirmative Action for Women, and the 1997 Elections," paper presented at the David Rockefeller Center for Latin American Studies, Harvard University, Cambridge, 1997.

72. Lisa Baldez, "Elected Bodies: The Gender Quota Law For Legislative Candidates in Mexico," *Legislative Studies Quarterly* 29, no. 2 (May 2004): 231–58; and María del Carmen and Alanis Figueroa, "Women and Politics," *Voices of Mexico* 56 (July–September 2001): 7–11; Kathleen Bruhn, "Whores and Lesbians: Political Activism, Party Strategies, and Gender Quotas in Mexico," *Electoral Studies* 22, no. 1 (2003): 101–19.

73. Victoria E. Rodríguez, "Women, Politics, and Democratic Consolidation in Mexico: Two Steps Forward, One Step Back," in the *Oxford Handbook of Mexican Politics*, ed. Roderic Ai Camp (New York: Oxford University Press, 2012), 446–65.

74. Leslie Schwindt-Bayer, "Gender Quotas and Women's Political Participation in Latin America," Papers from the AmericasBarometer Small Grants and Data Awards, 2011.

75. Roderic Ai Camp and Keith Yanner, "Democracy Across Cultures: Does Gender Make a Difference?" in *Citizenship in Latin America*, ed. Joseph S. Tulchin and Meg Ruthenburg (Boulder, CO: Lynne Rienner, 2006), 149–70.

76. Adriana Beltrán and Laurie Freeman, "Hidden in Plain Sight: Violence Against Women in Mexico and Guatemala, *WOLA Special Report*, March 2007, 2. The number of unsolved murders of women in Ciudad Juárez since 1993 has highlighted the level of violence against women in Mexico.

77. Eric Van Young, ed., *Mexico's Regions: Comparative History and Development* (La Jolla, CA: Center for U.S.-Mexican Studies, UCSD, 1992).

78. "Identidad Nacional," 1,200 respondents, +/–2.8% margin of error, September 17–21, 2009 and April 7–11, 2010, www.parametria.com.mx.

79. See Roderic Ai Camp, "Province Versus the Center: Democratizing Mexico's Political Culture," in *Assessing Democracy in Latin America: A Tribute to Russell H. Fitzgibbon*, ed. Philip Kelly (Boulder, CO: Westview Press, 1998), 76–92.

80. Joseph Klesner, "Democratic Transition? The 1997 Mexican Elections," *PS: Political Science and Politics* 30, no. 4 (December 1997): 703–11.

81. Russell J. Dalton, *Citizen Politics in Western Democracies: Public Opinion and Political Parties in the United States, Great Britain, West Germany, and France* (Chatham, NJ: Chatham House, 1988), 85ff.

82. Inglehart, Nevitte, and Basáñez, *Convergencia en Norte América*, chap. 1, 12.

83. Federico Batista Pereira, "Why are There More Partisans in Some Countries than in Others?," *AmericasBarometer Insights 2012*, No. 71, 1.

84. Carta Paramétrica, "Identificación partidista," www.parametria.com.mx, 2011.

85. World Values Survey, 2006.

86. Alejandro Moreno, "Asi votaron . . . ," *Reforma*, July 2, 2012, 12.

87. María Fernanda Boidi, "Political Knowledge and Political Attitudes and Behavior in Mexico," 13–14.

88. Secretaria de Gobernación, "Conociendo a los ciudadanos Mexicanos: Prinicipales resultados," 2005, 8.

89. Ibid., 8–9.

90. Michael Edwards, et al., "Political Tolerance in the Americas: Should Critics Be Allowed to Vote?," *AmericasBarometer Insights: 2011*, no. 67, 1.

91. María Fernanda Boidi, "Political Knowledge and Political Attitudes and Behavior in Mexico," 24–25.

5

Rising to the Top: The Recruitment of Political Leadership in a Democratic Mexico

> We find that despite operating in the same institutional environment, the three most important parties—the once-hegemonic Party of the Institutional Revolution (Partido Revolucionario Institucional, or PRI), the center-right National Action Party (Partido Acción Nacional, or PAN), and the center-left Party of the Democratic Revolution (Partido de la Revolución Democrática, or PRD)—deal with the challenges of candidate recruitment and selection in different ways, leading one to believe that constitutional and electoral institutions alone cannot explain candidate selection in Mexico.
>
> JOY LANGSTON, *"Legislative Recruitment in Mexico"*

Most citizens in a society where elections are typical participate by voting. A small number become involved in a political demonstration or join a party or organization to influence public policy actively. An even smaller number seek political office and the power to make decisions.

The structure of a political system, the relationships between institutions and citizens, and the relationships among various political institutions affect how a person arrives at a leadership post. The process by which people reach such posts is known as political recruitment.[1] An examination of political recruitment from a comparative perspective is revealing for what it tells us about leadership characteristics and, equally important, what it illustrates about a society's political process.

All political systems and all organizations are governed by rules that prescribe acceptable behavior. The rules of political behavior are both formal and informal. The formal rules are set forth in law and in a constitution. The informal rules often explain more completely the realities of the process, or how the system functions in practice as distinct from theory. The political process melds the two sets of rules, and over time each influences the other to the extent that they often become inextricably intertwined. Mexico has produced some dramatic changes in political recruitment as it evolved through a period of democratic transformation in the 1980s and 1990s, and embarked on a process of democratic consolidation since 2000. The characteristics of national politicians in all three branches of the national government, and among state governors, reflect the multiple consequences of intense electoral competition and informal recruitment practices, some of which extend back to the mid-twentieth century.

THE FORMAL RULES

Formally, the Mexican political system has some of the same characteristics of the U.S. system. It is republican, having three branches of government—executive, legislative, judicial—and federal, allocating certain powers and responsibilities to state and local governments and others to the national government. In practice, the Mexican system has been dominated by the executive branch, which has not shared power with another branch from the 1920s until the 1990s, and allocates few powers to state and local governments. While this pattern was the norm for nearly seventy years, political transformations are changing the structural balance of power nationally and between the federal and state governments, altering well-established recruitment patterns.

In a competitive, parliamentary system, such as that found in Britain, the legislative branch is the essential channel for a successful, national political career. The legislative branch is the seat of decision-making power and the most important institutional source of political recruitment. In the United States, decision-making power is divided among three branches of government although in the legislative policy process both the executive branch and Congress play equally decisive roles. Not only is the structure in the United States different, measured by the actual exercise of political authority, but historically two parties have alternated in power. Recent scholarship has pointed to Chile, Hungary, South Korea, and Taiwan as sharing more similarities to Mexico's democratic transition.[2]

The significance of these characteristics for recruitment is that they affect how candidates for office are chosen. The degree to which the average citizen participates effectively in the political process determines, to some extent, his or her voice in leadership selection. Of course, it is not just a choice between candidates representing one political organization or party versus another, but how specific persons initially become candidates. The possible paths followed by potential political leaders in Mexico contrasts, although undergoing significant change the last few years, with approaches in the United States. The approaches between the two countries, beginning in 2000, began to take on more similarities, yet numerous qualities peculiar to Mexico's recent past persist. The PAN's initial presidential victory brought an end to the dominance of a single political organization, the PRI and its antecedents, and a single leadership group within Mexico's political system, continuing to 2012. With the return of the PRI in control of the executive branch in 2012, the change of parties in power have reinforced structural changes that impact on Mexico's traditional recruitment patterns at the state and federal levels.

When individual people in a small group exercise power over a long period of time, they tend to develop their own criteria for selecting their successors.[3] Moreover, they personally exercise the greatest influence over the selection process. Students of political recruitment call this *incumbent or sponsored selection*.[4]

In the formal structure, given the monopoly exercised by the PRI historically, one would expect the party itself to be crucial to the identification and recruitment of future political leaders. Until 1994, its role was minimal. The reason is that the PRI was not created as—nor has it functioned as—an orthodox political party, that is, to capture power, until 2006. The PRI, as suggested earlier, was formed to help *keep* a leadership group in power. Yet even a tight leadership group that exercises power in an authoritarian fashion must devise channels for political recruitment. Not to do so would eventually deprive it of the fresh replacements necessary to its continued existence.

In Mexico, until the mid-1990s, most decision-making positions were obtained through sponsored selection, whether the position was appointive or elective. Beginning in 1994, however, two structural conditions began to change that ultimately affected the recruitment process. First, the incumbent party began to experiment with a more open form of selecting its candidates, especially those nominees for state governors and ultimately for president in 1999. Instead of the president of Mexico making that decision, typically the pattern in the past, President Zedillo began to voluntarily withdraw from that process. In 1999, the PRI, for the first time, held an open presidential primary, the only party to date which has used such a selection process, in which several leading politicians competed intensely for the party's nomination, eventually won by Francisco Labastida.[5] The National Action Party, which for some time had engaged in a closed primary in which party delegates voted for their presidential candidate, selected a party outsider, Vicente Fox, as their choice, in that same election year. Six years later, the PRI used a closed primary to select Roberto Madrazo, and the PAN used a much broader primary than in 2000, broken down into three different regional elections requiring that the candidate win in all three regions, which resulted in Felipe Calderón, a dark horse candidate, winning the nomination. Ironically, the PRD has remained the most authoritarian and closed in its selection process, announcing its candidates, Cuauhtémoc Cárdenas in 2000, and Andrés Manuel López Obrador in 2006. In 2012, only the PAN completed a formal primary election, and once again, the dark horse candidate, Josefina Vázquez Mota, won her party's nomination, becoming the first woman presidential candidate ever from a major party. López Obrador received the PRD's nomination a second time after a party survey that revealed he was overwhelmingly the choice of its partisans. The only other major candidate for the PRI nomination conceded to Enrique Peña Nieto, who had been leading public opinion polls as the likely PRI candidate by an overwhelming margin, to maintain party unity.

The second major structural change is that the electoral process itself became increasingly competitive in the 1990s. All opposition parties combined governed only 3 percent of the population at the state or local level in 1988. In just two years' time, after the strong showing by Cuauhtémoc Cárdenas in the 1988 presidential race, the figure tripled to over 10 percent of the population. By 1995, nearly a fourth of Mexico's citizens lived under leadership from the PRD and the PAN, and by 1997, when these two parties won control of the national legislative branch, PRD and PAN politicians governed half of Mexico's population.[6] In the last decade, the PRD and PRI combined, the opposition parties from 2000 to 2012, controlled far more state governments than did the PAN and PRD at the apex of their opposition to the PRI.

During the many decades in which the PRI dominated Mexican politics, the Mexican federal bureaucracy became the favored source of political leadership. The reason for this is that in reality, the legislative and judicial branches remained weak, and local and state governments were staffed by individuals who typically owed their careers to state and national leaders, respectively. Even the party's own leadership came from career bureaucrats beholden to Mexico's president, rather than from the party organizations. If we compare the three leading parties' national office-holders from 1935 through 2009, it is apparent how the competitive origins of the

PAN and PRD led to the influence of party careers in their backgrounds since 79 and 63 percent of the PAN's and PRD's national leadership, compared to only 30 percent of the PRI's, held party offices.[7] It is no accident that nearly all of the PAN's prominent leaders have been state party chairs and members of their party's national executive committee. Nevertheless, it is worthwhile to see the dramatic impact of the democratic transition and consolidation on the PRI. When Mexico's prior administrations are divided into pre-democratic (1934–1988), democratic transition (1989–2000), and democratic (2001–2009) presidencies, the figures for prominent PRI officeholders who were state party chairs changes significantly, from only 24 percent in the pre-democratic era to 37 and 60 percent respectively for the two democratic periods.[8]

For most of its history since 1939, the National Action Party produced a different type of leadership, and therefore, stressed different recruitment institutions. It shared more similarities with U.S. political institutions, since its leaders competed vigorously within and outside of party ranks to be nominated and, more significantly, to defeat the PRI's candidates for various positions. Its prominent leaders have had predominantly local party careers, and have come from elective office (see Table 5-1).[9]

Many of its top officials and candidates in the 1990s had been former members of Congress and, since the mid-1990s, governors. Vicente Fox himself illustrates this pattern, having served as a Congressman and governor of his home state; and Felipe Calderón was a two-time member of Congress, the leader of his party in the 2000 to 2003 Congressional session, the president of the PAN, and a candidate for governor of his home state. The winner of the 2012 presidential race, Enrique Peña Nieto, represented his hometown in the state legislature early in his career and served a full term as governor of the state of México.

Indeed, a comparative analysis of governors from 1988 to 2000 with those from 2000 through 2009 clearly demonstrates the impact of a democratic setting on the recruitment and selection process, foreshadowing and

Table 5-1 Party Experiences of Leading Politicians in the Executive and Legislative Branches

Party Position	Government Post %		
	Cabinet Secretary	Assistant Secretary	Supreme Court Justice
PAN CEN	53	31	100
PRI CEN	14	10	3
PAN other	72	75	100
PRI other	19	14	2

Source: Mexican Political Biographies Project, 2009.

replicating many of the characteristics Vicente Fox and Felipe Calderón represent. Since the leading presidential contenders in the 2006 race from the PRD and the PRI were also former governors, and again the PRI and PRD candidates repeated this experience in 2012, it further confirms the importance of such patterns. The majority of new governors from all parties began their careers locally, emphasizing the importance of local political origins.[10] Moreover, most governors today remain in their home states or nearby states for their college education, thus reducing networking ties with influential national politicians from Mexico City. Second, most governors have held elective office compared to a small percentage of national executive branch officials in the last two decades. Third, a huge shift occurred between the two periods in the percentage of governors who were born and raised in rural communities. Fourth, if we separate PAN governors from all other parties, we discover that they are not professional politicians; many make their living in the private sector and have had extensive experience in business as owners and managers, which accounts for the increase in such career experiences. Many also have provided leadership in business interest group organizations.[11] Such backgrounds explain the dramatic drop in college-educated governors and governors who achieved a graduate degree. Governors in the democratic era are not dominated by the technocratic generation with its advanced educational credentials, which characterized the 1980s and 1990s.

As party competition has increased, the PRI itself has been forced to emulate the recruitment patterns typical of the PAN. In fact, once it had lost control of the federal executive branch, the bureaucracy was no longer a natural source of PRI leadership. Instead, because it continued to control the majority of state governorships, political recruitment patterns within the PRI shifted back to state elective and appointive careers and to a lesser degree to local experience. It remains to be seen if this shift will continue with PRI control over the executive branch after 2012, but it is not likely to be reversed given the increase autonomy and influence of state governors. This local pattern was more common in the party's early history in the 1930s and 1940s. The important shift in recruitment patterns can be seen in the careers of the three major parties' presidential contenders in 2000. All three had been governors of their home state. In all the presidential races from 1964 to 2000, only one presidential candidate had served as governor. Fifth, and surprisingly, governors, even from the PAN and the PRD, are coming from political families in increasing numbers, linking them to one of the most pervasive informal rules of PRI-era politicians and governors. Peña Nieto highlights that informal family linkage, having been related to four governors by blood or marriage from Atlacomulco, the most influential community on leadership in the state of México.[12] López Obrador has no such family ties.

INFORMAL CREDENTIALS: WHAT IS NECESSARY TO RISE TO THE TOP IN MEXICAN POLITICS

Regardless of which individuals do the actual recruiting of future figures in prominent national political offices, specific institutional settings facilitate that process, making the contacts between certain persons possible. Strangely, the most important institution in the initial recruitment of Mexico's national political leaders in the twentieth century is the university.

Mexico's postrevolutionary leadership, building on the concept of a National Preparatory School introduced by the liberals in the mid-nineteenth century, used public education as a means of preparing and identifying future politicians. Some politicians who served in national posts in the 1920s and 1930s never obtained higher education; they were self-made, largely on revolutionary battlefields from 1910 to 1920. Many continued as career military officers in the new postrevolutionary army.

A rapid shift occurred in credentials between the revolutionary generation of political leaders (holding office from 1920 to 1946) and the postrevolutionary generation (holding office from 1946 through the 1960s). The importance of higher education in political recruitment after 1946 is clearly illustrated by the personal experiences of Miguel Alemán (1946–1952) and the persons he recruited to political office. Encouraged by his father to obtain a good education, he was sent to Mexico City where he studied at the National Preparatory School and then the National School of Law, graduating in 1929. Over four-fifths of Alemán's closest chosen political associates were classmates or professors at the two schools he attended in Mexico City.

Alemán established the overwhelming value of preparatory and university education as the institutional locus of Mexican political recruitment. The extraordinary importance of this institution as a locus of political recruitment became clear to me in the early 1970s when I interviewed Antonio Armendáriz, a classmate and friend of President Alemán. As we chatted in his home in Mexico City about the importance of the National Preparatory School, I asked him about the extent of the contacts he made in his student days. He turned to me, and without hesitation, recited in alphabetical order, the last names of every person in his classroom from half a century earlier. Among them were numerous cabinet members, governors, and Supreme

Court justices from 1946 to 1958. It is obvious in retrospect that Alemán introduced radical changes in emphasis on the most important institutions responsible not only for recruitment, but also for the professional and civil influences on future political institutions, and therefore public policy decisions.[13] I argued elsewhere that "Alemán's collaborators define and mold many patterns that generate long-term consequences for political elite recruitment, composition, socialization, and public policy orientations."[14]

Education's importance increased as greater numbers of future politicians began to attend the National Preparatory School and, more significant, the National University. Having attended the former reached an all-time high during the 1958–1964 administration, in which 58 percent of the politicians were graduates. From 1935 through 2009, over 30 percent of all cabinet secretaries and assistant secretaries and two-fifths of Supreme Court justices attended this institution. Graduates of the National University reached their highest level under President de la Madrid (1982-1988), when they accounted for 55 percent of his college-educated officeholders. In the executive branch, since 1935, 54 and 52 percent of cabinet secretaries and assistant secretaries were UNAM graduates. Two thirds of Supreme Court justices were alumni of the National University's Law School, and three out of ten leading members of Congress attended that one institution.

Alumni from private institutions have increased their presence dramatically since 2000, nevertheless, UNAM continues to account for three out of ten top decision-makers in the executive branch, a fourth of all Congressional deputies, and nearly half of Supreme Court justices. Since the democratic consolidation, however, private university alumni have continued to increase their presence in influential public offices, and for the first time, exceed the number of alumni from the National University, having accounted for only 7 percent of college-educated politicians as late as 1988 (see Table 5-2).

The university and preparatory school became important sources of political recruitment for two reasons. Many future politicians taught at these two institutions, generally a single course. Three-quarters of national political figures have taught at the college level. Politicians use academia in part as a means to teach students intellectual and political skills, helping them get started in a public career. Typically, they place a student in a government internship or part-time job, followed by a full-time position after graduation. Miguel de la Madrid is an excellent illustration of this, having started his career in the Bank of Mexico (Mexico's "federal reserve bank") on the recommendation of an economics professor.[15]

Vicente Fox did not continue the tradition of college teaching typical of his predecessors; he only completed his degree while campaigning for

Table 5-2 University Graduates by Presidential Administration

	Institution			
	National University (%)	Military (%)	Private (%)	Other (%)
Obregón, 1920–1924	50	9	0	41
Calles, 1924–1928	37	0	5	58
Portes Gil, 1928–1930	33	0	0	67
Ortiz Rubio, 1930–1932	43	21	0	26
Rodríguez, 1932–1934	50	0	0	50
Cárdenas, 1934–1940	27	4	2	74
Avila Camacho 1940–1946	35	6	4	53
Alemán, 1946–1952	51	3	4	42
Ruiz Cortines, 1952–1958	38	4	1	57
López Mateos, 1958–1964	44	6	2	48
Díaz Ordaz, 1964–1970	50	5	1	44
Echeverría, 1970–1976	53	6	2	39
López Portillo, 1976–1982	51	7	3	39
De la Madrid, 1982–1988	55	5	7	33
Salinas, 1988–1994	44	7	18	31
Zedillo, 1994–2000	31	7	26	36
Fox, 2000–2006	23	4	26	47
Calderón, 2006–2012	15	5	30	50

Source: Mexican Political Biography Project, 1995, 2009.

president. Nevertheless, his educational experiences at the prestigious Ibero-American University produced several influential ties to future, prominent Mexicans. More importantly, many of his cabinet members had been part- or full-time academics, including his treasury and foreign relations secretaries. What is distinctive about Fox's administration educationally is the fact that many top appointees graduated from or taught at distinguished private institutions, especially the Monterrey Technological Institute for Higher Studies (ITESM) in Nuevo León, popularly known as "Monterrey Tech," and the Autonomous Technological Institute of Mexico (ITAM), in the Federal District. Calderón deviated from Fox in his emphasis on higher education, but like his predecessor, he did not teach. He graduated from the Free Law School, Mexico's most prestigious private law school, and received an MA in public administration, similar to de la Madrid and Carlos Salinas, from Harvard University, and began a second MA at ITAM in economics, sharing some similarities with the technocratic generation. Peña Nieto reinforces the recent pattern of presidential graduates from private institutions, having graduated from the Pan American University in Mexico City in law, and completing an MA at the ITESM in business administration, the first PRI president since 1929 to graduate from a private school. Unlike his two predecessors, however, he reintroduced college teaching as part of his background, having taught briefly at his alma mater.

As suggested above, the second institution most influential in the initial recruitment of national politicians is the federal bureaucracy. Numerous prominent figures have begun their careers in lesser agency posts, sometimes as advisers or technical experts. If they decide to make politics their career, they develop contacts with other ambitious figures, typically a superior in their own agency or in a related organization. That individual, similar to the politician-teacher, initiates their rise within the national bureaucracy. In spite of the inroads made by local and state party and governmental bureaucracies, and by the PAN national party organization, the federal bureaucracy continues to rank second only to the university as a source of political recruitment. In contrast to the United States, the Democratic and Republican parties are often the source of nationally prominent politicians because they have traditionally been formative in the candidate-selection process and in the competition for offices that influence policymaking. As younger generations of politicians move into the most influential political positions, politicians with important career experiences in their respective parties are likely to become more influential in the 2010s.

An examination of Mexico's most influential politicians from 1970 to 2000 reinforces this interpretation. Mexican politicians rely on informal, personal contacts to develop their ties to a politician-teacher or a superior, which sociologists call networking. Ambitious Mexicans form strong personal ties to an individual mentor and may have different mentors at various stages of their careers. These networking patterns, which are examined in some detail below, occur in three common settings (see Table 5-3): educational institutions, career positions (primarily the bureaucracy for politicians), and within the family.

In Mexico few *national* politicians have been recruited through party channels, especially at the local and state levels, with the exception of numerous prominent PAN party figures and, to a lesser extent, younger leaders of the PRD. Many prominent figures at the state and local levels are recruited in such fashion, as suggested in our discussion of state governors. Because decision-making was centralized in the executive branch rather than in the legislative bodies before 2000, a career in the national bureaucracy was the foremost means of ascent.

The salience of the federal bureaucracy in the recruitment process contributes to another informal characteristic of upward political mobility in Mexico: the significance of Mexico City. Politicians who come from Mexico City, in spite of its tremendous size, are overrepresented in the national political leadership. This was true before the revolution of 1910,

Table 5-3 How Mentors and Protégés among the Mexican Elites Meet

Type of Power Elite	Sources of Mentor-Protégé Relationships		
	Education (%)	Career (%)	Family (%)
Political	45	42	13
Intellectual	76	15	9
Capitalist	1	5	94
Military	31	69	0
Clergy	63	25	11

Note: (N = 398) Data based on known relationships between a mentor and protégé among Mexico's power elite. *Education* refers to a mentor-protégé contact that occurred in any educational setting, typically between a student and a professor, between any two students, or between professorial peers. *Career* refers to a mentor-protégé contact that took place in an occupational setting, typically between two individuals working in an organizational bureaucracy, often in a superior-subordinate relationship. *Family* refers to mentor-protégé relationships established within the immediate family, including mentors who were grand-parents, in-laws, aunts and uncles, or parents.
Source: Roderic Ai Camp, *Mexico's Mandarins, Crafting a Power Elite for the Twenty-First Century* (Berkeley: University of California Press, 2002).

but those violent events introduced a leadership whose birthplaces deemphasized the importance of the capital. That remained true until the 1940s, when the presence of Mexico City in the backgrounds of national politicians increased substantially. By the presidency of Luis Echeverría (1970–1976), when fewer than one in ten citizens was born in Mexico City, one in four national political figures named it as a place of birth. In the past twenty years that figure increased dramatically. Since 1982, on average, a third of leading political figures have come from the capital. If we examine the change in the Federal District's representation among the most prominent politicians between those serving from 1935 to 1988, the pre-democratic period, with those who have held office since 2000, the importance of Mexico's capital is readily demonstrated. Among cabinet members only, nearly half today compared to only one-fourth earlier, are from the Federal District. Among Supreme Court justices the difference is even more extraordinary, half today compared to only 13 percent prior to 1988. Since similar distortions favoring the Federal District are found among assistant secretaries, and such individuals disproportionately become cabinet secretaries, this pattern is likely to continue from 2012 to 2018.

In all political systems, whom one knows has much to do with political recruitment and with appointment to an important political office. U.S. politics is replete with examples of prominent figures who sought out old friends to fill responsible political offices. In fact, knowing someone is often a means for obtaining employment in the private sector as well. In Mexico, whom one knows in public life is even more telling, given the fact that incumbent officeholders often decide who obtains influential posts. Mexicans with political ambitions can enhance personal contacts at school, in the university, or during their professional and public careers through family ties.

Americans have produced a few notable political families, for instance, the Adamses, Kennedys, Gores, Romneys, and the Bushes, but such families are numerous in Mexico.[16] Relatives in politics are important, as studies of British and U.S. politicians have shown, because children of political activists are more likely to see politics as a potential career than are children reared in a nonpolitical environment.[17] This is true of other careers too. For example, Catholic bishops in Mexico often come from families where parents or close relatives were nuns, priests, or deeply involved in religious activities and organizations.[18] It is natural that a youngster growing up in a political family would come in contact with many political figures. More than one in seven Mexican national politicians from 1934 to 1988, including President Salinas, were the children of nationally prominent political figures. Salinas's father, who served in the cabinet in the 1960s, helped his son's early career. Cuauhtémoc Cárdenas, PRD's leading figure from 1989 to 2000, is the son of President Lázaro Cárdenas. Enrique Peña Nieto, as mentioned above, is related to four other governors of his home state of México, and is the grandson of the mayor of his hometown, the source of numerous other leading political families since the 1930s.[19] Since 2000, given the opposition victories in the executive branch, that figure declined to one in eleven, as expected, since the fathers of leading PAN politicians would not have had nearly as many opportunities to serve in influential public office. If extended family ties are considered, two-fifths of all politicians from 1934 to 1988 were related to national political figures during the same period. Since 2000, over a fourth of prominent figures come from similar backgrounds. Numerous PAN leaders are the children of its founders and early presidential candidates, and many of their fathers were PAN candidates for the state and federal legislative posts. An examination of governors suggests that kinship ties to extended political families are extensive. Half of all governors boasted such ties in the pre-democratic era. During the democratic transition from 1988 to 2000, a third of governors shared such ties, but since 2000, those figures have increased once again, with more than two-fifths coming from such politically active families.[20]

Politically active families are not the only factor that makes family background important. Social and economic status is another. Studies of politicians worldwide, in both socialist and nonsocialist societies, reveal the importance of middle- and upper-middle-class backgrounds.[21] In Third World countries without competitive political structures, family origins become even more significant to career success. Higher socioeconomic backgrounds are helpful in political life because well-off parents provide opportunities for their children. Education is such a significant means of political recruitment that *access* to it enables making the right contacts and obtaining the necessary, informal credentials. There even exists a relationship between place of birth and middle class backgrounds, highlighted by the overrepresentation of the Federal District in politicians' birthplaces. During the last eight decades, a fourth of Mexican politicians came from working-class backgrounds, but only 7 percent of those born in the Federal District share such socioeconomic origins. The economic backgrounds of prospective politicians has become even more significant today, especially among Panistas, given the dramatic increase in graduates from leading private universities which offer few scholarships to needy students. Some Mexicans from working-class backgrounds manage to attend preparatory schools and even universities, but few actually complete degree programs. This explains why Mexico's youngest generation of national politicians, those born since 1940 (Presidents Salinas's, Zedillo's, and Fox's generation), 1950 (President Calderon's generation), and 1960 (President Peña Nieto's generation) are almost exclusively from middle- and upper-middle-class backgrounds (80 percent or more). President Zedillo, however, is an exception, the first chief executive in decades to come from a working-class family of modest means. Fox and Calderón, on the other hand, fit and reinforce the recent pattern.

THE RISE OF WOMEN

Another informal credential universal to political leadership in all countries is gender. Politics has been, and remains, dominated by men. Nevertheless, women have made substantial inroads in national political office. On the whole, women have been far more successful politically in Mexico than in many other countries, including the United States. For example, several women served on the Supreme Court in Mexico, long before Sandra Day O'Connor was appointed by President Reagan. Numerous women have held senate positions. By the 2009–2012 Congressional session women obtained 26 percent of the seats in the Chamber of Deputies and 23 percent in the Senate, compared to 17 percent women in both the United States Congress and Senate, illustrating comparatively the increased representation in Mexico.[22] However, cabinet posts have only occasionally been filled by women in Mexico; men have had a virtual lock on that domain, especially in the major agencies, although this has begun to change. President Zedillo increased the number of women in his cabinet to three, the highest number ever, including Rosario Green as his secretary of foreign relations, a figure exceeded by Presidents Fox and Calderón, who appointed four women to their cabinets, including the portfolios of foreign relations and social development. President Calderón later appointed Marisela Morales as the first female attorney general in 2011. Peña Nieto has maintained a similar level of representation, appointing three women to his initial cabinet, including for the first time, a female secretary of Health.

Slightly different recruitment patterns have traditionally been followed by women interested in politics (see Table 5-4). This fact worked against their obtaining the higher positions because they did not come in contact with current and future political figures who could assist them up the bureaucratic ladder.[23] For example, serving as a private secretary in the federal bureaucracy or secretary general (top post under the governor) in the state bureaucracy has led to national careers for many male politicians. The representation of women in national political offices (cabinet, subcabinet, and top judicial and legislative posts) did increase substantially after 1976, during the administrations of José López Portillo and Miguel de la Madrid, providing the foundation for stronger increases during the democratic transition and consolidation eras. Typically, women politicians have been found far more frequently in party posts during the PRI hegemony. Equally important in distinguishing women from men is their much greater likelihood of party militancy. As I have argued elsewhere, however, it remains to be seen whether or not such intense militancy is beneficial to democratic consolidation.[24]

Women traditionally have not been as well educated as men, but younger women have received much more university training, putting them on par with men holding influential posts in the 1970s and 1980s. By the 2005 to 2009 Mexican educational cycle, UNICEF reported that women's attendance in elementary school was equal to men's, and in secondary school, exceeded that of men.[25] In fact, women with secondary educations in Mexico exceeded their peers in Argentina, Brazil, and Costa Rica. As of the 2010 census, equal numbers of women and men had completed a preparatory education, and 16 percent of women compared to 17 percent of men had obtained a college education.[26] This comparative lack of education with men deprived them of the same level of recruitment contacts and mentors traditionally found in Mexican universities. On the other hand, college-educated women entering national political ranks bring far greater educational diversity and training than men since 2000.

Finally, women have been significantly deprived compared to men when measuring the likelihood of their coming from political families. They are nearly half as likely to have relatives in public office. Kinship ties, as demonstrated above, are a crucial factor in opening the door to higher office,

Table 5-4 Credentials of Prominent Politicians by Gender

Credential	Women (%)	Men (%)
Education		
Primary, secondary, preparatory only	19	16
Normal only	14	4
Subtotal	33	20
University	29	47
Graduate	38	34
Degree earned		
Law	29	44
Economics	17	13
Business administration and CPA	6	6
Medicine	3	7
Engineering	1	12
Other	45	19
Political office		
Private secretary	3	9
Union leader	11	11
Secretary-general	1	8
State legislator	21	15
Federal deputy	78	48
Mayor	6	11
Kinship ties		
Relative in public office	15	28
Father in politics	8	9
Party militancy		
PAN[a]	12	8
PRD[a]	7	5
PRI	39	27
Party leadership[b]		
PAN	77	82
PRD	78	93
PRI	68	29

Source: Mexican Political Biography Project, 2009.
[a]PAN and PRD include smaller parties on the right for PAN and the left for PRD.
[b]Party members only.

thus the lack of such relationships has placed them at a disadvantage compared to their male peers. Equally important in explaining why women have limited experiences in such important local offices such as that of mayor, an important stepping stone to becoming a governor, are the antagonistic attitudes of men holding traditional views of female roles, still being translated into sexual harassment and physical threats toward women with political ambitions, well-documented in a recent study of female mayors in Tlaxcala.[27]

The expansion of representation in the legislative branch as a consequence of electoral reforms contributed significantly to the rise of women politicians. As mentioned in the previous chapter, the PRD, similar to some

Scandinavian parties, began experimenting with a quota system. In 1993, they instituted a 30 percent rule, guaranteeing women that level of represen-tation among the party's candidates for office. After the implementation of this rule, women deputies from the PRD increased from 8 to 23 percent. The growing influence of the PAN also enhanced the likelihood of larger num-bers of women politicians. The PAN alone provided 45 percent of the 116 female members of Congress serving in the 2006–2009 legislative session.[28] The figures in Table 5-4 clearly demonstrate the huge difference in the leg-islative backgrounds of female versus male politicians at the state and federal level, which prepares women to function readily in a competitive, democratic polity.

In the 2003 Congressional elections, after the implementation of the new federal quota legislation, the number of female deputies increased signifi-cantly. In spite of this notable improvement, the implementation of the spirit of the law varied from party to party. Party candidates chosen in direct elections for Congressional and senate seats need not comply with the quota. Among the three major parties, 49 percent of their candidates were chosen through direct election. In spite of the fact that the gender quotas applied to only half of the candidates, women won 23 percent of the seats in the 2003–2006 legisla-ture, moving Mexico's ranking of the percentage of women in the legislative branch worldwide from 55 to 23, equal to Switzerland.[29] As of 2011, Mexico ranked thirty-second in the world in the percentage of women in both houses of Congress.[30]

Younger women who are politically ambitious are now taking on many of the characteristics of their male peers, thus increasing their opportunities for closer contact with potential future politicians. Women also typically continue to have much broader and deeper experiences in their parties and in civic and nongovernmental organizations. As Victoria Rodríguez has argued, "Women's involvement locally is often at the grassroots level or in political positions other than mayor, such as city council members or administrative appointees, and for these women such positions often represent their first step in learning and experiencing formal participation in the exercise of gov-ernment. Women's reasons for their commitment to public service at the local level vary; while many women actively involved in the political lives of their localities intend to use such activities as a stepping stone to higher political levels, others have no desire to do so. Moreover the majority of politically active women at the local level tend to focus their activities on local issues and participate in social movements rather than political office; in fact their involvement in politics is often motivated by a demand to meet the needs of the community or neighborhood."[31] These career differences, though working against female political recruitment in the past, may very well give women stronger skills in a changing, plural political context and thus an advantage in an increasingly democratic Mexico.[32]

THE CAMARILLA: POLITICAL NETWORKING IN MEXICO

Perhaps the most distinctive characteristic of Mexican politics, knowledge of which is essential to understanding the recruitment process, is the political clique, the *camarilla*. Prior to 2000, it determined, more than any other variable discussed, who goes to the top of the political ladder, what paths are taken, and the specific posts they are assigned. Many of the features of Mexican political culture predispose the political system to rely on camarillas. A camarilla is a group of people who have political interests in common and rely on one another to improve their chances within the political leadership (see Table 5-5).

The fundamental question that the two successive PAN presidential victories raise for this unique, informal process of Mexican political life is: Will the camarilla system continue to play a crucial role? The camarilla system has been altered substantially by the structural changes that the PRI defeat introduced, but it is unlikely to disappear altogether. The reasons why these informal, personal linkages are unlikely to disappear altogether include the following. First, the underlying cement of the camarilla system is the mentor-protégé relationship. As a recent study of Mexico's most influential leaders from all professions (including the armed forces, the clergy, cultural elites, capitalists, and politicians) illustrates, prominent Mexicans from all walks of life have relied heavily on mentors, who often were equally influential themselves, to promote their career success.[33] In fact, six out of seven influential Mexicans were known to have a mentor. Among politicians, the figure is 100 percent. Second, even if camarillas were to disappear altogether within the federal bureaucracy, an unlikely situation, they would still function at the state level, where the PRI continues to control the majority of governorships and, therefore, state patronage. The PRI's victory in 2012 at the federal level will help to reinforce its continued influence. Third, personal loyalties are a fact of Mexican life. Individuals are likely to rely on personal relationships to foster their career success, even if the extent of the rewards is altered by structural changes within the Mexican system.

A camarilla is often formed early, even while its members are still in college. The members place considerable trust in one another. Using a group of friends to accomplish professional objectives is a feature found in other

Table 5-5 Characteristics of Mexican Camarillas in the Twenty-First Century

1. The structural basis of the camarilla system is a mentor-protégé relationship, which has many similarities to the patron-client culture throughout Latin America.
2. The camarilla system is extremely fluid, and camarillas are not exclusive but over-lapping, relying on networking techniques found in other societies.
3. Most successful politicians are the products of multiple mentors and camarillas, that is, rarely does a politician remain within a single camarilla from beginning to the end of his or her career.
4. The larger the camarilla, the more influential its leader and, likewise, his protégés.
5. Some camarillas are characterized by an ideological flavor, but other personal qualities determine protégé ties to a mentor.
6. Protégés often surpass the political careers of their mentors, thus reversing the benefits of the camarilla's relationship and the logical order of camarilla influence.
7. Camarillas increasingly will be formed in diverse institutional environments, including state bureaucracies, the corporate world, international agencies, political parties, and civic organizations, as well as federal bureaucratic agencies.
8. Superior-subordinate institutional relationships will increasingly displace the importance of educational and familial contacts.
9. Most politicians continue to carry with them membership in an educational camarilla, represented by their preparatory, professional, and graduate school generation.
10. The rise of the nonprofessional politician increases the potential importance of networking across influential groups and professions, notably with the business world.

Source: Roderic Ai Camp, *The Metamorphosis of Leadership in a Democratic Mexico* (New York: Oxford University Press, 2011); *Mexico's Mandarins: Crafting a Power Elite for the Twenty-First Century* (Berkeley: University of California Press, 2002); and "Camarillas in Mexican Politics: The Case of the Salinas Cabinet," *Mexican Studies* 6, no. 1 (Winter 1990): 106–7.

sectors of Mexican society, including academia and the business community. A camarilla has a leader who acts as a political mentor to other members of the group. He typically is more successful than his peers and uses his own career as a means of furthering the careers of other group members. As the leader of a camarilla ascends within an institution, he places members of his group, when possible, in other influential positions either within his organization or outside it. The higher he rises, the more positions he can fill.[34]

All of the qualities described in Table 5-5 remain true for most national government officeholders. But the universality of these qualities will break down as PAN and PRD members acquire more posts, especially if those individuals are not career politicians, but have moved laterally into politics from other professions. Camarillas will not disappear, but other characteristics will increase in importance and other variables will moderate camarillas' influence.[35]

The role of the mentor and the political groups he creates take on added importance because the mentor establishes the criteria by which he chooses his disciples and because he plays a formative role in socializing his disciples. The implications for political recruitment are crucial. It has been shown that politicians, like most people, tend to recruit those with similar credentials or experience, who in many ways mirror themselves.[36] Over time, mentors can structure the recruitment process to favor certain credentials and institutions. In the past, the most successful camarillas reached the presidency. Presidents, because they exercise the most comprehensive influence over top political appointments, have the greatest impact on the recruitment process, affecting the entire political system.

The demise of the PRI's monopoly completely alters this pattern. The recruitment and promotion criteria will no longer be universal, but dispersed, depending on the political setting from which an individual emerges, for example, from state politics, the Congress, the bureaucracy, or from a nonpolitical career in business, international agencies, and civic organizations. Furthermore, President Fox did not show a strong tendency to appoint only influential cabinet members who mirrored his career and political experience. Instead, he diversified the recruitment process by selecting a range of individuals to direct governmental agencies who differed significantly in their career experiences. He also included many former members of the PRI in top posts. Those individuals, in turn, had the greatest opportunity to fill subordinate posts with their own choices. It remains to be seen whether they too will follow the pattern of their predecessors in choosing like types for the most influential positions, but it seems unlikely that they would deviate radically from that pattern. Felipe Calderón, as a career politician and public servant, gave greater weight to important PAN politicians, many of whom were long-time PAN figures with ties to the party from important states and the party bureaucracy in the Federal District. We don't know what preferences Peña Nieto will use, but we do know that he is a professional politician, has spent his entire career in the state capital of México, and boasts ties to one of the most influential multi-generational political families in the twentieth century. A number of his cabinet choices were officials who served in his administration in the state of México. In the foreseeable future, the majority of mid- to upper-level positions are still likely to be filled by individuals who have come from careers in the bureaucracy, since they have the expertise and experience necessary for many of these positions, evidenced by the fact that assistant secretaries were overrepresented in the backgrounds of many cabinet appointees from 2000 to 2012.

Politicians' educational and career characteristics have changed markedly in the past two decades. The most persistent change has been the constant increase in *level* of education. Not only are all national political leaders (with a few exceptions in the legislative branch) college educated, but the number of graduate-school-educated leaders has reached new highs. President Fox does not continue the pattern established by his predecessors, having completed only an undergraduate business administration degree. Because he was not a professional politician, nor employed in the federal bureaucracy, the broad recruitment criteria established by influential political mentors and presidents did not influence his preparation. Calderón, on the other hand, shares some similarities with recent PRI presidents. He comes from a political family, his father having been a founder of the PAN in 1939 who campaigned for the PAN in Michoacán, where he introduced his son to partisan, electoral politics. His brother and sister have served in Congress, and both were members of the PAN National Executive Committee, like the president. As mentioned previously, Calderón graduated from the Free Law School, a school that has graduated ten percent of top PAN politicians from middle-class families, and completed an MA from the Kennedy School at Harvard. Peña Nieto is the first graduate of the Pan American University (founded by the Catholic order Opus Dei and best known for its advanced business management course and for producing some leading PAN and PRI politicians) and holds an MA from ITESM, which has produced many leading economists in public life from both the PAN and PRI.

Fox's three predecessors reflect the importance given to advanced education in Mexican politics. Of the *new* national officeholders under de la Madrid, nearly half, like the president, had graduate degrees. Only six years later, beginning with the Salinas administration in 1988, 70 percent had received graduate training; many of them with PhDs. Of Zedillo's cabinet members, 66 percent claimed such educational credentials. Graduate education had become such a preferred credential that top political figures have been known to lie about having it. For example, there was a scandal involving Zedillo's first education secretary, who never completed his BA or his PhD.[37] In the top posts in the executive branch, during the democratic transition from 1988 to 2000, 60 percent of those officials boasted graduate degrees, and since 2000, during the democratic consolidation, that figure reached 70 percent. A similar level and pattern can be found among Supreme Court justices for these same two periods. Even two-fifths of the top legislators since 2000 have graduate degrees.

De la Madrid and Salinas introduced another informal credential into the recruitment process. Their camarilla selections emphasized politicians who had been educated outside Mexico, particularly at the graduate level. Zedillo did likewise. It can be said that Salinas was following in the footsteps of his father, who also graduated from Harvard with an advanced degree. Zedillo followed in the footsteps of his mentor, economist Leopoldo Solís, a Yale graduate. Even Fox, although he did not earn a graduate degree, obtained a diploma in advanced management from Harvard. The point is that numerous political figures began to study abroad, generally at the most prestigious universities in the United States. In 1972, 58 percent of Mexico's national political figures with PhDs received them from the National University and only 13 percent from U.S. universities. By 1989, only 29 percent had graduated from an institution in their native country, compared with 48 percent from U.S. institutions.[38] In the 1990s, 55 percent of national politicians received their PhDs in the United States. The data in Table 5-6 suggests that since 1935, a fifth of all cabinet secretaries and a fourth of all assistant secretaries had completed graduate degrees in the United States. The democratic transition, 1988 to 2000, covering the Salinas and Zedillo presidencies, reveals an increased number of top cabinet officials with graduate training in the United States. Since 2000, in the executive branch, those figures have increased significantly among cabinet secretaries, 37 percent of whom attended graduate programs north of the border. Combined with those who studied elsewhere outside of Mexico, graduates of foreign programs exceeded half of all top officials.

A third change in the educational background of contemporary politicians, and perhaps the most significant, is the discipline studied. Law, as in the United States, has always been the field of study of most future politicians, with engineering and medicine coming in second. This means that law school is the most likely place to meet future politicians and political mentors. The most remarkable change is a shift from law to economics in politicians' educational backgrounds. Salinas was the first president with that specialty, and his political generation was the first to count as many

Table 5-6 Graduate School Trends of Politicians since the Democratic Transition

Government Branch	Location of Graduate Training (%)			
	United States	Europe/Latin America	Mexico	None
Legislative				
All deputies	5	6	11	79
Democratic transition	6	11	13	69
Democratic consolidation	7	8	24	60
Executive				
All secretaries	20	12	13	56
Democratic transition	24	21	15	40
Democratic consolidation	37	14	18	30
All assistant secretaries	24	13	15	48
Democratic transition	29	18	18	36
Democratic consolidation	31	12	21	36
Judicial				
All Supreme Court justices	2	11	17	74
Democratic transition	4	19	21	56
Democratic consolidation	0	36	36	27

Source: Mexican Political Biographies Project, 2009.

economists as lawyers among its members. Zedillo duplicated this pattern personally and among his collaborators. Fox's degree in business administration is closely linked to the emphasis on economics, and one out of three members of his cabinet graduated in economics-related disciplines. An important explanation for why a degree in orthodox economic programs is uncommon among PAN politicians is that many of the public universities' schools of economics favored a neo-Marxist curriculum.

The emphasis on economics led to another significant change in recruitment characteristics: the elevation of private over public education. This characteristic is less pervasive than the others but even more remarkable. Between the administration of de la Madrid and Salinas, a six-fold increase in the percentage of private-school graduates took place. Instead of the National University and public universities maintaining their level of dominance, private institutions have begun to make serious inroads.

An important explanation for this can be seen from the data presented in Table 5-7, which suggests that in percentage terms, economics graduates of two of the leading private universities, ITAM and ITESM in Monterrey, accounted for 86 and 30 percent of politicians who were alumni of those schools. In contrast, only 13 percent of the more than one thousand politician alumni of UNAM were from the National School of Economics. This trend is enhanced by the fact that many PAN politicians are private school graduates, and as more businesspeople chose political careers, private university graduates increased. Vicente Fox is a case in point. His educational origins are reflected in his initial cabinet choices. Nearly half graduated from private schools, with Ibero-American University, his alma mater, the Monterrey Technological Institute of Higher Studies (ITESM), the Free Law School, the Autonomous Technological University of Mexico, (ITAM) and Anahuac University, the most important. Even more remarkable, three of his first cabinet members obtained undergraduate degrees from private universities in the United States. This is significant for political recruitment

Table 5-7 Leading Universities Attended by Mexican Politicians Who Were Economists

University Attended (# of Degrees Awarded)	% with Degrees in Economics
UNAM (1151)	12.9 (149)
ITAM (63)	85.7 (54)
ITESM (67)	29.9 (20)
University of Nuevo León (32)	25.0 (8)
University of Guadalajara (80)	11.3 (9)
National Polytechnic Institute (71)	11.3 (8)
Ibero-American University (54)	7.4 (4)

Source: Mexican Political Biographies Project, 2009.

because it changed not only informal credentials, but also the institutional locations where recruitment takes place. In fact, it contributes to the diversity of the recruitment process since 2000, a process that traditionally has relied on fewer, concentrated, public educational sources in Mexico, a pattern which is likely to continue under Peña Nieto, the first PRI president to graduate from two private institutions, from a Catholic university, and with one degree in business administration. Based on his initial cabinet choices, top private universities, including ITESM, ITAM, and Ibero-American University continue to be well-represented in their educational backgrounds.

THE RISE AND DECLINE OF THE TECHNOCRAT

As the recruitment process changed and the credentials of future politicians were modified, some scholars labeled the younger generation of politicians in Mexico as technocrats, *técnicos*. The rise of technocratic leadership took place throughout Latin America. A number of attributes have been associated with this class of leaders in Brazil and Chile, and many have been mistakenly applied to Mexico's leaders. This has generated some confusion about technocrats.[39]

Mexico's technocratic leadership is characterized by new developments in their informal credentials. In particular, they are seen as well educated in technologically sophisticated fields; as spending most of their careers in the national bureaucracy; as having come from large urban centers, notably Mexico City; as having middle- and upper-middle-class backgrounds; and as having studied abroad. By implication, in contrast to the more traditional Mexican politician, they have few direct ties to the masses and, in terms of career experience, lack elective office-holding and grassroots party experience.[40]

For some years the typical Mexican politician had been a hybrid, exhibiting characteristics found among *técnicos* and traditional politicians. The assertion by some scholars that technocrats lack political skills is incorrect and misleading. Technocrats as a group do not have an identifiable ideology. The political-technocrat, a more apt label, is primarily distinguished from the politician of the 1960s or 1970s by lack of party experience, by the fact that he or she has never held elective office, and by specialized education abroad. These characteristics, for example, are found in President Zedillo's own career. The implication of these three characteristics is that the politician-technocrat, although highly skilled, does not possess the same political bargaining skills as does the peer who has had a different career track and that such a person *may* be more receptive to political and economic strategies used in other cultures as a consequence of foreign education.

It has been convincingly argued that Salinas's economic cabinet, including Zedillo, whose members shared these technocratic characteristics, welcomed the economic liberalization philosophy of Western Europe and the United States because of their economic background and education abroad. As economists, they identified with an international profession based in the United States, with tools and concepts that were believed to be universally—and locally—transferable, and with the methodology and ideology dominant in leading Ivy League graduate programs.[41]

Much of the dissension in the Mexican establishment political leadership in the 1990s can be attributed to a division between the technocratic leadership and traditional political figures, popularly called *los dinos*, or dinosaurs. Essentially, the argument was that the *técnicos* replaced the traditional politicians; devalued their skills and experiences, primarily their electoral and party experiences; and opposed their unprogressive authoritarian practices with modernizing political and economic alternatives. The crux of the divisions was the alleged ideological differences between the two groups. In reality, as Miguel Centeno pointed out, the central issue introduced by this technocratic elite was not "an ideology of answers or issues but ... an ideology of method."[42]

The fundamental issue dividing the technocrat from the traditional political leadership, as is so often the case, was access to power. The traditional politician did not want to give up his control over the political system and PRI leadership to a technocratic elite, regardless of different ideological preferences. The dominance of the technocrats in the 1990s introduced an additional characteristic, a belief that the institutions they led were the undisputed arbiters of economic and political decision-making. Even so, they showed an inability to listen and an intolerance of their domestic opponents. This pattern increasingly isolated the technocratic leaders from other groups, both within and outside Mexico's leadership prior to 2000. Technocrats like Zedillo had smaller and smaller camarillas because their relative youth afforded them less political experience, and this experience covered a narrower range of institutions and agencies. Some of these characteristics can also be found among the technocratic elite in China, who were largely responsible for that country's economic transformation.[43]

Technocratic leadership might have remained entrenched for many years if the PRI had retained its dominance over national political leadership and a technocrat had been the PRI's presidential candidate. Fox's presidential victory, however, ensured the rapid decline of technocratic control over national political institutions. Fox's own career, when contrasted with that of Zedillo, makes the differences between the two men patently clear. Zedillo, who moved to Mexico City to continue his education, began a career in the federal bureaucracy even before he completed his undergraduate economics degree. Fox, on the other hand, remained in León, his hometown, for most of his education, and only upon graduation from college did he begin a career in the private sector. Zedillo quickly ended up in the forefront of the programming and budgeting secretariat, a crucial agency in the development of Mexican technocrats.[44] Fox, instead, spent his formative years working up the ladder of a multinational corporation, Coca-Cola of Mexico. Zedillo left Mexico in the 1970s to earn two graduate degrees from Yale and, like so many of his peers, began teaching part-time. Fox obtained a diploma from a short advanced management course at Harvard, but continued as a full-time employee of Coca-Cola, becoming its CEO. Zedillo continued his career in the Mexican federal government in a progression of posts, while Fox left Coca-Cola to go into business for himself. Zedillo joined Salinas's cabinet in 1988, and Fox won election as a congressman from his home state, before becoming governor in the 1990s.

In certain respects, Fox represents some of the same trends occurring within the PRI itself. The increased pluralization of the political system, and the intense electoral competition in the 1990s, contributed to the rise of politicians from all parties who incorporated experience in electoral politics. These structural changes also promoted the careers of politicians with broad experience, rather than a narrow range of technocratic career experiences. In an original, recent examination of 1,400 members of the Chamber of Deputies from 1997 to 2006, Joy Langston found that certain municipal and federal career experiences exerted similar consequences for both PRI and PAN legislators. As she bluntly concluded, "In Mexico, political futures heavily depend on past career choices."[45] Fox himself, and some of the collaborators he appointed, broadened the scope of these experiences further to include representatives of the private sector and even individuals with careers in international organizations. For example, more than two-thirds of his cabinet had previously pursued careers in the private sector. Surprisingly, even a large sample of politicians from the PRD, based on a study of 161 PRD and PAN candidates for Congress in 2006, came from business backgrounds, including 7 percent who owned their own firms, and 34 percent who managed a business for someone else. The next largest category was professional occupations. Among the PAN candidates, 17 percent owned their own businesses and 25 percent worked in management.[46]

Fox appointed several technocrats to his cabinet, notably his treasury secretary, and another technocrat continued his term as head of the Bank of Mexico. An international technocrat was in charge of his economic development agency. Calderón increased the representation of public figures with technocratic backgrounds, some of them former technocrats in Zedillo's administration. They were particularly well-represented in the technical and economic agencies. Technocratic types have retained considerable influence in economic decision-making, but they have lost control over the national political system. This does not mean, however, that some of the characteristics that technocrats reinforced or introduced also have disappeared. The most influential characteristic in decline is the predominance of public bureaucratic careers. Among those qualities that continued to be preeminent in the Calderón presidency were the increasing importance of private university education and the persistence of economics or economically related disciplines such as business administration and public accounting, as well as newer specialized fields unavailable to earlier generations in politicians' educational backgrounds. Engineering degrees in many more specialized sub-fields also have increased, equaling the figures under Salinas' presidency.[47]

CONCLUSION

Prior to 2000, the formal structure of Mexico's political system shed little light on how interested Mexicans pursued successful political careers. The political recruitment process was strongly affected by the centralization of political authority and the characteristics fostered by incumbent selection. Informal credentials typically replaced formal requirements as helpful or essential to the recruitment process. The PAN presidential victory, the PAN and PRD control over the national legislative branch, and the breadth of their influence at the state and local levels introduced different leadership characteristics and legitimized new recruitment practices. Even with the return of the PRI, which has adopted many of the institutional patterns relied upon by PAN and to a lesser extent PRD politicians, those democratic influences will continue. Democracy does alter recruitment patterns.

Informal credentials have long been associated with generations of political leaders since the 1920s. As mentors changed their own credentials, they passed on those changes to succeeding generations of politicians. They were responsible for such trends as higher levels of education, graduate education abroad, private undergraduate education, the importance of economics, the role of university teaching, and the impact of economic agencies in the federal government. All of these qualities, with the exception of the dominant influence of federal economic agencies, remain influential since 2000. Peña Nieto has continued these same patterns among his initial cabinet members, many of whom have studied in the United States, have Ph.D.'s or graduate degrees, are economists, and alumni of leading Ivy Leagues institutions. The continuation of their influence, however, depends on the nature of leadership at all levels of the federal government, and in particular successful presidential contestants. Governors increasingly have a stronger opportunity to obtain their party's nomination. Unlike Calderón, many of the successful governors emphasize other career, educational, and family characteristics, and such an individual in the presidency from 2012 to 2018 might, once again, alter the importance of some background characteristics over others.

In the past, the political clique or camarilla was the essential ingredient in the recruitment process. As we have seen, it is an informal structure built on several characteristics of the general culture, a structure emphasizing the use of a group of friends to enhance career success. The political camarilla, as crafted prior to 2000, will decline in importance, as new leadership types take over national positions. Fox himself, and many of his collaborators, suggests the continued importance of informal processes, including networking. These new politicians elevate networking that goes beyond the formation of political groups to establishing linkages between politicians and leaders from other sectors of society, including influential businesspeople and clergy. Calderón shifted the balance back toward a greater reliance on career politicians like himself, while continuing to retain links to nonprofessional public servants. Peña Nieto is likely to continue to reinforce this shift. Recent studies demonstrate unequivocally that many of Mexico's leaders in the twenty-first century have extensive ties, established through educational experiences, family, and career, with prominent figures from other leadership groups. For example, Fox went to school and became close friends with three members of Mexico's most influential capitalist families. Fox also became involved with a pro-democratic civic action organization, the San Angel Group, where he made contact with prominent intellectuals and civic leaders, including two of his future cabinet members.

Changes in the recruitment process, brought about by alterations in the political structure and type of leadership, have already introduced several important trends, particularly the importance of individuals from provincial and private sector backgrounds and the increase in private university training. These two features have several potential consequences. In the first place, the continued importance of private university education enhances the likelihood that Mexicans from business or professional backgrounds in the private sector will pursue political careers, since many of them come from those educational institutions. On the other hand, the exclusive nature of private institution student bodies, given the socioeconomic inequalities in Mexico and the lack of scholarship opportunities, will actually narrow rather than increase the range of recruitment pools especially if they increase their dominance over most levels of national political recruitment. If having a provincial background becomes increasingly important, and the next generation of mentors have such a background, then subsequent leaders also are likely to come from the provinces rather than from the Federal District, as reflected in the Fox presidency, and that of Peña Nieto, given his exclusive career in his home state. This characteristic could become part of a decentralization trend arising from democratic consolidation. Since Calderón restored the preeminence of politicians from the Federal District, it remains to be seen if this pattern is not just sustained, but decreased or increased by his successor. If the electoral process remains highly competitive, then mayoral, gubernatorial, and national legislative careers, all emphasizing geographic origins outside of Mexico's capital, will flourish. Such politicians will determine the future success of a democratic polity.

NOTES

1. Lester G. Seligman, *Recruiting Political Elites* (New York: General Learning Press, 1971).
2. Francisco E. González, *Dual Transitions from Authoritarian Rule: Institutionalized Regimes in Chile and Mexico, 1970–2000* (Baltimore, MD: Johns Hopkins University Press, 2008), 220ff.
3. Kenneth Prewitt, *The Recruitment of Political Leaders: A Study of Citizen-Politicians* (Indianapolis, IN: Bobbs-Merrill, 1970), 13.
4. See Ralph Turner, "Sponsored and Contest Mobility and the School System," *American Sociological Review* 25, no. 6 (December 1960): 855–56.
5. George W. Grayson, *A Guide to the November 7, 1999, PRI Presidential Primary* (Washington, DC: CSIS, 1999).
6. "Notable avance de la oposición en una década," *Diario de Yucatán*, November 22, 1999, www.yucatan.com.mx.
7. Roderic Ai Camp, *The Metamorphosis of Leadership in a Democratic Mexico* (New York: Oxford University Press, 2010), 47.
8. Mexican Political Biographies Project, 2009.Complete information on all of the politicians in this study are available in my *Mexican Political Biographies, 1935-2009* (Austin: University of Texas Press, 2011). Analysis of these patterns are found in *The Metamorphosis of Leadership in a Democratic Mexico*.

9. For more detailed information about the recruitment characteristics of PAN and PRD members, see my *Metamorphosis of Leadership in a Democratic Mexico*; and "The PAN's Social Bases: Implications for Leadership," in *Opposition Government in Mexico*, eds. Victoria Rodríguez and Peter M. Ward (Albuquerque: University of New Mexico Press, 1995); 65–80.

10. Christopher Díaz discovered that PRI gubernatorial candidates in the 1990s were less likely to have local grassroots careers. See his excellent "Electoral Competition in Mexico and Career Trajectories of PRI Gubernatorial Candidates, 1991–2001," *Politics and Policy* 33, no. 1 (March 2005): 36–52.

11. Roderic Ai Camp, "Political Recruitment, Governance, and Leadership in Mexico: Has Democracy Made a Difference?," in *Pathways to Power: Political Recruitment and Candidate Selection in Latin America*, eds. Peter Siavelis and Scott Morgenstern (University Park: Pennsylvania State University Press, 2008), 309.

12. He is related to governors Mario Sánchez Colín, Alfredo del Mazo Vélez, Alfredo del Mazo, and Arturo Montiel Rojas. Alfredo del Mazo Vélez and his son, Alfredo del Mazo, were in the cabinets of presidents Adolfo López Mateos and Miguel de la Madrid respectively. Both were internal candidates of the PRI for the party's presidential nominations in 1964 and 1988.

13. Roderic Ai Camp, "Political Leadership and Political Development, from the Alemán Generation to the Democratic Generation," in William Beezley, ed., *A Companion to Mexican History and Culture* (New York: Wiley-Blackwell, 2011), 468–79.

14. Roderic Ai Camp, "Political Institutionalization and Public Policy: The Impact of the Alemán Generation," *The Metamorphosis of Leadership in a Democratic Mexico*, 154–82.

15. Interview with Miguel de la Madrid, Mexico City, 1991.

16. Political families in the United States have not declined significantly in recent decades. Kimberly L. Casey, "Political Families in American Electoral Politics," paper presented at the Western Political Science Association, San Diego, California, December 11, 2008, www.allacademic.com/meta/p238293_index.html.

17. For the United States, see Alfred Clubok et al., "Family Relationships, Congressional Recruitment, and Political Modernization," *Journal of Politics* 31, no. 4 (November 1969): 1036.

18. Based on interviews with numerous bishops and archbishops of Mexico. Camp, *Crossing Swords: Religion and Politics in Mexico* (New York: Oxford University Press, 1997), 196.

19. www.eluniversal.com.mx, February 11, 2005. Atlacomulco has produced three cabinet members and four governors since the 1940s.

20. Such ties have been documented in detail by Javier Hurtado in *Familias, política y parentesco, Jalisco 1919–1991* (Mexico City: Fondo de Cultura Económica, 1993).

21. Thomas R. Dye, *Who's Running America? Institutional Leadership in the United States* (Englewood Cliffs, NJ: Prentice-Hall, 1976), 152; George K. Schueller,

"The Politburo," in *World Revolutionary Elites*, ed. Harold D. Lasswell and Daniel Lerner (Cambridge, MA: MIT Press, 1966), 141.

22. See the highly useful Global Database for Women: www.quotaproject .org, 2011.

23. For background information on women in Mexican national politics, see Anna M. Fernández Poncela, "El reto de la política y la apuesta de las mujeres," *Este País*, January 1995, 2–4; "Participación social y política de la mujer en México," in *Participación política: Las mujeres en México al final del milenio* (Mexico City: El Colegio de México, 1995); and Marta Lamas, "The Role of Women in the New Mexico," in *Mexico's Politics and Society in Transition*, eds. Joseph Tulchin and Andrew Selee (Boulder, CO: Lynne Rienner, 2003), 127–42.

24. *Metamorphosis of Leadership in a Democratic Mexico*, 125.

25. www.unicef.org/infobycountry/mexico_statistics.html, June 2011.

26. www.inegi.org.mx, June 2011. Women now account for 43 percent of all students studying in that field. Robert Duval-Hernández and F. Alejandro Villagómez, "Trends and Characteristics of Economics Degrees in a Developing Country: The Case of Mexico," *The Journal of Economic Education* 42, no. 1 (2011): 87–94.

27. Verónica Vázquez García, "Mujeres en campaña, Cómo postularse come candidate municipal sin morir en el intento," *Estudios Sociológicos* 29, no. 85 (2011): 131–57.

28. www.diputados.gob.mx, 2007.

29. Lisa Baldez, "Elected Bodies: The Gender Quota Law for Legislative Candidates in Mexico," *Legislative Studies Quarterly* 29, no. 2 (May 2004): 249. Also see her "Primaries vs. Quotas: Gender and Candidate Nominations in Mexico, 2003," *Latin American Politics and Society* 49, no. 3 (Fall 2007): 69–95.

30. Women in National Parliaments, www.ipu.org/wmn-e/classif.htm, April, 2011.

31. Victoria Rodríguez, "Women, Politics, and Democratic Consolidation in Mexico: Two Steps Forward, One Step Back," in *The Oxford Handbook of Mexican Politics*, ed. Roderic Ai Camp (New York: Oxford University Press, 2012), p. 461.

32. For an excellent discussion of women's civic participation and local government roles, see María Luisa Tarrés, "The Role of Women's Nongovernmental Organizations in Mexican Public Life," in *Women's Participation in Mexican Political Life*, ed. Victoria Rodríguez (Boulder, CO: Westview Press, 1998), 131–45; and Alejandra Massolo, "Women in the Local Arena and Municipal Power," in *Women's Participation in Mexican Political Life*, 193–203.

33. Roderic Ai Camp, *Mexico's Mandarins: Crafting a Power Elite for the Twenty-First Century* (Berkeley: University of California Press, 2002).

34. For an excellent description of this process, see Merilee S. Grindle, "Patrons and Clients in the Bureaucracy: Career Networks in Mexico," *Latin American Research Review* 12 (1977): 37–66.

35. Joy Langston, "Sobrevivir y prosperar: una búsqueda de las causas de las facciones políticas intrarrégimen en México," *Política y Gobierno* 2, no. 2 (1995): 243–77.

36. Kenneth Prewitt and Alan Stone, *The Ruling Elites: Elite Theory, Power, and American Democracy* (New York: Harper & Row, 1973), 142.

37. This person, Fausto Alzate, was forced to resign in disgrace. He claimed to have received a PhD from Harvard, where he did study but did not graduate.

38. Alfonso Galindo, "Education of Mexican Government Officials," *Statistical Abstract of Latin America*, vol. 30, pt. 1 (Los Angeles: UCLA, 1992), 599.

39. See my chapter and the editors' introduction: "Technocracy *a la Mexicana*: Antecedent to Democracy?," in *The Politics of Expertise in Latin America*, eds. Miguel Angel Centeño and Patricio Silva (New York: St. Martin's Press, 1997), 196–213.

40. For the evolution of technocrats, see my "The Time of the Technocrats and Deconstruction of the Revolution," in *The Oxford History of Mexico*, eds. William H. Beezley and Michael C. Meyer (New York: Oxford University Press, 2010), 569–97.

41. For detailed evidence of the formative role of U.S. higher education, see Camp, *Mexico's Mandarins*; and Stephanie Golob, "Crossing the Line: Sovereignty, Integration, and the Free Trade Decisions of Mexico and Canada," PhD dissertation, Harvard University, 1997.

42. Miguel Angel Centeño, *Democracy Within Reason: Technocratic Revolution in Mexico* (University Park: Pennsylvania State University Press, 1994), 209; Juan D. Lindau, "Technocrats and Mexico's Political Elite," *Political Science Quarterly* 111, no. 2 (1996): 295–322, offers still another view.

43. He Li, "Technocrats and Democratic Transition: the Cases of China and Mexico," *Journal of International and Area Studies* 8, no. 2 (2001): 67–86.

44. Eduardo Torres Espinosa, *Bureaucracy and Politics in Mexico: the Case of the Secretariat of Programming and Budget* (Brookfield, UK: Ashgate, 1999).

45. Joy Langston and Francisco Javier Aparicio, "The Past as Future: Prior Political Experience and Career Choices in Mexico, 1997–2006," CIDE Working Paper, Political Studies. No. 207, December, 2008, 28.

46. Katheleen Bruhn and Kenneth Greene, preliminary survey of PAN and PRD candidates for Congress, June 6 and June 30, 2006.

47. For the view of Mexican scholarship on leaders, see *Liderazgo político: Teoría y procesos en el México de hoy*, ed. Martio Bassols Ricárdez, et al. (Mexico: Universidad Autónoma Metropolitana Iztapala, 2008).

6

Groups and the State:
An Altered Relationship
in a Democratic Polity?

> The growth of electoral competition in Mexico has had uneven
> and ambiguous consequences on the role and shape of clien-
> telistic interest-intermediation arrangements. As elsewhere in
> Latin America, democratization has clearly failed to destroy the
> political centrality of clientelistic structures. Rising electoral
> competition has not left, however, clientelism unchanged. The
> combination of more open political contestation, fiscal strin-
> gency and market reform has introduced major changes in the
> nature and scope of clientelistic arrangements.
>
> BLANCA HEREDIA, *"Clientelism in Flux"*

All political systems, regardless of whether the struggle for political power
is highly competitive or strongly monopolized by a small leadership group
or single party, must cope with political interests and groups. In the United
States various interest groups, as they are labeled, express their demands to
the executive and legislative branches and contribute significant sums of
money to parties and candidates. In Mexico, because the political system's
structure is different from that of the United States, both the type of groups
and their means for influencing public policy are not the same.

THE RESIDUE OF CORPORATISM

The importance of corporatism to the Mexican political culture and
pre-2000 model was noted earlier.[1] Corporatism describes the more formal
relationship between selected groups or institutions and the government or

state. Since the revolution—that is, for most of the twentieth century—Mexico used an interesting structure to channel the most influential groups' demands, enabling the government to monitor the demands and mediate among them. The government sought to act as the ultimate arbiter and to see to it that no one group became predominant.

The corporatist structure was largely devised and put in place under President Lázaro Cárdenas (1934–1940). Cárdenas wanted to strengthen the state's hand in order to protect the interests of the ordinary worker and peasant, but he ironically created a structure that for the most part benefited the interests of the middle classes and the wealthy, not unlike that of many other political systems.[2] The reason for this outcome is that Cárdenas' commitment to the social welfare of the less well off was not shared by most of his successors, who have responded to other concerns and groups.

What is important, however, is that although the ideological orientation has changed and various economic strategies have been experimented with since the 1930s, the arrangement remained largely intact until the 1990s.[3] Only under President Salinas was there some interest in restructuring the corporatist relationship,[4] in response to Salinas's promises of political modernization and democracy. Critics argued that the corporatist structures presently provide the greatest stumbling block to a functioning Mexican democracy.[5] Some changes in the corporatist structure were introduced by recent presidents. Others, however, were the result of larger economic and political changes during the democratic transition and during the years of democratic consolidation since 2000. Not only did the government have fewer resources to offer various groups in the 1990s, but its electoral competitors achieved huge inroads on the PRI's monopoly regionally.[6] Fox's presidential victory clinched the demise of the traditional corporatist system, depriving a PRI-controlled federal government from directly subsidizing or rewarding various groups. Nevertheless, case studies of working class communities since 2000 illustrate that the practice of candidates from all parties rewarding voters in exchange for their votes is widespread and healthy.[7] Additionally, the PRI specifically continues to maintain corporatist linkages to traditional, pre-democratic organizations, including labor, and has not been replaced by the PRD or the PAN.[8]

Historically, the corporatist features of the political system allowed two types of channels for making political demands, and consequently two types of institutional representatives emerged prior to the 1990s. The institutional relationship with the government under this type of system was traditionally a formal one: The state established an organization, requiring those persons meeting the criteria of a special interest to belong to it. For example, the state created several business organizations to which businesses employing a certain number of employees must belong.[9] The state, however, even when the PRI enjoyed a political monopoly, was not able to control all institutions representing various groups. Those it controlled were considered to be quasi-governmental interest organizations, part of the traditional corporatist structure.

Some interest groups increased their influence over time, becoming more autonomous. They created their own organizations—as would typically be the case in the United States—which were independent of the government. For example, the business community established the Mexican Association of Employers (Coparmex), an influential private-sector voice, frequently expressing public opposition to government economic policies. Many of their members played a crucial role in supporting PAN electoral victories at the state and local level, especially in northern Mexico.[10]

The other kind of channel is the informal channel, which is characteristic of all government models. Certain groups in Mexico do not use formal institutions, independent or governmental, to exercise their considerable influence, but instead use informal channels. The informal channels may be incorporated in the governmental structure or remain independent of it. We cannot assert with complete certainty that the informal channels are more significant than the formal channels, but given the lack of relevant studies, most observers of Mexican politics believe that to be the case, even after the advent of democracy.

INSTITUTIONAL VOICES

The range of interest groups in the United States is formidable because of the political system's openness and the ability of multitudes of like-minded citizens and institutions to organize. Such collectivities in Mexico are fewer and weak, and do not figure as significantly in decision-making.[11] Remember that decision-making remains centered in the executive branch, thus blocking the ability of diverse interests to pressure the legislative branch despite its growing influence in modifying executive initiated legislation. Further, the prohibition against running consecutively for legislative seats limits the potential threat that interests can level against individual members of Congress. Nevertheless, interest groups gradually have increased in number and influence, addressing their concerns to Congress as it initiates greater numbers of bills. As members of the PAN and PRD took over as chairs of the committee structure in Congress, they showed an interest and autonomy in pursuing policy issues related to certain groups, including the armed forces and the Zapatista guerrillas. As a leading student of the Congress concluded, "the long period during which Congress neither mattered nor paid attention to government actions has come to an end."[12]

The most important groups incorporated formally and informally in Mexico's interest group structure are the military, the Catholic Church, business, organized labor, intellectuals and the media, nongovernmental organizations, guerrillas and indigenous communities, and drug trafficking organizations. Each has a different institutional relationship to the government.[13]

The Military

No group has played a more significant role in Latin American political life than the military. However, since the 1930s its pattern of influence in Mexico has been quite different from that found elsewhere in the region. Most important, the military has found it necessary to intervene politically in every Latin American country except Mexico since that decade, and in most countries the military seized power in the 1970s and 1980s.[14] Since the democratic transition in the region in the 1980s and 1990s, some important transformations in civil-military relationships have taken place. Interestingly, such changes, while not achieving a perfect balance between civilian superiority and military subordination, have been far more extensive in South America than in Mexico.[15] Since 2007, the armed forces' impact on public policy has reached new heights after President Calderón increased its responsibility for the challenging task of defeating the drug cartels.

The military's relationship to the Mexican state or government is different from that of all other groups. The reason is that the military does not function as a separate political actor; rather, it is incorporated into the government apparatus and operates under civilian leadership. This does not mean that the military does not pursue its institutional interests; rather, it publically subsumes its differences from those of the state.

Since the 1930s Mexico's civil-military relationship has been increasingly characterized by subordination of the military to civilian leadership.[16] How did its unusual relationship come about? The political leadership gradually reduced the military's political influence through a variety of techniques. In the first place, as James Wilkie demonstrated historically, each successive government reduced the military's allocation as a percentage of the federal budget from 1921 to 1964.[17] The size of the military in relation to the population, and the sum budgeted to the military per capita, was among the lowest worldwide, far below the figures for the United States,[18] but has risen significantly in the 1990s.

Under Zedillo, military expenditures averaged 5 percent instead of the typically 2 to 3 percent, placing it midway among all countries' per capita expenditures. Such expenditures increased dramatically since Fox became president. Between 2000 and 2008, Mexico's National Defense budget increased 338 percent.[19] The armed forces also increased significantly in size from 1988, when they numbered 179,000, to 258,000 at the end of the Calderón administration (see Table 6-1).[20]

Prior to the 1970s, in addition to gradually reducing the size and potential influence of the military, the state strengthened the legitimacy of political institutions, including the official party (PRI). Government politicians had the advantage of operating in a semiauthoritarian fashion within the electoral arena. Military intervention is generally facilitated by competing political groups in a society that are seeking allies in the military. In Mexico, however, the military had to be either for the establishment—that is, the civilian leadership—or against it, and it had no outside civilian allies after 1952. During the 1940s, 1950s, and 1960s, military officers who pursued political careers helped bridge the gap between civilian and military officials. In other words, these political military officers provided a significant, *informal* channel of communication, allowing the civilian leadership to solidify its control and to establish its legitimacy.

Civilian leadership also cemented its control over the military through the professional socialization process. Civilian politicians established several military schools, most notably the Heroic Military College, the Higher War College, and in 1981 the National Defense College, to train officers. One of the most important themes in the curriculum of the schools is respect for authority, for one's superior officer, and for the commander in chief, the president. All military schools tend to drill in their cadets the concept of subordination to authority, but Mexican military academies are famous for

Table 6-1 Changes in Mexico's Armed Forces by Administration

Administration	Size Last Year of Administration	Percentage Increase
2006–2011	258,088	3.2
2000–2006	250,125	5.5
1994–2000	237,025	9.7
1988–1994	214,681	16.4
1982–1988	179,305	35.2
1976–1982	116,050	29.3
1970–1976	82,500	18.3
1964–1970	67,100	37.3

Sources: George W. Grayson, *Mexico's Armed Forces: A Fact Book* (Washington, DC: CSIS, 1999), 39; Ernesto Zedillo, *Sexto informe: Anexo estadístico*, Disco 11, 2000; transparency request 0000700024708, Secretariat of National Defense; Sergio Aguayo Quezada, *México todo en cifras* (Mexico: Aguilar, 2008), 185.

the level of discipline they instill. The dominant value would be the individual's willingness to subordinate himself totally to those in authority over him and the expectation that submission would be rewarded and independence would be severely punished.[21]

The military has served the government in many capacities other than those traditionally subscribed to by the military in the United States.[22] The Mexican military's primary responsibility has not been national defense; rather, it has operated in many realms as an internal police force devoted to national security.[23] Not only does it provide the government with political intelligence, but it also has been used to maintain electoral peace, to settle contentious strikes, to repress incipient guerrilla movements, and to carry out anti-drug-trafficking missions.

Drug corruption and its consequences have become the most intractable problem facing Mexico's leaders for the foreseeable future, but the political issue refocusing attention on civil-military relations prior to this emphasis after 2000 was the attack by the Zapatista Army of National Liberation (EZLN) on January 1, 1994, on army encampments in the highlands of Chiapas. The response of the Mexican army was swift and repressive and led to numerous allegations of human rights abuses and summary executions. However, because of the extraordinary Mexican and foreign media coverage, President Salinas quickly reined in the military. This is historically significant because it presages the allegations of widespread human rights abuses by the armed forces in their anti-drug mission since 2000, and makes it evident that this issue has not been satisfactorily resolved.

The activities that will most affect the military's relationship to the state and increase or decrease its potential influence over the decision-making process are its current roles in the anti-drug-trafficking campaign and in maintaining public security, which had already emerged in the 1990s as national security issues of significant proportions.[24] In response to growing levels of crime and drug-related violence, President Zedillo established a National Public Security Council in 1996, giving for the first time "Mexico's military a role in decision-making and policy-setting in important domestic public security matters."[25] Vicente Fox, responding to the public's concern for personal security, created a new cabinet-level agency, Public Security, in 2000. He also appointed a brigadier general as attorney general, raising the issue in the minds of many Mexicans of the encroaching militarization of influential civilian agencies and their traditional tasks. As one observer remarks in her analysis of this period, it suggests the "contradictory process" of constructing a democracy."[26]

Civil-military relations changed significantly under President Fox's administration. The secretary of the navy and, to a lesser extent, the secretary of national defense instituted internal, structural changes affecting the promotion process, human rights training, and, in the case of the navy, drastic reductions in the top naval bureaucracy and a radical reduction in the number of admirals on active duty. The relationship between the attorney general and the armed forces was stronger under Fox than any recent, preceding president and led to extensive collaboration in the armed forces' anti-drug mission.[27] The application of the new transparency law beginning in June 2003 opened the military to greater public scrutiny by the media and scholars. The increasing interest of the legislative branch in military affairs resulted, for the first time in history, in testimony by a secretary of national defense in the legislative chambers, during which various deputies, with the media present, questioned the secretary extensively on a wide range of controversial issues.

The dramatic growth of the armed forces' anti-drug mission, however, grew exponentially during the Calderón administration when the president made a major national security policy decision to take on the drug cartels directly and aggressively by assigning mobile battalions to those cities and regions characterized by the highest levels of cartel activity. Calderón's anti-drug strategy ironically led to greater drug-related violence, dramatically influencing public opinion as to the most widely perceived national security issues. Drug cartels are constantly competing against each other for a larger share of the drug market, which can be achieved by taking control of important routes for shipping drugs through and from Mexico to the United States, as well as producing drugs in Mexico. Each time the armed forces succeeds in killing or capturing high ranking cartel leaders, it results in a leadership vacuum, exacerbating these internal conflicts and the consequent violence. Drug-related murders have gone up exponentially to the point where drug violence dominates Mexicans' views of the principal threats against their personal and national security. Half of all Mexicans believe that organized crime is the principal threat against their national security.[28]

In spite of the failure of the government's strategy to decrease the level of violence and increase personal security, Mexicans continue to view the Mexican armed forces in a positive light. This result is also surprising given the extent of human rights allegations against the armed forces. Of all the government institutions, including the National Human Rights Commission itself, the army is viewed most positively.[29] Comparatively speaking, it ranks third in the Western Hemisphere behind Canada and the United States in the level of trust Mexicans place in that institution.[30] Even though most Mexicans believe the government's current anti-drug strategy is a failure and will not succeed, they have not assigned the blame to the armed forces.

How have these new missions affected civil-military relations in the era of democratic consolidation? The fundamental, underlying issue is that "security is not just another issue in the public agenda in Mexico: It is the main challenge facing Mexican democracy. If the Mexican state is not able to provide security at the different levels, all the other national tasks cannot be performed."[31] This political situation in Mexico opens the door for an enhanced role to be played by the military. Despite this situation, the subordination to a civilian culture has not changed in the last decade. What needs to occur, and what appears to remain in flux, is the extent to which the armed forces are generating a democratic institutional culture within the military. As I have argued elsewhere, "In the long run it would be unhealthy, and threatening, to maintain a state institution built on a fundamentally authoritarian culture, generating authoritarian leaders, in the midst of a democratic society. It would create a danger within the heart of a democratic society to maintain such an institution."[32]

The armed forces compared to any other executive branch institution, maintains the greatest degree of autonomy from state control. This remains the case even though the legislative branch, beginning with the Fox administration, began taking a stronger interest in limiting some of the traditional areas of autonomy. This more aggressive posture by the legislative branch, as Jordi Díez has suggested, has been tempered under Calderón. Both senators and deputies, even when confronted with empirical evidence of the rapid increase in human rights violations, suggested to him that this issue was the responsibility of the Human Rights Commission.[33] In 2011, the Supreme Court ruled that the armed forces military code of justice needed to conform to international standards and that human rights cases should be tried in civilian courts. If this decision is implemented fully, it would provide a significant first step in limiting the armed forces' autonomy. Most human rights officials are not optimistic.[34] The National Defense Committee of the Senate approved such a judicial reform and sent it to the full body in April 2012.[35] To date, "The military continues to operate with little oversight and control. The 'war' against organized crime unleashed by the Calderón administration, and the security crisis it provoked, has strengthened the standing, budget and influence of the armed forces in Mexican politics and it appears that, in this area, Mexico's democratic transition remains unfinished."[36]

The Church

Mexico legally established and, in practice, enjoys freedom of religion, yet Mexicans, as we noted in Chapter 4, are overwhelmingly Catholic, products of a Catholic, Christian culture.[37] The Catholic Church exercised extraordinary political influence in Mexico and elsewhere in the region during the colonial period and continued to do so in much of the nineteenth century and part of the twentieth.[38]

The government broke this pattern of influence by implementing virulent anticlerical provisions in the 1917 constitution in an attempt to limit the church's ideological influence over the socialization of citizen values. Articles 3 and 130 specified these restrictive clauses, which limited religious influence in education, spelled out numerous restrictions on clergy's political involvement, and clearly established state superiority over the church. Clergy's and Catholics' resistance to the implementation of these provisions under President Calles led to the Cristero War from 1926 to 1929, during which time many priests were persecuted and murdered, masses were suspended, and seminaries were closed. In my personal interviews with dozens of bishops, many of whom were raised or were enrolled in seminaries during the 1920s and 1930s, they pointed to these personal or family experiences as determining their decision to become priests.

The church, unlike the military, operated as an institution fully independent of the government yet severely hampered in theory and practice by the constitution. The state reached an informal understanding with the church after 1930 that in effect allowed it to carry out the spiritual and pastoral functions within the purview of all churches in return for its remaining publicly quiet about political and social issues. The understanding remained in effect until 1992, and in practice was fairly well followed by both parties until the early 1980s.

President Salinas moved, as part of his modernization plans, to make the Catholic Church a more open actor in the political system. Many politicians resisted any changes in the constitutional restrictions on the church, but Salinas believed the relationship was outdated and needed refashioning. Demonstrating his new posture, he invited leading clergy to attend his inauguration in December 1988 and then appointed a former political figure as his personal representative to the Vatican. He also made Pope John Paul a welcome guest in Mexico in the summer of 1991, creating even closer relations between the government and the church. In 1992, Salinas revised several major constitutional provisions, one of which now permits recognition of all churches as legal entities. However, the reforms did leave several major constitutional issues unresolved, among them "religious education in public schools, access to electronic means of mass communication, [and] fiscal measures for religious associations."[39]

The church's role as an interest group was limited because of the antichurch rhetoric that was incorporated into the public education of each child in Mexico. The church and clergy were at a disadvantage compared with some other groups in the corporatist arrangement because of the legal limbo they occupied. For example, the church as an institution had no legal standing until 1992, the only institution among the organized groups under discussion. Before 1992, clergy of all faiths and nuns did not have a legal right to vote, although many actually did.[40] I first learned of such commonplace violations from Angela Gurria, a leading Mexican sculptor whose home served as the local balloting station in her upscale neighborhood, the same location where President Miguel de la Madrid cast his ballot. Numerous sisters from a nearby religious order often voted in her home.

As Chapter 4 pointed out, Mexicans nonetheless remain very religious: Many are practicing Catholics, and most have a high regard for clergy and the church as an institution. By 2007, Mexico boasted the presence of three sitting cardinals. Moreover, nearly half of all Mexicans report that they participate in meetings of religious groups, twice that of such countries as Uruguay, Argentina, Chile, and Venezuela, and well above the United States.[41] Because respect for the church is high and political organizations did not provide adequate channels for people to express their political demands, some Mexicans turned to the church for guidance and, more important, as an institutional vehicle to convey their political frustrations.[42] Currently, many Mexicans believe that the Catholic Church can have some or a lot of influence on the president (66 percent), a governor (53 percent), the Chamber of Deputies (46 percent), and members of the Supreme Court (43 percent).[43]

This trend is reinforced by the fact that Mexican priests overwhelmingly favor speaking out in support of democracy. Nine out of ten priests believe the church should support democratization and eight out of ten priests believe it should support a just society even if they produce conflicts with the government.[44] Catholic bishops have begun to speak regularly and critically, illustrating the view expressed by Cardinal Norberto Rivera Carrera of the Mexico City archdiocese that a "silent Church does not serve God nor humanity."[45] By 2010, half of all Mexicans believed the church should speak out on social and political issues, while the other half opposed such actions. Moreover, half of all citizens responded favorably to the concept of separation of church and state, while more than a third continued to oppose such a separation. This latter position may be due to the high regard Mexicans have for the church and for priests in direct contrast to their impressions of the presidency.[46]

The church, as is true of other groups, such as businessmen, does not speak with a single voice. Despite its image as a centralized, hierarchical institution, it is decentralized at the level of individual dioceses, of which there are seventy-three dioceses and sixteen archdioceses in Mexico.

Dioceses and archdioceses are territorial subdivisions that serve as organizational units, and each is governed by a bishop or archbishop. Collectively, these men are the extremely autonomous hierarchy of the church.

The leadership of the church in Mexico in terms of policy influence is the episcopate—the body of bishops, archbishops, and cardinals—which in conference recommends policies on issues ranging from the purely theological to foreign debt, the maldistribution of income, and drugs. The episcopate meetings result in the publication of pastoral letters and enunciations of recommended positions.

It is apparent from recent events in Mexico that the geography and the social and economic composition of a diocese often affect the attitude and orientation of its priests and bishops. The most extreme example of this was Bishop Samuel Ruiz in Chiapas, whose clergy represented rural, indigenous interests in San Cristóbal de las Casas. Ruiz's firm stance in defense of the Indians, both before and after the Zapatista uprising in 1994, engendered criticism as well as support within episcopal ranks.[47] The Vatican ordered his diocese to stop ordaining secular Indian deacons in an effort to dismantle Ruiz's ideological influence.[48]

The most important issue nationally in the 1990s that unified bishops nationally, however, was democratization. Not only did individual bishops circulate numerous pastoral letters on this topic, as early as the late 1980s, but the episcopate itself adopted several of these letters as its official position. In particular, bishops addressed several specific issues, especially the obligation to vote, electoral fraud, and the so-called "fear vote." The episcopate declared in 2000, shortly before the election, that it was a sin for any party to use scare tactics as a means of encouraging partisan support.[49] The Mexican Episcopate, recognizing the importance of the 2000 presidential race, produced a pamphlet entitled *Democracy Isn't Possible Without You*, in which it urged all Mexicans to vote according to their conscience and to select candidates they believed most ideal to serve the nation.[50]

The church's interest in secular, political issues related to democracy has continued unabated. When the Fox government attempted to thwart the presidential candidacy of Andrés Manuel López Obrador in 2006, the five bishops of the social pastoral committee of the episcopate, including the former head of the episcopate, condemned the government's actions, viewing it as contrary to a democratic transition.[51] "They couched their request in terms of protecting human rights and establishing a balance of power and moderation among the branches of government. They further argued that his removal, by violating his rights, would violate the rights of all Mexicans in the 2006 elections."[52] Their support was crucial in the attorney general's decision to withdraw the legal complaint, thereby clearing the way for López Obrador to become the PRD's candidate. The episcopate also ran national newspaper ads suggesting that the 2006 elections "represent an opportunity and a challenge to consolidate the significant advances" of an incipient democracy.[53] It was the first time they placed such an ad during a presidential campaign. During the two-month period immediately following the election, when the results were vociferously disputed by López Obrador, the episcopate issued several declarations supporting the electoral institutions, the electoral process, and the institutional resolution of electoral disputes.

The other major issue that has significant implications for public policy is the Church's stance on drug cartel violence, and armed forces' human rights abuses.[54] With the exception of some regional dioceses, the leadership of the church universally has not offered clear and strong positions of condemnation toward such abuses comparable to their posture on democracy, nor have they questioned the increased violence as a result of the government's anti-drug strategy.[55] In 2011, Cardinal Francisco Robles Ortega, of the Monterrey archdiocese, which has witnessed extraordinary levels of violence, demanded that the state government improve its security operations to avoid open gun battles in the city.[56] An outspoken exception to most bishops has been José Raúl Vera's public comments from the Saltillo diocese, who has stated openly that the government's military-led strategy is a serious mistake.[57] Many priests have been threatened by drug cartels, thus dampening outspoken comments from many clergy.[58]

The church generally does not openly lobby for its political positions; rather, it requests and receives audiences with the state officials. Typically, party presidential candidates meet with bishops during their campaigns.[59] Church personnel also meet with various members of the executive branch on matters of mutual concern. On the state level, bishops frequently exchange views with state governors and collaborate with the government on social welfare projects. Relations are good as a rule and have improved considerably since 1989, but at the local level in certain instances, such as in the southern state of Chiapas, they may be quite conflictual. Chiapas witnessed the deportation of priests, armed attacks on the bishop, conflicts among various religious groups, and the intervention of outside national and international actors, including the Vatican envoy, during the 1990s.

The social policy arena that most concerns the Catholic Church in Latin America and in Mexico, as one might assume, is its public posture on such orthodox church dogma as abortion and euthanasia. The president and secretary general of the Mexican Episcopate sent out a detailed statement to the media of their opposition to anyone, religious or not, supporting either of these policy issues.[60] Furthermore, many Mexicans believe that the church influences their opinion on this issue. For example, 44 percent are influenced to some degree by what priests have to say about abortion, while only 27 percent would consider their priests' views on political parties.[61] In the last decade, a number of state legislatures have attempted to implement laws, pro or con, for and against, legalizing abortion. The most notable legislation in this regard was passed by the Federal District legislature legalizing abortion, in spite of active opposition from the church and its allies, with legislators primarily from the PRD and PRI voting for the law and PAN legislators against.[62] Mexicans living in the Federal District favored the legislation 44 to 38 percent. Outside of the capital, only 23 percent of Mexicans agreed with the new law versus 58 percent who were opposed. A large majority of Mexicans are in favor of abortion in the case of rape, endangering the mother's life, or the presence of a malformed fetus.[63] The other social issue commonly linked to religious dogma is euthanasia. In Mexico, 39 percent approve of its use in cases of incurable, terminal illnesses while 46 percent are opposed.[64]

The open posture of church leaders in advocating civic participation, and stating their views on broad national policy, has extended to the position of individual politicians too. Leading bishops have called on politicians to profess openly their religious faith, thus setting a spiritual example for other Mexicans.[65] President Fox himself provides the most prominent example of this recent pattern. When the pope visited Mexico in 2002 in celebration of the canonization of a Mexican saint, critics charged that Fox, the first president to attend a public religious act presided over by the pope, should not have attended the mass nor demonstrated publicly his respect for the pope by kissing his hand. The Mexican public, however, overwhelming supported (more than 80 percent) the president attending the mass, publicly demonstrating his religious devotion, and exercising the same religious rights as any ordinary Mexican.[66]

Raising the visibility of religious beliefs among the population at large, and politicians specifically, might well affect public policy. A unique study of Mexican congresspersons demonstrates significant differences in their levels of religiosity, measured by church attendance (see Table 6-2). PAN members of Congress are more religious and more Catholic than the Mexican population. Ninety-seven percent are Catholic and 3 percent Protestant. PRD congresspersons, on the other hand, express low levels of religiosity, with two-thirds declaring no religious affiliation; the other third are Catholic. The PRI deputies are most representative of the population generally, with 87 percent Catholics, 10 percent no religion, and 3 percent

Table 6-2 Religious Attendance among Members of Congress

	Frequency of Attendance (percentages)				
Party Affiliation	Once a Week	Monthly	Infrequently	Rarely	Never
PRI	13	9	28	34	16
PAN	58	27	8	7	0
PRD	5	0	13	22	60

Source: Based on interviews with members of the 1994–1997 legislature. See Antonia Martínez, "Diputados, clivajes (cleavages) y polarización en México," *Perfiles latinoamericanos,* 11 (December 1997): 57.

Protestants. The attendance patterns reflected in Table 6-2 demonstrate that PAN politicians practice their religious faith more intensely. These religious beliefs, as the author of this research argues, may affect politicians' views on important issues, including such controversial topics as divorce and abortion, on which the deputies from each party take substantially different positions.

The tone of many bishops' commentaries also has changed in recent years. Numerous bishops now believe it is their responsibility to take stands on significant social, economic, and political issues extending well beyond democracy itself, a belief that has produced implicit and explicit criticism of government actions. In fact, since 2000 the episcopate warned the government not to fail to help the citizenry, especially poorer Mexicans. Bishops continued this critical posture throughout the Fox administration, raising critical questions about such issues as the government's labor reforms and complete liberty of expression for all Mexicans, including clergy. The church does not foment dissent; rather, it mirrors its constituency's existing frustrations. With the exception of social issues, notably abortion, its views have not been as prominently circulated during Calderón's presidency. However, the church's openly critical posture on those specific social policy issues, when it deems it necessary, has continued under Calderón, and has led to petitions to both the Vatican and the government to prevent bishops from interfering in internal political affairs.[67]

Business

The private business sector combines some of the features of a governmental institution, the military, with those of an autonomous institution, the church. As pointed out earlier, an array of organizations present their demands to the government. The most important quasi-governmental organizations, established by the government itself, were a group of federations that included the National Chamber of Industries (Canacintra, or CNIT), the National Chamber of Commerce (Concanaco), and the National Federation of Chamber of Industries (Concamin). These organizations have been considerably weakened since 1996, when the Supreme Court ruled against obligatory chamber membership, leaving them insufficient revenues from membership fees and dependent on secretary of commerce subsidies. The most important autonomous organizations, in addition to Coparmex, are the Mexican Insurance Association (AMIS), the Mexican Council of Businessmen (CMHN), and the Mexican Bankers Association.

The private sector, historically, has labored under conditions similar to the constraints on the church, although not nearly as extreme. The government prior to 2000 allowed labor, professional organizations, and peasants to be formally represented in the PRI, but it purposely excluded the private sector. It did so because private-sector interests did not coincide with the rhetoric of the postrevolutionary leadership, even if in reality their interests typically have been shared.[68]

Recognizing the advantage of collective representation, at least on certain issues, businessmen created a unitary body to represent the top organizations: the Businessmen's Coordinating Council (CCE). The CCE, however, is not representative of its own members, even though it speaks for them. The most influential business organization in Mexico is the semi-secret CMHN, which is made up of thirty-nine prominent capitalists. The members meet frequently with cabinet members, and occasionally with the president. Just three weeks after his election, president-elect Fox met with members of the council at the Bankers' Club. The meeting was arranged by one of its members, a long-time friend and school companion of Fox from the Ibero-American University.[69] It is clear from the literature that the CMHN rarely makes direct demands on the government or the president; rather, membership in this elite organization is used to gain individual access to the president or the appropriate government official.[70] What is ignored by analysts, however, is the fact that the council serves as an influential vehicle through which capitalists network and advance their own business interests. In short, it functions as an informal interest group between politicians and leading capitalists and a crucial personal link among capitalists.

A structural condition in Mexico that explains the added importance of capitalists, facilitating informal processes including business-government networking, is that the majority of Mexico's top corporations remain in the hands of a small number of wealthy families. Whether they are listed on the stock exchange in Mexico or in New York, these families dominate Mexico's manufacturing, industrial, and technological economy. Consequently, individual capitalists influence corporate decision-making to a greater extent than found in most postindustrial societies, including the United States.

During the democratic transition, smaller independent business groups under Coparmex's vociferous leadership advocated a more energetic political activism for businessmen, including open support for opposition parties. These groups began to campaign for candidates of the National Action Party, and members even ran for state and local offices, especially in northern Mexico.[71] Their position was symbolized in the 1988 presidential race when a successful northern businessman, Manuel Clouthier, a former president of both Coparmex and the CCE, opposed Salinas on the PAN ticket. The direct involvement of businessmen in political campaigns has continued and increased, and several prominent businessmen served as advisers to Fox during his presidential race, becoming members of his administration after his election. The most significant case of this influence occurred in the 2006 presidential election, and some analysts believe that businesses, using the Internet, produced condemnations of López Obrador, likening him to Hugo Chávez, the radical president of Venezuela.[72] Thus, one can argue that under Fox and more so under Calderón, business interests were well represented directly within the most important decision-making institutions such as the Chamber of Deputies, and that they were "able to move from the boardroom to the Chamber."[73]

Businessmen, more than any other group in Mexico with the exception of the political leaders themselves, have the capability of influencing government decisions, especially in the economic realm. They have not been able to do so consistently. Government economic policy, which has favored business's interests more frequently than those of organized labor, has emerged as much from the self-interest or preferences of government leaders as from private-sector pressures. Given Fox's macroeconomic preferences, and his business background, this did not change. On the other hand, numerous conflicts have occurred between the Fox and Calderón administrations and the private sector over major policy issues, indicative of divisions within the business community.[74]

It can be argued that recent governments must pay closer attention to business's demands, at both the state and national levels, especially given the increasing electoral competitiveness and business's greater ability to determine the outcome of elections. Because the former quasi-governmental organizations have formed alliances with the autonomous groups to criticize government economic policies, business organizations no longer can even be considered remotely corporatist.[75] This greater activity marks a significant change in entrepreneurial political behavior and, if adapted elsewhere in Mexico, will cause major alterations in state-group relations.

Careful analysts of business influence in post-democratic Mexico have suggested that their influence has increased rather than decreased. Strom Thacker, who has followed business interests for two decades, argues that "One might expect democracy to ameliorate the uneven power structures and sharp inequalities inherited from authoritarian rule. But business, or at least certain well-organized, powerful segments of it, has proven to be relatively agile at adapting to the new rules of the game and has, if anything, enhanced its relative influence in the political system and exacerbated existing political and economic inequalities."[76] He goes on to argue that the business community is in an advantageous position to lobby Congress given their resources and the weak staff structure among non-repeating officeholders. There is no question that a consolidating democracy has introduced additional changes that affect the private sector, but big business in particular has made use of market power, legal maneuvering, political participation, and material resources to protect itself from democratic incursions while maximizing its freedom to maneuver politically. Finally, democracy has introduced a major structural change in the relationship between business and the government, refocusing their attempts at affecting policy decisions away from the executive to the legislative branch. This does not imply that big business is always successful in their lobby efforts.

Organized Labor

Of all the groups with political influence in Mexico, organized labor best met the criteria of an ideal, traditional corporatist group. Organized labor in Mexico is quite different from that in the United States. The first distinguishing characteristic is the preponderance of government employees, most of them federal, who account for more than a third of all organized workers. The second characteristic is that organized labor is made up of unions called confederations, similar to the chambers of the business organizations. Nearly half of organized laborers are members of these broad confederations. The third differentiating characteristic of labor is the lesser presence of purely industrial-based unions such as those of miners, electricians, and petroleum workers. These characteristics have undergone significant change since the PRI's defeat in 2000.

The most important labor organization, the Mexican Federation of Labor (CTM), was established under President Cárdenas. He and his successors maintained a close relationship with union leaders that amounted to government control.[77] The control was cemented by incorporating the CTM as the foundation of one of the three sectoral pillars of the National Revolutionary

Party—a role that continues to this day. More than any other characteristic, organized labor's status within the party placed it in the semi-corporatist fold. Unlike business, the church, or even the military, which is incorporated into the state itself, organized labor has had a prominent role in the PRI. Between 1979 and 1988, for example, 21 to 25 percent of the PRI's federal deputies were labor leaders, most commonly from the CTM.[78] Since President Fox's election, the percentage of labor deputies as a proportion of PRI members of Congress has declined dramatically, accounting for a mere 7 percent in 2009 to 2012.[79] This does not mean that it influenced the decision-making process but, rather, that its relationship with the government in the past, through the party, was formalized, legitimized, and visible.

This pattern changed under Fox. It is apparent that even international protests against conditions in multinational corporations in Mexico has led to newly independent union representation among some firms, and that their leadership, at least initially, is responsive to worker demands.[80] It became clear that independent unions would make significant inroads after 2001, when the Supreme Court, following a series of other court decisions, ruled against provisions in the Federal Labor Law giving preference to the established, corporatist unions affiliated with the PRI.[81] Regardless of the structural changes which have occurred within organized labor, only 18 percent of Mexicans view unions as democratic.[82]

In the past, the government often promoted new unions and leaders to keep established unions in line. The removal of PRI-affiliated politicians from the national government in 2000, however, effectively eliminated the government's ability to continue such policies. The corporatist system of integrating most of organized labor within the PRI required that it control the government bureaucracy, providing resources for patronage and the establishment of new unions. The government also subsidized favored unions, creating a dependent relationship, because most unions were unable to charge dues.[83]

It is ironic that when the PAN was in opposition it criticized government interference in labor unions. Both the Fox and Calderón administrations have maintained a confrontational posture toward organized labor, represented in their antagonistic and protracted relationship with the Mexican Mining and Metalworkers' Union. Perhaps the most influential sources of change within the labor movement are the recent decisions by the Supreme Court. For example, one of the regulations the court overturned in the federal labor law allowed employees to be fired if they left a union that held a collective contract with the employer. This and other decisions are significantly changing Mexican labor culture. In response to these decisions, the Federal Workers Union (FSTSE) recently told members they could affiliate with any party of their choice.[84] The Calderón administration also dissolved the

Table 6-3 Labor Strike Petitions and Strikes
in Federal-Jurisdiction Industries

Years	Strike Petitions	Strikes	Ratio of Strikes to Petitions
1989–1994 average	7,021	138	.020
1995–2000 average	7,825	46	.006
2001–2006 average	6,488	44	.007
2007–2009 average	11,022	23	.002

Source: Adapted from Graciela Bensusán and Kevin T. Middlebrook, "Organized Labor and Politics in Mexico," in *The Oxford Handbook of Mexican Politics,* ed. Roderic Ai Camp (New York: Oxford University Press, 2012), Table 3.

Central Light and Power Company in Mexico City in 2009, its predominant supplier of power, and fired all 45,000 workers, most of whom were members of the Mexican Electrical Workers Union, gutting the union's membership. One can obtain a sense of organized labor's efforts by reviewing its recent history of strikes in Table 6-3.

The data in Table 6-3 suggest that in spite of the major increase in requests to recognize the legal right to strike (petitions), the number of actual yearly strikes decreased substantially in the first three years of the Calderón administration, suggesting an increasingly negative climate toward unions and strike activity. The initial downward trend started under President Zedillo, suggesting that it cannot be attributed to partisan change alone, but to an altered economic ideological position.

From an economic perspective, it is clear that over the last two decades labor never benefited in real terms from rising wages, although the government did provide some subsidies for consumer goods and housing. In real terms, the minimum wage is less today than it was in 1994, and has remained essentially stagnant for years. The average daily minimum wage was 13.98 pesos in 1994, and by midway through the Calderón administration it declined to 10.6 pesos, or 72 on a 100-point scale of the purchasing power in 1994.[85] The inability of organized labor and working class Mexicans generally to improve their income through a real increase in the minimum wage demonstrates the limits of their policymaking influence on governmental institutions, including the executive and legislative branches.

One union that is an exception to this pattern and has exerted itself politically since 2005 is the National Teachers Union, the largest single organization among government workers' unions, and one of the most important groups in Mexico. Formerly an integral member of PRI-controlled unions, its longtime leader, Esther Elba Gordillo, was forced out of the PRI leadership in 2004. Pursuing an independent political position, Gordillo successfully crafted the New Alliance Party (PANAL), and supported Calderón for the presidency. "Gordillo instructed union members to split their ballots in order to support Calderón's presidential candidacy and still elect PANAL candidates to federal and state legislative seats. President Calderón recognized the SNTE's electoral effectiveness by giving Gordillo and her allies a significant voice on educational policy issues, granting them de facto control over such prominent offices as the Social Security Institute for State Workers (Instituto de Seguridad y Servicios Sociales de los Trabajadores del Estado) and the cash-rich National Lottery, and by ignoring repeated denunciations of internal union corruption."[86] Gordillo basically has demonstrated how major union organizations can use their membership to achieve political ends more directly by seeking and winning legislative seats in Congress.

Intellectuals and the Media

The intellectual community has an amorphous relationship with the government. Some of its formal organizations are patronized by the state; others are independent. None speaks for the intellectual community, but they do provide some public prestige. The most salient quasi-governmental organization is the National College, a publicly supported institution founded in 1946, whose purpose is to disseminate its members' work. Members are prominent figures in all fields, including law, sciences, humanities, social sciences, and fine arts.

The relationship of the intellectual community to the state is much more a product of the relationship between the government and intellectual employment than between the government and intellectuals' organizations. Three sectors of the economy employ the vast majority of intellectuals: government, academia, and publishing. Unlike intellectuals in the United States, Latin American intellectuals—Mexican intellectuals among them—have a long history of employment in public life, either in a federal bureaucracy, especially the Secretariats of Foreign Affairs and Education, or in various political posts as governors, party leaders, and cabinet members.[87]

The lack of employment opportunities in Mexico has encouraged intellectuals to work for the government. This means that the government does not have to incorporate intellectuals formally into institutional relationships with the state because the majority have been state employees since the 1920s. Many intellectuals, desirous of maintaining greater autonomy, have sought employment in the most prestigious universities, especially those in Mexico City. They hold teaching and administrative positions at the National Autonomous University, the Autonomous Technological Institute of Mexico, the Ibero-American University, the Center for Economic Research and Teaching, and at the Colegio de México. Intellectuals have advantageous ties to the government because many were classmates of future politicians and others have been their teachers. Politicians often identify prominent intellectuals as having been their most influential professors.

If intellectuals influence societal ideas, they typically do so through the written word. Intellectuals in Mexico, as in the United States and other countries, establish magazines to circulate their views. Magazines dedicated to particular schools of thought are typically the product of a group of people who share certain ideological principles. Some of the more prominent contemporary intellectual groups in Mexico include those of the late Octavio Paz, who contributed to his journal *Vuelta* and its successor, *Letras Libres*, headed by Enrique Krause; Héctor Aguilar Camín, who from 1983 to 1995 directed the popular monthly *Nexos;* Julio Scherer García, president of the board of *Proceso;* and Federico Reyes Heroles, who is an editorial board member of *Este País*, Mexico's first magazine devoted to survey research, but with a strong intellectual bent. Many intellectuals earn a portion of their income contributing essays to newspaper editorial pages.

The intellectual community has increasingly sought new channels in the electronic media, mainly in television. Some prominent Mexican figures, including Enrique Krause, Octavio Paz, and Rolando Cordera, have used this medium to reach a larger audience and to discuss controversial political and social topics. The proliferation of public opinion polls, the association of some leading figures with these survey research efforts, and most important, their analysis of the findings in both the print and electronic media extend intellectuals' influence to the electoral arena, as polling results become identified with the party and the candidate.[88]

Intellectuals are also making use of the Internet. Many who write for leading journals and newspapers include their e-mail address with their names. All of the leading magazines and journals now have websites, including *Proceso* and *Letras Libres*, which increases the reach of intellectual ideas and provides more feedback from public audiences to intellectual contributors. Others have created their own blogs. A comprehensive world poll suggests that the Internet will become the primary source of news and other information for citizens of many countries in the next decade. In Mexico, 5 million citizens were using the Internet when the country began its democratic consolidation in 2000. By 2009, 28 million Mexicans, an increase of over 500 percent, were using this new technology. Seventy percent of those users were members of social networks, nearly a third on Facebook, reflecting an increase in spending on social network advertising in just one year from 2007 to 2008 of 366 percent. A 2011 study of Facebook and Twitter users found that nearly two-thirds are under twenty-nine, that nine out of ten have high school or college degrees, that an equal number are urban residents, that they have much lower confidence in all institutions than nonusers especially among Twitter subscribers, who expressed more than twice as much a strong interest in politics.[89] Twitter users, primarily college students, used the medium in the last two weeks of May during the 2012 presidential race to organize peaceful demonstrations to protest the electronic media bias in favor of Peña Nieto, and the possible return of the PRI to the presidency.

These figures represent a dramatic change in the existence of a "digital culture" in Mexico. Seventy-eight percent of Mexicans now believe that the Internet gives them more freedom compared to 72 percent of Germans and 85 percent of Americans. Interestingly, however, is the fact that only half of Mexicans agree that it is a safe place to express their opinions, which does not seem important to Internet users in more developed economies such as France or Japan. Mexicans also believe strongly that the Internet should not be regulated by any level of government.[90]

The government's relationship to the intellectual community is also reflected in its attitude toward the media.[91] Mexico has freedom of speech, but freedom of the press does not have a strong tradition. Government controls over radio and television programming are quite strict, nevertheless, television is the most important medium politically, and selected intellectuals and commentators, as suggested above, have developed national recognition. Television is significant because it is second only to family as a basic source of political attitudes.[92] The print media, which has operated under far fewer restrictions, has existed within a professional culture that until recently has not advocated investigative journalism. Journalists have been more effective since 2003, when the Fox administration implemented the new Transparency Law, giving ordinary citizens and reporters access to a wide range of governmental information and statistics.

Most of the censorship in Mexico today is self-censorship from publishers who are afraid to antagonize their sources, governmental and nongovernmental, or advertisers.[93] The most significant threatening source of self-censorship involves publishers and editors trying to protect their reporters and editorial writers from being threatened, kidnapped, and murdered by drug cartels. By 2006, Mexico had replaced Colombia as the most dangerous country in Latin America for reporters and the practice of journalism. This pattern continued unabated through 2012. This new phase of censorship in a democratic context has serious implications for democratic consolidation:

> Killing and threatening journalists with impunity has negative consequences for the consolidation of a modern democratic state and the rule of law. The right of a citizen to be informed is violated every time a reporter is killed, abducted, attacked or forced to resort to self-censorship to protect his or her

life. No story is worth a life. In many places in Mexico issues that affect the daily lives of ordinary people, drug trafficking, crime, corruption and ineffective governance, are not being covered. Citizens are being deprived of essential information that enables them to make informed decisions on public policies of direct concern to them. They are being deprived of the type of investigative reporting that makes the press in the United States, and many other democratic nations, "watch dogs" of democracy.[94]

The increasing violence against Mexican journalists (more than forty-eight have been murdered or disappeared since Calderón introduced his strategy) led to a ten point-agreement among more than seven hundred media outlets to find ways to protect their reporters and to avoid glorifying crime bosses, and urged news organizations to unite against such threats by jointly publishing stories.[95] In 2012, the Senate unanimously approved a constitutional amendment to make attacks on journalists a federal crime, which human rights activists hailed as a legislative milestone.[96]

Journalists, according to a study by Sallie Hughes, began emulating journalistic practices in the United States during the democratic transition. By the early 2000s, Hughes documented the changing attitudes of professional journalists and editors toward "civic journalism" through numerous interviews with them in the field.[97] Despite advances in civic journalism, scholars view the media's role as not having fulfilled its democratic potential, especially because of the monopolistic control over media exerted by influential corporations such as Televisa. Hughes believes that all aspects of media's contribution to democratic development, ranging from how issues are framed to the diversity of ideas presented, affect the country's ability to consolidate its democratic processes and even the way citizens participate.[98]

Television, for example, appears to have played a significant role in the 2000 presidential election. During the campaign, 84 percent of the voters watched television news, and two-thirds of those viewed news programs at least four or more times weekly. Several NGOs and the Federal Electoral Institute examined media bias. The parties and candidates can obtain television and other media coverage in two primary ways: advertising and news commentaries. Because of significant changes in the electoral laws, the major parties in 2000 were roughly equal in their ability to advertise, especially on the dominant television networks. Even when coverage is equitably distributed, it may well be biased. In a comprehensive examination of television news coverage in the 2000 election, Hughes and Lawson discovered that privately owned stations offered more balanced political news than state-run stations, that both were subject to bias, and that the inclinations and values of owners and journalists influenced electoral coverage.[99]

In the 2006 presidential race, analysts argued that negative campaigning and advertising did work to the disadvantage of López Obrador.[100] The two televised debates favored Calderón's candidacy against the PRI candidate Roberto Madrazo, who was unable to best Calderón on stage. Most observers believe López Obrador made a serious error in attending only the first of the two debates. The only comprehensive study of the campaign itself indicates that "López Obrador did not do significantly worse among those who watched the debate, but his absence from the second debate did tend to confirm the PAN's portrayal of him as high-handed and autocratic. In other words, the debate did not prejudice people against AMLO, but he might have helped himself by showing up. The day after the debate, online gamblers put Calderón ahead of AMLO for the first time in the campaign."[101] Additional studies of Mexico City voters during the 2006 president campaigns found that audiences interpreted television news through class-based lenses, accepting information that reinforced prior notions about candidates and politics, and rejecting information that did not reinforce those notions.[102] In 2012, the two televised presidential debates largely were viewed by surveys and the media as a wash.[103]

The dependence of intellectuals and journalists and the institutions that employ them on the largesse of the state affected their relationship to the government before 2000. But the coming to power of a different political party eliminated the monopoly of a single party-state relationship. Furthermore, the growing professionalization in television and the media increasingly restricts governmental influence from any one source. Finally, the rise of independent educational institutions, as alternative sources of employment for present and future intellectuals, also provides greater potential autonomy in intellectual employment. However, some sectors of the intellectual community continue to rely heavily on the government to support their activities, thus continuing a pattern of dependence. Most importantly, the reliance of many Mexicans on electronic media for political news and information, and the increasing use of intellectuals to make use of that media, increases the importance of who controls those sources of communication in spite of the fact that Mexicans rank near the very bottom of Latin American countries in their level of news consumption, regardless of the medium.[104] Rather than government exercising an overwhelming influence on the content of media, the monopolization of the leading media sources exercises a greater potential threat to biased sources in the future. This situation, combined with the dark shadow over press freedom exerted by the drug cartels, which neither the government nor the media organizations have been able to thwart, poses serious obstacles to the traditional functions performed by media sources, and their actors, in a democratic society.

VOICES OF DISSENT

Even when Mexico's political model was a more or less orthodox example of a corporatist structure, the government never successfully incorporated all potentially influential groups into its fold, nor all members of the groups just discussed. Indeed, many of those who opposed the government politically were formerly its supporters. These included both intellectuals and political opposition leaders.

Mexico allowed dissent, but successfully controlled its level and tone prior to 2000. The government had a structural advantage in terms of continuity of leadership and the dominance of its party, the PRI, over the voting process. In an underdeveloped economy, the state's economic resources are overwhelming, and in Mexico those resources were used to disarm and co-opt dissidents, be they peasant leaders, lawyers, labor organizers, or intellectuals. Yet the state, including the presidency and the federal bureaucratic leadership—contrary to its impression as a monolithic and all-powerful institution—demonstrated in practice that it was "a heterogeneous concoction of social classes and political factions holding little consensus over critical issues."[105] In the past, the government often coopted dissidents. *Cooptation is the process by which the government incorporates an individual person or group into its ranks.* Groups find it difficult to counter government influence over their leaders. Few people can resist the attraction of political power or money, and the government often rewards cooperation with prestigious posts. Some persons accept posts for financial reasons; others because of the possibility of working within rather than outside the system.

The attitudes of each administration toward various groups and individual leaders varied. Since 1989, the state gave greater attention and consequently prestige to business, the military, and the church, and less attention to labor. Since 2000, however, although both Fox and Calderón followed a similar pattern toward each of these institutions, they also have paid more attention to what might be described as the voices of dissent, many of which increased their influence during the democratic transition, and have taken on the role of established institutions.

Nongovernmental Organizations

Mexico has witnessed a flowering of popular movements since 1989. This is not a new phenomenon. Many groups with political, economic, and social interests grew out of the general malaise of the 1968 student movement and the subsequent government repression, and such organizations were given an additional boost in Mexico City after the 1985 earthquake. Also, after 1968, women were given more influential roles in these organizations, particularly in urban areas. In the 1988 presidential elections, many of these movements began linking themselves more closely to political parties.[106]

Critical voices have been a presence among most of these groups for decades. But a set of organizations over which the government has been unable to exercise much control has been nongovernmental institutions. Nongovernmental organizations range in scope from civic action groups, similar to the League of Women Voters in the United States, to religiously affiliated human rights advocacy organizations. Scholars argue that such organizations not only have increased significantly in numbers, but they have contributed to functional specialization and to civic diversity through a process of modernizing the composition of civil society groups.[107] By the mid-1990s, more than five thousand such groups existed in Mexico, half of them in Mexico City, and an additional 25 percent in four cities: Guadalajara, Tijuana, Oaxaca, and Saltillo.[108] By the mid-2000s, their numbers had grown to an estimated 20,000 NGOs operating in Mexico, although only 8,500 had a legal structure. Comparatively speaking Mexico's situation is disappointing, since Chile boasts 50,000 registered NGOs.[109] Interestingly, one of the few studies of the composition of these organizations in Mexico finds that they are largely from the middle class, approximately half are over the age of fifty, and they attribute their involvement in civic groups to a critical political event, which was 1968 for the over-fifty group, 1988 for the thirty-to-fifty-year-old members, and 2006 for the under-thirty members. In terms of personal values, they score higher than the average citizen on preference for an active government, level of community involvement, and gender equality.[110]

Among the most notable of these organizations in the 1990s was an umbrella group, the *Alianza Cívica*, or Civic Alliance, which coordinated dozens of other organizations. Directed by Sergio Aguayo, Civic Alliance represented Mexicans seeking democratic change, in particular clean and fair elections. It recruited election observers from four hundred nongovernmental and civic groups to watch five thousand polling places. In 2000, it concentrated its electoral observation program on two hundred districts in twenty-seven states, using more than seven thousand volunteers. Even intellectuals became involved in the electoral outcome, when a loosely organized elite, calling itself the San Angel group, acted as a watchdog of the 2000 election.

Human rights groups, during the first two years of the Fox administration, were among the most influential organizations in effecting changes in domestic policies. Among the most important of these changes has been increased access to government files, similar to the U.S. Freedom of Information legislation. This new access has led to numerous revelations about past abuses, including the massacre of student demonstrators in Mexico City in 1968, and the disappearance of leftist and alleged leftist activists in the 1970s and 1980s, during Mexico's own version of the region's "dirty wars."[111] On the other hand, a number of government security files, including one on myself, because I had corresponded with many opposition figures in the 1970s and 1980s, disappeared before 2000. The president appointed a special prosecutor and promised to prosecute and punish officials responsible for the murders. Many human rights activists remain critical of the Fox administration for the slow pace of reforms, and the inadequacy of protection for activists and judges, citing the murder of a leading human rights figure, Digna Ochoa, in October 2001 in the capital. These actions by Fox did not produce any significant prosecutions or results.

The limited impact of human rights NGOs continued during the Calderón administration. Their efforts became even more significant to public policy as human rights abuses increased dramatically from 2006 through 2012, and the armed forces became a notable agent of human rights allegations. As Mariclaire Acosta suggests, the U.S. Department of State's 2009 report on human rights in Mexico summarizes the situation in the following terms: "Unlawful killings by security forces; kidnappings; physical abuse; poor and overcrowded prison conditions; arbitrary arrests and detention; corruption; inefficiency, and lack of transparency of the judicial system; confessions coerced through torture; violence and threats against journalists leading to self-censorship. Societal problems included domestic violence, including killings of women; trafficking in persons; social and economic discrimination against some members of the indigenous population, and child labor."[112] Leaders from human rights organizations publicly expressed their criticisms, including direct communications to President Calderón.[113] There is no question that national and international human rights NGOs were critical to the federal government's response on this issue which led to new legislation, but was rejected by the Supreme Court in 2011.

Nongovernmental groups, without a doubt, also played a crucial role in the increasing competitiveness of Mexico's electoral process and in Vicente Fox's benchmark electoral victory. Their growth is one of the most significant political changes in Mexico since 1988, and they are likely to play a critical role in contributing to the give and take of democratic politics, especially in their relationship to the legislative branch. In recognition of this role, the chamber of deputies passed a law in 2004 "to encourage citizen activities performed by civil organizations, which sets forth certain benefits such organizations may obtain from the government, as well as establishing opportunities for collaboration between civil associations and the government. In short, such groups are now formally registered."[114] At present, however, most nongovernmental groups are characterized by their lack of partisan political attachments. They also have created a network of channels from which to work outside the party system altogether. Finally, they have contributed significantly to an expansion of international influences in Mexico.[115]

Scholars who have examined the role and impact of civic organizations since 2000 are typically in agreement that they have largely failed to increase their influence beyond the 2000 presidential election. One of the reasons for this is the continued influence of corporatist relationships that can be found in numerous "authoritarian enclaves."[116] Overall, the track record of NGOs in various policy arenas has been mixed. Jonathan Fox, who has studied these organizations for years, examined the extent to which a consolidating democracy has enhanced the abilities of NGOs to benefit the interests of poor, rural Mexicans. He concludes from three detailed case studies that they have benefitted from increased associations more so than from competitive, democratic elections.[117] In general terms, by the end of the Calderón administration, "Time and the disappointing failures of the post-transition decade have shown that civil society organizations, and especially NGOs, are important actors, but that they still lack the strength and the tools to have a sustained effect on shaping public policy."[118]

Collectively, with the exception of religious organizations, more Mexicans typically are involved in civic or nongovernmental organizations and associations than in any other form of participation. The organizations that attract the greatest percentage of regular participation in Mexico and elsewhere in Latin America typically are parent-teacher associations. Not surprisingly, those Mexicans who are most likely to attend parents' meetings express a greater interest in politics and participate in political activities. The lack of personal security has actually increased the level of participation in these associations.[119]

Participation in various organizations during and after the democratic transition has led to a strongly held belief among a majority of Mexicans that they individually, rather than by formal participation through a wide range of interest groups, or through elected representatives, should be able to determine or influence public policy. In short, the concept of direct democracy has taken hold (see Table 6-4).

Support for direct democracy procedures has increased significantly since 2007. For example, support for the second of these procedures in Table 6-4 increased from 50 to 73 percent from 2007 to 2009. However,

Table 6-4 Citizen Support for Direct Democracy

Questions	Those in Favor (%)
Should the majority of Mexicans be able to reject laws proposed by a majority of deputies and senators?	84
Should the president be able to approve laws supported by a popular referendum that were rejected by Congress?	73
Should citizens be able to initiative legislative proposals?	79

Source: "Tiene democracia directa amplio respaldo ciudadano," 1,200 respondents, +/−2.8% margin of error, December 17–21, 2009, www.parametria.com.mx.

recent scholarship suggests that while active involvement in associations impacts positively on institutional relationships that reinforce democracy, surprisingly their evidence suggests that "the impact associations have on the quality of democracy does not run through their impact on the behavior or values of individual active citizens."[120]

Occasionally, direct democracy is exercised by a single individual. In Mexico, the poet Javier Sicilia, whose son was a victim of criminal violence, publicly demanded that the government alter its anti-drug strategy and recognize the high cost in Mexican lives, producing public demonstrations in support of his criticism, and more significantly, a personal encounter with President Calderón at Chapultepec Castle in a "Dialog for Peace," which could only be described as a transparent, widely publicized conversation between individual citizens and the president.[121] His movement, which became the Movement for Peace, attracted national and international support, and in 2011 and 2012, made contact with numerous other groups, including the Zapatistas.

Social Movements

Another source of civic influence occurs through social movements that evolve into more formal organizations. Mexico and Latin American boast a long history of such movements. Scholars have discovered recently that confrontations against the political system itself have declined while other, more institutionalized forms of participation, such as petitions and public demonstrations, are on the increase.[122] Democratic politics in Mexico and elsewhere in Latin America appear to have encouraged and "normalized" protest politics among citizens who share an interest in politics and are involved in their communities, which now can be considered a conventional form of political expression.[123] Mexico, compared to all other countries in Latin America, ranked lowest in their level of participation in protests during the Calderón administration, less than half the level of participation of the United States and less than a third of the Argentineans who protest.

A notable example, made up of individuals and groups who were part of the old corporatist structure, is the El Barzón movement, composed of small businessmen, agriculturalists, and middle-class people opposed to government financial policies. Specifically, many people were caught in a credit crunch and became part of a broad debtors' protest. Analysts claimed that they may have reached as many as two million members by the late 1990s. What is significant about this group is that it transformed itself into a typical interest organization, making demands on state and federal governments, and using a range of techniques to express its views. More importantly, it created a multiplier effect, because it weaved "together, more or less simultaneously, events ongoing in the farthest corners of Mexico."[124] As Shannan Mattiace concluded, "Movements like El Barzón widened their protest activities to include opposition to private companies, such as banks, in addition to protesting governmental policies. Forging cross-class alliances and coalitions became a real possibility for many social movement organizations, freed up from the hierarchical structure of the corporatist system that discouraged intersectoral alliances. El Barzón capitalized on the decline of the corporatist system to expand its social base, as the impact of the debt crisis spread to virtually every sector of the Mexican economy after 1994."[125]

The failure of Mexican administrations—local, state, and national—to resolve many long-standing problems, particularly in rural communities, came to a head on January 1, 1994, with far-reaching national and international consequences. A different kind of social movement, willing to use force to obtain redress for decades of abuse and exploitation of indigenous peasants in the highlands of Chiapas, emerged in the form of the Zapatista Army of National Liberation (EZLN), which launched guerrilla attacks and seized villages near San Cristóbal de las Casas.[126]

The Zapatistas' beliefs are laid out very clearly in their official paper, *El Despertador Mexicano* and their website, and cover many issues, including women's rights. Their principal focus is on agrarian and economic reform, and some of their requests echo the voice of their inspiration, Emiliano Zapata, such as limits on land ownership and the redistribution of excessive land holdings.[127] The rebellion had at least three underlying causes: disappointment with the government for changing the provisions for agrarian reform in Article 27 and ignoring peasants as a client group, the peasants' declining economic status in the rural community, and their exclusion from the political process.[128]

The enigmatic spokesperson for the EZLN, Subcomandante Marcos, Rafael Sebastián Guillén, a former university professor and non-Indian, captured the national and international media's attention.[129] It immediately became clear that although most Mexicans opposed the guerrillas' use of force, they sympathized strongly with their goals. The EZLN uprising influenced the pace of electoral change for the remainder of 1994, leading to more electoral reforms favorable to the opposition parties, and set the tone for this period as one of increasing political instability and violence, especially after the PRI presidential candidate, Luis Donaldo Colosio, was assassinated. The Zapatistas showed other popular movements that even small, well-organized groups can have tremendous political influence. The guerrillas demonstrated the importance of electronic media, illustrating their ability to defeat the military and the government in the media war, affiliating themselves with national and international NGOs through e-mail. They continue to maintain an updated website, as they quickly evolved into a peaceful, popular movement.[130]

The government and the Zapatistas signed an agreement in February 1996, the San Andrés accords, but President Zedillo never implemented these provisions. Among the provisions, the government agreed to permit Indian communities to establish local governments, to educate themselves using indigenous languages, and to mandate indigenous representation in legislative bodies. President Fox made settling the Zapatista impasse a primary campaign issue, stating publicly in a nonchalant fashion that he would settle this issue "in fifteen minutes." In spite of many concessions, including withdrawing the military in 2001, the guerrillas remain intractable. Further debate of constitutional reforms linked to a National Indigenous Law (2001) suggested the difficulties of democratic pluralism in addressing these and other long-neglected issues.[131]

The greatest impact of the EZLN, however, has been its encouragement of other civic and specifically indigenous rights groups. On the negative side, their point of view advocating communitarian attitudes has tended to dominate indigenous issues in Mexico. As suggested in a previous chapter, Mexico has witnessed an important movement among local communities to incorporate their traditions and customs as part of their political decision-making process, with mixed results, especially for women.[132] Todd Eisenstadt's extraordinary field research surveying more than five thousand respondents demonstrated that in Oaxaca, in contrast to Chiapas, indigenous and non-indigenous peasants adopted similar attitudes toward property rights, the result of differing historical experiences between the two states, rather than indigenous versus nonindigenous viewpoints alone, divided along communitarian versus individual property rights.[133]

The emergence of the Zapatistas also produced an environment more favorable to other groups willing to use violence to achieve their goals. In the summer of 1996, an organization calling itself the People's

Revolutionary Army (ERP) initiated attacks on isolated police outposts and military patrols in the southern state of Oaxaca and elsewhere in central Mexico. They have been traced back to dissident leftist groups founded in the 1960s, and to an organization associated with Lucio Cabañas, a guerrilla leader killed in Guerrero in the 1970s. Unlike the Zapatistas, the ERP has been unwilling to negotiate with the government. Other armed groups are also operating in many rural regions. None of these groups achieved the Zaptista's level of success politically, nor has any established international linkages.[134] Increased participation and democratic competition since 2000 have not necessarily provided adequate channels for the demands of all Mexicans.

The advent of electoral democracy in Mexico has not been accompanied by increased security, by political institutions that represent the interests of the majority, or by a notable reduction in the socioeconomic inequalities highlighted elsewhere in this book. "Given this, social movements are as necessary today as they have ever been in raising issues ignored by policymakers and in forcing leaders to listen to voices not heard within more formal institutions. In sum, many of the substantive demands that gave rise to the social movements that emerged after 1985 in Mexico remain unresolved, providing a continued raison d'être for social movement activism today."[135]

Drug Trafficking Organizations

A decade ago, it would never have occurred to any analyst of the Mexican political scene to list drug trafficking organizations (DTOs) as an influential political actor in determining Mexican public policy. These criminal organizations have gone well beyond the typical range of criminal activities to become perhaps the most influential organized institution affecting government actions (as it relates to public security) and electoral outcomes (the 2009 congressional races and the 2012 presidential election). As John Bailey convincingly argues:

> DTOs have crossed a number of thresholds to create a three-dimensional crisis of governance. First, some DTOs have acquired the power and political savvy to overwhelm the state's police-justice system and even confront its military forces. The horrific violence employed by the DTOs against each other and against both state and society, and the state's apparent inability to repress the gangs, has sown deep anxiety in the public. Second, trafficking groups have infiltrated the government, society, and economy in various regions of the country to the point that they exercise decisive power over aspects of public policy and civil society activities. They have penetrated

national-level agencies as well, mainly in the police-justice-military sector, and exercise significant influence. Third, the governing party and opposition parties have failed to forge a united front against the traffickers and continue to seek partisan advantage in the crisis. Thus, the most serious threat to democratic governance is whether the government can deliver minimally acceptable public safety throughout the national territory.[136]

Three quarters of Mexicans have indicated three out of four of the most important issues confronting Mexico are crime, illegal drugs, and corrupt politicians.[137] Increasingly, sophisticated analysis by leading political scientists and economists are describing drug cartels' extraordinary impact on social, economic, and political facets of Mexican life, dominating numerous aspects of the domestic and international agendas. Drug trafficking is not a recent phenomenon in Mexico, but the increased presence of drug cartels paralleled the democratic transition that began in 1989. When the government arrested Félix Gallardo in 1989, considered the "godfather of Mexican cartels," it opened the door for the development of independent cartels, which have come and gone until the present, but also have expanded in size and influence, to where they are now employing, by United States intelligence estimates, some 450,000 Mexicans.[138]

Socially, drug cartels have exerted an important impact on the culture. They are sophisticated in marketing themselves and in providing economic assistance to nonprofit institutions and governmental works in poorer, rural communities. Mexican attitudes toward the cartels suggest the depth and potential they exercise on Mexican society (see Table 6-5). Many drug traffickers have been romanticized in popular musical ballads known as *narcocorridos* in concerts and on the radio.[139] As the answers in Table 6-5 suggest, many Mexicans actually view drug cartels in a positive light, from being Robin Hood–type criminals to producing economic opportunities, employment, and good works in their communities. In 2011, the Knights Templar cartel gave away copies of a twenty-two-page pamphlet described as a code of conduct in which they claim to be fighting poverty and injustice.[140]

Economically, drug trafficking organizations increasingly have infiltrated legal businesses, broadening their criminal activities well beyond that of producing and trafficking in illegal substances. Moreover, the violence they have generated has produced serious economic consequences for ordinary Mexicans. From 2006 through 2010, 2 percent of the Mexican population over the age of eighteen (1,265,000) have been forced to leave their homes to seek refuge elsewhere in or outside of Mexico.[141] William P. Glade has provided the most original analysis of the cartels as economic monopolies, describing them in the following terms: "Viewed as an oligopolistic set of multi-product firms, popularly called the regional drug cartels,

Table 6-5 Mexican Attitudes toward Drug Trafficking Organizations

Questions	Percentage Answering Yes
Listened to a *narcocorrido*	90
Narcocorridos reflect reality	69
Drug trafficking generates employment	41
Listened frequently to a *narcocorrido*	37
Drug traffickers do more public works in communities than governments	34
Drug trafficking generates progress in the communities where they live	33
If drug trafficking weren't violent, it would be beneficial to your state	27
Narcocorridos distort reality	24
Drug trafficking is a necessary evil	23
Don't know if they are heroes or criminals	17
Drug cartel leaders are heroes	15
It is not bad to produce or sell drugs	11
It is not a bad thing to consume drugs	10

Source: Parametría, four hundred respondents, +/−4.9% margin of error, February 12–16, 2011.

the narcotics industry per se has been backed up by an astonishingly efficient production regime for such side products as assassination, intimidation, human trafficking (moving illegal migrants of Mexican and other origin) across the northern frontier, extortion, lucrative kidnapping-for-profit schemes, money laundering, and increasingly grisly massacres over wider stretches of the Republic."[142] Glade goes on to identify numerous other social and economic costs, including expenditures on security, judicial reform, infrastructure, and the flight of capital or the lack of investment. J.P. Morgan of Mexico estimated the drug-related violence and security is costing the country 1 to 1.5 percent of its gross domestic product, 210 billion pesos yearly.[143] In fact, a survey by a leading security firm in Mexico in 2011 revealed that two-thirds of American company executives in charge of security describe conditions in 2011 as less secure than 2010, 58 percent attribute the security situation primarily to organized crime, 27 percent reconsidered future growth plans because of the situation, and 8 percent considered moving their operations to another country.[144]

Finally, drug trafficking organizations have created a political conundrum for Mexico. The exponential increase in drug-related homicides, even though they are concentrated in only 6 percent of Mexico's more than 2,400 municipalities, raises serious issues about the degree of sovereignty exercised by government authorities at the local and state levels.[145] Mexico's leading criminologist estimates the penetration of organized crime in 73 percent of the country's municipalities. Authorities are unable to protect public prosecutors, journalists, police, mayors, political candidates, and potential witnesses from drug cartel retributions. The vast majority of Mexicans believe the government cannot defeat the drug cartels, and nearly two-thirds believe that corruption, not the United States' demand for drugs, is the primary explanation for the failure of the government's anti-drug strategy.[146] There are instances where the national leadership of the major political parties actually chose gubernatorial candidates in order to prevent drug cartels from influencing the choice locally.[147]

CONCLUSION

From the leadership's viewpoint prior to the 1990s, Mexico developed a successful corporatist structure for engaging and controlling society's most important interest groups. The corporatist system was never comprehensive or complete, but channeled many political demands through quasi-governmental institutions. It was an essential ingredient in Mexico's one-party state.

Various groups in Mexico, including the military, the church, business, labor, intellectuals, and the media, have maintained somewhat different relations with the government, depending on the legal and institutional role given to them by society. Interestingly, whether their relationship was established and visible or more autonomous and independent, the informal channels that their leaders use carry more weight in the decision-making process than do the formal channels. That aspect of the relationship has not changed significantly since the advent of democratization. Prior to 2000, the political system used and abused certain interest-group institutions to mobilize the rank and file for their own purposes rather than, for the most part, to hear group demands. The removal of a single-party elite from controlling the state, and electoral competition, destroyed this well-established pattern of interest-group relations.

The groups sharing the most institutionalized relationship with the government through their incorporation in the PRI party structure had the least influence on the decision-making process. Groups excluded from the party, such as business, the church, and the military, influenced the decision-making process more heavily. Of the major interest groups in most Western polities, business has produced the most influence on Mexican government policies, primarily in the area of economic policy. Recently, they have exerted a concrete impact on electoral outcomes as candidates for public office and as sources of electoral propaganda. Electoral competition, and the increasing strength of the legislative branch, will continue to enhance the importance of these three institutional actors.

The state itself often has pursued its own policies, not in response to demands or pressures from any particular group, but because of self-interest or its interpretation of societal interests.[148] In this sense, the state too has been an actor in the decision-making process. It had the greatest potential for influencing the outcome of policymaking because it operated in a semi-authoritarian environment prior to 2000, mediating among the more traditional, competing interests.

Electoral democracy, multi-party control, and different executive branch leadership have dealt a deathblow to certain characteristics of the traditional, semi-corporatist structure in Mexican politics. The most influential structural change that alters this relationship is that the state and the party are no longer interchangeable. The ability of a small, circulating elite, affiliated with the PRI, to retain control for decades over the federal bureaucracy, was the source of this pattern in state-group relations prior to democratic consolidation. The party itself was a hollow skeleton, funded by the state. Breaking that link destroyed the ability of government officials to keep groups loyal to their party or to the state. Indeed, scholars argue that the inability of the state to reward economically its corporatist allies was the primary explanation for the decline of the PRI and its eventual defeat in the 2000 presidential election.[149] As we have seen, however, certain groups, especially labor, may retain ties to specific political parties, including the PRI, but the competition for interest group loyalties has intensified, making such linkages more difficult to sustain.

The pattern that is least likely to be affected in state-interest group relations in the foreseeable future, at least until the legislative branch unequivocally demonstrates its decision-making influence on the national level and amends the constitution to permit consecutive reelection, is the informal process through which elites use their networking ties to raise issues, seek out crucial information, and obtain access to critical policymakers. Indeed, the most perverse example of this is the support of many Mexicans for the government's use of a "negotiation strategy" with the drug cartels, especially with the PRI capturing the presidency in 2012, based on the alleged assumption that the PRI successfully used such informal means to achieve an arrangement with the drug traffickers prior to 2000. Certain existing formal institutions, however, are well placed to continue using the elite networking patterns to convey their demands, especially capitalists in the private sector, while at the same time participating in a partisan manner as individuals or groups in the electoral process. The Catholic Church also has demonstrated before and after Fox's election that it is an influential actor. More than any other institutional interest group, it has a reservoir of support among average Mexicans, and it often articulates the interests of less influential Mexicans. Consequently it will remain the most critical voice of government economic policies that do not address the issue of poverty and redistribution of wealth.

The least influential groups in the democratic consolidation phase of Mexico's political model have been the NGOs. They currently have the greatest potential for exercising their influence through former members who have reached decision-making posts in the executive branch, and more frequently as members of the Chamber of Deputies.[150] In particular, female politicians, with far greater prior experience in NGOs, have contributed strongly to this outcome. Why haven't NGOs established more institutionalized relationships with the legislative branch? At least two important explanations come to mind. In the first place, because politicians refuse to institute consecutive reelection in the legislative branch, there is essentially no continuity in congressional leadership, committee membership, or congressional staff. Therefore, a structural obstacle impedes the establishment of longterm relationships between interest group actors and public servants. A second explanation, alluded to above, is that informal contacts through noninstitutional channels is typical. María Luis Tarrés predicted this pattern among female NGOs in 1998, arguing that such civic organizations would decline in importance after democratization took hold because these groups had developed informal, alternative channels of communication under the semiauthoritarian regime, and would not easily adjust to typical institutional channels characteristic of democratic models.[151]

NOTES

1. For the Mexican version, see Ruth J. Spalding, "State Power and its Limits: Corporatism in Mexico," *Comparative Political Studies* 14, no. 2 (July 1981): 139–61.

2. Nora Hamilton provides additional insight to these changes from the 1970s through 2010 in *Mexico: Political, Social, and Economic Evolution* (New York: Oxford University Press, 2011), 293.

3. Howard J. Wiarda, "Mexico: The Unravelling of a Corporatist Regime?" *Journal of Inter-American Studies and World Affairs* 30, no. 4 (Winter 1988–1989): 1–28.

4. Luis Rubio, "Economic Reform and Political Change in Mexico," in *Political and Economic Liberalization in Mexico: At a Critical Juncture?*, ed. Riordan Roett (Boulder, CO: Lynne Rienner, 1993), 35–50.

5. James Sánchez Susarrey, "Corporativismo o democracia?" *Vuelta* 12 (March 1988): 12–19.

6. Blanca Heredia, "Clientelism in Flux: Democratization and Interest Intermediation in Contemporary Mexico," paper presented at the National Latin American Studies Association, Guadalajara, 1997.

7. María Magdalena Tosoni, "Notas sobre el clientelismo político en la ciudad de México," *Perfiles Latinoamericanos* 29 (January–June, 2007): 67.

8. Aldo Muñoz Armenta, "El sindicalismo corporativo mexicana y los partidos políticos en tiempos de alternancia," *Revista Nueva Antropología* 20 (July 2006): 133–55.

9. Robert J. Shafer, *Mexican Business Organizations* (Syracuse, NY: Syracuse University Press, 1973), explains these requirements in some detail.

10. For detailed evidence of this influence, see Vikram K. Chand, *Mexico's Political Awakening* (Notre Dame, IN: University of Notre Dame Press, 2001), 208 ff.

11. Judith A. Teichman, *Policymaking in Mexico: From Boom to Crisis* (Boston: Allen & Unwin, 1988).

12. Luis Carlos Ugalde, *The Mexican Congress: Old Player, New Player* (Washington, DC: CSIS, 2000), 160.

13. Miguel Basáñez, *La lucha por la hegemonía en México, 1968–1990*, 8th ed. (Mexico City: Siglo XXI, 1990), 35ff.

14. Abraham Lowenthal and J. Samuel Fitch, *Armies and Politics in Latin America*, rev. ed. (New York: Holmes & Meier, 1986), 4ff.

15. James Burk, "Theories of Democratic Civil-Military Relations," *Armed Forces and Society* 29, no.1 (2002): 7–29.

16. Franklin D. Margiotta, "Civilian Control and the Mexican Military: Changing Patterns of Political Influence," in *Civilian Control of the Military: Theories and Cases from Developing Countries*, ed. Claude E. Welch Jr. (Albany: State University of New York Press, 1976).

17. James W. Wilkie, *The Mexican Revolution: Federal Expenditure and Social Change Since 1910*, 2nd ed. (Berkeley and Los Angeles: University of California Press, 1970), 100–06.

18. Merilee Grindle, "Civil-Military Relations and Budget Politics in Latin America," *Armed Forces and Society* 13 (Winter 1987): 255–75.

19. Roderic Ai Camp, "Armed Forces and Drugs: Public Perceptions and Institutional Challenges," in *Shared Responsibility: U.S.-Mexico Policy Options for Confronting Organized Crime*, eds. Eric L. Olson, David A. Shirk, and Andrew Selee (Washington, DC: Woodrow Wilson International Center for Scholars, 2010), Table 5, 301.

20. Roderic Ai Camp, "Militarizing Mexico, Where is the Officer Corps Going?," (Washington, DC: CSIS, 1999).

21. Michael J. Dziedzic, "Mexico's Converging Challenges: Problems, Prospects, and Implications," unpublished manuscript, U.S. Air Force Academy, April 1989, 34.

22. See Roderic Ai Camp, *Generals in the Palacio: The Military in Modern Mexico* (New York: Oxford University Press, 1992), for an analysis of these roles.

23. Phyllis Greene Walker, "The Modern Mexican Military: Political Influence and Institutional Interests" (master's thesis, American University, 1987), 76.

24. For evidence of this, see José Luis Reyna, "Narcotics as a Destabilizing Force for Source Countries and Non-Source Countries," in *The Latin American Narcotics Trade and United States National Security*, ed. Donald A. Mabry (Westport, CT: Greenwood Press, 1989), 123–35.

25. Graham H. Turbiville, Jr., "Law Enforcement and the Mexican Armed Forces: New Internal Security Missions Challenge the Military," *Low Intensity Conflict & Law Enforcement* 6 (Autumn 1997): 69–83.

26. Sigrid Arzt, "The Shaping of Mexico's Civil-Military Relations under the Fox Administration in Light of the Law Enforcement Challenges," paper presented at the Latin American Studies Association, Washington, DC, September 2001.

27. Jordi Díez and Ian Nicholls, *The Mexican Armed Forces in Transition*, Strategic Studies Institute, January 2006, 38–41.

28. Sistemas de Inteligencia en Mercado y Opinión, June–August, 2009, "Encuesta seguridad nacional," 1,250 interviews nationally, July 24–27, 2009, +/–1.9% margin of error, www.parametria.com.mx, April, 2010.

29. Ibid.

30. Daniel Montalvo, "Do you Trust Your Armed Forces?," *AmericasBarometer Insights 2009*, No. 27, Figure 1, 1.

31. Jorge Chabat, "Mexico: The Security Challenge," in *Canadian and Mexican Security in the New North America: Challenges and Prospects*, ed. Jordi Díez (Montreal: McGill-Queen's University Press, 2006), 68.

32. "Challenges to Civil-Military Relations in the 21st Century," in *Canadian and Mexican Security in the New North America, Challenges and Prospects*, ed. Jordi Díez (Montreal: McGill-Queen's University Press, 2006), 98–99.

33. "Legislative Oversight of the Armed Forces in Mexico," *Mexican Studies* 24, no. 1 (Winter 2008): 113–45.

34. Cara Elizabeth Urwin Gibbons, "The Inter-American Court's Mexican Tetralogy on Military Justice: A Case for Principled Jurisprudence," MA Thesis in Law, University of Toronto, 2011, 52.

35. "Military Justice," *Justice in Mexico*, News Report (April 2012), 19–20.

36. Jordi Díez, "Civil-Military Relations, the Unfinished Transition," in Camp, ed., *Oxford Handbook of Mexican Politics*, 265–85.

37. Soledad Loaeza, "La iglesia católica y el reformismo autoritario," *Foro Internacional* 25 (October–December 1984): 142.

38. The relationship is outlined in Karl Schmitt, "Church and State in Mexico: A Corporatist Relationship," *Americas* 40 (January 1984): 349–76.

39. Roberto Blancarte, "Religion and Constitutional Change in Mexico, 1988–1992," *Social Compass* 40, no. 4 (1993): 567.

40. For an excellent example, see Matt Moffet, "In Catholic Mexico, a Priest's Power Is Limited to Prayer," *Wall Street Journal*, December 6, 1989.

41. José Miguel Cruz, "Social Capital in the Americas: Participation in Religious Groups," *AmericasBarometer Insights 2009*, No. 15, 1.

42. "La crisis de la iglesia católica," www.parametria.com.mx, August, 2010.

43. "Divide a Mexicanos estado laico," www.parametria.com.mx, August, 2010.

44. Adapted from Oscar Aguilar Ascencio, "La iglesia católica y la democratización en México," in *La iglesia católica y la política en el México de hoy*, ed. José de Jesús Legoretta Zepeda (Mexico: Ibero-American University, 2000), 171.

45. "Una Iglesia muda no sirve, dice Mons. Rivera," *Diario de Yucatán*, September 6, 1999, www.yucatan.com.mx; and "La crisis de la Iglesia Católica II," www.parametria.com.mx, August 2010.

46. www.parametria.com.mx, one thousand respondents,+/–3.1% margin of error, July–August, 2010.

47. Michael Tangeman, *Mexico at the Crossroads: Politics, the Church, and the Poor* (Maryknoll, NY: Orbis Books, 1994).

48. Ginger Thompson, "Vatican Curbing Deacons in Mexico," *New York Times*, March 12, 2002.

49. "También es un pecado grave saber que ocurre esa y no denunciarla, censura de la Iglesia al vote del miedo," *Diario de Yucatán*, May 10, 2000, www.yucatan.com.mx.

50. Conferencia del Episcopado Mexicano, *La democracia no se puede dar sin ti, elecciones del 2000* (Mexico: CEM, 2000), 12.

51. José Antonio Roman y Alonso Urrutia, "Condena comisión episcopal desaseo contra AMLO: La CEM se deslinda," *La Jornada*, April 5, 2005.

52. Roderic Ai Camp, "Exercising Political Influence, Religion, Democracy, and the Mexican 2006 Presidential Race," *Journal of Church and State* 50, no. 1 (Winter 2008): 101–22.

53. Associated Press, "Bishops Urge Mexicans to Vote in July," June 13, 2006.

54. Camp, "Armed Forces and Drugs," 323–24.

55. "La Arquidiócesis pide el retiro del Ejército," *El Universal*, December 4, 2009, "Nuevo arzobispo manda mensaje al crimen organizado," *El Heraldo de Chihuahua*, October 27, 2009, and "Preocupación creciente del episcopado mexicana," www.caritas.tn/index, 2010.

56. Alberto Medina Espinosa, "Pide Iglesia evitar balaceras," *El Porvenir*, April 29, 2011.

57. Josh Allen, "Growing Catholic Divide over Mexico Drug War," *Christian Science Monitor*, January 13, 2012.

58. Roderic Ai Camp, "Church and Narcostate," *Foreign Policy* (August 13, 2009): 1–3; and Jennifer González, "Sacerdotes católicos no escapan a flagelo del narcotráfico en México," www.elNuevoHerald.com, March 22, 2012.

59. Interviews with former presidents José López Portillo and Miguel de la Madrid, Mexico City, summer 1990.

60. Los obispos de México, "Baluarte de la democracia, la mujer mexicana," *Diario de Yucatán*, April 21, 2007.

61. Bimsa, "Imágen de la Iglesia Católica," 1,000 respondents, +/–3.8% percent margin of error, November 25–December 4, 2005.

62. James C. McKinley, Jr., "Mexico City Legalizes Abortion Early in Term," *The New York Times*, April 25, 2007.

63. "Mexico polarizado por debate sobre derecho al aborto," www.parametria.com.mx, April 10, 2007.

64. "Eutanasia: Mexicanos ante la muerte asistida," www.parametria.com.mx, November 27, 2006.

65. "Los políticos deben profesar públicamente su fe," *Diario de Yucatán*, November 6, 2000, www.yucatan.com.mx.

66. "La visita del Papa y el respeto a la ley," *Este País*, September 2002, 53–54.

67. "Una misiva del Vaticano, prohiben a Mons. Cepeda Silva hablar en nombre del Episcopado," *Diario de Yucatán*, September 7, 2000, www.yucatan.com.mx; and "El PRD pide a Gobernación que 'meta en orden' al Cardenal Rivera Carrera," *Diario de Yucatán*, August 29, 2000, www.yucatan.com.mx. Alejandro Díaz Domínguez, "La regulación religiosa en materia electoral mexicana: una explicación alternativa sobre sus diferencias," *Economía, Sociedad y Territorio* 6, no. 22 (2006): 431–56.

68. Hamilton, *Mexico: Political, Social, and Economic Evolution*, 135.

69. *Reforma*, June 10, 1996, A1.

70. Ben Ross Schneider, "Why Is Mexican Business So Organized?" *Latin American Research Review* 37, no. 1 (2002): 77–118.

71. Graciela Guadarrama S., "Entrepreneurs and Politics: Businessmen in Electoral Contests in Sonora and Nuevo León," in *Electoral Patterns and Perspectives in Mexico*, ed. Arturo Alvarado (La Jolla, CA: Center for U.S.-Mexican Studies, UCSD, 1987), 83ff.

72. Kathleen Bruhn, "López Obrador, Calderón, and the 2006 Presidential Campaign," in *Consolidating Mexico's Democracy: The 2006 Presidential Campaign in Comparative Perspective*, eds. Jorge I. Domínguez, Chappell Lawson, and Alejandro Moreno (Baltimore, MD: The John Hopkins University Press, 2009), 175–76.

73. Ibid, 126.

74. Matilde Luna, "Business and Politics in Mexico," in *Dilemmas of Political Change in Mexico*, ed. Kevin J. Middlebrook (London: Institute of Latin American Studies, University of London, 2004), 350.

75. Kristin Johnson Ceva, "Business-Government Relations in Mexico Since 1990: NAFTA, Economic Crisis, and the Reorganization of Business Interests," in *Mexico's Private Sector: Recent History, Future Challenges*, ed. Riordan Roett (Boulder, CO: Lynne Rienner, 1998), 125–57.

76. "Big Business, Democracy, and the Politics of Competition," in Camp, ed., *The Oxford Handbook of Mexican Politics*, 319.

77. George W. Grayson, *The Mexican Labor Machine: Power, Politics, and Patronage*, Significant Issues Series 19 (Washington, DC: CSIS, 1989), 12.

78. Juan Reyes del Campillo, "El movimiento obrero en la Cámara de Diputados (1979–1988)," *Revista Mexicana de Sociología* 52, no. 3 (July–September 1990): 139–60.

79. Graciela Bensusán, "A New Scenario for Mexican Trade Unions: Changes in the Structure of Political and Economic Opportunities," in *Dilemmas of Political Change in Mexico*, ed. Kevin J. Middlebrook (London: Institute of Latin American Studies, University of London, 2004), 254.

80. Ginger Thompson, "Mexican Labor Protest Gets Results," *New York Times*, October 8, 2001, www.nytimes.com.

81. Katrina Burgess, "Mexican Labor at a Crossroads," in *Mexico's Politics and Society in Transition*, ed. Joseph S. Tulchin and Andrew D. Selee (Boulder, CO: Lynne Rienner, 2003), 99.

82. Carta Paramétrica, "Reforma Laboral 2012," 500 interviews, +/– 4.4% margin of error, September 22–26, 2012, www.parametria.com.mx.

83. Kevin J. Middlebrook, "The Sounds of Silence: Organised Labour's Response to Economic Crisis in Mexico," *Journal of Latin American Studies* 21 (May 1989): 195–220.

84. "Labor: Another Flank Demanding Reform," *Review of the Economic Situation of Mexico* (May 2001), 207–08.

85. Graciela Bensusán and Kevin T. Middlebrook, "Organized Labor and Politics in Mexico," in Camp, ed., *The Oxford Handbook of Mexican Politics*, Table 1.

86. Ibid., 354.

87. Fred P. Ellison, "The Writer," in *Continuity and Change in Latin America*, ed. John J. Johnson (Stanford, CA: Stanford University Press, 1964), 84.

88. For discussions of its influence, see Juan Carlos Gamboa, "Media, Public Opinion Polls, and the 1994 Mexican Presidential Election," in *Polling for Democracy: Public Opinion and Political Liberalization in Mexico*, ed. Roderic Ai Camp (Wilmington, DE: Scholarly Resources, 1996), 17–36.

89. Consulta Mitofsky, "Pérfil de usario de redes sociales en Internet, Facebook y Twitter," December 2011.

90. "Internet considered by 27,973 citizens of the world," Mund, Opinion and Policy Report, Series 10, Bulletin No. 11, March 12, 2010.

91. Albert L. Hester and Richard R. Cole, eds., *Mass Communication in Mexico* (Brookings, SD: Association for Education in Journalism, 1975).

92. Roderic Ai Camp, "Learning Democracy in Mexico and the United States," *Mexican Studies* 19, no. 1 (Winter 2003): 17.

93. Jeffrey Staub, "Self-Censorship and the Mexican Press," *Mexico Policy News*, no. 9 (Fall 1993): 30–34. Background information on these relationships can be found in Ilya Adler, "Press-Government Relations in Mexico: A Study of Freedom of the Mexican Press and Press Criticism of Government Institutions," *Studies in Latin American Popular Culture* 12 (1993): 1–29.

94. "Protecting Press Freedom in an Environment of Violence and Impunity," in Olson et al., eds., *Shared Responsibility: U.S.-Mexico Policy Options for Confronting Organized Crime*, 271–72.

95. Ken Ellingwood, "Mexico News Companies Agree to Drug War Coverage Guidelines," *Los Angeles Times*, March 25, 2011.

96. Tim Johnson, "Mexico Acts to Toughen Law against Attacks on Journalists," *Kansas City Star*, March 13, 2012.

97. See her outstanding analysis of these changes in *Newsrooms in Conflict: Journalism and the Democratization of Mexico* (Pittsburgh, PA: University of Pittsburgh Press, 2006), 191ff.

98. "Democracy in the Newsroom: The Evolution of Journalism and the News Media," in Camp, ed., *The Oxford Handbook of Mexican Politics*, 367–97.

99. Sallie Hughes and Chappell Lawson, "Propaganda and Crony Capitalism: Partisan Bias in Mexican Television News," *Latin American Research Review* 39, no. 3 (October 2004): 82.

100. Chappell Lawson, "Introduction, The Mexican 2006 Election in Context," in Domínguez et al., eds., *Consolidating Mexico's Democracy: The 2006 Presidential Campaign in Comparative Perspective*, 11–13.

101. Kathleen Bruhn, "López Obrador, Calderón, and the 2006 Presidential Campaign," 179.

102. Sallie Hughes and Manuel Alejandro Guerrero, "The Disenchanted Voter: Emotional Attachment, Social Stratification, and Mediated Politics in Mexico's 2006 Presidential Election." *International Journal of Press/Politics* 14, no. 3 (July 2009): 353–75.

103. For an interesting analysis on the level of interest in that debate, see Carta Paramétrica, "Encuesta Parametría: Debate presidencial," April 30, 2012, and Carta Paramétrica, "Encuesta Parametría: Saldo del debate," May 14, 2012.

104. Arturo Maldonado, "Who Consumes News Media in Latin America and the Caribbean?," *AmericasBarometer Insights: 2011*, no. 70, 1.

105. Diane E. Davis, *Urban Leviathan: Mexico City in the Twentieth Century* (Philadelphia, PA: Temple University Press, 1994), 320.

106. These and other arguments are developed by contributors to Joe Foweraker and Ann L. Craig, eds., *Popular Movements and Political Change in Mexico* (Boulder, CO: Lynne Rienner, 1990); for human rights, see Edward L. Cleary, "Human Rights Organizations in Mexico: Growth in Turbulence," *Journal of Church and State* 37, no. 4 (Autumn 1995): 793–812.

107. Adrian Gurza Navalle and Natália S. Bueno, "Waves of Change within Civil Society in Latin America, Mexico City and São Paulo," *Politics & Society* 39, no. 3 (2011): 417.

108. Alberto Olvera, "Civil Society in Mexico at Century's End," in *Dilemmas of Political Change in Mexico,* ed. Kevin Middlebrook (La Jolla, CA: U.S.-Mexico Studies Center, 2004), 428.

109. Mariclaire Acosta, "NGOs and Human Rights," in Camp, ed., *The Oxford Handbook of Mexican Politics*, 440.

110. MUND, "Who is Active in the Civic Resistance, and Why?," Opinion and Policy Report, Series 6, No. 14, October 18, 2006.

111. The most recent, comprehensive account of the dirty war era in Mexico can be found in Fernando Herrera Calderón and Adela Cedillo, eds., *Challenging Authoritarianism in Mexico: Revolutionary Struggles and the Dirty War, 1964–1982* (New York: Routledge, 2012).

112. U.S. State Department, *2009 Human Rights Report: Mexico*, www.state .gov, 2009; Mariclaire Acosta, "NGOs and Human Rights," 428.

113. An excellent outline of his administration's failures on this issue can be found in José Miguel Vivanco, Executive Director of the Americas Division, Human Rights Watch, letter, September 24, 2010.

114. Cristina Puga, "Associations and Governance in Mexico," paper presented at the Latin American Studies Association, Las Vegas, Nevada, October 2004, 10–11.

115. Douglas A. Chalmers and Kerianne Piester, "Nongovernmental Organizations and the Changing Structure of Mexican Politics," in *Changing Structure of Mexico: Political, Social, and Economic Prospects*, ed. Laura Randall (New York: M.E. Sharpe, 1996), 253–61.

116. Ilán Bizberg, "La sociedad civil en el nuevo régimen político," *Foro Internacional* 47, no. 4 (2007): 785–816.

117. *Accountability Politics: Power and Voice in Rural Mexico* (New York: Oxford University Press, 2007).

118. Mariclaire Acosta, "NGOs and Human Rights," 440.

119. José Miguel Cruz, "Social Capital in the Americas: Participation in Parents' Associations," *AmericasBarometer Insights: 2009*, No. 24.

120. Peter P. Houtzager and Arnab K. Acharya, "Associations, Active Citizenship, and the Quality of Democracy in Brazil and Mexico," *Theory and Society* 40 (2011): 29.

121. Héctor Aguilar Camín, "El diálogo que sí fue," *Milenio*, June 24, 2011.

122. Ma. Fernanda Somuano Ventura, "Más allá del voto: modos de participación política no electoral en México," *Foro Internacional* 45, no. 1 (January–March 2005): 83.

123. Mason Moseley and Daniel Moreno, "The Normalization of Protest in Latin America," *AmericasBaromoter Insights 2010*, No. 42, 4.

124. Gabriel Torres, "The El Barzón Debtors' Movement: From the Local to the National in Protest Politics," in *Subnational Politics and Democratization in Mexico*, eds. Wayne A. Cornelius, Todd A. Eisenstadt, and Jane Hindley (La Jolla, CA: Center for U.S.-Mexican Studies, UCSD, 1999), 146.

125. Shannan Mattiace, "Social and Indigenous Movements in Mexico's Transition to Democracy," in Camp, ed., *The Oxford Handbook of Mexican Politics*, 406ff.

126. Thomas Benjamin, *A Rich Land, a Poor People: Politics and Society in Modern Chiapas* (Albuquerque: University of New Mexico Press, 1989); and Tom Barry's perceptive exploration of the agrarian issues in *Zapata's Revenge: Free Trade and the Farm Crisis in Mexico* (Boston: South End Press, 1995).

127. *El despertador mexicano*, no. 1, December 1993, 1–20. Kara Zugman Dellacioppa, *This Bridge Called Zapatismo: Building Alternative Political Cultures in Mexico City, Los Angeles, and Beyond* (Lanham, MD: Lexington Books, 2009).

128. See Niels Barmeyer, *Developing Zapaatista Autonomy: Conflict and NGO Involvement in Rebel Chiapas* (Albuquerque: University of New Mexico Press, 2009); Richard Stahler-Sholk, "Globalization and Social Movement Resistance, The Zapatista Rebellion in Chiapas, Mexico," *New Political Science* 23, no. 4 (2001): 493–516; and George A. Collier's "The New Politics of Exclusion: Antecedents to the Rebellion in Mexico," *Dialectical Anthropology* 19 (May 1994): 1–44.

129. Alma Guillermoprieto, "The Unmasking," *New Yorker*, March 13, 1995, 40–47; and Ann Louise Bardach, "Mexico's Poet Rebel," *Vanity Fair*, June 1994, 69–74, 130–35.

130. See Ruth Urry, "Rebels, Technology, and Mass Communications: A Comparative Analysis of EZLN and FMLN Media Strategy," Tulane University, 1996.

131. Martha Singer Sochet, ed., *México: Democracía y participación política indígena* (Mexico: Ediciones Gernika, 2007).

132. Jonathan T. Hiskey and Gary L. Goodman, "The Participation Paradox of Indigenous Autonomy in Mexico," *Latin American Politics and Society* 53, no. 2 (Summer 2011): 61–86, concluded that the autonomy of these traditional governance processes has actually reduced participation in national elections.

133. Todd A. Eisenstadt, *Politics, Identity, and Mexico's Indigenous Rights Movements* (Cambridge, UK: Cambridge University Press, 2011); Comisión Nacional de Derechos Humanos, *Participación política de la mujer en México* (Mexico: CNDH, 2009).

134. Gustavo Hirales Morán, "Radical Groups in Mexico Today," Policy Papers on the Americas, Center for Strategic and International Studies, Washington, DC, September 2003.

135. Mattiace, "Social and Indigenous Movements in Mexico's Transition to Democracy," 415.

136. John Bailey, "Drug Traffickers as Political Actors in Mexico's Nascent Democracy," in Camp, ed., *The Oxford Handbook of Mexican Politics*, 467.

137. Pew Global Attitudes Project, "Most Mexicans See Better Life in U.S.— One in Three Would Migrate," September 23, 2009, 1,000 interviews nationally, May 26 to June 2, 2009, +/–3.0% margin of error.

138. The best comprehensive discussion of the drug war and cartels in Mexico is Olson et al., eds., *Shared Responsibility: U.S.-Mexico Policy Options for Confronting Organized Crime*. The most comprehensive monograph in English is George Grayson, *Mexico: Narco-Violence and a Failed State?* (New Brunswick: Transaction Publishers, 2009).

139. See Luís Astorga, "Drug Trafficking in Mexico: A First General Assessment," UNESCO, Discussion Paper 36, 1999, 22–24, for a discussion of narcocorridos. www.unesco.org.

140. www.latindispatch.com, July 20, 2011.

141. "México y sus desplazados," 500 respondents, +/–4.4% margin of error, May 1–2, 2011, www.parametria.com.mx.

142. William P. Glade, "Economy as Grand Guignol: The Postreform Era in Mexico," in Camp, ed., *The Oxford Handbook of Mexican Politics*, 723.

143. *June News Report*, Justice in Mexico, Trans-Border Institute, June 2011, 8.

144. The American Chamber of Commerce in Mexico and Kroll Mexico, "The Impact of Security in Mexico on the Private Sector," 550 respondents, +/–5% margin of error, November 29–January 31, 2011.

145. Viridiana Ríos and David A. Shirk, "Drug Violence in Mexico, Data and Analysis through 2010," Trans-Border Institute, University of San Diego, February 2011.

146. Four hundred interviews nationally, March 28–31, 2009, +/–4.9% margin of error, www.parametria.com.mx. Laurie Freeman, "State of Siege: Drug-Related Violence and Corruption in Mexico: Unintended Consequences of the War on Drugs," *A WOLA Special Report*, Washington Office on Latin America, June 2006.

147. Shannon O'Neil, "The Real War in Mexico: How Democracy Can Defeat the Drug Cartels," *Foreign Affairs* 88, no. 4 (July–August, 2009): 63–77; and Vanda Felbab-Brown, "The Violent Drug Market in Mexico and Lessons from Colombia," Policy Paper No. 12, Brookings Institution, March 2009.

148. For support of this view, see Rose J. Spalding, "State Power and Its Limits: Corporatism in Mexico."

149. Beatriz Magaloni, *Voting for Autocracy: Hegemonic Party Survival and Its Demise in Mexico* (Cambridge, UK: Cambridge University Press, 2006), 259.

150. For the civic and social movement impact on political parties, S. Ilgu Ozler, "Out of the Plaza and into the Office: Social Movement Leaders in the PRD," *Mexican Studies* 25, no. 1 (Winter 2009): 125–54.

151. María Luisa Tarrés, "The Role of Women's Nongovernmental Organizations in Mexican Public Life," in *Women's Participation in Mexican Political Life*, ed. Victoria Rodríguez (Boulder, CO: Westview Press, 1998): 193–203.

7

Mexico's Political Institutions: The Structure of Decision-Making

> At least in formal terms, Mexico has been one of the most centralized countries in Latin America. From the 1930s to the early 1980s, a single party dominated almost all aspects of political life, including holding most elected positions. Between 80 and 90 percent of all public resources in the early 1980s were spent through national government agencies despite the nominal existence of a federal system. By the new millennium, however, Mexico had become a multiparty democracy and almost half of all public resources were managed at the state and local level. State and local governments, which had appeared to be mere appendages of an overwhelmingly dominant central state, now had a degree of discretion in spending and policymaking they had not enjoyed in decades. Even more important, this process of decentralization took place in the context of a gradual process of democratization in which the country instituted truly competitive elections for the first time in decades.
>
> ANDREW SELEE, *Decentralization, Democratization, and Informal Power in Mexico*

Every political system devises a set of structures and institutions to facilitate political decision-making. Studies of decision-making reveal that there are a number of interrelated steps in the process. The steps begin with a problem requiring a political solution and pass through a series of institutions in which the problem is ignored or resolved, often legislatively. Some institutions primarily channel demands from society through the political system. Other institutions contribute to the selection and election of political leadership. Still others carry out the solutions proposed by the political system.

Each political model performs the steps in decision-making differently, although many models have certain similarities. Mexico, as has been suggested earlier, evolved a political system that formally resembled that of the United States but centralized much greater authority in the executive branch. The powers of the executive branch combined with the dominance of a leadership group represented by a single party—the PRI and its antecedents—led to a government dominated by the executive, largely in the person of the president. Since 2000, the executive branch's influence on decision-making has declined. The first political institution that assumed a larger voice in the decision-making process during the democratic transition was the legislative branch, largely because political parties other than the PRI began in 1997 to win control of these institutions. The second political institution, beginning with the reforms Zedillo introduced in 1994, the Supreme Court, representing the apex of the judicial branch, achieved independence from the executive branch and slowly began to hand down legal decisions independent of the presidency. Its independence accelerated under Fox and more so under Calderón. The newest of important actors, who now wield considerable influence on federal government policy and on executive branch leadership, are state governors, suggesting their importance in Mexico's democratic consolidation. Finally, although they are not nearly as visible or demonstrably influential on government policy, other local actors are exerting influence, especially mayors and state legislators. The importance of mayors can be measured by the fact that most members of Congress in Mexico would readily give up their seat to lead medium and large cities, a phenomenon that would occur only rarely in the United States.

The most important reason for examining political institutions in Mexico is that they are fundamental to achieving democratic consolidation. Recent research in Latin America and Mexico demonstrates that citizen confidence in institutions is transferred to their confidence in democracy. Most scholars and Mexicans believe that their institutions are tainted by deeply embedded levels of corruption, making it difficult if not impossible to increase the public trust. Stephen Morris argues that institutional reforms are critical to reducing the level of corruption.[1] In other words, political institutions themselves are essential to solving this fundamental obstacle to achieving a functioning democracy. Other observers have argued that the recent focus on fair elections, to the neglect of establishing strong and new foundations for democratic institutions, has led to renovating leadership while largely retaining unaltered political processes.[2]

THE EXECUTIVE BRANCH

The seat of the Mexican government is Mexico City, in the Federal District, a jurisdiction with certain similarities to the District of Columbia in the

United States. Mexico City, unlike Washington, DC, combines the qualities of New York City, Chicago, and Los Angeles, for Mexico's political capital is also overwhelmingly its intellectual, artistic, and economic capital. It is the most populated metropolitan area in the Western Hemisphere and accounts for nearly a fifth of the country's population.

The executive branch of the government houses two types of agencies: those that have counterparts in most First and Third World countries, such as departments of foreign relations and national defense, and others that are idiosyncratically Mexican, called decentralized or parastatal agencies. Parastatal agencies are a product of Mexican nationalism, Mexicanization, and state expansion from the 1940s through the 1980s.

The preeminent parastatal agency in Mexico, recognized internationally, is Petróleos Mexicanos (Pemex), the national petroleum company. Pemex was born when President Lázaro Cárdenas nationalized foreign-owned petroleum companies in 1938.[3] Since then the government has controlled the development of petroleum resources, including exploration and drilling, and the domestic retailing of petroleum products. Because of the vast Mexican oil reserves and their rapid exploitation in the 1970s and 1980s, Pemex became Mexico's number one company.

The formal cabinet consists of seventeen agencies: Attorney General of the Republic; Secretariat of Agrarian Reform; Secretariat of Agriculture, Livestock, Rural Development, Fishing and Nutrition; Secretariat of Communications and Transportation; Secretariat of the Economy; Secretariat of Energy; Secretariat of the Environment and Natural Resources; Secretariat of Foreign Relations; Secretariat of Government; Secretariat of Health; Secretariat of Labor and Social Welfare; Secretariat of National Defense; Secretariat of the Navy; Secretariat of Public Education; Secretariat of Social Development; Secretariat of Tourism; and Secretariat of the Treasury and Public Credit.

The agencies of greatest standing in the executive branch are those sharing long histories. In the 1920s, 1930s, and 1940s, the Secretariat of National Defense carried far more weight than it does today, because it often was the source of presidential leadership. With the centralization of power in the hands of a civilian president and, as we have seen, the importance of individual, federal bureaucratic agencies as sources of political recruitment prior to 2000, a relationship developed between decision-making influence and the degree to which individual agencies were the source of high-level personnel. In the 1950s and 1960s, the Secretariat of Government, an agency devoted to internal political affairs, replaced the Secretariat of National Defense as a source of presidential leadership and as a major voice in policy decisions.[4] A month before Peña Nieto took office, he received the approval of congress to combine the functions of the secretariat of public security, a cabinet agency created by President Fox to direct greater attention to the growing issues of crime and violence, with that of Government. Thus, this agency will exercise even greater influence during the 2012-2018 administration than previously.

Despite the roles played by these two agencies, the Secretariat of the Treasury wielded considerable influence, and its head received significant attention in each cabinet. He became arbiter in the allocation of funds to other agencies and to state governors in connection with the federal revenue-sharing program.[5] Other than the president, the treasury secretary became the key figure in distributing economic resources, as well as in determining financial policies. Other economic agencies in the government also increased their influence with the onset of hard times. By the 1980s, the Secretariat of Programming and Budgeting (combined with Treasury in 1992), the Secretariat of the Treasury, and the Bank of Mexico (the federal reserve bank) became a troika in setting economic policy.[6]

The most interesting of these three agencies and the most politically influential during its short life (1977–1992), was the Secretariat of Programming and Budget, which produced three consecutive presidents: de la Madrid, Salinas, and Zedillo. More important, it introduced a cadre of important political-technocrats who dominated the Salinas-Zedillo camarillas, their political generation, and economic decision-making.[7] One of their members, Francisco Gil Díaz, became Fox's treasury secretary.[8] Another figure, Guillermo Ortiz Martínez, served as governor of the Bank of Mexico in both the Fox and Calderón administrations. The president's desire to streamline economic policymaking and the ultimate decline of technocrats among the political leadership ensured the demise of this agency.[9]

To streamline cabinet coordination and facilitate policymaking, Miguel de la Madrid organized subcabinet groups along policy lines, including an economic cabinet. Salinas added another category, national security, giving it heightened visibility. It includes the Secretariats of Government, Foreign Relations, National Defense, Navy, and the Attorney General of the Republic. This subcabinet group provided the basis for Fox's new public security secretariat.[10] Under Felipe Calderón, given his aggressive, proactive strategy against the drug trafficking organizations, these agencies, with the exception of Foreign Relations, have received greater visibility and achieved more influence than at any other time in the last four decades.

Groups in Mexican society who have played a role in national policy decisions, as noted in the previous chapter, have made their concerns and interests known to the executive branch at the highest possible level. What has changed in this process since the democratic consolidation is the growing importance of the legislative branch in the outcome of policy initiatives, and therefore, the increased influence of political parties represented there. A consensus among scholars is that President Fox weakened the presidency significantly during his administration, focusing on a personal relationship with the public while neglecting to develop and strengthen channels of communication with the legislative branch.[11] From an institutional perspective, other explanations for this decline include divisions within his presidential staff, the heavy reliance of the presidency on cabinet agency staffs,[12] and his "outsider" status as a candidate without strong attachments to the PAN, producing serious ideological divisions between Fox and PAN traditionalists.

When Calderón won the presidency in 2006, the initial expectation was that he would achieve greater success than Fox in his policy initiatives, given the fact that he boasted a long history in top PAN party leadership, that he had served in Congress, and that he held a cabinet post, therefore having prior firsthand experience in the decision-making process at the highest levels. Early on he was more successful than his predecessor, but Calderón increasingly ran into difficulties as a consequence of his inability to obtain adequate support from the PRI and the PRD to implement major legislation, most of which was watered down if it received legislative approval.

The cabinet secretary remains the key figure in initiating policy proposals, and his staff thoroughly studies the issues and collects information relevant to the formulation of policy. He may be responding to a presidential request or pursuing matters associated with his agency's mandate under broad guidelines outlined to him by the president and presidential advisers. Those Mexicans who have access to the president himself are even more successful in influencing decisions than are those whose highest-level contacts are cabinet figures.

Because the decision-making structure has been so hierarchical and the president exercised so much influence (or presently is expected to exercise authority over the system even though his power is significantly limited), considerable pressure is put on channels of access to the presidency. The president's chief of staff, whose position is essentially a cabinet-level appointment, has the complete confidence of the president. Because he acts as a gatekeeper in denying or granting requests to see the president, he performs a crucial role in the decision-making process.

President Fox introduced few changes to the formal cabinet structure in Mexico, continuing the concept of interagency coordination, dividing his cabinet into three broad groups: economic, political and security, and social.

However, he created an entirely new arrangement of formal advisers, called coordinators, who reported to an overall Coordinator of Public Policies, who in turn reported directly to the president. Fox used these coordinators to draw attention to major policy issues, appointing a number of prominent figures to these posts. Most observers have concluded that these coordinators, many of whom resigned during the first half of Fox's administration, never exerted significant influence on policy, and that the traditional cabinet agency leadership has continued to maintain its preeminence in the executive branch decision-making process through the Calderón administration.[13]

Prior to the PAN's electoral victory in 2000, the presidency specifically, and the executive branch generally, were viewed as the primary voice in the decision-making process. Analysts described the Mexican presidency as having "meta-" constitutional powers, or as "hyper-" presidentialism. The president's and the executive branch's role in the decision-making process can be illustrated by a pre-2000 example. The worst fears of critics of the Mexican semiauthoritarian decision-making process were borne out in 1982 when President José López Portillo announced without warning the nationalization of the banks. The circumstances surrounding the decision have been well documented, and according to the few people López Portillo consulted, he did not consider the views of any of the groups that would be affected.[14] The fact that a single political actor, in consultation with two or three others, could make a decision that would have major reverberations throughout the economy and bring relations between the private sector and the state to a breaking point demonstrates the dangers inherent in centralized power.[15]

Typically, however, presidents have not operated in solitary splendor. Diane Davis, in the only extensive case study of recent presidential decision-making even before Fox took office, discovered that the president often failed to get his way.[16] There is no question that until 2000, decision-making was centralized and that the president personally exercised greater influence over the outcome of policies than does a U.S. president. As Benito Nacif aptly has argued, during the period when the PRI dominated the executive branch, the president was not only "the Chief Executive but chief legislator as well."[17] Even with the advent of multiple-party control in the Chamber of Deputies, the percentage of legislation passed initiated by the executive branch remained remarkably high.

Although the executive branch is likely to see the majority of its bills passed, it is the opposition parties that are introducing the vast majority of the legislation (see Table 7-1). Even the PRI, which essentially had no history of introducing legislative initiatives, "were it not for the democratic transition" likely would not have adjusted quickly to this new legislative

Table 7-1 The Process of Legislation in the Chamber of Deputies

Legislature	President		Deputies		State Legislatures		Total	
	Initiated	Approved	Initiated	Approved	Initiated	Approved	Initiated	Approved
(1991–94)	124	122	117	26	2	1	243	149
(1994–97)	84	83	165	24	2	1	251	108
(1997–00)	32	28	549	108	25	1	606	137
(2000–03)	61	50	1060	210	86	15	1207	275
(2003–06)	36	21	2677	487	113	16	2891	563
(2006–09)	37	32	2595	398	10	0	2770	458

Source: Adapted from Benito Nacif, "The Fall of the Dominant Presidency: Lawmaking under Divided Government in Mexico," in *The Oxford Handbook of Mexican Politics*, ed. Roderic Ai Camp (New York: Oxford University Press, 2012), 240.

role.[18] For example, the number of legislative proposals from the opposition parties increased dramatically from the 1991–1997 sessions to the 1997–2000 session. After Fox became president, the total number of bills presented before Congress exploded, reaching nearly three thousand in the 2003–2006 congressional session, compared to only 606 in the last legislative session under Zedillo (1997–2000). The approval rate overall declined to 19 percent, although President Fox was able to receive approval for 60 percent of his bills compared to only 18 percent for members of Congress. Calderón improved on Fox's record, getting 86 percent of his bills passed, compared to 13 percent of legislation initiated largely by PRD and PRI deputies, and 20 percent by members of his own party.

A comparison of the number of initiatives per member of Congress reveals that the legislative branch had not achieved such a comparable level since the 1920s, even before the PRI existed. These figures demonstrate that competitive elections, a multiparty system, and shared legislative control, will expand the number and range of sources for legislative proposals, thereby expanding access to the decision-making process among various groups, including political parties, interest groups, and legislators themselves. Given this outcome alone, scholars argue that the democratic consolidation process is working in Mexico to produce greater diversity among those actors who are participating in the decision-making process, and that analysts should view this as a democratic success. Caroline Beer, in a recent study of this phenomenon at the state level, also demonstrated a pronounced increase in legislative staff, bills, and discussion in those states where electoral competition was intense.[19]

A valid criticism of Mexico's democratic consolidation of a presidential system combined with a multiparty legislative branch is that the tradeoff remains that major, innovative legislation, which Mexico requires to achieve far greater economic success (for example a significant reduction in

monopolistic control in numerous sectors of the economy), are not forthcoming because they are blocked in the legislative process by the very
heterogeneity of democratic actors.[20] Indeed, these types of policy inactions
actually are perpetuating antidemocratic behaviors in other aspects of
Mexican institutional life. As a recent study of Calderón's proposed major
reforms during the first legislative session suggests, the president was
"forced to accept profound changes in his original projects in return for
support and approval. The reform of PEMEX is perhaps the most telling
example. *The approved bill shows little resemblance to the initial presidential proposal* [emphasis mine], which included private participation in both
producing and distributing natural gas and oil, and falls very short of what
the president and experts considered essential to turn the oil monopoly into
a competitive company. Much the same can be said of the fiscal and judicial
reforms and, to a lesser extent, of the pension's bill."[21]

Presidentialism, the cornerstone of the Mexican political system and the
decision-making process for decades, has taken on many new features during
the past two PAN administrations.[22] It is readily apparent that the president
and his individual cabinet members face many difficulties in persuading
Congress to approve major portions of their individual legislative proposals,
and success requires considerable political skills and negotiation. The fact
that many policy debates are now within the public's view and are extensively covered in the media affects the style of the decision-making process.
Given the presidency's long history of dominance, however, the expectation
still exists in many quarters that the president should remain a strong figure
and that the presidency, not the legislative branch, should continue to initiate
the most influential bills. In fact, however, "divided government opposition
parties have become the main source of law change."[23]

THE LEGISLATIVE BRANCH

Mexico's national legislature is bicameral, with a Chamber of Deputies and a
Senate. Deputies are elected on the basis of roughly equally populated districts, of which there are three hundred. In 1970 one hundred seats were
added for deputies selected from party lists based on the proportion of the votes
cast for the parties. The purpose of the increment was to increase the opposition's representation, owing to the overwhelming dominance of the PRI in
the regular legislative seats. In the reforms in the 1980s, another hundred
seats were added; now three hundred deputies represent individual districts
and two hundred represent parties. These party or plurinominal deputies are

elected at large, based on the proportion of votes received in five designated regions each containing forty seats. A case can be made for the benefits of plurinominal seats, but in Mexico, as one astute observer concludes: "In terms of democracy, . . . proportional representation exacts a heavy cost for minimal benefits. Formulas which ensure minority representation, while bringing opposition to the legislature, are at best distorting and at worst anti-democratic."[24] This system breaks the link between voters and their representatives. Even more surprising, all three parties are using these relatively "safe seats" to elect party leaders to the Chamber, a pattern continued to date.[25]

The Senate, which has fewer powers than the Chamber of Deputies, has two senators from each state and the Federal District, a total of sixty-four, and in 1994 added sixty-four additional seats, thirty-two to be assigned to the party with the second highest vote count in each state in 1994, and the remaining thirty-two as national proportional representation seats in 1997, for a grand total of 128. Senators are elected for six-year terms, all of which came up for election together for the first time in 2000. The Chamber of Deputies and the Senate each have numerous committees, some with names like those found in the U.S. Congress. Deputies and senators cannot be reelected to consecutive terms; seniority does not exist, at least regarding committees, for all members are new to a particular legislature. Recent research suggests, however, that those members of Congress who have served previously in either chamber are more likely to hold committee chairs than first-time members.

The legislative branch was long controlled by the PRI, whose members accounted for more than 90 percent of the district seats in the Chamber of Deputies and, until 1988, all Senate seats (see Table 7-2). Until 1997, when the PRI first lost majority control of the lower chamber, the president appointed a congressional leader (equivalent to the majority leader in the U.S. Congress), who headed all the state delegations. Each state's delegation in the Chamber was usually headed by someone who had served before or by a rising star who was given the post for the first time. Many deputies from the PRI complained that decisions were made in an authoritarian fashion by the leadership and that as individuals they played a minor role.[26] Since the PRD and PAN won control of the Chamber of Deputies in 1997, the deputies have elected their own leader. Depending on their distribution among deputies, all three major parties' and some minor parties' members now chair various committees. Committee chairs do play a significant role in the legislative process.[27] The Senate also has a leader, and the senior senators from each state form the internal governing body. The Senate has taken on a more plural character since 1994, when the PAN and PRD obtained thirty-two party seats, 25 percent of the total, a figure they

Table 7-2 Representation in the Legislative Branch, Mexico, 1994–2012

	Deputies											Senators							
	District Seats				Party Seats				Total			State Seats[b]		Party Seats			Total		
Party[a]	1994	1997	2000	2003	1994	1997	2000	2003	1994	1997	2000	1994	2000	1994	1997[c]	2000	1994	1997	2000
PRI	277	165	131	163	23	74	78	61	300	239	209	64	32	32	13	28	96	77	60
PAN	18	64	141	82	101	57	67	71	119	121	208	0	28	24	9	23	24	33	46
PRD	5	70	28	55	66	55	23	40	71	125	51	0	4	8	8	13	8	16	17
PT	0	1	0	—	10	6	9	—	10	7	9	0	0	0	1	0	0	1	0
PVEM		0	0	—		8	15	—		8	15	0	0	0	1	0	0	1	5
Others				—			8	28			8	0	0			0			0
	300	300	300	300	200	200	200	200	500	500	500	64	64	64	32	64	128	128	128

	Deputies						Senators		
	District Seats		Party Seats		Total		State Seats	Party Seats	Total
Party	2006	2009	2006	2009	2006	2009	2006	2006	2006
PRI	65	184	41	53	106	237	29	6	35
PAN	136	69	70	73	206	142	41	11	52
PRD	91	38	36	31	127	69	26	5	31
PT	2	3	9	10	11	13	0	3	3
PVEM	0	4	17	17	17	21	0	4	4
Others	6	1	27	16	33	17	0	3	3
	300	300	200	200	500	500	96	32	128

Source: 2006.

[a] PRI = Institutional Revolutionary Party, PAN = National Action Party, PRD = Democratic Revolutionary Party, PT = Labor Party, PVEM = Green Party.
[b] The state seats were all elected in 1994.
[c] Only 32 seats were allocated in 1997.

increased in the 2000 elections to sixty-eight seats, or 53 percent. These percentage distributions among the three leading parties change with the parties' fortunes at election time.

Earlier discussion indicated that the legislative branch traditionally had little to say in the decision-making process, unlike the U.S. Congress. The reason for this was that each legislator who was a member of the PRI was beholden to the political leadership, and indirectly the president, for his or her position. If such a legislator wanted to pursue a public career, he or she needed to follow presidential directives. The post-2000 legislators are not controlled by the president, regardless of their party affiliation. None of the three parties since 1997 have obtained a simple majority of seats (251), thus legislative alliances have become a fact of life in passing legislation.

The role of the legislative branch in the Mexican decision-making process has changed dramatically since late 1997. In the past, Congress primarily examined presidential legislative initiatives and made recommendations to the executive branch for alterations. Theoretically it could have rejected a presidential initiative, but most presidential legislation, as we have seen, was approved, typically overwhelmingly (see Table 7-1).

The dominance of parties in the legislative branch that do not control the executive branch led to other important changes. The legislators have significantly altered bills proposed by the executive branch before their approval. Indeed, the legislative branch has either modified or rejected all of Fox's and Calderon's major bills, including significant fiscal and political reforms. Constitutional changes have the lowest chance of passage, followed by political reforms. By the end of the Fox administration, budget and fiscal proposals only were being approved at a 20-percent rate.[28] Deputies have created a much more contentious environment for debates, and they have increased attention to bills that originate from within the Chamber. Given deputies' increased importance, cabinet members have sought to court them, using many of the same techniques found in the relationship between the executive and legislative branches in the United States. "Lobbyists who used to focus all their efforts on the president now schmooze with members of Congress."[29] Nearly two-thirds of deputies reported some or a lot of lobbying in the Chamber.[30]

The legislative branch also serves to legitimize, rather than just approve, executive legislation. When opposition parties began obtaining significant representation in the Chamber of Deputies, the government lost its ability to readily amend the constitution; the PRI did not have two-thirds of the seats in the lower chamber, the number necessary to do so. Mexican presidents and the executive branch have used constitutional amendments to give major, controversial legislation an extra measure of legitimacy.

Since it cannot even achieve a simple majority, the government cannot any longer use this technique without first achieving a coalition to pass legislation or amend the constitution.

Despite the significantly increased role of the legislative branch in Mexican politics, there are two important structural conditions that inhibit its policymaking influence. The first of these, mentioned above, is the continued prohibition on consecutive reelection.[31] Consecutive reelection would enhance legislative power by permitting members to increase their expertise and to develop stronger ties with their constituencies. In the 2000–2003 session, for example, only 15 percent of members of Congress had any previous state or national legislative experience. An examination of sessions since 2003 indicates little change in these percentages.[32] Mexican legislators proposed eliminating the reelection prohibition as early as 1995. More than two-thirds of both chambers favored such a change during the first years of the Fox administration, a figure sufficient to amend the constitution, but the reelection prohibition remained in place. In the 2003–2006 session, 75 percent favored reelection. During the Calderón administration, a *Reforma* survey of members of Congress found that 71 percent still favored the consecutive reelection of legislators.[33]

Why has this significant structural change in the legislative branch, given overwhelming support for such a reform among federal deputies, not occurred? The explanation is twofold. First, Mexicans in general are strongly opposed to such a change, even though their support for eliminating it has increased in recent years. Fewer than a fifth of Mexicans favor reelection even though a third or more believe it would produce a better representative.[34] Their attitude is largely determined by the erroneous view that a prohibition on consecutive reelection in the legislative branch was a principle of the revolution ingrained in the 1917 constitution. In reality, Mexico's legislative branch reelected deputies and senators until 1933, when the constitution was amended to restrict their reelection to nonconsecutive terms. The second explanation is that members of Congress have not shown a willingness to take the lead on this reform and educate their constituencies about its history as well as its institutional benefits.

The only structural change in the Chamber of Deputies the public appears to favor is reducing its size (79 percent favor one hundred or two hundred deputies instead of three hundred from individual districts), and a nearly equal percentage favor a reduction in senators. A comparison between Mexico and the United States based on the ratio between the total population and the combined number of senators and representatives shows Mexico well below the American ratio of one for every 566,000 citizens compared to one for only 173,000 for Mexico.[35]

The second institutional feature linked to reelection is legislative expertise. Not only do most legislators lack congressional experience, they are unable to rely on the staff expertise that American members of Congress take for granted. The importance of legislative staff is becoming a hallmark of the new, democratic consolidation era, even at the state level. Staff sizes are likely to increase significantly among all parties in the Congress, and a staff culture in legislative bodies increasingly is becoming the norm. A second condition is the limited budget devoted to congressional staff in contrast to congressional pay, which exceeded that of its counterparts in the European Union and in Canada, and was just below that of salaries in the United States.[36] The Chamber of Deputies counted approximately sixty researchers for five hundred legislators in the Calderón administration, and like their employers, many leave at the end of three years. By contrast, the executive branch has several thousand full-time permanent staff.[37]

Each of these structural weaknesses, which impact on the efficacy of the legislative branch, has contributed to the inability of that branch to increase its prestige among the general public. In survey after survey the legislative branch ranks at the bottom among all other institutions measured. Interestingly, a comparison between legislative bodies in the United States and Mexico from 2002 to 2011 demonstrates that the disapproval of the way in which Congress has performed its work has gone from only a third to three-quarters of all Americans compared to two-fifths to half of all Mexicans.[38] What is important to observe in the Mexican case, however, is the inability of this body after an entire decade of democratic politics to improve its standing more than a few percentage points.[39] In fact, many Latin Americans and Mexicans appear to blame their legislature for failures in governance. One in five Mexicans believes that its Congress "obstructs the power of the president," a figure lower than found in many Latin American countries, including Argentina and Uruguay.[40]

Mexicans' lack of enthusiasm for the legislative branch also is reflected in their recent views on a significant role for ordinary citizens in the legislative process. Three-quarters or more of all Mexicans believe strongly in direct democracy, indicating that a majority of citizens should be able to reject laws approved by deputies and senators and that they should be able to initiate legislative proposals.[41] The strength of these beliefs among ordinary Mexicans suggests how democratic consolidation has socialized the populace to a Mexican version of democratic processes, while maintaining largely traditional views of many aspects of weaker governmental institutions, namely the federal legislative branch.

The legislative branch can also be viewed more broadly as an important source of political patronage and as a training ground for future political leaders. It has been used in the past to reward people prominent in quasi-governmental interest groups and among the labor, peasant, and popular professional sectors.[42] Among some opposition parties from 2000 to 2012, such as the PRD and the PRI, it remained the only national venue for their leaders. Professional people predominate among the legislators, but peasant and labor leaders, as well as women, who might not obtain higher political office in the executive branch, are well represented. In fact, as indicated previously, more women now serve in Mexico's Congress than in the U.S. Congress.[43] Even more important, the legislative branch provides upward mobility to a different type of politician: those who are more likely to have come from a working-class background, from the provinces (because of the district representation), from electoral careers, and with less formal education. In short, greater percentages of persons who are excluded from executive branch careers, even at mid-level, can find places in the legislative branch. The fact that some channels are open to these kinds of Mexicans, who in many background characteristics correspond more closely to the population in general, is important to social mobility and leadership fluidity. This recruitment function is more significant since 2000 because holding a national, legislative post, as we have demonstrated, is increasingly significant in the policy process. If we conceptualize a consolidated democracy as a polity characterized by increased diversity in the backgrounds of political leaders, then the legislative branch, of the three branches of government, contributes most heavily to that quality.

The legislative branch also can be described as a school for political skills. Among national government institutions, some opposition leaders and parties are represented only in the legislative branch. To date, with a few exceptions, no leading figures from the PRD have served in the executive branch at the cabinet level. Negotiating skills will be more and more valued in the decision-making process as legislative seats remain divided among the three major parties. Most officials in the executive branch have little or no experience in such skills; hence persons whose careers have brought them through the legislative bodies are likely to be in greater demand in the future.

THE JUDICIAL BRANCH

A major principle in the U.S. government structure is the balance of power. The founding fathers were concerned that the executive branch might take on dictatorial aspects and hence sought to apportion power among the executive, legislative, and judicial branches in such fashion that none would dominate. Mexico's judicial branch, while sharing some structural similarities to its counterpart in the United States, plays a significantly different role in governance. The constitution of 1917 assigns the Supreme Court power over the judicial structure, which consists of the Supreme Court, circuit courts, and district courts.

The Supreme Court, according to Article 94, consists of twenty-one justices. When it meets, its hearings are open to the public, except in special cases. Justices are appointed by the president of Mexico with the approval of the Senate. Circuit court judges and district court judges are appointed by the Supreme Court to a four-year term, after which they may be reappointed. Each justice is responsible for a certain number of circuit and district courts, and is required to inspect them periodically to ensure they are performing their duties as prescribed by law.

A judicial branch influences the decision-making process when it is independent of legislative and executive authority and when it can legislate through judicial rulings. Mexico's legal system is less adversarial than that of the United States, and was designed to supplement a system of administrative laws and procedures, thus channeling legal conflicts into this domain, that is the executive branch, rather than the judicial system. The federal court system considers legal disputes that arise out of actions or laws by government authorities that violate individual guarantees spelled out in the constitution, actions or laws by federal authorities that encroach on the sovereignty of states, and actions or laws by states that invade federal authority. Legislating through judicial precedent had not been a viable procedure in Mexico until 1994. For the Supreme Court to establish a binding precedent, it was required repeatedly to reach identical conclusions about precisely the same issue. In other words, the decision would only affect the appealing party, not any other citizen. The high bench typically has ruled on appeals of individual persons, not on matters of constitutionality, and they have only rarely ventured into political issues.

The remaining serious limitation of the judicial system is that the lower levels are tainted by corruption and outside political manipulation.[44] An absence of consistency and integrity makes it difficult, if not impossible, for the average citizen to resort to the system to protect his or her rights. The criminal justice subsystem has incorporated the use of torture in obtaining confessions. These circumstances combine to create a lack of respect for the law, a crucial element in a viable legal system and democracy.

How does the average Mexican view the culture of law in Mexico, the justice system, and the likelihood that they will receive appropriate treatment in the legal system? Recent surveys suggest serious reservations among Mexicans about the legal system as well as a distorted view of the legal process and their own behavior in response to the law. The range of statements in Table 7-3 captures numerous facets of Mexican interpretations of justice and their legal system. The answers reveal three components of Mexican attitudes toward the justice system. First, little confidence exists among nearly all Mexicans that they would be treated fairly by the court system in Mexico. Second, few Mexicans view the courts as adequately performing their constitutionally assigned responsibilities. Third, despite their largely negative views of the judicial process, they do not view accused individuals as innocent until proven guilty, as is the case in the United States, and furthermore, typically believe the accused should be incarcerated. In the Western Hemisphere, Americans have the highest regard for the criminal justice system, along with such countries as Jamaica, Panama, Colombia, and Canada, whereas Mexicans are at the very bottom, along with Ecuador and Peru. Two of the most influential variables that adversely affect Mexican and Latin American views of the judicial process are having been a victim of crime and one's perception of the level of corruption or crime. Furthermore, the level of confidence one has in the executive branch, and the national police specifically, also impacts on trust in the judicial process.[45]

Table 7-3 Mexicans Views of Justice and the Culture of Law

Questions or Statements	Percentage Agreeing
Do you believe justice in Mexico is prompt, complete and impartial as set forth in the Constitution?	14
In Mexico, laws benefit the criminals.	48
Are you confident you would be treated fairly if you were accused of a crime?	22
The Supreme Court has fulfilled its constitutional tasks in an effective manner.	18
Laws in Mexico apply equally to everyone.	12
When an individual is declared guilty of committing a crime, he has done so voluntarily.	13
When a person is suspected of committing a crime he should be considered guilty until demonstrating his innocence.	41
While awaiting trial, should a person be jailed?	56
If a family member or close friend commits a crime and only you know about it, should you report him to the authorities?	59
Did you know that the state is obliged to provide you with a public defender if you were on trial?	44

Source: "Presunta justicia," four hundred respondents, +/–4.9% margin of error, February 12–16, 2011, www.parametria.com.mx.

A second broad issue that affects the culture of law is citizen attitudes toward legality and illegality. For example, a fourth of all Mexicans have indicated that purchasing something without a receipt in order to avoid paying the sales tax does not violate the law. Other examples of behavior that 15 to 20 percent of Mexicans did not consider illegal included throwing trash on the street, buying pirated goods, and not using a seatbelt.[46] A deeper exploration of typical attitudes toward obedience to the law and one's conceptualization of corruption suggests the degree to which ordinary Mexicans either encourage or tolerate violations of the law, making it more difficult to enforce the law and to eliminate corrupt behavior at all levels of society and among governmental and nongovernmental institutions. Responses supportive of changing attitudes toward the application of the laws and a reduction in corruption suggest that Mexicans overwhelmingly recognized bribery as a corrupt act that should be punished. Similarly, small acts of disobeying the law, such as riding public transportation without paying, are viewed as unacceptable. However, a series of other responses suggest difficulties legal reforms alone cannot address. Most important of these are Mexicans' lack of respect for legal and governmental institutions, viewed as arbitrary and disrespectful toward individual citizens. Finally, three out of ten Mexicans consider fellow citizens who obey the laws when there are no consequences for doing so as foolish or stupid, thus establishing a cultural norm encouraging the opposite behavior. Moreover, laws are unquestionably viewed as having a clear social class bias.[47] These attitudes have led the most perceptive scholars of corruption and the law to argue that authoritarianism may have created the lack of respect for the law, but democracy in practice has not only failed to reverse this pattern, but seems to have actually exacerbated it.[48]

The public's feelings of the inadequacy of judicial institutions, especially in smaller, rural communities, or in poor neighborhoods in metropolitan areas, has produced a significant increase in vigilantism in the past decade.[49] From 1984 to 2001, nearly three hundred cases of actual or attempted lynching occurred in Mexico. Roughly a fifth of Mexicans actually openly expressed "support for vigilante justice."[50] Citizens who are most likely to support such non-system solutions to crime have low confidence in governmental institutions and high levels of interpersonal trust. Finally, another aberration in the citizen views of justice is the acceptance or encouragement of illegal behavior by authorities in pursuit of criminals. Mexicans and Americans share a similar view on this issue, with seven out of ten citizens agreeing the "authorities should always respect the law."[51] This response is particularly significant given the fact that police, especially before the democratic consolidation began, rarely have conformed to such a standard, and that the level of criminal violence, perceived or real, remains at the all-time highest level. Their response to this question suggests contradictory responses or incomplete understanding of the rule of law. High levels of interpersonal trust, low perception of insecurity, and lower levels of victimization all contribute to higher levels of support for authorities respecting the law.

The Supreme Court began to take on a more influential role in the governing process after 1994, when a series of judicial reforms were introduced. The first of these reforms, passed with the support of the PAN, altered the control that the president exercised over Supreme Court appointees, requiring that he obtain a two-thirds majority in the Senate and that appointees could not hold influential political office in the year immediately prior to their nomination. Even more important, the law introduced a new form of judicial review, the "action of unconstitutionality," which allowed the court to declare laws or administrative acts unconstitutional. If a required number of justices support the decision, it becomes the law for all citizens. Only specified government officials and legislators may initiate this type of case.[52]

Symbolically, the court's independent and activist role began to receive attention from the public when it "stunned Mexicans by ruling against Zedillo in a dispute with Congress [similarly increasing the autonomy of the legislative branch]. The court ordered Zedillo's administration to release records from Banco Unión, which was part of a massive government bailout of failed banks in 1995."[53] Under Fox, the court blocked the president's attempt to make minor changes to the rules on private electricity generation.

The data presented in Table 7-4 support the conclusions of recent scholars that the Supreme Court indeed has become an effective political force in Mexico. This new role is indicated dramatically in the increase of constitutional cases, using the actions of unconstitutionality law, since Fox became president. Furthermore, the rulings themselves show a dramatic increase in favor of the plaintiff versus the government, from only 2 percent

Table 7-4 Recent Decisions by Mexico's Supreme Court

Important Cases	1994–1997	1997–2000	2000–2003	2006
Constitutional controversies	3	3	23	34
Actions of unconstitutionality	9	14	20	38
Totals	12	17	43	72

Source: Julio Ríos-Figueroa, "Fragmentation of Power and the Emergence of an Effective Judiciary in Mexico, 1994–2002," *Latin American Politics and Society* 49, no. 1 (April 2007): 42; "Observatorio Judicial," *Este País,* June 2007, 62.

from 1995 to 1997 to 9 percent from 1997 to 2000 to 25 percent from 2000 to 2003.[54]

President Fox made the institutionalization of the legal system a hallmark of his first months in office by refusing to settle a dispute in a state electoral body, instead referring it to the Supreme Court, which ruled in favor of the Federal Electoral Institute. Furthermore, he openly praised the high court, assuring Mexicans that it has not received a political line from any source.[55] Fox also proposed additional reforms to the justice system in 2004, including making legal proceedings public, introducing plea bargaining, and making the attorney general's office a strictly investigative agency.[56] But as Julio Ríos-Figueroa, a leading student of the judiciary, suggests, while it was the judicial reforms that were most important in changing the justices' behavior, "they modified their behavior after noticing the change in the distribution of power among political parties in the two elected governmental branches: the legislative and the executive. The emergence of an effective judiciary in Mexico is linked to the increment in the degree of fragmentation in the elected branches of government."[57]

The most important reforms to date can be attributed to the Calderón administration, which began implementing a revolutionary judicial reform on a state-by-state basis in 2008. The most critical component of this reform are radical renovations in criminal trials, introducing the system of oral trials, an adversarial culture, and a criminal process which requires evidence beyond the traditional suspect confession, typically forced from an individual through police abuse. As the most comprehensive survey of the implementation of all aspects of the judicial reform concluded, they "involve sweeping changes to Mexican criminal procedure, greater due process protections, new roles for judicial systems operators, and tougher measures against organized crime. . . . However, by no means do recent reforms guarantee that Mexico will overcome its current challenges and develop a better criminal justice system." The authors argue that success will depend less on these procedural changes and more on efforts to address other long-standing issues associated with traditionally weak and corrupt institutions.[58] Calderón's government also produced another important reform in 2011, which broadens the *amparo*, the most important writ (somewhat similar to that of habeas corpus) assigning constitutional rights to ordinary citizens.[59]

It is apparent that the court has taken a more activist role, and it has further strengthened the circuit courts, giving them complete autonomy to decide the constitutionality of local laws.[60] Over time, it has decided on an increasing number of cases, which increased dramatically from 2000 to 2006. In 2006 alone, the number of cases far exceeded those in the previous three years combined (see Table 7-4). Despite these significant changes, the judicial system faces an uphill battle against a criminal justice system and police agencies riddled with corruption.[61]

FEDERALISM

Technically, Mexico's 1917 constitution established a federal system, which allocated certain rights to states and municipalities. The basic structure of municipal and state governments is established in Article 115. Each municipality is governed by a municipal president and a council chosen by direct popular election. Municipalities are autonomous in the administration of their finances, but the taxes they collect are decided upon by the state legislatures, not the municipality itself. Similarly, governors and state legislatures are chosen by direct popular election. The same prohibition against reelection applies to governors (who are elected for a six-year term) and municipal presidents (who are elected for a three-year term) as applies to the presidency.

Historically, the federal executive branch, similar to its control over the other national branches of government, exercised highly centralized control over the states and municipalities. Prior to 1994, it accomplished this control in several ways. First, in terms of state political leadership, the president typically chose or influenced the choice of state governors. It is important to recall that no governor from an opposition party won office from 1929 to 1989, thus giving the PRI a monopoly over state governments. The governor of each state exercised control over the legislative and judicial systems analogous to presidential control over the federal branches of government. Moreover, the relationship between municipal leadership and the state executive branch was equally analogous to the relationship between the federal executive and state leadership.

Fiscal policy was an equally important variable in determining the subordinate relationship among local, state, and federal authorities. According to students of intergovernmental fiscal relations, a decision reached at the 1947 national tax convention became the driving force behind the loss of local autonomy. That meeting "proposed that local governments be given exclusive authority to the federal government in exchange for a guaranteed share of federal tax revenues. In later years, the federal government further concentrated financial authority in its hands," culminating in the creation of a National Tax Coordination System, which guaranteed states a share of the federal value added tax provided they relinquished authority over additional state-level taxes.[62] Although the constitution did not force state politicians to accept this offer, given the PRI's monopoly over successful state and national political careers, few were willing to risk such a loss in revenues. Essentially, given the extensive control the federal government had over the allocation of tax revenues, it basically could determine the funding for most government initiated projects at the state and local levels, accounting for 85 percent or more of the public revenues. Since the 1920s, the federal government has often allocated a disproportionate share of income to the wealthier states, thus reinforcing their economic position, while simultaneously depriving poorer states adequate funding. Beginning in the 1990s, this pattern changed, and poorer states began receiving larger shares of federal funds.

The fundamental issue in decentralizing decision-making from the federal to the state and local level since the PRI's monopoly was broken is the distribution of fiscal resources. Shortly before the end of the Zedillo administration, the governors collectively, in collaboration with the legislative leaders from the PAN, PRD, PT (Labor Party), and PVEM (Ecologist Green Party of Mexico), asked the federal executive branch to set aside more monies for the states. Public sentiment also favors the federal government allocating more of its revenues to the states to decide how those monies should be spent. The federal executive's position is enhanced in the overall process because revenues are collected by the executive branch and then reallocated back to the states. Under multiple party control since 1997, Congress has changed these figures twice, reducing the federal portion to 75 percent. By 2004, the federal government was transferring 31 percent of the national budget directly to the states. Municipalities depend on the federal government for two-thirds of their total funds.[63] The first examination of the revised federal revenue system concluded that regional disparities in the 1990s and the early 2000s were gradually being reduced, while at the same time arguing that further decentralization might actually limit this process rather than allowing a central authority to redistribute resources to the poorest entities.[64]

Recent scholarship also demonstrates the important relationship between democratic electoral politics and public works on the local level. Alone, competitive elections introduced by democratization is not adequate to alter budget behavior, but it has been demonstrated that alternating control over municipalities does influence positively local investment in public works.[65] In spite of the increased percentage of monies over which local governments have control, in reality it appears that state administrations continue to exercise influence over most of those allocations. The only significant source of revenue over which cities have exclusive control are local property taxes, but the amounts are paltry by United States standards.[66] Developed economies typically collect 3 to 4 percent of GDP at the local level, while in Mexico the figure falls below 0.4 percent and in numerous municipalities is 0.2 percent.[67] Whether or not municipalities or states control a larger share of local funds, the presence of those funds have attracted greater interest in municipal decision-making while at the same time producing unwanted or unexpected consequences, including the inability of local authorities, often lacking in technical and financial training, to administer those funds effectively.[68]

Increased control over a larger share of revenues provides an incentive for individuals, institutions, and groups to seek help from state governments and to influence the outcome of state legislation beneficial to their interests. In 2001, states were providing on average only 5.6 percent of their own revenue for their yearly budgets.[69] By the 2010 census, those figures reached 21 percent.[70] Since 2000, states increasingly have exerted an influence on national policy, especially fiscal policy. In 2002, a group of twenty-two governors from the PRI and PRD formed a National Conference of Governors (CONAGO) to lobby the executive branch and Congress for more funds and to continue increasing the percentage of transfers. This organization included governors from all three parties and initially became a significant voice in federal-state relations. By 2005, state governorships were roughly divided between those controlled by the PAN and PRD and those controlled by the PRI. The PRI increased its control by 2012 to twenty out of thirty-two, with more states undergoing alternation in party control during the Calderón administration (as of June 2012, nine states out of thirty-two have only had PRI governors: Campeche, Coahuila, Colima, Hidalgo, México, Quintana Roo, Tabasco, Tamaulipas, and Veracruz), suggesting the continued strength of the PRI throughout the democratic transition and consolidation. The majority of governorships were controlled by parties other than the PAN from 2000 to 2012, setting the stage for policy conflicts between states and the federal government. The distribution of party control in state legislatures midway through the democratic consolidation were: 42 percent PRI, 28 percent PAN, and 20 percent PRD, with other parties capturing 1 percent of the seats and plurinominal deputies the remaining 9 percent.

Scholars view the role of governors as increasingly important in Mexican policymaking and politics, but are divided as to just how significant that influence might be in the future.[71] Those who view their role as more limited in the medium term suggest the following obstacles. First, municipalities, as suggested above, have expanded their voice and consequently their influence as a competitive, decentralized actor. Second, a majority of

PRI governors openly opposed the designation of Roberto Madrazo as the party's presidential candidate in 2006, yet failed to prevail, even after creating a dissident faction known as the Democratic Union. Third, initially CONAGO was a more influential body, but internal factions have reduced its collective strength in policy confrontations with the executive branch.[72]

Scholars who view governors on a trajectory of increased influence point to a number of alterations in federal-local processes. Rogelio Hernández Rodríguez, who has followed governors more than any other scholar, argues that the most significant strategy which governors can pursue, especially in pursuit of altering the federal government's distribution of revenues to the states, is establishing a collaborative alliance with Congress. Congress's independence of the executive allows them to modify the federal budget, thus they are a more appropriate channel for governors to pursue.[73] In many cases, as he correctly points out, and reinforced in my own research, members of Congress are beholden to their respective state governors, which enhances these relationships on a personal level.[74] The most recent scholarship also argues that governors are exercising extraordinary levels of political autonomy. Congress has been "extremely generous" in allocating funds to states, thus allowing governors to fund projects without imposing state taxes.[75] Further, they have dispensed these federal funds with little if any accountability, forcing the federal treasury to propose restrictions on how funds should be spent and require accountability. George Grayson, for these and numerous other reasons, has labeled governors as the "nation's new feudal lords."[76]

Citizen attitudes toward state and local governments suggest some interesting patterns regardless of how observers assess the political and policy impact of state and local actors. In the first place, ordinary Mexicans know even less about their local than their national political institutions. For example, in 2005 only half of all Mexicans were sure that state legislatures actually existed. Since an equal number were aware that it was the responsibility of the national Congress to make laws, it is unlikely that few would know the role of the state legislatures. Indeed, the principles of the separation of powers and federalism are not well understood by the average citizen since one-third believed the state legislature was dependent on the national Congress, and only a fourth knew definitively that it was independent of the national congress. Moreover, only 38 percent believed that Congress was independent of the president, and 36 percent believed the state legislature was independent of the governor. Interestingly, Mexicans have slightly more confidence in their state legislatures than the national Congress (30 to 24 percent), although their overall confidence in both is low, as is the case of most political institutions. What is most important, however, is that nearly twice as many Mexicans believed their state legislator is more concerned with problems in their state than their federal representative (27 versus 15 percent), suggesting the greater potential for taking their problems to their state rather than to their national representative.[77]

CONCLUSION

The rise of federalism within the context of a period of democratic consolidation has produced numerous consequences, both for political processes at the national and local level, and on Mexican attitudes toward their respective governmental institutions. Mexico's executive branch has been the largest loser in the reallocation of power among the branches of government and between federal and regional actors.

The actor with the most rapidly expanding role in policymaking at the federal level is the national legislature. Since 1997, its influence has been apparent, whether it initiates, alters, or approves legislation. The expanding role of the legislative branch contributes to a changing role in group-state relations. As the analysis of interest groups in the preceding chapter suggests, leaders are more likely to seek out individual decision makers in the executive branch, even though they are increasingly making demands through new channels on legislative leaders and committee chairs.

Mexico is rebuilding its political institutions structurally and symbolically. Many of these institutions retain vestiges from the past. Scholars view many features of Mexico, both political and economic, as a reflection of a "contradictory democracy."[78] For example, now that the electoral process is competitive, the rationale for having two hundred plurinominal deputies remains questionable. The parties, as one observer concluded, are using these positions as an internal "family affair" to place party loyalists in legislative posts.[79] Two-fifths of the lower chamber and one fourth of the senate are not accountable to any specific constituency. Despite democratic consolidation, approval ratings of Congress remained near the bottom compared to all other institutions, and Mexicans were at the top of the list among all other Latin Americans suggesting that the president should govern without the legislative branch if that body hindered government decision-making.[80]

The dramatic rise of the role of the legislative branch, while fulfilling the expectations of democratic theory, has created numerous political difficulties for Mexico's consolidating democracy. In the first congressional session (2000–2003), a stalemate emerged between the president and the

Chamber of Deputies over significant policy issues, complicated by the president's difficult relations with his own party. The PRI faction in Congress issued a statement spelling out mechanisms for improving political negotiations and achieving policy consensus between the two branches of government. Among them they included new channels for direct exchanges between the legislative and executive branches, direct dialogue between state governors and the executive branch so that state officials could present their policy preferences to the federal government, and a requirement that executive branch priorities be fully transparent to the public.[81] Fox complained that the authoritarian presidency was in danger of being "replaced with an inflexible Congress."[82] Calderón's administration repeated the pattern of his predecessor. No party won a simple majority in the 2012 election, insuring the likelihood of similar problems between the two branches of government for the next three years.

Decentralization of power has definitely increased the number of institutions, groups, and individuals desirous of influencing the decision-making process, providing them with an increasing number of avenues to affect institutions that determine actual policy outcomes. In many cases, they may continue using informal forms of access more than formal, open institutional channels, regardless of their greater opportunities. An expanded legislative and judicial role in decision-making also increases the potential of groups, less influential in the past, such as NGOs or even articulate and skillful individuals, to enhance their impact on the policy-making process. However, it is not likely in the foreseeable future for individuals to channel their demands through the legislative branch. Two out of five Mexicans cannot name any branch of government, only one in three knows the senate is part of the legislative branch, three-quarters could not name a single member of Congress, and 92 percent could not name a senator.[83] State governors also have increased their influence on national policy, adding to the expanding list of political actors.

Why has federalism produced significant changes in the distribution of decision-making authority but largely has been unsuccessful in achieving a functioning democracy as part of the consolidation process? There exists considerable agreement as to the explanations for this failure.[84] An important explanation, and perhaps the most cynical, views the institutional reforms as emanating from political and economic elites to create competition among themselves, suggesting that local activists took advantage of the fresh democratic space to introduce their own version of democracy, a version that is more in line with traditional democratic theory and a culture based on diversity. In other words, the most influential actors never intended extensive political participation at all levels, beyond that of voting.[85]

A second view is that Mexican values and attitudes are not strongly supportive of a federalist structure. Scholars speculate that political culture is an important variable, but that such a federal culture remains under-developed.[86] A third, complementary view to the first argument, also suggests that federalism dispersed power and created new spaces for democratization. It too argues that the strengthening of federalism is "not always inter-twined with the fortification of democracy. In a nutshell, federalism can be seen as enabling democracy (because it fosters pluralism and protects minorities) or as constraining it (when a minority has a veto power over the will of the majority through the Senate or local legislatures)."[87] Because the mechanisms for federalism were never developed prior to the 1990s, these newly forged mechanisms have encountered many obstacles and produced contradictions within a federal system.

NOTES

1. Stephen D. Morris, *Political Corruption in Mexico: The Impact of Democratization* (Boulder, CO: Lynne Rienner, 2009).

2. Carol Ciriaco, "Democracy in Mexico: The Past, Present and Future," Council on Hemispheric Affairs, July 18, 2011, 2.

3. George Grayson, *The Politics of Mexican Oil* (Pittsburgh, PA: University of Pittsburgh Press, 1980); and Edward J. Williams, *The Rebirth of the Mexican Petroleum Industry: Developmental Directions and Policy Implications* (Lexington, MA: Heath, 1979).

4. Miguel Alemán, 1946–1952; Adolfo Ruiz Cortines, 1952–1958; Gustavo Díaz Ordaz, 1964–1970; and Luis Echeverría, 1970–1976 were civilians and came from the Secretariat of Government.

5. See the introduction by Antonio Carrillo Flores in Eduardo Suárez, *Comentarios y recuerdos, 1926–1946* (Mexico City: Porrúa, 1977).

6. Eduardo Torres Espinosa, *Bureaucracy and Politics in Mexico: The Case of the Secretariat of Programming and Budget* (Burlington, VT: Ashgate Publishing, 1999).

7. Miguel Angel Centeño and Sylvia Maxfield, "The Marriage of Finance and Order: Changes in the Mexican Political Elite," *Journal of Latin American Studies* 24, no. 1 (February 1992): 84.

8. Francisco Gil Díaz was part of the original group of economists in the presidency in the early 1970s. He was the teacher of Pedro Aspe, the architect of economic neoliberalism under President Salinas, and was responsible for obtaining a position for Zedillo early in his career. *Proceso* (January 13, 1992), 13.

9. Torres Espinosa, *Bureaucracy and Politics in Mexico.*

10. Raúl Benítez Manaut, "La seguridad nacional en la indefinida transición: Mitos y realidades del sexenio de Vicente Fox," *Foro Internacional*, 48, no. 1–2 (January–July 2008): 184–208.

11. Soledad Loaeza, "Vicente Fox's Presidential Style and the New Mexican Presidency," *Mexican Studies* 22, no. 1 (Winter 2006): 29–30.

12. José Luis Méndez, "La oficina presidencial y el liderazgo político en México y Estados Unidos: Incertidumbre competitivo o certidumbre cooperativo?," *Foro Internacional*, 47 , no. 4 (October–December 2007): 839–67.

13. *Review of the Economic Situation of Mexico*, (December 2000), 499.

14. Carlos Tello, *La nacionalización de la banca en México* (Mexico City: Siglo XXI, 1984).

15. Roderic Ai Camp, *Entrepreneurs and Politics in Twentieth-Century Mexico* (New York: Oxford University Press, 1989), 128–33.

16. Diane E. Davis, *Urban Leviathan, Mexico City in the Twentieth Century* (Philadelphia: Temple University Press, 1994), 316.

17. Benito Nacif, "The Fall of the Dominant Presidency: Law Making under Divided Government," in Roderic Ai Camp, ed., *Oxford Handbook of Mexican Politics* (New York: Oxford University Press, 2012), 241.

18. Christopher Díaz, "Do 'Nuevo PRI' Deputies in Mexico Legislate Differently than Their 'Dinosauro' Predecessors?: A Preliminary Analysis of Bill Initiation in the Mexican Chamber of Deputies," paper presented at the Latin American Studies Association, Las Vegas, October 2004, 13.

19. Caroline Beer, *Electoral Competition and Institutional Change in Mexico*, (Notre Dame, IN: University of Notre Dame Press, 2003).

20. For examples from the Fox administration, see *El gobierno panista de Vicente Fox: La frustración del cambio*, ed. Francisco Reveles Vázquez (Mexico: UNAM, 2008).

21. María Amparo Casar, "Executive-Legislative Relations: Continuity or Change?," in *Mexico's Democratic Challenges, Politics, Government, and Society*, eds. Andrew Selee and Jacqueline Peschard (Washington, DC: Woodrow Wilson Center Press, 2010), 133.

22. Jeffrey Weldon, "The Political Sources of *Presidencialismo* in Mexico," in *Presidentialism and Democracy in Latin America*, ed. Scott Mainwaring and Matthew Shugart (Cambridge: Cambridge University Press, 1997), 225–58.

23. Benito Nacif, "The Fall of the Dominant Presidency: Lawmaking under Divided Government in Mexico," 238.

24. For excellent background on the legislative structure, see Michael C. Taylor, "Constitutional Crisis: How Reforms to the Legislature Have Doomed Mexico," *Mexican Studies* 13, no. 2 (Summer 1997): 319.

25. Roderic Ai Camp, *The Metamorphosis of Leadership in a Democratic Mexico* (New York: Oxford University Press, 2010), 51ff.

26. Alonso Lujambio, *Federalismo y congreso en el cambio político de México* (Mexico: UNAM, 1995); and Luis Carlos Ugalde, *The Mexican Congress: Old Player, New Power* (Washington, DC: CSIS, 2000).

27. Jeffrey A. Weldon, "Committee Power in the Mexican Chamber of Deputies," paper presented at the National Latin American Studies Association, Chicago, September 1998.

28. Víctor Hernández, "Legislative Work in the Chamber of Deputies: 57th, 58th, and 59th Legislatures," *Review of the Economic Situation of Mexico* (August 2005), 377.

29. Kevin Sullivan, "Gentrifying Mexico's 'Bronx': With Power Shifting, Backbenchers Mind Their Manners," *Washington Post*, April 27, 2001, A18.

30. Jordi Díez, *Political Change and Environmental Policymaking in Mexico* (New York: Routledge, 2006).

31. See my "Mexico's Legislature: Missing the Democratic Lockstep," in *Legislatures and the New Democracies in Latin America*, ed. David Close (Boulder, CO: Lynne Rienner, 1995), 17–36.

32. Rosa María Mirón Lince, "El PRI post-hegemónico: Liderazgos y decisiones en el Congreso," paper presented at the Latin American Studies Association, Las Vegas, Nevada, October 7–9, 2004, 19.

33. "Avizoran cambios en el sistema electoral," *Reforma*, April 14, 2007.

34. "Crece apoyo a reelection, pero sin convecer," 1,200 respondents, +/−2.8% margin of error, December 17–21, 2009, www.parametria.com.mx.

35. "Reducción de legisladores: Aprobación desinformada," December 2009, www.parametria.com.mx, 1–2.

36. Alberto Morales, "Diputados del país ganan más que los de Canadá y la UE," *El Universal,* June 18, 2007.

37. Dulce M. Liahut Baldomar, "The Role of the Research Services in the Modernization of the Mexican Congress," paper presented at IFLA Council and General Conference, Jerusalem, August 13–18, 2000.

38. "Evaluación legislativo," five hundred respondents, +/−4.4% margin of error, March 26–30, 2011, www.parametria.com.mx.

39. Barry S. Levitt, "Institutional Trust and Congressional Autonomy in Latin America; Expectations, Performance and Confidence in Peru's Legislature," *Journal of Politics in Latin America* 3, no. 2 (2011): 73–105.

40. Margarita Corral, "Not Happy? Blame Your Legislature," *Americas-Barometer Insights: 2009*, No. 26, 1–2.

41. "Encuesta nacional: Reforma del Congreso," Bimsa, 1000 interviews, +/−3.5 margin of error, April 1–5, 2005.

42. See Peter H. Smith, *Labyrinths of Power: Political Recruitment in Twentieth-Century Mexico* (Princeton, NJ: Princeton University Press, 1979), 217ff.

43. At the state legislative level, in 2003, women held 14 percent of the 1064 seats nationally. See Lisa Baldez's excellent "Elected Bodies: The Gender Quota Law for Legislative Candidates in Mexico," *Legislative Studies Quarterly* 29, no. 2 (May 2004): 251.

44. G. Ferreyra Orozco, "Understanding Corruption in a State Supreme Court in Central Mexico: An Ethnographic Approach," *Human Organization* 69, no. 3 (Fall 2010): 248ff.

45. Stefanie Herrmann, Dillon MacDonald, and Robert Tauscher, "Confidence in the Criminal Justice System in the Americas," *AmericasBarometer Insights: 2011*, no. 62, 4–6.

46. "Mexicanos y su contacto con la ilegalidad cotidiana," Consulta Mitofsky, March 2011.

47. CIDAC, "Encuesta valores: Diagnóstico axiológico México," February 2, 2011.

48. Stephen D. Morris, "Mexico's Political Culture: The Unrule of Law and Corruption as a Form of Resistance," *The Mexican Law Review* 3, no. 2 (2011): 327–42.

49. George W. Grayson, "Threat Posed by Mounting Vigilantism in Mexico," Strategic Studies Institute, U.S. Army War College, September 2011.

50. Daniel Zizumbo-Colunga, "Explaining Support for Vigilante Justice in Mexico," *AmericasBarometer Insights: 2010*, No. 39, 2.

51. José Miguel Cruz, "Should Authorities Respect the Law When Fighting Crime?," *AmericasBarometer Insights: 2009*, No. 19, 3–5.

52. An excellent discussion of these changes can be found in Fabrice Lehoucq et al., "Political Institutions, Policymaking Processes, and Policy Outcomes in Mexico" (Mexico: CIDE, 2005), 44ff.

53. Kevin Sullivan and Mary Jordan, "Mexican Supreme Court Refuses to Take Back Seat," *Washington Post*, September 10, 2000, A31.

54. Jodi Finkel, "Supreme Court Decisions on Electoral Rules after Mexico's 1994 Judicial Reform: An Empowered Court," *Journal of Latin American Studies* 35 (2003): 777–99.

55. "El Tribunal, última instancia ante los excesos del poder público," *Diario de Yucatán*, April 19, 2001.

56. Chris Kraul, "Fox Tries to Balance Scales of Mexican Justice," *Los Angeles Times*, March 30, 2004, A3.

57. Julio Ríos-Figueroa, "Fragmentation of Power and the Emergence of an Effective Judiciary in Mexico, 1994–2002," *Latin American Politics and Society* 49, no. 1 (April 2007): 49.

58. Matthew Ingram and David A. Shirk, *Judicial Reform in Mexico, Toward a New Criminal Justice System*, Special Report, Trans-Border Institute, University of San Diego, May 2010, np.

59. Francisca Pau Giménez, "Judicial Review and Rights Protection in Mexico: Accessing Recent *Amparo* Constitutional Reforms," paper presented at the Latin American Studies Association, San Francisco, May, 2012.

60. "Inconstitucionalidad de leyes," *Diario de Yucatán*, September 18, 2000.

61. George Grayson, "Running After a Fallen Fox," *Harvard International Review* 27, no. 1 (Spring 2005): 22.

62. Lehoucq, "Political Institutes, Policymaking Processes, and Policy Outcomes in Mexico," 47.

63. Carlos Rosales, "Mexican Federalism and Municipal Finance: Bases of Interpretation," *Review of the Economic Situation of Mexico* (April 2003), 156–61.

64. Horacio Sobarzo, "Esfuerzo y potencialidad fiscal de los gobiernos estatales en México: Un sistema fiscal representativo," *El Trimestre Económico* 73, no. 4 (October–December 2006): 809–61.

65. Carlos Moreno Jaimes, "Gasto publico y elecciones: Una explicación política," *Foro Internacional* 47, no. 2 (April–June 2007), 431.

66. Steven Barracca, "Devolution and the Deepening of Democracy: Explaining Outcomes of Municipal Reform in Mexico," *Journal of Latin American Studies* 37, no. 1 (February 2005): 28.

67. MUND, "Municipalities: Seedbed of Political Alternation in Mexico," Opinion and Policy Report, Series 10, No. 5, February 8, 2010, 6. This article also points out the fact that municipalities, in spite of the existence of the Federation of Municipalities of Mexico, are "woefully underrepresented in lobbying."

68. José Hernández-Díaz and Anabel López Sánchez, "La construcción de la ciudadanía en la elección de autoridades municipales: El caso de Concepción Pápalo," *Estudios Sociológicos* 24, no. 71 (2006): 392.

69. Emily Edmonds-Poli, "Decentralization under the Fox Administration: Progress or Stagnation?," *Mexican Studies* 22, no. 2 (Summer 2006): Table 1. One needs to subtract the "state" revenues generated by the Federal District, which account for nearly half of all state revenues and 41 percent of its own revenues, completing distorting the state average.

70. www.inegi.org.mx, May, 2012.

71. Rogelio Hernández Rodríguez, "The Renovation of Old Institutions: State Governors and the Political Transition in Mexico," *Latin American Politics and Society* 45, no. 4 (Winter 2003): 97–127.

72. These arguments are carefully laid out by Magali Modoux, "Geografía de la gobernanza: La alternancia partidaria como factor de consolidación del poder de los gobernadores en el scenario nacional mexicano," *Foro Internacional* 46, no. 3 (July–September 2006): 525ff.

73. "Presidencialismo y gobiernos estatales en México," *Foro Internacional* 46, no. 1 (January–March 2006): 119–21.

74. *The Metamorphosis of Leadership in a Democratic Mexico*, "Governors: National Democrats of the Future?," 243–270.

75. Guillermo Rosas and Joy Langston, "Gubernatorial Effects on the Voting Behavior of National Legislators," *Journal of Politics* 73, no. 2 (2011): 477–93.

76. "Mexican Governors: The Nation's New Feudal Lords," Mexico under Calderón Task Force, November 10, 2010. For additional recent criticisms, see Luis Rubio, "México: ¿Cambio de regímen con los nuevos gobernadores?," *América Economía*, February 11, 2010.

77. "Percepción del Congreso de la Unión y los Congresos Estatales," 960 respondents, +/−3.2%, November 2004, www.parametria.com.mx.

78. See Jon Shefner's argument in "Development and Democracy in Mexico," *Latin American Research Review* 47, no. 1 (2012): 204.

79. Luis Carlos Ugalde, "El Congreso mexicano: Una mirada a la última década," *Este País*, (April 2001): 102.

80. Diana Orces, "Popular Support for a Government without Legislatures," *AmericasBarometer Insights: 2009*, No. 25, 1–2.

81. "La oposición exige al Presidente que ponga las bases para lograr acuerdos," *Diario de Yucatán*, March 9, 2002, www.yucatan.com.mx.

82. Richard Boudreaux, "Fox Loses Mexico Budget Battle," *Los Angeles Times*, November 21, 2004, A19; Nydia Iglesias, "The Political Scene," *Review of the Economic Situation of Mexico* (December 2004).

83. "El poder legislativo en México," 1,000 interviews from 100 legislative districts, April 23–27, 2005, +/−3.5% margin of error, www.consultamitofsky.com.mx, 2005; and "La reforma política," 1,000 interviews from 100 legislative districts, March 16–19, 2007, +/−3.1% margin of error, www.consultamitofsky.com.mx, 2007.

84. For an interesting analysis of the impact of the drug war on federalism and the judicial branch, see Juan Lindau, "The Drug War's Impact on Executive Power, Judicial Reform, and Federalism in Mexico," *Political Science Quarterly*, 126, no. 2 (2011): 177–99.

85. John Stolle-McAllister, "What *Does* Democracy Look Like? Local Movements Challenge the Mexican Transition," *Latin American Perspectives* 32, no. 4 (July 2005): 33.

86. John Kincaid and Richard L. Cole, "Citizen Attitudes Toward Issues of Federalism in Canada, Mexico, and the United States," *Publius, The Journal of Federalism* 41, no. 1 (2010): 71–72.

87. Alain De Remes, "Democratization and Dispersion of Power: New Scenarios In Mexican Federalism," *Mexican Studies* 22, no. 1 (Winter 2006): 197.

8

Expanding Participation: The Electoral Process

> The victory of the PAN at the presidential level is a watershed in Mexico's political history. On one level, it marks the conclusion of a prolonged transition to democracy. The election of Vicente Fox is in effect the last brick in the centripetal path to democracy, one started at the local level and gradually moved toward the center. By accepting its defeat, the PRI acknowledged that fair elections are now the only legitimate means of gaining access to power. Although this seems obvious and simple, it is quite a substantial accomplishment if one considers that only a few years ago there was not a general and accepted consensus in the country on this matter.
>
> YEMILLE MIZRAHI, *"From Martyrdom to Power"*

A little over two decades ago, most political analysis would have given little space to elections and electoral politics in Mexico. Elections have been a feature of the political landscape since the time of Porfirio Díaz, but with the exception of Francisco Madero's election in 1911, they never functioned as the crucial determinant of political leadership or furnished a policy mandate.

Beginning in the mid-1970s, elections took on a new dimension. At first, the uncharacteristic emphasis could be tied to the desire of some establishment figures to strengthen the PRI's image and that of the political system by promoting the opposition's fortunes. In essence, the government itself, through a series of electoral reforms, tried to stimulate the opposition. It provided opposition parties with an incentive to challenge the PRI's dominance by increasing their potential rewards but without extending the possibility of real victory.

ELECTORAL REFORMS

Some government strategists believed it was smart politics to increase opposition representation in the Chamber of Deputies through implementation of a plurinominal deputy system (deputies selected on the basis of their party's total regional vote); others were committed to actual reforms. The latter, who hoped to democratize the elections, believed that genuine competition would strengthen the political model and increase participation, a change for which they believed Mexicans were ready.

The 1977 reforms, incorporated into the Federal Law of Political Organizations and Electoral Processes (LOPPE), altered several constitutional provisions. The law increased majority districts for federal deputies (similar to United States congressional districts) from approximately two hundred to exactly three hundred seats. It also specified that an additional one hundred seats be assigned to opposition parties in the Chamber of Deputies through a complex mathematical formula that allocated seats proportional to each party's national vote totals. In effect, this meant that opposition parties, after the LOPPE went into effect, garnered approximately 26 percent of the seats in the lower house and were guaranteed a minimum of one-quarter of all the seats.

These reforms, designed to increase the presence of opposition party representatives in the legislative branch, essentially the only prominent political position available to members of those parties, produced an unintended consequence that continues to affect the composition of the legislative branch to the present. The most important opposition party during these years was the PAN, which "collectively, from 1949 to 1988, nearly forty years, . . . was only able to win 47 competitive district seats, reinforcing ties between their candidates and their local district constituencies, compared to 282 party seats, accounting for 86 percent of all PAN congressional seats."[1] This distortion in representation enhanced the control of the PAN's central party leadership in Mexico City, who were and remain responsible for choosing the party and plurinominal deputy lists. This pattern was replicated among PRD and PRI members of Congress, and affected significantly the composition of the legislative branch since plurinominal deputies typically are longtime professional politicians with strong ties to party leadership.

In 1986 de la Madrid introduced his own electoral law, including the following provisions, which had significant consequences in the 1988 presidential elections:

1. The winning or majority party is never to obtain more than 70 percent of the seats in the lower chamber.

2. The seats allotted to deputies on the basis of a proportional percentage of their total national vote are to be increased from one hundred to two hundred, increasing the total number of seats from four hundred to five hundred (three hundred by district and two hundred by proportional representation).

3. Opposition parties may obtain 40 percent (two hundred of the five hundred) seats without winning a single majority district.

4. The party winning the greatest number of majority seats would retain a simple majority in the entire chamber; that is, the party would be allotted additional seats through the proportional representation system.[2]

The law increased the opposition's presence in the Chamber of Deputies, but it was an increase *allocated by the government*, rather than an increase that the government permitted the opposition to earn.

It can be argued that economic and political conditions did more to boost opposition fortunes and to give elections greater political importance in Mexico than did internal reforms during this interim. Leading students of how the PRI maintained its monopoly, and why it lost it, have focused on two explanations. The PRI's monopoly on incumbency provides the leading political explanation. The underlying economic argument is that "government ownership of economic assets declined so rapidly that in 2000 public enterprise accounted for just 5.5% of the GDP, almost half of what it was during the previous presidential election, and almost one-fifth of its share of the economy at its height seventeen years earlier. At the same time, the electoral code for 2000 made the parties more reliant on legal public funding by explicitly forbidding contributions from government entities and sharply reducing the limit on private contributions. Although illicit campaign funding remained [as it does today], it fell far short of the PRI's wholesale use of public funds for partisan purposes in prior years."[3]

The imposition of PRI victories on the subnational level reached a high point with the gubernatorial and local elections in the state of Chihuahua, a next-door neighbor of Texas. Ciudad Juárez, one of Mexico's largest cities, lies on the border and traditionally was a PAN stronghold. The PRI claimed victories in the state capital and in Ciudad Juárez, as well as in the state gubernatorial race.[4] The scope of fraud was so great and citizen resistance so palpable that prominent intellectuals and Catholic bishops denounced the results in a full-page ad in Mexico's leading daily, *Excélsior*, calling for the election to be annulled. As mentioned earlier, northern bishops announced they would cancel masses if the federal government did not respond. The Vatican delegate to Mexico, at the prompting of Mexico's secretary of government, persuaded the clergy to withdraw their threat.[5]

The overall political environment laid the groundwork for the most significant change in the PRI and led to the events that characterized the 1988 presidential election, a benchmark in Mexican electoral politics. Certain persons in the establishment leadership, in disagreement with the economic direction of the de la Madrid government and the timidity of his reforms, attempted a reform of the party's structure. In 1986 they constituted themselves as the Democratic Current. Among the most prominent members were Cuauhtémoc Cárdenas, son of President Lázaro Cárdenas, the major political figure in the 1930s, and Porfirio Muñoz Ledo, former president of the National Executive Committee of the PRI. They and other PRI dissidents formed the National Democratic Front (FDN), selecting Cárdenas as its presidential candidate. Because the FDN joined the race too late to have its credentials legally recognized, several of the PRI's tiny splinter parties selected Cárdenas as their nominee, thus giving the FDN a place on the ballot.

THE DEMOCRATIC TRANSITION AND THE 1988 AND 1994 PRESIDENTIAL ELECTIONS

The electoral process during the democratic transition from 1988 to 2000 is characterized by three important patterns that established a template for how this process contributed to the consolidation of Mexican democracy from 2000 to the present. Most important is the fact that 1997 marks the date when the party in charge of the executive branch no longer can achieve a simple majority of the vote in the legislative branch. Indeed, since 1997, no party—and the PRI came closest to this in 2009—has been able to muster a simple majority of deputies in the Congress without forming alliances. Second, despite the declining fortunes of the PRI during these twelve years, most clearly demonstrated in 1988 and 1997, no clear opponent is established as the victor during these years. Third, the pace of electoral reforms increases, and moves from a dominant majority initiated strategy of encouraging increased electoral opposition, so as to give the impression of an electoral democracy, to structural reforms which impact on the quality and fairness of the electoral process.

The 1988 presidential election illustrated a longtime pattern in Mexican electoral politics: The strongest opposition movements were often led by dissidents from within the PRI. As will be seen in the brief histories of leading major opposition parties, most were founded by persons who abandoned government leadership because of policy and personal disagreements. This was true of the PAN and the PRD. Opposition party building did, however, include grassroots components, too, especially during the democratic transition era.

The 1988 presidential election took place when the government and the PRI were at a low in terms of their legitimacy among Mexicans. The selection of Salinas as the PRI candidate, the least popular choice among party leaders, further eroded the PRI's position. Given these conditions, the opposition began a vigorous campaign against Salinas. The PAN selected a charismatic businessman from the north, Manuel J. Clouthier, who provided energetic, if somewhat bombastic, leadership during the contest. Cárdenas was off to a rocky start, but with his name recognition, notably in rural Mexico, he began to build a strong following. Three leftist parties, which typically had attracted only small numbers of Mexican voters (see Table 8-1), eventually joined Cárdenas's battle against the PRI candidate: the Popular Socialist Party (PPS), the Cardenista Front for National Reconstruction Party (PFCRN), and the Mexican Socialist Party (PMS). Of the eight parties on the 1988 presidential ballot, four supported Cárdenas.

To most analysts' genuine surprise, the populist and leftist Cárdenas alliance generated a widespread response among Mexican voters. Cárdenas, according to official tallies, received 31 percent of the vote, the highest figure given to an opposition presidential candidate since the revolution; Salinas obtained 51 percent, barely a simple majority; and Clouthier captured 17 percent, the typical PAN percentage in a presidential election. Contrary to most observers' expectations, the left, not the right, altered the face of the election. In effect, the 1982 voters who defected from the PRI six years later cast their ballots for Cárdenas, not the PAN.

It is important to remember that the 1988 election took place under the 1986 law, which allowed, for the first time, the majority party (the PRI) to increase its representation in the Chamber of Deputies from some of the two hundred plurinominal seats. The PRI needed to implement the provision because it obtained only 233 majority district seats, 18 short of a simple majority of 251. It allocated itself 27 plurinominal seats, which added to the 233 majority district seats gave it a slight majority (260 out of 500). Table 8-1 illustrates the extraordinary shift in the parties' representation in the legislative branch. Until 1988 the highest percentage of seats obtained by the opposition, combining majority districts and plurinominal seats, was 28 percent. In 1988, however, the opposition achieved 48 percent of the total, a 71 percent increase in just three years.

Most observers of the 1988 election believe that the PRI engaged widely in fraudulent practices. Some—PRD figures among them—believe that Cárdenas actually won. The majority, however, although agreeing with charges of fraud, believe that Salinas actually did win—but that his percentage of the total vote was lower.

Table 8-1 Seats in the Chamber of Deputies by Party, 1949–2012

Year	PRI	PAN	PPS	PARM	PDM	PSUM	PS[f]	PRT	PMT	PRD	PT	PVEM	Totals
1949 Districts	142	4	1	—	—	—	—	—	—	—	—	—	147
1952[b] Districts	152	5	2	—	—	—	—	—	—	—	—	—	159
1955 Districts	155	6	1	—	—	—	—	—	—	—	—	—	162
1958[b] Districts	153	6	1	1	—	—	—	—	—	—	—	—	161
1961 Districts	172	5	1	—	—	—	—	—	—	—	—	—	178
1964 Districts	175	2	1	—	—	—	—	—	—	—	—	—	178
Party	—	19	10	4	—	—	—	—	—	—	—	—	36
1967 Districts	177	1	0	0	—	—	—	—	—	—	—	—	178
Party	—	16	9	5	—	—	—	—	—	—	—	—	34
1970 Districts	178	0	0	0	—	—	—	—	—	—	—	—	178
Party	—	20	10	5	—	—	—	—	—	—	—	—	35
1973 Districts	189	4	—	1	—	—	—	—	—	—	—	—	194
Party	—	21	10	6	—	—	—	—	—	—	—	—	37
1976 Districts	195			2	—	—	—	—	—	—	—	—	197
Party	—	20	12	9	—	—	—	—	—	—	—	—	41
1979 Districts	296		4	—	—	—	—	—	—	—	—	—	300
Plurinominal	—	39	11	12	10	18	10	—	—	—	—	—	100
1982 Districts	299	—	1	—	—	—	—	—	—	—	—	—	300
Plurinominal	—	50	10	0	12	17	11	—	—	—	—	—	100
1985 Districts	289	9	—	2	—	—	—	—	—	—	—	—	300
Plurinominal	—	32	11	9	12	12	12	6	6	—	—	—	100
1988[c] Districts	233	38	4	5	—	—	5	—	—	15			300
Plurinominal	27	65	27	24	—	—	46	—	—	11	—	—	200
1991 Districts	290	10	—	—	—	—	—	—	—	—	—	—	300
Plurinominal	31	80	12	14	—	—	23	—	—	40	—	—	200
1994 Districts	277	18	—	—	—	—	—	—	—	5	—	—	300
Plurinominal	23	101	—	—	—	—	—	—	—	66	10	—	200
1997 Districts	164	65	—	—	—	—	—	—	—	70	1	—	300
Plurinominal	74	57	—	—	—	—	—	—	—	55	6	8	200
2000 Districts	131	141	—	—	—	—	—	—	—	28	—	—	300
Plurinominal[d]	78	67	—	—	—	—	—	—	—	23	9	15	192
2003 Districts	163	80	—	—	—	—	—	—	—	55	—	—	298
Plurinominal[e]	62	73	—	—	—	—	—	—	—	40	6	14	198
2006 Districts[g]	65	137	—	—	—	—	—	—	—	96	2	—	300
Plurinominal	41	70	—	—	—	—	—	—	—	36	9	17	173
2009 Districts[h]	184	70	—	—	—	—	—	—	—	39	3	4	300
Plurinominal	53	73	—	—	—	—	—	—	—	31	10	17	184

Source: Adapted from Héctor Zamitiz and Carlos Hernández, "La composición política de la Cámara de Diputados, 1949–1989," *Revista de Ciencias Políticas y Sociales* 36 (January–March 1990): 97–108; "Electoral Analysis: How the Votes were Cast," *Review of the Economic Situation of Mexico* (July 2000), 257–263.

[a]PRI = Institutional Revolutionary Party; PAN = National Action Party; PPS = Popular Socialist Party; PARM = Authentic Party of the Mexican Revolution; PDM = Democratic Mexican Party; PSUM = Mexico's United Socialist Party; PST = Socialist Workers Party; PRT = Revolutionary Workers Party; PMT = Mexican Workers Party; PRD = Democratic Revolutionary Party; PVEM = Green Party.

[b]Three other seats were won by members of the Federación de Partidos Populares Mexicanos and the Partido Nacionalista Mexicano.

[c]Three deputies were classified as independents, and one deputy among the PRD majority transferred his loyalty to the PRD after being elected on the PRI ticket.

[d]The Convergence for Democracy (part of the PRD Alliance for Mexico), obtained three seats; the Nationalist Society Party (part of the PRD Alliance for Mexico), obtained three seats, and the Social Alliance Party (part of the PRD Alliance for Mexico), obtained two seats.

[e]The Convergence for Democracy obtained five seats.

[f]The PST changed its name to the PFCRN (Cardenista Front for National Reconstruction Party) in 1988.

[g]All other parties combined won twenty-seven plurinominal seats.

[h]All other parties combined won sixteen plurinominal seats.

The 1988 elections appeared to suggest the end of Mexico's one-party-dominant system, the increased importance of pluralism in the political culture, and, as suggested in Chapter 7, the greater importance of the legislative branch, where the PRI would have to negotiate with the opposition to obtain alliances sufficient to gain passage of major legislation. The 1988 elections were a departure from a pattern, but the 1991 congressional elections temporarily dampened expectations of a permanent augmentation of opposition strength.

Nevertheless, the 1994 presidential elections established a new benchmark in the Mexican electoral process. In some ways, they were just as important as the 1988 elections to the democratic transition, and in creating a favorable context for the crucial 2000 elections. First, the political context was more challenging and less stable than in 1988. Beginning with the surprise uprising of the Zapatista Army of National Liberation on January 1, 1994, followed two months later by the assassination of the PRI's presidential candidate in Tijuana, Baja California, on March 23, in mid-campaign (the first presidential candidate to be assassinated since 1929), the fear of political instability became widespread among all social classes. Second, these events led to the formation of the Pact for Peace, Justice, and Democracy by eight political parties to promote electoral reforms, later approved by the Congress. In addition to these changes, the Congress altered the composition of the IFE, giving to six "citizen" councilors, who had no party affiliation, the balance of power in the eleven-member body.[6]

The election results themselves were widely anticipated not only in Mexico but abroad as well. Public opinion polls taken immediately before election day predicted a PRI victory, but what was not expected was the extraordinary turnout, 78 percent, of registered voters, the highest ever recorded in Mexico and well above national averages elsewhere; the active participation of independent voters; and the proportion of independent voters casting ballots in favor of the PRI. Most Mexicans believed that the PRI actually won these elections, an important change in the credibility of the electoral process.[7]

The presence of international and trained national observers from numerous civic and nongovernmental organizations helped validate the outcome, despite the evidence of some fraud, the lack of secrecy in casting actual ballots, and many technical violations. In retrospect, most critics agreed that although the voting on election day itself was among the cleanest in recent Mexican history, the larger electoral context, including financing and access to media, created an unfair playing field favoring the PRI's fortunes.[8]

In 1996, the PRI-controlled Congress passed further electoral reforms.[9] Among these, the IFE was further modified, becoming completely independent of government control. The General Council increased from six to nine independent citizens, party representatives were removed as voting members, and an independent was appointed head of IFE. As Armand Peschard suggests, perhaps most important among these reforms was the decision to allocate larger amounts of public monies for campaign expenditures, approximately 264 million dollars, 30 percent distributed equally among eight contending parties, and 70 percent according to their share of votes in the 1994 election.[10] The IFE provided free television and radio advertising, also allocated on the same 30/70 percent formula. Finally, for the first time in many years, majority congressional districts were reallocated to correspond more closely to shifting demographic patterns.

Prior to the 2000 presidential elections, two-fifths of Mexicans continued to believe elections would be unfair. Such attitudes toward elections were and remain crucial to Mexican conceptions of democracy, and the legitimacy of a democratic process of governance. When asked what was most important to achieve a better democracy, nearly two-thirds of all Mexicans said clean elections.[11]

THE ESTABLISHMENT OF ELECTORAL DEMOCRACY: A STEPPING STONE TO DEMOCRATIC CONSOLIDATION

Throughout the preceding chapters, frequent reference has been made to the presidential victory of Vicente Fox and the PAN in the July 2000 elections. This election is the major landmark in Mexico's political evolution for many reasons. The victory of a party other than the PRI essentially stood the Mexican political model on its head, destroying permanently the incestuous, monopolistic relationship between state and party. Such a relationship no longer exists. The future of the Mexican electoral process from 2000 forward relies heavily on the behavior and organizational strength of the three leading political parties, the PAN, PRI, and PRD, and on citizen perceptions of their candidates. It also relies on citizen views of the performance of the parties' candidates in office, particularly in executive posts.

Analysis of the PAN electoral victory in 2000 suggests a number of explanations for Vicente Fox's defeat of the PRI's candidate, the first time this party lost a presidential race since 1929. The most obvious explanations for the Fox victory are fascinating, but many of them are part of much longer-term trends in Mexican politics, trends that explain the rise of the

Map 8.1 Party Winning the Most Votes by State in the 2000 Election

opposition generally and of the PAN specifically. These trends extend back to the 1940s. Three variables contributed to the evolution that led to the 2000 PAN victory. They are regionalism, urbanization, and level of economic and social development.[12]

An examination of the four presidential elections prior to 1994, in 1946, 1952, 1982, and 1988, when the opposition was strongest, reveals that the opposition collectively obtained at least 30 percent or more of the votes in seven states: Baja California, the Federal District, Guanajuato, Jalisco, México, Michoacán, and Morelos. In 1994, the opposition dominated in México, Jalisco, Morelos, the Federal District, and Michoacán, where it won more than half of the votes cast. It also won more than 45 percent of the vote in Guanajuato, but lost Baja California, Zedillo's home state.

There are many reasons for the long opposition to the PRI in these states. For some—Baja California, the Federal District, Nuevo León, and México—growth, income, urbanization, and development are important, as they are among the seven states with the highest per capita income. Economic growth produced the most influence on opposition strength over the long term. It has been argued that economic growth and development are statistically related to election results.[13] In Mexico, when economic performance translates into higher standards of living, those who live in regions benefiting most have voted for the opposition, contrary to expectations. This pattern suggests the importance of political freedoms and a democratic polity to Mexicans who were recipients of higher incomes and greater levels of education.

Why was the opposition stronger in states benefiting economically under the PRI's long leadership? A number of reasons stand out. First, the PRI was much better organized in rural areas, and low-income states typically are the most agrarian. The PRI accentuated this relationship in the 1990s through resources allocated by Pronasol (Solidarity) and by Procampo, a peasant-subsidy program.[14] Second, educated Mexicans, who are more sophisticated about participation and more likely to vote for an opposition candidate, lived in greater numbers in high-income states. Third, supervision of voting in urban centers, often located in the high-income states, was characterized by fewer reports of fraud and hence fairer.

Since 2006, regional differences have become even more influential. They continue to represent the greatest demographic differences among the 2012 presidential candidates. For example, the PRD's candidate obtained his greatest support from the center, because he overwhelmingly received the majority of votes from the Federal District. However, his support among voters residing in the north is only two-fifths of that from the center. The PAN candidate demonstrated the reverse pattern, doing best in the north and the center-west, but poorly in the south and the center. The PRI, on the other hand, performed extremely well in the north and the center-west, well in the south, and less well in the center.

Historical experience also had much to do with the level of opposition support in various states, generally in connection with poor relationships. Strong opposition in Guanajuato, Jalisco, and Michoacán stem historically from the importance of Catholicism and church-state relations in those states during the 1920s. When the federal government strictly applied constitutional provisions relative to religion, it provoked resistance from staunch Catholics and some clergy in the region, including these three states. This movement in defense of religious rights became known as the Cristero rebellion. Memories of the events are still fresh in the minds of the people who were children in the 1920s. The region contributes heavily to the priesthood and hierarchy, and a disproportionate number of bishops at the end of the twentieth century were graduates of the Morelia seminary in the heart of Michoacán.

The long-term variables that contributed to the strength of the political opposition enhanced other, specific variables that made possible the PAN victory in 2000. Polls indicated that the PRI and PAN candidates were running neck-and-neck up to the day their campaigns officially ended. Who voted for Vicente Fox in 2000, and what were the special characteristics of the Fox voter? Attitudes toward democracy played a crucial role. Among the traditional, historical variables determining opposition support, three stood out.

Educated voters were extremely influential in determining the outcome of the 2000 presidential race: 58 percent of Mexicans who voted in that election completed a secondary or higher education. These voters cast their ballots overwhelmingly for Fox. Fox, who received 42.5 percent of the vote nationally, obtained 49, 53, and 60 percent of the secondary, preparatory, and university educated voters, respectively. In contrast, Francisco Labastida, the PRI candidate, who won 36.1 percent of the national vote, obtained only 34, 28, and 22 percent, respectively, among the same three educational categories. Labastida did quite well among voters with a sixth-grade or lower education, but they accounted for only two-fifths of the voters.

In terms of broad regions, Fox did well throughout Mexico, but especially in the north and center-west, the location of many of the same states that traditionally supported opposition parties. The most important geographic factor, however, was not found among the voters in broad, multistate regions, but among those voters who lived in areas the Mexican census classifies as urban, mixed (combined rural/urban populations), and rural, accounting for 70, 10, and 20 percent of the voters, respectively. Obviously, the party that does best among urban voters has the greatest potential for winning the largest number of votes. Fox did best among these voters, and interestingly, his pattern of support and that of his leading opponent, Francisco Labastida, were exactly the opposite of each other. Labastida did well in rural areas and poorly in urban centers. Fox did as well as Labastida in rural areas, but much better among urban voters, among whom he received nearly half of the votes.[15]

A different variable, or at least a variable that was measured for the first time, was the impact of those Mexicans who were most desirous of democracy. The growth of the opposition generally, and the change in the electoral playing field, encouraged many Mexicans' expectations about a democratic model. Those voters who believed that Mexico was not a democracy at the time of the election largely voted for the PAN. In other words, they believed a Fox victory would introduce a democratic government to Mexico.

The most significant, unique influence on the outcome of the 2000 election was the voter who favored change, an individual most willing to risk change. In a post-election poll conducted by *Reforma*, the data make it clear that change was the fundamental variable in determining voter preferences (see Table 8-2). Apparently, "change" broadly referred to a change in party control of the executive branch, a change in the political model in the

Table 8-2 Why Mexican Voters Cast Their Ballots for President in 2000

Reasons for Voting	Candidate (percentages)				
	Fox	Labastida	Cárdenas	Others	Total
His proposals	37	42	17	4	22
The candidate	28	50	18	4	9
By custom	12	82	5	1	7
Other	34	43	22	2	6
Party loyalty	8	79	12	1	5
Least bad	37	40	20	3	4
Obligation	31	56	13	0	2
Don't know	27	55	14	3	2

Source: Roderic Ai Camp, "Citizen Attitudes Toward Democracy and Vicente Fox's Victory in 2000," in *Mexico's Pivotal Democratic Election*, ed. Jorge I. Dominguez and Chappell Lawson (Stanford, CA: Stanford University Press, 2004), 33.

direction of greater pluralism, and possibly a change in the type of leadership. More than two-fifths of Mexican voters gave change as their primary reason for voting. Only a fifth indicated the candidate's proposals as significant in their choice. Of the citizens who gave change as their reason for voting, the vast majority voted for Fox. "The fact that so many Mexican voters identified with change, and that democracy permitted them to make this choice, produced the Fox victory. Mexicans were not voting for Fox, they were not voting for PAN, they were not voting for substantive policy issues; they were voting for change, conceptualized pragmatically as an alteration in power, replacing incumbent politicians and the party they represented with something different."[16]

Another group that influenced the 2000 electoral outcome was younger, first-time voters. In fact, voters who were eighteen to twenty-four made up the largest single-age cohort among Mexican voters, a "baby boomer" group. This age group accounted for 18 percent of all voters. They had high expectations for Vicente Fox; and half of these young people, many of them students, voted for the PAN. Fox did better than either of his competitors in every age group except the fifty-five-or-older Mexicans, who gave their vote disproportionately to the PRI candidate.

Significant changes in the electoral "playing field," notably public financing of the elections, media coverage of the candidates, and the independence of the Federal Electoral Institute, affected voter perceptions and participation in 2000. The most significant of these changes was public financing, which distributed the bulk of actual campaign monies more evenly among the three leading parties, based on absolute amounts for each party and on their performance in the 1997 elections. Only 10 percent of campaign funds could come from private sources. Because both the PAN and PRD formed electoral alliances, they increased their overall portion of public monies, which disproportionately favored the smaller parties. Therefore, although the PRI received the largest amount of funding for the 2000 election, some $52 million, PAN's Alliance for Change received almost the same amount. The PRD received only $4 million less than the other two parties.[17]

Fox also changed the image of the PAN, broadening its appeal politically and socially, and strengthening its grassroots appeal through a personal organization, the Friends of Fox. Much of the grassroots support for the PAN, and Fox's ability to increase the PAN's appeal geographically in Mexico, stems from the impact of his personal organization. Much of the PAN's partisan strength is recent and turned out to be tenuous, given how citizens viewed him personally and their attachment to his Friends of Fox organization, not the PAN. Furthermore, this organization became a critical source of private campaign donations, adding to the PAN's significant level of public monies.

DEMOCRATIC CONSOLIDATION AND THE ROLE OF ELECTIONS

The 2000 elections clearly demonstrated that Mexico had reached a new plateau in its democratic transition, and could be viewed as having taken the important step toward achieving a democratic political model through a competitive, electoral process. But what role have elections since 2000 exercised in assisting Mexico to accomplish the much more difficult and complex goal of achieving a consolidated, functioning democracy? The period between 2000 and 2012 suggests several important trends to keep in mind that impacted on this process. First, Mexico continued the pattern that emerged in the democratic transition where none of the leading parties controlled the legislative agenda, nor exercised control over both the executive and legislative branches simultaneously. This was the consequence of a multiple party system produced by competitive, electoral democracy. Second, the electoral process also continued to reflect the unpredictable fortunes of the three major parties as political forces in the polity. The postelectoral period was characterized by extreme fluidity of voter preferences for the three leading parties at the presidential level and increasingly at the regional level. Third, the margin of plurality by which the leading party won control of the executive branch declined significantly from 2000 to 2006 but increased slightly in 2012 from 36 to 39 percent. The extraordinary closeness of the outcome in 2006 between the PAN and the PRD accentuated electoral controversies, which tested severely the legitimacy of the democratic model and the political institutions. Fourth, and finally, electoral reforms have shifted to a stage where they attempted to address numerous issues about the behavior of parties during electoral campaigns, and specifically reflect procedural behaviors that address the type of democracy Mexicans desire.

As Mexico prepared for the 2006 presidential race, the first presidential election since its citizenry had an opportunity to experience more deeply a democratic process with a divided executive and legislative branch, a number of important patterns became apparent, many of which may have medium- to longer-term implications for politics generally. In the first place, as commentators have noted in analyzing the results of the 2003 congressional elections, Mexicans shared extremely unfavorable views of all political parties. Two-fifths of Mexicans viewed them negatively, in contrast to only one-fifth who viewed parties positively, a figure that persisted through 2012. The most negative views of political parties are shared by those who live in the south; poorer, rural, and indigenous people; independents; well-educated Mexicans; those who live in the center of the country (including the Federal District); and those who favor a PRD-controlled executive branch.

In spite of their strongly negative views of political parties, only three out of ten Mexicans considered themselves nonpartisan, although that figure increased to 40 percent of likely voters in 2006. As of 2005, the PRI claimed 28 percent of party loyalists, followed by 21 percent for the PAN and 16 percent for the PRD. However, among citizens who intended to vote in 2006, the PRI received 31 percent to the PAN's 27 percent. The PRD, on the other hand, obtained 21 percent of the support. Furthermore, in what Mexicans call the *voto duro*, those individuals who always vote for the same party, the PRI boasted an even stronger base, with 47 percent and 29 percent, respectively, intending to vote for the PRI and PAN. The PRD captured 17 percent of these likely voters. Thus the PRI had an advantage over the PAN and PRD, measured by its core support, going into the presidential election. Similar distributions of partisan support were true at the beginning of the 2012 presidential race, with the PRI boasting 33 percent, the PAN 21 percent, and the PRD only 12 percent.[18]

All parties need to attract significant support from independent voters, but the PRI needs fewer of those than does the PAN and especially the PRD. Furthermore, local and state election data make clear that loyalty to incumbent parties has declined dramatically and that voters are concerned with a candidate's performance, not his or her party label. From 1988 through 2002, incumbent parties holding mayoralty posts were at an advantage over their opponents, but that advantage declined from their winning 90 percent of the time in 1988 to only 48 percent in 2003.[19] "While the PRI continues to dominate roughly half of all municipalities, by 2006 almost 90 percent of all municipalities had seen at least one change in the governing political party, which suggests a high degree of competition. Without doubt, there is more competition in larger municipalities. All of the largest twenty-five municipalities have gone through at least one change in the political party in government. However, even in municipalities with fewer than fifteen thousand inhabitants (which are primarily rural) there is a great deal of political party competition, and over 80 percent have undergone at least one change in the party in power. This finding suggests that citizens can reward or punish the party in power for its performance at the next elections, even if not the specific mayors responsible for policies."[20]

When voters were asked to identify specific attributes with individual parties, surprisingly they made no distinctions among the three on good government or improving the future, nor significantly on the issue of being concerned with that particular ability. Major differences are associated with perceptions of corruption. Half of the respondents identified the PRI with corruption, the highest single response associated with any party. Only 14 and 12 percent, respectively, identified this variable with the PAN and the PRD. On the issue of economic growth, the PAN received stronger support, but the PRD and the PRI ranked similarly on that issue. Finally, nearly a third of the respondents identified the PRI and the PRD as conflictual compared to only 16 percent who assigned the PAN that label. As noted, independents, as they did in 2000, would determine the outcome of the 2006 election. When they were asked that same questions, they provided a decidedly different response on several crucial attributes, attributes that affected their votes in 2006. They ranked the PRI significantly lower in providing good government than the PAN or PRD, and they ranked it equally low on producing a better future, while giving higher marks to the PRD. Especially important is the fact that independents, by a huge margin, believed that the PRD was interested in people like them (32 percent compared to only 16 percent for PAN and 12 percent for PRI). Independents, similar to all voters, viewed the PAN as the party most strongly associated with economic growth and least identified with conflict.[21]

The three leading presidential candidates in 2006 were Manuel López Obrador of the PRD, Felipe Calderón of the PAN, and Roberto Madrazo of the PRI. Of the three, López Obrador was by far the most popular among the partisan voters of any party, and led in the presidential horserace in national polls for nearly two years. By the end of 2005, López Obrador and

Calderón were neck and neck among voters. For the first three months of 2006, however, López Obrador built a solid lead over his competitors, reaching 8 to 10 percentage points ahead of Calderón by mid-March. But at the end of that month, once again, the two leading candidates were in a technical tie, with Madrazo closely behind. In one respect, the 2006 election parallels that of 2000. For any candidate to win the presidency, he personally would have to attract votes and carry his party to victory, similar to Fox's achievement. The PRD's candidate, however, had to increase his party's base most dramatically, given that the PRD is a distant third among the three major parties in partisan supporters, just as it was in 2012, whereas the PAN provided Fox with a larger partisan base. As José Antonio Crespo noted, López Obrador began organizing support committees in 2005, similar to the Friends of Fox, the crucial organization in Fox's campaign success in 2000.[22] Furthermore, even in the 2004 elections, after the PRD improved its congressional representation a year earlier, it remained the most concentrated of regional parties, and in half of the states where elections took place, it received only 10 percent or fewer of the votes.

In professional aptitudes, voters in 2006 ranked Calderón and López Obrador more positively than they did the PRI's candidate, Roberto Madrazo. In 2000, the candidates' professional abilities were not important variables in determining the outcome. The electorate opened the door for another outside candidate, similar to Fox, indicating they would prefer a qualified citizen to a professional politician as their president (52 to 38 percent). They also desired a strong president who would pursue the appropriate policy even when it is unpopular. Interestingly, when asked to classify the three candidates as historical personages, half the voters identified Madrazo as a villain, and nearly a third identified López Obrador as a reformer and hero.[23]

López Obrador, as suggested earlier, took a strong lead among the presidential candidates by early 2004. One of the reasons his strength persisted is because a large percentage (42 percent) of swing voters from the other parties and independents who voted for Fox in 2000 supported him. Equally important, López Obrador initially received strong support from the middle class. Although his support began to waver, Fox, with the help of the PRI in Congress, decided in 2005 to bring legal charges against López Obrador for abusing his power as governor of the Federal District by ignoring repeatedly a court order over a right-of-way. The legal violation was clear, and the legal matter itself, by Mexican standards, minor, but the populace, and indeed many politicians, perceived the charge against López Obrador to be entirely politically motivated, so as to remove him as a potential presidential candidate (candidates may not be under formal legal proceedings). The strategy backfired completely. López Obrador revived his candidacy and became a stronger frontrunner until April 2006.

The 2006 presidential race proved to be as exciting to observers as was the case six years earlier. Despite the fact that López Obrador took an early lead—in part because he demonstrated much stronger name recognition long before Calderón became a candidate—his PAN opponent was able late in the campaign to catch up and briefly took a small lead over López Obrador in April and May, 2006. For the last six months of the campaign, the PRI nominee, Roberto Madrazo, essentially remained a static candidate with a solid but unchanging percentage of support among slightly more than one-fourth of intended voters, primarily PRI partisans. His candidacy, nevertheless, raises several implications for the electoral process. First, given the fact that Madrazo represented the traditional wing of his party, his poor showing in the race forced the PRI's leadership to struggle over the kind of candidates they hope to nominate in the future. Unlike the other two political parties, support for the PRI nationally was essentially stronger than its candidate, and its congressional candidates performed better than its presidential nominee (28 to 22 percent).

If we compare voter support for the leading candidates in 2006 with voter support for the PRI and PAN candidates in 2000, we can identify some significant strengths and weaknesses of the candidates (see Table 8-3). Fox received 43 percent of the vote in 2000, but he performed most successfully among the following groups: well-educated voters achieving high school, preparatory, and college educations (49 to 60 percent of voters); citizens residing in the north and the center-west (49 percent); younger voters, ages eighteen to thirty-nine (47 to 50 percent); and urban residents (48 percent). Among actual voters on July 2, 2006, Calderón—who obtained almost 36 percent of the vote—received strong support from younger voters (who accounted for 79 percent of all voters) under age forty-nine (38 percent), those residing in the north and center-west (43 and 47 percent), university-educated Mexicans (42 percent), higher-income voters (43 and 50 percent), urban residents (40 percent), beneficiaries of social programs (41 and 44 percent), and most decisively, those who thought their personal economic situation would improve (60 percent).[24] López Obrador, in contrast, appealed to older voters (37 percent), lower income groups (34 and 39 percent), voters on the left (62 percent), independents (43 percent), residents of the center and south (44 and 40 percent), and those Mexicans who expected their economic situation to worsen (52 percent).

The campaign itself became a crucial factor in determining the changing fortunes of the two leading candidates during the final weeks of the race. The months of April and May witnessed a change in the PRD candidate's

Table 8-3 Demographic Variables and the Presidential Vote in 2006 (Percentages)

Variable	Calderón	Madrazo	López Obrador
Gender			
Male (52%)	36	22	37
Female (48%)	38	23	32
Age			
18–29 (30%)	38	21	34
30–49 (49%)	38	21	35
50+ (21%)	34	26	37
Education			
Basic	34	29	33
Middle	37	21	35
Higher (22%)	42	14	38
Income (monthly in pesos)			
–2000	31	30	34
2000–3999	32	24	39
4000–6499	36	21	37
6500–9199	43	16	36
9200+	50	14	30
Residence			
Urban	40	20	35
Rural	31	28	36
Presidential approval			
Approved fox's performance	17	26	51
Did not approve	8	31	56
Ideology			
Left	18	16	62
Center	37	24	31
Right	48	25	24
Partisan supporters			
PRI	11	74	12
PAN	89	4	5
PRD	3	3	93
Independents (35%)	34	10	43
Region			
North	43	27	24
Center-West	47	20	27
Center	34	15	44
South	27	29	40
Beneficiaries of social programs			
Oportunidades	41	26	29
Seguro popular	44	25	26
View of future personal economic situation			
Improve	60	15	20
Same	30	24	40
Worse	12	31	52
Vote in 2000			
Fox	57	8	29
Labastida	13	64	19
Cárdenas	7	4	88
New voters	36	19	37

Source: Reforma, exit poll, 5,803 voters, July 2, 2006, $+/-1.3\%$ margin of error.

growing lead. Data from survey research reveal shifting voter preferences during this brief period. The most notable changes among voter perceptions of the candidates in those weeks include the following. First, Madrazo's strongest base of support, other than voters who supported the PRI's candidate in 2000, was among residents of the seven northern states led by PRI governors. But his support there declined dramatically after March, shifting strongly in favor of Calderón. Between the last polls in mid-June and the vote on July 2, some 20 percent of his intended voters abandoned the PRI candidate, many of them in the north. On the other hand, Calderón, whose stronghold could be found in the nine PAN-controlled states for most of the campaign, lost significant support there two months before the election, support that initially split in favor of the PRI and PRD candidates, but revived in favor of Calderón at the close of the presidential race. López Obrador witnessed declines in the PRD-controlled states and the PRI-dominated south-center states, where he polled strongest. In general terms, from March to June, López Obrador converted more support from southern Mexico and Calderón acquired increased voter preferences from the north.[25]

Unlike the presidential debates in the 2000 race, most pollsters believe the televised debates in 2006 did not produce a major shift in voter preferences, a pattern repeated in 2012. In the first debate, López Obrador, by declining to participate, reinforced a growing negative image among voters of a candidate who was arrogant, symbolized for all viewers to see by his empty podium. Calderón was perceived to have won the debate by a sizeable margin, but small party candidates benefited most. López Obrador's decision to exclude himself, combined with his rude criticisms of President Fox, helped to reinforce an aggressive, negative PAN advertising campaign painting him as a "danger to the republic."[26] Each of these factors contributed to López Obrador's decline in the polls. The second debate, in June, essentially reinforced existing voter perceptions, which already favored, once again, López Obrador, despite Calderón being perceived as the winner.[27] It is clear from Kenneth Greene's analysis of the election, that the lack of strong party attachments, and the importance of a candidate's image among voters, enhances the impact of media during the campaign to alter the views of voters significantly, thus altering presidential electoral outcomes.[28] These conclusions also demonstrate, that electoral democracies in countries such as Mexico do not mirror behavior that typifies established democracies such as the United States.

Learning a lesson from Calderón, López Obrador began his own negative advertising campaign against the PAN candidate, quadrupling his ads in May and June.[29] This led to a major decline in how voters viewed Calderón's integrity, which prior to the ads was rated the most positive of the three leading candidates. Just three weeks before the election, López Obrador (compared to Calderón) was able to reestablish himself as being most capable or characterized by the following qualities: helps people most, most able to solve problems, most able to improve voter's economic situation, and most able to combat poverty.

Despite López Obrador's stronger showing in the final polls carried out in early to mid-June, Calderón was able to eke out a narrow victory of about one half of a percentage point (.58) over his opponent (35.89 percent over 35.31 percent, or approximately 244,000 votes). López Obrador accused the PAN of electoral fraud, refusing to accept the results, and requested an official recount of the entire vote by the Federal Electoral Tribunal, Mexico's special election court, which is responsible for all election disputes. After examining the PRD's allegations, it conducted an official recount of 9 percent of the polling stations. The court released its decision in September 2006 and declared Calderón the official winner, after finding no evidence of intentional fraud, only errors by all parties typical of Mexican elections. López Obrador, and a minority of his core supporters, refused to accept the court's decision and to recognize the legality of Calderón's presidency. Other forms of fraud, however, did occur in the 2006 election, most notably vote buying, being offered something for one's vote. An extensive survey of voters concluded that 9 percent received such an offer. These forms of "voter bribery" have occurred in elections from 2009 to 2012.[30]

The 2006 elections produced several significant consequences that impacted on Mexico's effort to consolidate its democratic model. From an electoral perspective no candidate won a simple majority of the votes and no party controlled Congress. Calderón was inaugurated with the weakest mandate of any president in recent history, matched by a small plurality in the legislative branch (41 percent of the seats). Thus Mexico, as argued in the previous chapter, was characterized by frequent political impasses between the executive and legislative branches, demonstrating that such a small plurality reinforced by a three-party system has not augured well for governance or for reinforcing increasingly positive views of Mexican democracy.

The unwillingness of López Obrador and many partisans of the PRD to accept the electoral results tested the legitimacy of the Mexican electoral process and the institutions devised by successive electoral reforms to administer elections and to litigate contested outcomes.[31] This outcome repeated the pattern in 1994 and in 2000 in which the strongest partisans of the losing party views the election as fraudulent or unfair. In 2006, however, López Obrador carried this dissatisfaction to an entirely new level.[32] Nevertheless, although citizen confidence in the Federal Electoral Institute and the Federal Electoral Court initially declined, both institutions regained the confidence of the majority of Mexicans, legitimating government institutions and the processes that govern their behavior.[33] Finally, López Obrador's decision to operate as a political force outside of the PRD for the entirety of the Calderón administration led to the rapid decline of the PRD as the second major force in partisan party politics, making it more difficult for López Obrador to defeat Peña Nieto in 2012. Only 16 percent of the voters in the 2012 presidential race were PRD partisans, compared to 28 percent and 19 percent partisans of the PRI and PAN.

The 2012 elections became the first presidential elections where major changes in the electoral laws were implemented. Passed in 2007, these reforms first were applied in the 2009 elections. They include numerous, significant changes based on electoral experiences and complaints dating from 2000. The most influential of changes included: no special interest groups, such as labor unions, can be attached directly to parties; substantial cuts in the public funding for elections and a significant alteration in the funding formula for each party, of which 30 percent is an equal amount assigned to all parties and the other 70 percent is based on each party's vote totals received in the prior election; parties must present regular financial and campaign reports to the IFE; the campaign lengths have been shortened to only ninety days for congressional campaigns in presidential years and ninety days for presidential candidates, and sixty days for congressional campaigns alone; parties may only use publicly funded slots to advertise themselves to potential voters; candidates may not use language in their statements about their opponents that slanders or denigrates those individuals; and they may contribute only an additional 20 percent of the total amount they receive from the IFE.[34] A number of analysts have viewed some of these changes as impinging on democratic behavior, rather than encouraging it. For example, "slanders" and "denigrates" have not been well-defined, thus preventing candidates in the 2012 race from making more critical comments about their opponents' past performance or public policy positions.[35]

This election reinforced some electoral patterns from the two previous elections, while introducing significant new shifts in voter behavior and voting patterns. First, and most important in terms of the democratic consolidation, it returned power at the federal level back to an opposition party, the PRI. Thus, in terms of electoral democracy, it further defines Mexican political behavior in the electoral arena as democratic. Second, it demonstrates once again the fluidity of partisan support in Mexico, demonstrating that the first and second parties in each of the three races has gone from PAN/PRI, to PAN/PRD, to PRI/PRD. Each of the three major parties has been represented twice as the top two contenders. Mexican voters, as they have clearly demonstrated at the local level for the last twelve years, are pragmatic voters, who readily switch parties when their expectations are unfulfilled by those in power. The surprise expressed by many observers and analysts in Mexico that the PRI should be able to make such a comeback was unfounded. Anyone closely following the success of the party at the state and local levels throughout the Fox and Calderón administrations would have detected its underlying electoral strength, consistently representing the largest plurality of votes at both levels. The question that should have been asked about the PRI is not how could voters return the PRI to power, but rather why shouldn't they vote for the PRI?

Third, for the first time in Mexican political history, one of the three major parties, the PAN, and surprisingly the most socially conservative of the leading parties, chose a woman, Josefina Vázquez Mota, as its flag bearer. This choice was more significant than might otherwise have been the case because since 2009, women have been voting in much larger percentages than men. They accounted for 56 percent of all actual voters (41 percent of men versus 47 percent of women in 2009), and in some states, the difference between female and male voters was 10 percent.[36] In 2012, however, the split between them was only 49 to 51 percent (see Table 8-4).

Table 8-4 Demographic Variables and the Presidential Vote in 2012

Variable	Vazquez Mota	Peña Nieto	López Obrador	López Obrador 2006
	Percentages			
Gender				
Male (49%)	25	37	36	37
Female (51%)	27	41	29	29
Age				
18–29 (31%)	23	36	37	34
30–49 (44%)	27	41	30	35
50+ (25%)	28	40	30	37
Education				
Basic (49%)	24	48	26	33
Middle (21%)	28	33	37	35
Higher (30%)	29	29	39	38
Income (monthly in pesos)[a]				
–785	24	45	28	31
786–1,517	24	39	34	38
1,518–3,03423	45	29	37	—
3,035–4,551	25	41	30	32
4,552–7,585	21	38	37	33
7,586–15,170	25	36	37	34
15,171–20,000	26	35	35	31
20,000+	26	33	40	29

(continued)

Table 8-4 (*continued*)

Variable	Vazquez Mota	Peña Nieto	López Obrador	López Obrador 2006
	Percentages			
Residence				
Urban	26	37	34	35
Rural	26	44	29	36
Presidential approval (Calderón's performance)				
Yes	37	36	25	26
No	7	44	47	56
Ideology				
Left	11	20	67	62
Center	23	40	32	31
Right	36	50	13	24
Partisan supporters				
PRI	5	90	4	12
PAN	85	6	7	5
PRD	2	4	93	93
Independents (37%)	22	32	41	43
Region				
North	33	40	25	24
Center-West	29	44	25	27
Center	19	35	43	44
South	20	39	40	40
View of future personal economic situation				
Improve	55	26	17	20
Same	24	43	30	40
Worse	10	43	45	52
The most important problem in Mexico[b]				
Economy	22	35	29	—
Security	23	37	25	—
Vote in 2006				
Calderón	49	29	20	29
Madrazo	6	82	10	19
López Obrador	5	12	83	88
New voters	22	38	36	37
Reason for their vote				
Their ideas and proposals	25	42	30	—
Change	20	32	45	—
Honesty	30	20	48	—
Always for same party	25	63	11	—
Continuity	87	9	4	—
Help the people	17	50	32	—
The least bad choice	36	27	32	—

Source: Reforma, exit poll, July 1, 2012, 3,096 voters, +/−1.8% margin of error, courtesy of Alejandro Moreno.

[a]This question and the answers came from Parametría's exit polls. See Carta Paramétrica, "Cambios de perfil en los votantes de 2006 and 2012," July 1, 2012, p. 5. 6,026 voters were interviewed.

[b]This question and the answers came from Consulta Mitofsky's exit poll. See "México: 1o de julio 2012, perfil del votante," July 2012, p. 14. More than 20,000 voters were interviewed.

Fourth, the presidential elections of 2000 and 2006 clearly revealed that the campaign determined the outcome, that the individual who was in the lead at the beginning of the campaign ended the race as the runner-up on election day. In 2012, however, Enrique Peña Nieto was able to maintain his lead throughout the entire campaign, and the only change determined by the race resulted in Andrés Manuel López Obrador becoming the most important opponent of the PRI candidate, after starting in third place behind the PAN candidate, narrowing the gap to only 7 percent behind Peña Nieto. Nevertheless, 37 percent of voters made their choice during the campaign itself or on election day, and more importantly, 56 percent of those individuals who voted for López Obrador, did so during the campaign or on July 1st.[37] Fifth, once again, independent voters played a crucial role, accounting for 37 percent of the electorate. What is most remarkable about their role was the fact that they outnumbered the combined partisan voters from the PRD and PAN, and more importantly, provided two-fifths of all the voters who cast their ballots for López Obrador.

Sixth, the most interesting event in the race was determined by the use of social media, specifically the "Yo soy 132" student demonstrators, who relied on Twitter to organize themselves to protest the candidacy of Peña Nieto and the favorable manipulation of his candidacy by Televisa, the dominant national television station. Their efforts succeeded in briefly closing the gap between Peña Nieto and López Obrador in the final weeks of the campaign, but they were not able to sustain their influence nor persuade other voters in large numbers outside of their age group to support their position. Seventh, 63 percent of Mexicans voted in this election, the highest turnout for a presidential election since 1994, suggesting that an increasing percentage of Mexicans are taking their civic responsibilities seriously.

The 2012 presidential election, by comparison with the 2000 and 2006 elections, could be accurately described as bland and uninteresting. Why was Peña Nieto able to maintain his lead, largely uncontested, against the other two leading candidates? López Obrador was not able to fully capitalize on initially closing the gap in May and June, although he came much closer after the last polls just before July 1. At least three explanations help to explain his inability to defeat the PRI. The most important variable was voters' memory of the 2006 campaign. Voters were asked one week before the 2012 campaign began if they recalled the campaign accusation from PAN that "López Obrador is a danger for Mexico." Sixty-two percent remembered the phrase, and more importantly, a third of voters continued to believe that assertion was true. When voters' favorable opinions of López Obrador were subtracted from their negative opinions, he ended up with a favorable opinion of only 1 percent.[38] While López Obrador was able to actually reduce his negative ratings later in the campaign, he was not able to overcome such a substantial margin of negative views. In the final poll before the election, his negatives exceeded his positives by –9 compared to Peña Nieto's +6.[39] Second, many Mexicans, both supporters and non-supporters from 2006, were strongly disaffected with his unwillingness to accept the electoral outcome for years after the Federal Electoral Court's decision. Indeed, the level of dissatisfaction with his behavior is reflected by the fact that only 15 percent of Mexicans in 2012 were even willing to admit that they had voted for López Obrador, less than half of those citizens who actually supported his candidacy (35 percent) in 2006. Shortly before the campaign began, 90 percent of those who voted for the PRI in 2006 said they would support the PRI in 2012, while 27 and 22 percent of PRD and PAN voters in the previous election favored the PRI. Third, many Mexicans viewed López Obrador as out of touch with the electorate. Ironically, even though university student protests, primarily in Mexico City, boosted his chances, his social media following did not compare with either Peña Nieto's or Vázquez Mota's following throughout the campaign.

As the data in Table 8-5 demonstrate, López Obrador seriously neglected the use of Facebook, by far the most frequently used form of social media in Mexico. Three weeks before the election, López Obrador boasted fewer than half a million "likes" compared to 3 million for Peña Nieto and 1.7 million for Vázquez Mota. Among Twitter users, his following was more comparable to his two opponents, but Peña Nieto, in spite of the support for López Obrador from many students, remained ahead of his opponent but slightly behind Vázquez Mota. The importance of social media to López Obrador's performance is suggested by the fact that on the day of the election, 39 percent of voters were using the internet to communicate political

Table 8-5 Social Media Followers in the 2012 Presidential Election

	Facebook Likes				Twitter Followers			
Candidate	1/12	4/12	5/12	6/10	1/12	4/12	5/12	6/10
Peña Nieto	1.3 mil	1.8 mil	2.9 mil	3.0 mil	319,000	473,000	736,000	794,000
Vázquez Mota	94,000	1.4 mil	1.5 mil	1.7 mil	233,000	385,000	793,000	840,000
López Obrador	78,000	330,000	423,000	488,000	214,000	330,000	600,000	687,000

Note: Vázquez Mota was still a primary candidate in January 2012. Exact dates are January 16, April 1, May 29, and June 10.

Sources: From author's own calculations from actual candidates' accounts; Eric L. Olson and Diana Murray Watts, "Social Media in the 2012 Presidential Elections: A Testing Ground," Mexico Institute, Woodrow Wilson Center for Scholars, April 30, 2012; and from Alejandro Moreno, taken from *Reforma,* January 16, 2012.

questions, 40 percent of them daily, and of the one out of ten Mexicans who obtained their political information from the internet, nearly two thirds voted for López Obrador, three times that of Peña Nieto.[40] Perhaps most important in explaining why the "Yo soy 132" movement did not catch on with other Mexicans is the fact that half of all Mexicans at the beginning of June believed a political party or candidate was behind the movement. Indeed, only one in three Mexicans considered them to be genuine student protests.[41]

Early in the campaign, Vázquez Mota was the strongest opponent. She had two potential advantages. First, she had very low negative ratings. In poll after poll in April and May she was the most frequent second choice of voters favoring both the PRI and the PRD candidates. Second, given the disproportionate participation in Mexico among female voters, she also demonstrated early on an ability to capture their support. Twenty percent more women supported her candidacy while an equal percentage did not support López Obrador. In spite of these potential pluses, she squandered these advantages initially with a disorganized campaign, and by presenting an unclear campaign that distinguished her from her two PAN predecessors. Further, some observers also believe that the public's dissatisfaction with the quality of the public educational system, widely publicized in the last year of the Calderón administration, reflected badly on her career bona fides as secretary of public education from 2006 to 2009. She should have strongly identified herself with the antipoverty programs she directed under Fox, and with both administrations' health program, Seguro Popular. Nearly nine out of ten voters share positive views of these two programs under PAN.[42] Given the large number of beneficiaries of both programs, she should have been able to capitalize significantly on such an association.

As the data in Table 8-4 illustrate, Peña Nieto demonstrated several important strengths among the electorate. If we analyze the typical demographic variables, he performed strongly among women, while his two opponents split the remainder of their vote; he did well among the largest age group, ages thirty to forty-nine, capturing 41 percent of those voters, but also did equally well among older Mexicans, a group the PRD captured in 2006; he performed even more strongly among less educated voters who account for half of all voters, receiving half of their votes; he substantially reduced the PRD's stronger showing among rural Mexicans in 2006, reestablishing the PRI's traditional influence; and he edged out López Obrador's first place position among new voters in 2006. Equally important, given the fact that two-fifths of Mexicans chose their candidate on the basis of their ideas and proposals, followed by a fourth who wanted change, Peña Nieto attracted two-fifths of those citizens, whereas López Obrador did equally well among voters desiring change. Perhaps most striking, however, is that half of all voters who chose someone on the basis of their helping people, selected the PRI candidate. Finally, Peña Nieto and López Obrador essentially split the vote among individuals who viewed their economic situation as worse or the same, although Peña Nieto did much better among those who viewed it as the same. Regardless of when people made up their minds about their choice, before or during the election, or on the day they went to the polls, Peña Nieto won in every category.

PARTIES: THEIR ORIGINS AND FUTURE IN A DEMOCRATIC POLITICAL CONTEXT

National Action Party

Mexican electoral politics is dominated by three parties: the PAN, the PRI, and the PRD. Given the persistence of electoral democracy, the parties' ability to survive, adjust, and eliminate their weaknesses will determine their success in the second decade of the twenty-first century. All three parties have something in common: Their leadership is divided and they boast various factions favoring different party platforms. The most important of the three parties from 2000 to 2012, given its control over the national executive branch, was the National Action Party, which, until its victory in 2000, was Mexico's longest-lived opposition party. The PAN was founded in 1939 by Manuel Gómez Morín, a former national figure in government economic policymaking, and Efraín González Luna, a lawyer and Catholic activist. As is true of so many of Mexico's opposition parties, leadership often came, at least initially, from disgruntled establishment elites. In some cases it was persons who had their own political ambitions cut short; in other cases it was a question of policy differences. The PAN's formation is an example of the latter's bringing together diverse individuals who were against the statist, populist economic policies of President Lázaro Cárdenas (1934–1940).

The PAN first put up candidates against the PRI on the local level. It also supported several opposition presidential candidates, but it did not run its own candidate until 1958. Ten years after its founding, it captured less than 3 percent of the legislative seats (see Table 8-1). After the first electoral reforms went into effect in 1964, it began obtaining roughly 10 percent of the seats, assisted by its share of party deputies. Its representation stabilized around that figure until 1988, when it doubled its share to 20 percent.

The PAN ideological banner has shifted over time. Initially, party leaders, many of whom were well connected financially or had ties to Catholic Action Youth or other Catholic movements, were described as conservative, in some cases reactionary, pro-business, and pro-church. By the 1960s the party evolved gradually into a Mexican variant of a Christian Democratic organization.[43] However, like the PRI and especially the left-of-center parties, the PAN suffered from internal dissent. At various points its leadership wavered between those desirous of playing more or less by the rules of the political game, as set down by the government, or those who advocated a more aggressive stance vis-á-vis the PRI.

The new PAN activists since the 1980s, sometimes referred to as neo-Panistas, have taken a more conservative stance ideologically and have often allied themselves with combative businessmen willing to run under the PAN banner. As Soledad Loaeza suggested in her analysis of the 1988 presidential election, the neo-Panistas broke new ground "by challenging the unwritten rules of Mexican politics—in particular, the idea that industrialists should not participate in politics."[44] When President Salinas took some of the thunder out of traditional PAN issues, like statism, labor corruption, and outmoded church-state relations, the PAN centered its major criticism on political modernization, notably genuine electoral reform, a popular issue with the electorate.

The PAN's growth nationally was never dramatic. It remained the major opposition party, except during the 1988 presidential race, but its strength in presidential contests from 1982 to 1993 stabilized at approximately 17 percent. In 1994, it established a stronger presence, accounting for half of all opposition votes cast, a fourth of the electorate. Its organizational strength and the narrowness of its platform made it viable primarily in urban centers. Vicente Fox significantly increased the PAN's support, especially strengthening the party in rural areas, although most new voters were supporting Fox, not the party. Indeed, it would be accurate to call the PAN a regional, urban party. In 1988, the first time that the PAN won more than 10 percent of the legislative majority districts, the thirty-eight seats it obtained were in the major cities, including Ciudad Juárez; Mexico City; León; Guadalajara, the capital of Jalisco; several districts in the industrialized section of the state of México; San Luis Potosí and Mérida, both state capitals; and Culiacán. In fact, four-fifths of its legislative seats were in just five Mexican cities. The PAN repeated the same pattern in 1994, but more than half its eighteen seats were from Jalisco and five from the north. Two-thirds of the districts it captured were from León, Guadalajara, and Mérida. By 2000, it more than doubled the number of seats, to 141, and although Fox helped expand its representation to other districts, more than half the seats were from the Federal District, Guanajuato, Jalisco, and México.

PAN's potential in the future is strongest at the local and state levels. One might have expected it to grow most dramatically in the North, where many of its original supporters in the business community gave it national prominence.[45] By 2005, PAN politicians had governed twelve different states, eight of them in regions other than the north. In 2008, the PAN controlled governors in eight states (22 percent of the population) compared to six states by the PRD (21 percent of the population) and eighteen by the PRI (57 percent of the population).

The PAN's national future, in spite of its presidential victories, is less sure. There are several reasons for this. First, as suggested previously, Vicente Fox was an outsider, a populist version of a Panista, who used his personal charisma and his own organization to complement the PAN's appeal, building on the small but solid base of partisan supporters. Three out of ten Mexicans were partisan supporters of the PAN in 2000, but the PAN was unable to retain those voters as core supporters. A third of its partisans converted to the PAN in 2000. The 2006 elections demonstrated that the PAN had not expanded permanently beyond its partisan core, and its support declined significantly among all voters from 43 to only 36 percent in 2006, and a second time from 36 to 25 percent in 2012.[46]

Second, the PAN has preserved control of the party bureaucracy by promoting figures whose political experience was in the national, legislative

Map 8.2 Party Winning the Most Votes by State in 2006

branch. Most of these individuals boasted kinship or personal ties with the party's founders or leadership. Unlike his predecessor, Calderón represented this type of politician. The PAN always has selected its presidential candidate democratically, but the selection process was internal, limited to a group of active party delegates.[47] Politicians inside the party wanted to renovate what they have described as an aristocracy among the leadership and to promote a more open process in policy debates and a direct, secret, universal vote of party members for both candidates and leaders. The PAN has moved away from the more restrictive selection process to one that incorporates all registered party members, not just delegates, and in 2006, it introduced this new regional primary composed of three regional contests.[48] In 2012, while altering several conditions, and holding the primary on a single date, it continued this new, broader tradition, choosing Josefina Vázquez Mota from three candidates.

The third reason why the PAN faces an uphill battle to maintain and increase its national strength is the reason why most voters, other than traditional PAN partisans, voted for the party and its presidential candidate in 2000. The vast majority of new PAN partisans voted for the party because it represented a change from the PRI. At least since 1990, many voters have viewed the PAN as the primary alternative to the PRI, rather than as a party whose ideology corresponds to their personal views. The PAN's growth, therefore, depends heavily on its performance in office, whether it is at the national, state, or local levels. This interpretation was documented by the 2006 presidential race, in which most analysts agree that the election was López Obrador's to lose. Calderón squeaked by with a narrow victory, but the mixed success of his party in the presidency barely helped him achieve that victory. As suggested earlier, incumbency does not favor the PAN or any party at the local level, unless it achieves demonstrable policy results. In 2012, Vázquez Mota faced an uphill battle because of voter frustrations with economic conditions and levels of drug-related violence under Calderón.

Democratic Revolutionary Party

The second national party is the Democratic Revolutionary Party. The PRD has a short history; it constructed itself on a foundation of smaller leftist parties that flowered during the 1970s. Elements of the Mexican Communist Party (PCM), founded in 1919, and the Mexican Socialist Party (PMS), founded in 1987, provided the formal organizational base. The PRD came into being after the 1988 presidential election. Many of its founders, as in the case of the PAN, were PRI dissidents.[49] Some of its members in the

Chamber of Deputies and in the Senate previously held political posts as Priistas or as leftist-party members.

The results of the 1988 election were deceptive in terms of PRD strength. The immense popularity of Cuauhtémoc Cárdenas's father among many sectors of the population made it difficult to distinguish support for Cárdenas candidacy as a symbol of his father from support for the principles of his coalition. Those who voted for the PRD, as in the case of the PAN, were primarily interested in change. But the PRD, even more than the PAN, owing to its origins from a loosely connected alliance of small parties, found it difficult to maintain its cohesion.

From 1991 through 1997, PRD electoral strength left it in third place behind PRI and PAN (see Table 8-1). The PRD faced electoral conditions involving fraud, and many of its active supporters were physically threatened, injured, or killed. In fact, PRD members constituted the single largest group of victims in national and international Human Rights Commission reports in the early 1990s. The PRI also was successful in 1994 in convincing many voters to associate electoral violence with the PRD. That fact, combined with Cárdenas's poor performance in the first televised presidential debate, ensured PRD's third-place position.

The 1997 midterm elections offered both Cárdenas and the PRD an opportunity to revive its electoral fortunes. Cárdenas became the party's standard-bearer in the most significant race, that of the newly elected head of the Federal District, Mexico's most influential urban center. Changing his campaign style and benefiting from deteriorating social and economic conditions, as well as a poor campaign by his PAN opponent, Cárdenas easily defeated the PRI's candidate. Using the Federal District's thirty congressional seats as a base, the party swept to victory in twenty-nine districts and recaptured its original strength in México, Michoacán, and Morelos, states where it did well in 1988. It won nearly the same percentage of votes as the PAN nationally, 26 percent, but it did slightly better in the plurinominal regions, thus receiving more seats, narrowly giving it second place after the PRI in the Chamber of Deputies. In 2000, however, the PRD's national strength remained stagnant at 17 percent of the vote for president (one-tenth of a percent less than in 1994), as the PAN's increased and the PRI's declined significantly. The PRD won only twenty-eight districts in Congress, one less than in 1997. It could claim significant representation congressionally only in Michoacán, Cárdenas's home state, Tabasco, and Zacatecas.

Cárdenas used his position as head of the Federal District to make a third run for the presidency in 2000. By imposing himself as the party's candidate, Cárdenas further accentuated divisions within its leadership. Those divisions spilled into the public arena. In addition to the serious problems inside the party, the PRD appeared hypocritical to many Mexicans, advocating democracy in the broader political arena, but not entertaining it within the party itself. The PRD's candidate selection process contrasted with the PRI's decision to hold an open primary, allowing any registered voter to cast a vote for its presidential candidate. In 2005, the PRD approved new internal regulations, including a decision to hold an open primary to select its presidential candidate. In 2006, Cuauhtémoc Cárdenas indicated that he would compete against Manuel López Obrador in the new, open primary, but he ultimately withdrew his candidacy, and López Obrador was declared the official candidate without holding the primary.[50] Similarly, in 2012, Marcelo Ebraud, the popular PRD governor of the Federal District, withdrew his candidacy as the party's presidential candidate when a party-sponsored poll indicated López Obrador remained the favorite of PRD partisans.

After the party's poor performance in the 2000 presidential race, the leadership divisions multiplied in intensity and number. In 2001, three major groups existed within the party leadership: the Refoundation wing headed by Cuauhtémoc Cárdenas and Rosario Robles, the New Left group led by Jesús Ortega and Jesús Zambrano, and the Amalistas, directed by Amalia García, a former party president, and Raymundo Cárdenas. None of the three groups dominated the party, and therefore its governability relied on compromises among these three factions.[51] The party continued to be characterized by internal splits and dissension, but after the decision by PAN and PRI members of Congress to deprive Manuel López Obrador of his immunity, party leadership put aside its differences and decided to maintain a united front through the 2006 presidential elections.[52]

The PRD was unable to maintain that unity after the election when López Obrador announced his strategy of not recognizing the Federal Electoral Court's decision or Felipe Calderón's presidency. Many PRD politicians decided to pursue a moderate course, withdrawing their support for López Obrador. By 2011, as the parties and potential candidates began jockeying for support for the 2012 presidential race, PRD fortunes had declined dramatically. From December 2009 through 2011, only 15 percent of the population on average indicated they would support a PRD candidate for the presidency, the poorest showing for any of the leading parties since Mexico began its period of democratic consolidation after 2000. Worse, only 9 percent of Mexicans indicated that they identified with the PRD in 2011, compared to 34 percent for the PRI and 22 percent for the PAN. In fact, the public perception of the PRD, held by six out of ten citizens, was that PRD leaders were more occupied with internal conflicts than their ability to solve the country's problems.[53]

The PRD's ideology is difficult to characterize because the party's ranks are an amalgam of political groups professing views ranging from Marxist to populist. Some issues prominent in the PRD platform and that have distinguished it from the PRI include electoral reforms, fiscal reforms, broad social programs, women's rights, and free education. In short, the PRD advocated the diversification of economic relations, increased political pluralism in the electoral arena, programs to mitigate the negative effects of NAFTA, and thoroughgoing electoral reforms. With electoral democracy in place, the PRD's most distinctive position is that it favored economic policies that cater less to business interests and advocate the traditional importance of the state in economic affairs.[54] While most analysts agree that it offers an "interesting alternative in the Mexican political arena,"[55] as the 2012 presidential race began only one in six Mexicans preferred it to all other parties.

Interviews with 484 PRD delegates at the VIII Party Congress in Mexico City in 2004, characterized the party in the following terms: (1) Three-fifths of those delegates identified at least eleven different political currents within the party. (2) The delegates were most disgusted with the conflicts among the various leadership groups. (3) They considered their most important task to attract new voters. (4) Militants believed the party should focus its resources on expanding its geographic base. (5) Two-thirds of the delegates believed the PRD should maintain its political programs. (6) Four-fifths supported differentiating itself ideologically from the other parties. (7) Ninety percent supported the candidacy of López Obrador as president. (8) Party members favored democracy followed by economic development as priorities for the country but overwhelmingly favored social justice over economic development and democracy. (9) Finally, party members agreed that the state had the responsibility for achieving social justice, even if it meant public instability.[56]

The PRD's future is conditioned by three significant elements. First, it will depend on the ability of its leadership to resolve major issues in party governance since 2006. Second, it will have to reorganize from its grassroots base and rely on its local party activists and leaders for recruits to national political positions, just as its delegates suggested, reinforcing an earlier decision to use its base committees as the foundation for a bottom-to-top reorganization.[57] Third, voter support on the left represents a minority of Mexicans and shows no signs of expanding. As Mexico approached the 2006 presidential race, even though its candidate, López Obrador, initially led the field by a large margin, only 19 percent of the voters said they would vote for the PRD. López Obrador, during the election, demonstrated the same abilities as Fox in attracting support from other partisans and independents alike.

He remained the most well known PRD candidate for the presidential nomination in 2012, but López Obrador's appeal among the general public had altered significantly, with 49 percent of Mexicans viewing him negatively compared to only 40 percent positively. To his credit, despite beginning the campaign well behind the second place candidate, Josefina Vázquez Mota, López Obrador did increase support for the PRD by the second month of the campaign, ultimately finishing in a strong second place. But an analysis reveals that half of his support comes from partisan PRD voters, and nearly all the rest from independents and approximately 8 percent of individuals who previously supported the other two major parties. Nevertheless, the PRD demonstrated that it still appeals to a solid third of the electorate, not all that different from the PRI or PAN, suggesting that an appealing candidate from the left can win the presidency. To be successful on the national level after 2012, the PRD needs to strengthen its organization on the local level, to expand its strength regionally in the west and north, and to select a new generation of leaders and candidates.

Institutional Revolutionary Party

Much of the history of the PRI, Mexico's third party, already has been discussed as a component of the evolution of Mexico's authoritarian governmental leadership. In the post-2000 democratic electoral era, the PRI shares similar problems with the other two parties. The PRI went into the election as a transitional party whose leadership depended nearly completely on the incumbent president and whose candidates were selected internally by party leaders, the president, and PRI governors. The PRI has been forced to cut its umbilical ties financially and structurally with the state. Since July 2000, it has begun operating as an independent political organization and after its debacle in 2006, taking on features that are products of democratic electoral competition.[58]

The party's leadership is broadly divided into two factions; the first is a younger group who wants to transform the party into a competitive political organization by democratizing its leadership and making it responsive to its grassroots members. The second faction, dominated by a group of traditionalist governors, wants to keep the party's leadership under tighter control and continue some of the practices from the party's nondemocratic past. Ideologically, they are opposed to some of the features of economic neoliberalism. The democratic reformist wing, led initially by President Zedillo himself, partially transformed the image of the party by implementing, for the first time in the party's history, a democratic selection process for its presidential candidate.[59] The party chose to use an open primary, the first and only time any party in Mexico had opened up its presidential candidacy to all registered voters. It could not hold a closed primary because it did not have a complete list of members. Francisco Labastida, the eventual victor, was opposed by the then-PRI governor of Tabasco, Roberto Madrazo, a leading politician from the traditionalist wing, and the campaign was fierce.[60]

Six years later, under the leadership of Madrazo, the PRI's presidential candidate, the party withdrew from its wide-open primary system, and instead implemented a selection process long used previously by the PAN, a secret vote of party delegates.[61] Nevertheless, electoral competition, and decentralized candidate selection of congressional and gubernatorial candidates, marked an important change in how the PRI conducts its business since the beginning of the democratic consolidation.[62] In 2012, it initiated a compromise between the two previous primary methods, conducting a primary opened to militant members and partisan sympathizers of the PRI, in which Peña Nieto's only significant opponent withdrew in favor of party unity.

The PRI's National Political Council met in 2001 after losing the election to Fox, and authorized its National Executive Committee to organize a national assembly at the end of the year. The assembly represented an innovative decision on the part of the party leadership because at least 30 percent of the participants were elected through a direct and secret vote at municipal and district assemblies. The party leadership, in recognition of Fox's appeal to younger voters, required that a third of the party activists attending the assembly be under thirty years of age. The party leadership also decided, after protests from PRI activists to expand the selection of the party's second in command, the secretary general, to an open, elective process inside the party.[63] After the party held its national assembly in November 2001, it passed several significant resolutions, among them that 40 percent of the party's candidates would be women and 30 percent would be individuals under thirty years of age.

The question that interested most analysts of Mexico is what would happen to the PRI when it no longer controlled the national executive branch and, therefore, was deprived of a huge source of patronage and financial influence for twelve years. The party demonstrated, in spite of its significant leadership divisions and poor showing in the 2006 presidential elections, a continued ability to evolve into an independent political organization. If it truly relies on its grassroots political activists, it will not only survive as Mexico's strongest national party, but has the potential to evolve and grow, solidifying its local and regional base. Indeed, this explains, in part, its ability for a dramatic comeback in the 2009 elections, establishing it as the party to beat in the 2012 presidential race.

Despite its dramatic defeat by the PAN in 2000, the PRI continued to maintain the strongest presence at the state level, demonstrating its political power to recover and to defeat the PAN in the 2003 congressional elections, winning 53 percent of the three hundred districts, twice that of the PAN. A comparison between its 2006 performance at the regional level, with that of 2009, demonstrates the breadth and depth of its presence throughout Mexico. In 2009, it won one or more seats in twenty-eight of the thirty-two entities in Mexico, and gave up only six of the districts it retained in 2006. Its greatest weakness was in Chiapas, where it lost two districts to the PRD, making Chiapas the most volatile state among the three major parties since 1997. It won five or more seats in Coahuila, Jalisco, México, Puebla, Tamaulipas, Veracruz, Guerrero, and Oaxaca, and an overwhelming thirty-two seats from the state of México alone. Equally important, it captured a similar proportion of seats from the other two leading parties, 58 percent from the PAN and 51 percent from the PRD.[64] It remains a majority or strong plurality party at its base, which it used to translate into an equally strong presidential candidacy in 2012. To maintain this grassroots strength in the future, it needs to do what the PAN accomplished in the 1990s—demonstrate to the electorate at the state and local level that it can govern effectively and be accountable to the people. In the municipal elections of 2008, the PRI demonstrated just that strength, capturing 59 percent of the mayoralty positions up for election.[65] In 2012 it won four of the seven gubernatorial races, Chiapas, Jalisco, Tabasco and Yucatán, taking back Jalisco from the PAN and Chiapas from the PRD.

CONCLUSION

Mexico's electoral landscape has changed completely since July 2000. No party has a lock on Mexico's political future. In fact, one characteristic they all share is that Mexicans have little confidence in political parties. This has been the case for decades, and the PAN's victories in 2000 and 2006 have not changed that view. Fewer than one out of four Mexicans has any confidence whatsoever in the three major parties.[66] Support for parties is low throughout the region, but Mexico, Canada, Chile and Colombia rank among those countries with the highest level of trust.[67] It is important to remember that even with the extraordinary advances of the PAN, and to a much lesser extent the PRD at all levels—local, state, and national—no incumbent party is secure in any of its posts. Recent historical experience clearly demonstrates that despite their initial popularity, newly incumbent parties have failed to convince voters to return them to office in the next election if their performance does not meet voter expectations.[68] The reasons for voter disenchantment are often the same as those given for citizen dissatisfaction with the PRI when it was the incumbent party: incompetence, unfulfilled campaign pledges, and corruption. Thus, the PRI's ability to stage a comeback depends not only on its performance but on that of its opponents, once they have garnered elective office. The PAN's loss to the PRI in the 2003 and the 2009 congressional elections, and the 2012 presidential election, clearly demonstrates the impact of those variables on electoral outcomes. As one study concluded during the first decade of Mexico's democratic consolidation, "Over 90 percent of the Mexican federal electoral districts" were competitive among two or more parties."[69] On the positive side, Mexicans are among the most likely citizens of Latin America to believe that their parties actually represent their views.[70]

The most important consequence of electoral politics in Mexico's era of democratic consolidation is that citizen confidence in elections, based largely on electoral outcomes, affects their views of democracy's existence. For example, in the aftermath of the controversial 2006 presidential elections, when comparing Mexicans' responses to the question, "Is Mexico a democracy today?," the number of people who considered it a democracy declined 14 percent (from 64 to 55 percent) between the time immediately before the election and shortly after the Federal Electoral Tribunal's final decision about the outcome. Over a third of Mexicans did not consider their country to be a democracy in September 2006. Even though three-quarters of Mexicans thought it was the best form of government, only slightly more than a third of citizens considered the type of political institutions important if their quality of life improved.[71] The relationship between elections and democracy, both in 2000 and 2006, is linked to whose candidate wins rather than to the inherent legitimacy of the process.

The broader issue of voter perception of the fairness and integrity of the elections is of even greater importance in the development of institutional legitimacy within a democratic context. In 2011, twenty years after the creation of the Federal Electoral Institute, only 49 percent of Mexicans believed that the victorious candidate in the most recent election really received the majority of votes! An equal percentage of citizens agreed with the statement that in their state, elections were free, clean, and fair. Yet, when pollsters asked respondents if they had witnessed any fraudulent action during an election, only 7 percent replied in the affirmative.[72] Only half of the adult population believes the local electoral councilor members are impartial, and that the PAN (43 percent) and PRI (27 percent) are the most favored parties, with the PRD (6 percent) at a distant third.[73] Ironically, it can be argued that these critical responses replicate accurate views of how the incumbent PRI ran elections prior to 2000. These figures also explain why López Obrador once again challenged the veracity of the IFE's vote count in 2012. Their immediate recount of half the balloting places in Mexico produced nearly exactly the same totals: 38.3 percent for the PRI, 31.5 percent for the PRD, and 25.5 percent for the PAN.

The potential relationship between elections and democracy is also reversible. Statistically speaking, an analysis of all Latin American countries found that the most important explanatory variables for increased trust in elections in order of importance were: support for democracy, voted for the presidential winner, identification with a political party, and level of interpersonal trust. Not surprisingly, citizens from long-standing countries with democratic electoral systems such as Costa Rica and Uruguay expressed the greatest level of trust in elections, while Mexico and the United States ranked at the bottom of the top half, with Mexico ahead of the United States.[74] This finding suggests that the United States' long and pre-eminent reputation as a functioning democracy is not, by itself, adequate to ensure citizen trust in elections.

Another important, if indirect, consequence of Mexican attitudes toward political parties distinct from the electoral process that impinges on the fulfillment of democratic goals is related to citizen views of political parties. As indicated in the chapter on political participation, direct involvement with political parties compared to numerous other organizations is relatively limited. Data from Latin America suggest that is a widespread pattern among all countries, but Mexico ranks in the bottom third. Surveys reveal that Mexicans and Latin Americans typically are dissatisfied with parties because they lack trust in them as political institutions and they do not believe parties are listening to the people.[75] Poorer Mexicans, even when they do participate, have been ineffective in communicating their demands.[76] Mexicans' low interest in politics, and the degree to which they strongly identify with any political party, also explain the nature of their relationship with parties. The low regard in which Mexicans hold parties is also reflected in the high level of support, which has increased in recent years to nearly two-thirds of all Mexicans, for independent candidates unattached to any party to run for office. Only a fifth of Mexicans believe that parties should provide the exclusive channel for ambitious individuals to run for office.[77]

A more sophisticated analysis of the competitive electoral process as a required ingredient in the conceptualization of a consolidated democracy tests the relationship between electoral competition and effective governance. As Matthew R. Cleary discovered in his analysis of this issue at the local level, "It seems clear that the uncritical acceptance of U.S. electoral theory in the Mexican context is imprudent. The electoral connection in Mexico labors under the strain of institutions and practices that impede mechanisms of accountability. These problems include extreme centralization

within the municipal government, a constitutional prohibition against reelection, and a three-year term of office."[78] He goes on to suggest that if
observers of Mexico properly theorized the problems Mexican institutions
introduced, they would not readily have predicted qualitative outcomes
resulting from electoral competition.[79]

NOTES

1. Roderic Ai Camp, *The Metamorphosis of Leadership in a Democratic
Mexico* (New York: Oxford University Press, 2010), 51.

2. María Emilia Farias Mackey, *The Reform of Electoral Policy* (Mexico:
Congreso de la Unión, 1987), 8–9.

3. Kenneth F. Greene, *Why Dominant Parties Lose: Mexico's Democratization in Comparative Perspective* (New York: Cambridge University Press, 2007),
253; and Beatriz Magaloni, *Voting for Democracy: Hegemonic Survival and Its
Demise in Mexico* (New York: Cambridge University Press, 2006).

4. Vikram K. Chand, "Politicization, Institutions, and Democratization in
Mexico: The Politics of the State of Chihuahua in National Perspective," PhD dissertation, Harvard University, 1991.

5. For a detailed analysis of this conflict and its national consequences, see
Vikram K. Chand, *Mexico's Political Awakening* (Notre Dame, IN: University of
Notre Dame Press, 2001).

6. These and other changes are outlined in detail in George Grayson's excellent summary, *A Guide to the 1994 Mexican Presidential Election*, CSIS Election
Studies Report (Washington, DC: CSIS, 1994), 8–10; and in John J. Bailey, *The
1994 Mexican Presidential Election*, CSIS Election Studies Series (Washington, DC:
CSIS, 1994).

7. "Mexico's Electoral Aftermath and Political Future," summary of a conference at the Mexican Center, University of Texas, Austin, September 2–3, 1994; and
in Enrique Calderón Alzati and Daniel Cazés, eds., *Las elecciones presidenciales de
1994* (Mexico: UNAM, 1996).

8. "The Prospects for a Free, Fair and Honest Election in Mexico," A Report to
the Business Coordinating Council, August 15, 1994; the Washington Office on Latin
America, "The 1994 Mexican Election: A Question of Credibility," Washington, DC,
August 15, 1994; and the Instituto Federal Electoral, "Main Criticisms to the Electoral
Roll and the Nominal Lists" (Mexico City: IFE, 1994).

9. For an excellent analysis, see Joseph Klesner, "Electoral Reform in
Mexico's Hegemonic Party System: Perpetuation of Privilege or Democratic
Advance?" Paper presented at the American Political Science Association meeting,
Washington, DC, 1997.

10. Jacqueline Peschard, "Control Over Party and Campaign Finance in
Mexico," *Mexican Studies* 22, no. 1 (Winter 2006): 83–105.

11. *Este País*, May 1998, 16.

12. See my "Mexico's 1988 Elections: A Turning Point for Its Political Development and Foreign Relations," in *Sucesión Presidencial: The 1988 Mexican Presidential Elections*, eds. Edgar W. Butler and Jorge A. Bustamante (Boulder, CO: Westview Press, 1991), 98ff.

13. Barry Ames, "Bases of Support for Mexico's Dominant Party," *American Political Science Review* 64, no. 1 (March 1970): 153–67.

14. Kathleen Bruhn, "Social Spending and Political Support," *Comparative Politics* 28, no. 2 (January 1996): 151–77.

15. See "The Voter Profile," *Review of the Economic Situation of Mexico*, (July 2000), 267.

16. Roderic Ai Camp, "Citizen Attitudes Toward Democracy and Vicente Fox's Victory in 2000," in *Mexico's Pivotal Democratic Election*, ed. Jorge I. Domínguez and Chappell Lawson (Stanford, CA: Stanford University Press, 2004), 34.

17. José Antonio Crespo, *Raising the Bar: The Next Generation of Electoral Reforms in Mexico* (Washington, DC: CSIS, 2000).

18. Carta Paramétrica, "Identificación partidista," www.parametria.com.mx, November, 2011.

19. Carlo Varela, "The Electoral Processes Have Begun," *Review of the Economic Situation of Mexico* (June 2004), 220–24.

20. Andrew Selee, "Municipalities and Policymaking," *The Oxford Handbook of Mexican Politics*, ed. Roderic Ai Camp (New York: Oxford University Press, 2012), 101–18.

21. Bimsa, "Imágen de los partidos políticos," 1,000 respondents, February 9–14, 2005, +/−3.1% margin of error.

22. José Antonio Crespo, "The Party System and Democratic Governance in Mexico," Policy Paper on the Americas (Washington, DC: CSIS, 2004), 35.

23. "Dividen votos por región," *Reforma*, February 28, 2005, 8A; and "Alcanza Calderón a AMLO," *Reforma*, November 21, 2005.

24. A fresh argument on the importance of voter income on partisan support based on a useful methodological conceptualization of social class categories, see Dennis Gilbert, "Social Class and Voter Preference in Mexican Elections," paper presented at the Latin American Studies Association, San Francisco, May, 2012.

25. Roderic Ai Camp, "Democracy Redux, Mexican Voters and the 2006 Presidential Race," in *Consolidating Mexico's Democracy: The 2006 Presidential Campaign in Comparative Perspective*, eds. Jorge I. Domínguez, Chappell Lawson, and Alejandro Moreno (Baltimore, MD: Johns Hopkins University, 2009), 29–49.

26. Allyson Lucinda Benton's excellent "Quién está preocupado por López Obrador: Las respuestas del mercado a las tendencías electorales durante la campaña presidencial mexicana del 2006," *Colombia Internacional*, 64 (July–December): 68–95.

27. Kathleen Bruhn, "López Obrador, Calderón, and the 2006 Presidential Campaign," in Domínguez et al., eds., *Consolidating Mexico's Democracy*, 179.

28. Kenneth F. Greene, "Campaign Persuasion and Nascent Partisanship in Mexico's New Democracy," *American Journal of Political Science* 55, no. 2 (April 2011): 413.

29. Ibid., 180–81.

30. Carlos Vilalta, "Vote-Buying Crime Reports in Mexico: Magnitude and Correlates," *Crime, Law, and Social Change* 54, no. 5 (December 2010): 326.

31. Todd A. Eisenstadt and Alejandro Poire, "Explaining the Credibility Gap in Mexico's 2006 Presidential Election, Despite Strong (Albeit Perfectable) Electoral Institutions," paper presented at the Center for Democracy and Election Management, November 8, 2006.

32. Consulta Mitofksy, "La Resistencia civil postelectoral: Hasta dónde?," September 2006. Two-thirds of Mexicans agreed that all Mexicans should accept Calderón as president, whereas 31 percent disagreed. 1,200 respondents, $+/-2.8\%$ margin of error, September 8–12, 2006.

33. Chappell Lawson, "How Did We Get Here? Mexican Democracy after the 2006 Elections," *PS: Political Science and Politics* 40 (January 2007): 47.

34. www.ife.org.mx, 2012; Julio Juárez Gámiz, "El papel de la publicidad política en la nueva ley electoral: Una mirada crítica," *Sociológica* 25, no. 72 (January–April 2010): 43–70.

35. Gilles Serra, "The Risk of Partyarchy and Democratic Backsliding: Mexico's 2007 Electoral Reform," *Taiwan Journal of Democracy* 8, no. 1 (July 2012): 31–56.

36. This pattern is true in all states and in urban or rural settings. Consulta Mitofsky, "Una verdad: Las mujeres votan más que los hombres," www.consulta.mx, October 2011.

37. Carta Paramétrica, "Cuándo deciden su voto los Mexicanos?," www.parametría.mx.com, July, 2012.

38. Carta Paramétrica, "Evaluación de las campañas de 2006," www.parametria.mx.com, April 2012.

39. Consulta Mitofsky, "Preferencias Ciudadanias," No. 28, www.consulta.mx, June 26, 2012.

40. Carta Paramétrica, "Uso de internet y redes sociales en la elección presidencial," 1,474 respondents, $+/-2.6\%$ margin of error, July 1, 2012, www.parametria.com.mx.

41. Carta Paramétrica, "Encuesta Parametría—Yo soy 132," one thousand respondents, $+/-3.1\%$ margin of error, May 29-June 1, 2012 www.parametria.com.mx.

42. Carta Paramétrica, "Pierde levadura el PAN," one thousand respondents, $+/-3.1\%$ margin of error, April 11–15, 2012, www.parametria.com.mx, 2012.

43. Leticia Barraza and Ilán Bizberg, "El Partido Acción Nacional y el régimen político mexicano," *Foro Internacional* 31, no. 3 (January–March 1991): 418–45.

44. Soledad Loaeza, "The Emergence and Legitimization of the Modern Right, 1970–1988," in *Mexico's Alternative Political Futures*, ed. Wayne Cornelius, Judith Gentleman, and Peter H. Smith (La Jolla, CA: Center for U.S.-Mexican Studies, 1989), 361.

45. See Yemile Mizrahi, *From Martyrdom to Power: The Partido Acción Nacional in Mexico* (Notre Dame, IN: University of Notre Dame Press, 2003), 68ff.

46. "Encuesta simpatizantes rumbo al 2006," *Reforma*, May 16, 2005, 6A.

47. José Antonio Hernández Company, "The Legacies of Authoritarianism: The Institutionalization of Opposition Parties and Their Electoral Strategies in Mexico," paper presented at the Latin American Studies Association, San Francisco, May, 2012.

48. Steven Wuhs, "Democratic Rules and the Anti-democratic Implications: Presidential Candidate Selection in the PAN and PRD for the 2006 Elections," Special Issue No. 2, *Política y Gobierno* (2009): 51–75.

49. Carlos B. Gil, *Hope and Frustration: Interviews with Leaders of Mexico's Political Opposition* (Wilmington, DE: Scholarly Resources, 1992), 155ff.

50. David Shirk, "Choosing Mexico's 2006 Presidential Candidates," in Domínguez et al., eds., *Consolidating Mexico's Democracy*, 129–51.

51. "PRD 6th National Congress," *Review of the Economic Situation of Mexico* (May 2001): 198–200.

52. Víctor Hugo Martínez González, *Fisiones y fusiones, divorcios y reconciliaciones: La dirigencia del Partido de la Revolución Democrática (PRD), 1989–2004* (Mexico: Plaza y Valdes, 2005).

53. "Caída y crisis del PRD," 1,000 respondents, +/−3.0% margin of error, February 19–23, 2011, www.parametria.com.mx, 2011.

54. Javier Farrera Araujo and Diego Prieto Hernández, "Partido de la Revolución Democrática: Documentos básicos," *Revista Mexicana de Ciencias Políticas y Sociales* 36 (January–March 1990): 67–95.

55. Tina Hilgers, "Causes and Consequences of Political Clientelism: Mexico's PRD in Comparative Perspective," *Latin American Politics and Society* 50, no. 4 (Winter 2008): 148.

56. "Estudio de opinión sobre el Partido de la Revolución Democrática," April 16, 2004, www.olivaresplata.com.

57. "PRD 6th National Congress," 199.

58. Guadalupe Pacheco Méndez, "Hacia la cuarta etapa del Partido de la Revolución? La elección interna de dirigentes del PRI en febrero de 2002," *Foro Internacional* 46, no. 2 (April–June 2006): 303–52.

59. Adam Brinegar, Scott Morgenstern and Daniel Nielson, "The PRI's Choice: Balancing Democratic Reform and Its Own Salvation," *Party Politics* 12, no. 1 (January 2006): 77–97.

60. "PRI Primaries," *Review of the Economic Situation of Mexico* (December 1999): 478–83.

61. Party statutes approved by the 19th National Assembly of PRI and by IFE, April 2005. See www.pri.mx.gov.

62. Joy Langston, "The Changing Party of the Institutional Revolution, Electoral Competition and Decentralized Candidate Selection," *Party Politics* 12, no. 3 (May 2006): 395–413.

63. "PRI," *Review of the Economic Situation of Mexico* (May 2001): 201–202.

64. "Hypotheses on the July 5th Elections: PRI Takes from PAN and PRD," MUND, Opinion and Policy Report, August 14, 2009.

65. "Observations and Hypotheses on the 2009 Congressional Elections in Mexico," MUND, Opinion and Policy Report, January 8, 2009.

66. "Rumbo a la elección del 2000," *Este País*, (November 1999), 17.

67. Margarita Corral, "(Mis)Trust in Political Parties in Latin America," *AmericasBarometer Insights: 2008* (2008): 1.

68. Yemile Mizrahi, "Dilemmas of the Opposition in Government: Chihuahua and Baja California," *Mexican Studies* 14, no. 1 (Winter 1998): 151–89; and David Shirk, *Mexico's New Politics: The PAN and Democratic Change* (Boulder, CO: Lynne Rienner, 2004).

69. Joseph Klesner, "Electoral Competition and the New Party System in Mexico," *Latin American Politics and Society* 47, no. 2 (Summer 2005): 103–42.

70. Margarita Corral, "Political Parties and Representation in Latin America," *AmericasBarometer Insights: 2010*, No. 36 (2010): 16.

71. "Divide a Mexicanos 'el efecto 2 de julio,'" *Excélsior*, November 10, 2006.

72. Brian M. Faughnan and Elizabeth J. Zechmeister, "Vote Buying in the Americas," *AmericasBarometer Insights: 2011*, no. 57, 1.

73. "La desconfianza en las eleciones," 500 respondents, +/–4.4% margin of error, March 26–30, 2011, www.parametria.com.mx.

74. Mathew L. Layton, "Trust in Elections," *AmericasBarometer Insights: 2010*, No. 37, 1, 3.

75. Margarita Corral, "Participation in Meetings of Political Parties," *AmericasBarometer Insights: 2009*, 1.

76. Claudio Holzner, "Voz y voto: participación política y calidad de la democracia en México," *América Latina Hoy* 45 (2007): 84.

77. "Aumenta apoyo a candidaturas independientes," 1,200 respondents, +/−2.8% margin of error, December 17–21, 2009, www.parametria.com.mx.

78. "Electoral Competition, Participation, and Government Responsiveness in Mexico," *American Journal of Political Science* 51, no. 2 (April 2007): 296.

79. Carlos Moreno-Jaimes, "Do Competitive Elections Produce Better-Quality Governments? Evidence from Mexican Municipalities, 1990–2000," *Latin American Research Review* 42, no. 2 (June 2007): 136–53.

9

External Politics: Relations with the United States

Growing interdependence between the United States and Mexico beginning in the last decades of the twentieth century transformed a traditionally arm's-length relationship into one characterized by mutual dependencies that have narrowed the range of viable policy options for both countries. At the same time, the gradual emergence of shared ideas about economics, politics, and most recently narcotics control has encouraged each country to perceive the challenges and policy solutions for a key set of national interests in a similar light. This has reduced the range of situations in which Mexico follows a policy approach unacceptable to U.S. national interests and which might thereby stimulate the natural impulse of the powerful to exploit its position to gain cooperation through coercion. Shared ideas and policy approaches have also encouraged the United States to see Mexico as a kindred state worthy of the benefit of the doubt. Finally, as interdependence has amplified Mexico's impact on U.S. domestic concerns, the role of the U.S. Congress in bilateral affairs has increased. The bias of this institution, and especially the House of Representatives, toward domestic instead of international concerns weakens the restraining influence that interdependence and shared ideas can have on the interventionist impulse. Members of the U.S. Congress are thus prone to demand and even require the exercise of U.S. power to force Mexico to help resolve a U.S. domestic policy problem. As a consequence, Mexico has repeatedly found its policy autonomy constrained in situations where Congress has interests.

PAMELA K. STARR, *"U.S.-Mexico Relations and Mexican*
Domestic Politics"

Throughout this book I have emphasized the impact of the United States on Mexico and the historical relations of the two countries. My focus has been on domestic politics, but the pervasive influence—if only psychological—of the United States, in addition to politics of place, culture, and economics, has helped mold, indirectly and implicitly, Mexican political behavior. This does not mean that Mexico is not concerned with foreign relations elsewhere in the region, especially since 2007. Rather, the dominance of the United States in foreign policy issues important to Mexico usually outweighs the latter's interests in other external actors. This role has become more pronounced under President Calderón, as his administration embarked on an aggressive, proactive, confrontational strategy against drug cartels, often with the encouragement of the United States. Europe's rejection of Mexico's request for investment and aid in the late 1980s, in favor of concerns in Eastern Europe, led the Mexican leadership to pursue a strategy of closer economic ties to the United States, thus ensuring even greater interdependency. Vicente Fox's administration accentuated a relationship begun by his predecessors, but Fox attempted to diversify trade relations, signing a European Union Free Trade Agreement in 2000. In spite of the extraordinary increase in trade between the United States and China in recent years, the enormous growth in trade with the United States continues to reinforce Mexico's relationship with its neighbor.[1] As Sidney Weintraub noted during the Calderón administration, Mexico sent more than 80 percent of its merchandise exports to the United States, which constituted about 1 percent of the U.S. Gross Domestic Product, whereas those exports accounted for a fourth of Mexico's GDP. China replaced Mexico as the second largest exporter to the United States, but Mexico remains the second largest market for American goods.[2] Indeed, Mexico purchases 13 percent of all American exports. It is also crucial to point out that two-fifths of the parts on average from Mexican exports to the United States are American made.[3]

The proximity of the United States to Mexico has affected their relationship in the past, often to Mexico's disadvantage, and continues to determine their current relationship. Mexico always has struggled to retain a strong sense of self-identity in the shadow of its more powerful neighbor. Indeed, Mexico's nationalism is in part a response to its experiences with the United States, and its postrevolutionary foreign policy also, in part, is based on its relationship with the United States. For example, in both international and regional forums, such as the United Nations or the Organization of American States, Mexico has tried to become an independent actor in foreign policy matters vis-à-vis the United States. Under Fox, Mexico won a temporary seat on the United Nations Security Council in 2001, reinforcing the president's desire to pursue a more active role in international politics. Mexico used its new position to oppose the U.S. position on Iraq, while at the same time it helped to forge a more moderate consensus among other Security Council members.[4] Under President Calderón, Mexico increased its international presence as a member of the Security Council from 2009 to 2010, but also as a leader in global environmental issues in the Major Economies Forum on Climate Change, in regional development through the Mesoamerican Development Project, and in international financial institutions through the G-20 countries.[5] Mexico established a Mexican Agency for International Development Cooperation to implement some of its projects.[6]

Recently, scholars discovered a number of attitudes among leaders and ordinary Mexicans that help to explain many of the observations in this chapter (see Table 9-1). Mexican leadership and citizens generally are most strongly in agreement in how they view their own national identity, including the level of pride expressed in being Mexican, their broader view of identifying themselves regionally as Latin Americans, their agreement that Mexico should seek a special relationship with the United States, and their ranking of some of the most important international issues globally.

Table 9-1 Mexican Views Impacting Foreign Policy Issues

	(Percentages)	
Statement	Elites	Non-Elites
Proud to be Mexican	78	81
Consider themselves to be Latin Americans	54	51
Consider themselves to be world citizens	32	26
Most important international threats		
Drugs and crime	91	82
Global warming	80	80
Scarcity of food	72	80
National disasters	70	78
Poverty	79	76
Mexico should actively participate in world affairs	96	68
Accept UN decision to solve an international issue	21	51
Free trade is good for Mexico	73	63
Foreign investment benefits Mexico	92	79
Permit foreign investment in the petroleum sector	64	37
Mexico should seek a special relationship with the United States	51	49
Mexico should be a regional leader	50	35
Mexicans with family members living abroad	—	52
Mexican families that receive half or more monthly income from abroad	—	30
Immigration is good for the receiving country	76	57
Emigration is good for Mexico	29	44
The United States should legalize undocumented Mexicans	19	33
Mexico should generate employment to reduce emigration	53	26
Mexico should negotiate a temporary workers program with the U.S.	18	23

Source: Guadalupe González González, et al., *México: Las Américas y el mundo 2010*, "Política exterior: Opinión pública y líderes" (Mexico: CIDE, 2011).

Most Mexicans are overwhelmingly unenthusiastic about their country assuming a leadership role in the region. Only a third of Mexicans consider this to be an appropriate pursuit for their country. Leaders are more accepting of such a role, but it is only barely half who do so. Yet two-thirds and nearly all elite Mexicans believe their country should actively participate in world affairs. Mexicans have become more accepting of global linkages is in its economic relationships with other countries. Mexicans share a revolutionary heritage of anti-foreignism, but most overwhelmingly agree that foreign investment benefits their country, and to a lesser extent, that free trade is good for Mexico. Fewer Mexicans support foreign investment in the petroleum sector even though two thirds of elites now believe in that economic policy.

Analysts of Mexican foreign policy have long argued that the Mexican government's nationalistic foreign policy stance permitted its leadership to grant concessions to the Mexican Left at little political cost. Although the Mexican Left had few opportunities to pursue their agenda in domestic politics, they could claim greater success in the foreign policy. Such concessions created friction with the United States, but it allowed Mexican leadership to retain strong nationalistic symbols and to reinforce their legitimacy as a protector of Mexican sovereignty.[7]

Nationalism remains a significant issue in Mexico, especially in the context of the United States' bilateral relationship, but nationalism is much more complex in the twenty-first century than previously. One reason for this is the physical movement of vast numbers of Mexicans across the northern border. This has led to a number of fascinating consequences, complemented by increasing economic integration and even cultural influences fomented by technological change, the most influential of which is the Internet. Economic, political, and cultural globalization patterns have pressured most countries into looking outward, not inward. Mexicans have responded to these trends, and comparative surveys demonstrate their decreasing emphasis on nationalistic conceptualizations. For example, only 60 percent of younger Mexicans express pride in being Mexican, 20 percentage points below the national norm (see Table 9-1).[8]

A comparison of how Americans and Mexicans perceive each other reveals other, complex components of nationalism (see Table 9-2). These responses alone suggest the complexity of how citizens in each country view each other, their institutions, and broader economic and political concepts. Sometimes they can be quite similar. For example, they both overwhelmingly agree that community is more important than the individual. This view is essential to establishing and maintaining a democratic polity and to constructing legitimate institutions, a component of a consolidated democracy.

Table 9-2 Mutual Views of Americans and Mexicans

Statements	Percentage of Those Agreeing	
	Americans	Mexicans
Have favorable impression of Mexicans/Americans.	85	35
Have unfavorable impression of their (MX/US) government.	48	66
Free trade can benefit both countries.	75	50
Mexico should not permit Mexican presidential campaigns in the U.S.	62	47
Distant neighbor best describes how the U.S. sees Mexico.	49	36
Corruption explains why Mexico is much poorer than the U.S.	35	37
Its government explains why Mexico is much poorer than the U.S.	35	36
Child or sibling marrying a Mexican/American.	81	52
Community is more important than the individual.	72	69

Source: "Como miramos al vecino," Encuesta CIDAC-ZOGBY México y Estados Unidos, 2010 respondents, $+/-3.2\%$ margin of error, February 3–7, 2006.

Many analysts would not have expected American and Mexican responses to coincide on this statement. Even though some state and local governments, such as the state of Arizona, have introduced controversial legislation against undocumented immigrants directed primarily against Mexicans and Hispanics, suggesting racist undertones, it might surprise readers that Americans overwhelmingly are unopposed to their child or sibling marrying a Mexican. Instead, Mexicans are much more resistant to the reverse pattern. Both populations also recognize the importance of learning each other's language, placing it far ahead of any other potential second language.

The Mexican government has recognized many components of the altered global setting and has responded in several ways. One of the ways in which it responded formally was to establish in 1990 the Program for Mexican Communities Abroad. This program officially took note of this "transborder embrace" in "an attempt to recruit migrants in the United States as members of the national diaspora."[9] Fox highlighted this commitment to Mexicans living in the United States by implementing a policy to allow such nationals to vote in Mexican presidential elections. Even though an unexpectedly small number of Mexicans in United States voted in the 2006 election (although at the norm for a newly franchised voter living abroad), such Mexicans are legitimized and linked to the country of origin by this governmental policy.

Under President Calderón, the Mexican government pursued a more drastic step in challenging its long history of ultranationalism. As part of the president's aggressive anti-drug strategy, which increasingly included the active participation of multiple agencies of the United States government, ranging from the Department of Defense to the Attorney General, Calderón signed a major security agreement known as the Mérida Initiative in 2008, which provided direct American assistance to Mexico as well as security and legal training in both countries.[10] Large numbers of Mexicans accepted these antinationalistic agreements because of serious concerns with personal security and criminal activity.

It can be argued that the most significant transformation in attitudes has occurred among ordinary Mexicans, creating what David Gutiérrez masterfully describes as a Third Space. He argues that the processes associated with free-market global capitalism "have the inevitable effect of transnationalizing the identities of people who habitually travel through the social spaces transformed by these trends." As a result, the people who have grown up on both sides of the border often feel as "at home" in one place as another.[11] The number of Mexicans who fit into this category is astonishing; one out of two Mexicans claim to have a family member living abroad, nearly all of whom resided in the U.S. (see Table 9-1). Equally significant, because of the economic and cultural implications, three in ten Mexicans received half or more of their monthly income from abroad!

In this transnational context, traditional as well as new issues confront the bilateral agenda between the two countries. The most controversial issues facing both countries in the twenty-first century are drug trafficking and immigration. These can be subsumed under three general categories: national security concerns involving drug trafficking, terrorism, political corruption, and political development; basic economic issues, especially trade, investment, immigration, and debt; and cultural influences, values, language, and the arts. The other significant policy issue is economic integration, which goes well beyond the NAFTA agreement.

Indeed, border management, involving local and state interests, in many respects has become the most complex problem.[12] Recently, the two countries outlined in detail many joint projects to improve transportation, commerce, and security screening at the border. Anyone who used to cross the border between the two countries prior to September 11, 2001, wishes longingly for those bygone times, when encountering the long, often frustrating delays returning to the United States, even as ordinary tourists.[13] The commercial traffic at the multiple ports of entry has increased exponentially since the implementation of NAFTA, and cross-border trucking has finally been achieved as part of that agreement, further increasing the volume of traffic. When I travel south from Los Angeles County paralleling the train tracks headed for the small community of Calexico, California, opposite Mexicali, Baja California, it is almost as if there exists a continuous two hundred mile chain of freight cars moving constantly in a giant circle, transferring products between the two countries.

NATIONAL SECURITY ISSUES

The national security issue of greatest significance and long duration in bilateral affairs is that of illegal drugs. The two countries have been collaborating since President Richard Nixon declared his War on Drugs in the 1960s.[14] In the 1990s, Mexico shifted from a minor producer of drugs consumed in the United States, to an increasingly important source. Today, it is the leading source of marijuana and heroin consumed by Americans. Because of the country's geographic location, it has become the major site for the transshipment of drugs from elsewhere in Latin America: more than two-thirds of the cocaine entering the United States passes through Mexico.[15]

It is very important to remember that the drug problem originated in the United States, the largest illegal drug market in the world, where approximately one of eleven Americans over twelve uses illegal drugs.[16] As a leading expert on drug consumption suggests, "Mexico's principal drug problems, the violence and corruption related to trafficking, are the consequence of the large U.S. market for cocaine, heroin, marijuana, and methamphetamine. If the U.S. market disappeared, Mexico's problem would diminish dramatically, even with its own domestic consumption remaining. Thus, it is easy to argue that the key to reducing Mexico's problems is vigorous efforts to reduce consumption in the United States."[17] Instead, the United States has pursued an interdiction strategy without significant success for four decades, strongly encouraging Mexico to join its efforts in using a similar strategy. A Department of Defense funded study nearly two decades ago reached the conclusion that monies devoted to prevention and to a lesser degree rehabilitation were far more effective.[18] One dollar spent on prevention equaled seven dollars spent on interdiction.[19] America's drug czar under Obama, when asked how he would spend an additional $10 billion if it magically appeared in his budget, responded "I'd spend it on prevention and treatment. I think law enforcement and interdiction need strong support, and we've continued to do that. We just really have not put the resources into prevention and treatment that we should."[20]

President Calderón's decision to pursue an aggressive strategy against the Mexican cartels has contributed importantly to the public's views of the most important threats to their national security. It can be easily argued that the top five threats listed by Mexicans, organized crime, public insecurity, kidnapping, corruption, and armed groups—accounting for more than four out of five of all the responses—could be subsumed under organized crime.[21] This emphasis, at least from the Mexican point of view, is not likely to change after 2012, since the lack of public security and the level of drug-related violence remains the number one issue in 2011 and 2012.

Americans' demand for drugs has created many national security problems for Mexican-U.S. relations. Mexico has made considerable efforts to stop the shipment and production of illegal narcotics, but it has made little headway in stemming the flow of drugs across the border. The implementation of NAFTA has only made this task more difficult with the long-delayed introduction of cross-border trucking beginning in 2011. The expansion of drug trafficking has produced numerous, significant consequences: First, because of the amounts of money changing hands and the profits to be made, with estimates ranging between $15 and $30 billion yearly (the lower figure exceeds the total amount of funds spent by the Calderón administration on their security budget from 2006 through 2011),[22] and second, corruption of government officials is inevitable, as is also true in the United States.

Mexicans' income and standard of living are much lower than in the United States, thus corruption has been both broader and deeper there. Through the Mérida Initiative, the United States has invested in the institutional strategy of reforming the police, which has been extended to local police. Yet, at the end of 2011, the 1,100-member police force in Veracruz, a major port, was disbanded because of corruption.[23] A year later, the Mexican government announced that it had screened 180,000 members of the 430,000 state and local police, and fired 65,000 who failed integrity exams.[24] As critics point out, "significant reform in Mexico requires a holistic approach that reaches far beyond the institutions to address the profound economic, sociological and cultural problems that are affecting the country today. Indeed, given how deeply rooted and pervasive these problems are and the geopolitical hand the country was dealt, Mexico has done quite well."[25] Furthermore, drug traffickers, especially in rural communities, have been effective in persuading many Mexicans that they also are responsible for improving the lives of ordinary citizens. Two-fifths of Mexicans believe traffickers create jobs, and a third agree that they create more public works than do local governments, producing progress in their communities.[26]

There is widespread concern in Mexico that drug traffickers are establishing stronger ties to government officials, even though hundreds of government officials, police, and members of the armed forces have given their lives to defeat the cartels. Surprisingly, by 2009, most Mexicans (63 percent) believed that political corruption, not United States demand (26 percent), was the primary explanation for their drug-related problems.[27] Equally important, Mexicans consider corruption (68 percent), crime (81 percent), and illegal drugs (73 percent) as the major domestic policy problems, ranking ahead and just behind that of economic issues (75 percent).[28] These rankings of the major domestic policy issues continued through 2012.

President Calderón attempted to destroy the drug cartels by confronting them directly, relying much more heavily on members of the armed forces. He used mobile battalions to confront cartels, trying to reduce the power of the individual cartels and to capture their leaders.[29] Even though the armed forces and federal police, in collaboration with the United States, arrested and captured numerous leaders, drug-related violence actually increased significantly throughout most of the Calderón administration.[30] In those states where the armed forces intervene, the homicide rate increases significantly.[31] Ironically, the successes achieved by this confrontational strategy created a vacuum among the leading cartels, as they intensely battled each other to take over lucrative drug trafficking routes.[32] The cartels also branched out into numerous other activities, ranging from kidnapping and illegal migration to extortion and money laundering businesses. The cartels are part of a huge global network of organized crime,[33] and have moved into Central America.[34] The fluid nature of the cartels, and their links to corrupt officials, has made it difficult for the government to exert sovereignty over many local communities in Mexico.[35]

Mexicans also are concerned about issues of sovereignty in relation to combating drug trafficking in Mexico, specifically the extent of collaboration between governmental agencies from both countries. Mexico's willingness to allow unarmed U.S. drug enforcement agents to operate on its soil led to numerous controversies earlier in the drug war. During the Calderón administration, the dramatic increase in drug-related violence, and the public's concerns with public security, altered significantly long-standing attitudes toward United States participation in a campaign on Mexican soil. These changing views, however, raise new concerns about Mexican sovereignty. From 2009 through 2012, the Pew Foundation completed a yearly, broad survey, including specific questions involving the armed forces, finding that 74 to 78 percent of Mexicans favored the training of personnel by the United States, 57 to 64 percent would accept money and weapons from the United States, and most surprisingly, 26 to 38 percent actually supported deploying American troops to Mexico.[36] The last figure increased 12 percentage points from 2010 to 2011. In 2010, half of all Mexicans supported the involvement of such organizations as the FBI or United Nations troops in their country if the Mexican government could not resolve the problems of insecurity.[37]

Interestingly, only 26 percent of Americans favored American troops operating in Mexico. By 2011, two-thirds of Mexicans agreed that Mexico should accept intelligence and police or military support from the United States, nearly half said they should accept arms, and even one in five would permit armed American agents to fight against the cartels.[38]

Since September 11, 2001, after which the United States created Northern Command, it desired active cooperation between Mexican, Canadian, and U.S. armed forces. Mexico consented to formal participation in the Department of Defense's new regional structure, but did not become involved in any active manner until the secretary of its navy assigned a captain as a formal liaison in 2009. The following year, the Mexican Army followed suit. The collaboration between the militaries of both countries reached its highest level ever in 2012. Mexico is using its relationship with the United States to obtain intelligence leading to locating and capturing drug cartel leadership. Since 2011, the Obama administration has been sending drones "deep into Mexican territory to gather intelligence that helps locate major traffickers and follow their networks, according to American and Mexican officials."[39] Both countries also have established two "fusion" centers staffed with nationals representing intelligence and military agencies from both governments. In a completely new strategy in 2011, the United States allowed Mexican police to stage cross-border raids from inside the American border. Specifically, Mexican commandos "assembled at designated areas and dispatched helicopter missions back across the border aimed at suspected drug traffickers."[40]

Most Mexicans, especially political leaders, do not want Homeland Security involved directly in solving their national security problems any more than Americans want Mexican intelligence agencies or actors intervening in U.S. domestic affairs. Unfortunately, transnational patterns include issues such as drug production and transportation that cross national borders and become the security problem of the country next door, or for that matter, thousands of miles away. As experts on United States-Mexican security issues warned in advance, militarization of the border, which occurred when President Obama sent 1,200 National Guard troops to the southwestern region, is now an additional issue in bilateral tensions.[41] From a Mexican perspective, the inability of the United States to prevent the flow of arms to Mexico, which provides 90 percent of the traceable weapons used in drug-related homicides, has become a major complaint.[42] Given partisan domestic attitudes about gun control in the United States, this becomes an intractable issue when developing a counter-narcotics strategy in Mexico.[43] Further, an estimated $10 billion a year is laundered by the cartels in the United States and transported back across the American border to Mexico. Many analysts have argued that both sides should focus more significantly on forensic financial criminal activities. From a United States perspective, there exists serious concern about the potential for "spillover violence" along the border.[44] Gangs in Mexican and major American cities are essential to the successful distribution and sales of drugs throughout the region.

An entirely new issue in the bilateral national security agenda is international terrorism. It is a topic that is deeply enmeshed in other longstanding issues including drug trafficking (as a means of financing such activities) and immigration (the ease with which individuals can cross into the United States from Mexico). The September 2001 terrorist attacks on the United States set off a series of reactions in Mexico that reflected the complexity and history of the two countries' relationship. Fox's first secretary of foreign relations, Jorge Castañeda, expressed strong support for the United States and for its right to defend itself, a position that was not widely supported by Mexicans. In response to public opinion, President Fox provided only tepid support for the United States.[45] The relationship between the two countries continued to deteriorate as the Bush administration pursued an aggressive policy and initiated the war with Iraq, a war condemned by an overwhelming number of Mexicans.

Contrary to what some public commentators might believe, as early as 2004, Mexicans shared similar concerns with Americans about national security issues. Ordinary citizens overwhelmingly believed drug trafficking, the world economic crisis, chemical and biological weapons, and international terrorism were major threats to Mexican security. Furthermore, they were much more likely to favor certain policies than their leaders, including collaboration with American officials. For example, they favored increased requirements for entering and exiting Mexico; increased control over goods through Mexico's borders, ports, and airports; and allowing American agents to work with Mexican counterparts to protect borders, airports, and ports.[46]

Terrorism and border security policies linked to that issue have produced new institutional structures in the bi-national relationship. The establishment of a Homeland Security Agency, which coordinates numerous existing U.S. agencies, altered previously established institutional patterns. The potential terrorism threat implies increased collaboration among the armed forces, among health-related agencies that would cope with bioterrorism, and among intelligence agencies, just to name a few.[47] Both countries are further linked together in solving these new bilateral issues because both countries' citizens and infrastructure will have to bear the likely consequences of such attacks along the border. More importantly, with drug trafficking organizations expanding into multiple illegal activities, one of which is establishing control over illegal migration routes, is that they would be much more likely to use their skills and sophisticated channels to transport terrorists. As of 2012, no evidence exists to document such a linkage.[48]

CULTURAL INTERFACE

As suggested above, one salient contextual explanation of Mexico's willingness to consider an economic and even a political union with Canada and the United States is that some of the three countries' basic economic and political values are converging. In eleven of fifteen values measured by the World Values Survey between 1981 and 1990, Ronald Inglehart and his collaborators discovered that the three countries were simultaneously moving in the same direction.[49] The three most important goals of Mexicans and Americans were the same two decades ago: raise children, have a successful career, and be happily married. In 2007, they reexamined the trends among the three countries, again using World Values Survey data. In recent years, their values have become more divergent. For example, national pride among Canadians and Mexicans have continued to increase since 1990, while Americans declined significantly. Whereas respect for authority has declined among Canadians and in the case of Americans, significantly, it has risen dramatically among Mexicans. In short, while broadly their values are converging there exists greater diversity than previously. Even though Mexicans admire many qualities of their neighbor to the north, not least its political system, they share many reservations as well.

The attitudes expressed by the citizens of both countries are surprising, even to Mexican experts. For example, contrary to a traditional stereotype of Mexicans, three-quarters of Mexicans and Americans view them as hardworking. Other than both countries believing the other's language is overwhelmingly the most useful second language, the view of Mexicans as hardworking elicited the strongest agreement from both countries. By contrast, the sharpest disagreement between the two occurred with their views on tolerance and racism. Americans and Mexicans agree on the level of Mexican tolerance, but Americans view themselves as less tolerant than Mexicans, and Mexicans view them as far less tolerant. A similar pattern occurs with racism; both Americans and Mexicans view the latter as rarely racist. Americans, on the other hand, are twice as likely to see their country as racist, and Mexicans are twice as likely as Americans to see Americans as racist. This is a persistent image (see Table 9-3).

Table 9-3 American and Mexican Cultural Views of Each Other

Statements	Percentage of Those Agreeing	
	Americans	Mexicans
Mexicans are hardworking	78	75
Americans are hardworking	56	26
Mexicans are honest	42	49
Americans are honest	41	22
Mexicans respect the law	34	33
Americans respect the law	46	40
Mexicans are racists	18	17
Americans are racists	35	73
Mexicans are tolerant	44	45
Americans are tolerant	36	17
Spanish/English is the best second language for children to learn	78	89

Source: "Como miramos al vecino," Encuesta CIDAC-ZOGBY México y Estados Unidos, 2010 respondents, +/–3.2% margin of error, February 3–7, 2006.
Questions: Except for the last question, all questions were asked using a 5-point scale, with 5 being "very" and 1 being "not at all." These percentages are a sum of the 4 and 5 responses.

Mexico's distrust of the United States because of the latter's involvement historically in Mexican affairs is complemented by cultural and economic relationships between the two countries. There is a lively commerce in ideas, music, art, fashion, cuisine, and so on. The influence of U.S. culture can be found worldwide, but it is more intense in Mexico by virtue of closeness. Heavy tourist traffic runs in both directions. More Americans report visiting Mexico than any other developing country or region.[50] Twenty-two million tourists visited Mexico in 2010, 79 percent of them from the United States and Canada.[51] In the last decade, more than half of Americans reported having visited Mexico previously, and 70 percent indicated they would like to visit the country.[52]

The reverse pattern is equally striking. Fifty-six percent of all foreign visitors to the United States come from Canada and Mexico. During 2008, 13.7 million people entered the United States from Mexico. Canadians and Mexicans spent $22 billion. A fourth of all Mexicans have already visited the United States, and nearly 60 percent indicate they would like to travel to it again. The proximity of place also has contributed to the fact that more Americans reside in Mexico than in any other Third World country, and more Mexicans reside in the United States than in any other country (32 million in 2010). Los Angeles has a higher concentration of people (4.5 million in 2010) of Mexican descent than any city except Mexico City.[53] English is studied and spoken by many Mexicans.[54] Spanish is the foreign language studied most often in U.S. high schools. American music permeates the airwaves.

On the other hand, Mexican-American musicians and music originating from Mexico have increased in popularity in the United States. Los Tigres del Norte, from San Jose, California, have generated a large following among music fans. American performers from rock stars to magicians are headliners in major Mexican cities. Television is saturated with shows and movies from north of the border, and the well-to-do who subscribe to satellite reception have access to a complete range of programs. The United States constitutes an almost unavoidable presence in the daily lives of most Mexicans.

Culturally, the relationship is unequal. Nevertheless, because Spanish is the second most frequently spoken language in the United States, and Mexicans— along with Central Americans, Cubans, and other Latin Americans—have spread throughout the United States, their culture is influencing the United States' culture.[55] Some Americans have reacted with heightened nationalism. The English First movement in the 1980s was an effort to reassert the supremacy of English and of traditional, nonminority values in the face of what is deemed to be an onslaught of Hispanic values and language. Oscar Martínez observed that "Groups such as U.S. English and English First have campaigned hard to convince a large portion of the American public that the use of languages other than English fosters fragmentation in the country and threatens future political stability. Led by California, by the mid-1980s about twelve states had declared English as their official language, sending a message to Hispanics and other language minority groups that they should rid themselves of their native tongues as quickly as possible."[56]

Politically and culturally it is the United States that has exercised the greatest long-term influence between the two countries, but the asymmetry each exercises on the other is shifting in favor of Mexico. Nevertheless, America's influence in the world, while in decline, continues to assign it substantial prestige. This allows its political processes and to some extent its political values to acquire a certain degree of legitimacy in the eyes of many Mexicans, including politicians, hence the implicit influence of the United States model. In the past, some Mexicans have felt uncomfortable supporting democratization because they sensed it was a goal of the United States.[57] In fact, the majority of Mexicans do not favor the United States policy of promoting democracy elsewhere in the world. Today, however, as demonstrated elsewhere in this book, Mexicans, like Latin Americans and all residents of the Third World, are judging democracy overwhelmingly on its effectiveness as a political model, not on its origins or associations with the United States.

In the second decade of the twenty-first century, however, it may be Mexicans who begin to exert a profound influence on the United States, especially in California and Texas. Their impact politically was clearly illustrated in the outcome of the United States presidential election in 2012. The growth in the Hispanic population generally, and Mexicans specifically, as reported in the demographic statistics from the 2010 census, has been nothing short of extraordinary. The growth exceeded all predictions from just a decade ago, when leading scholars estimated 25 million Mexicans and 41 million Hispanics in the United States in 2010.[58] Instead, by 2009, the figures were 31 and 48 million respectively. By 2050, Hispanics will account for 128 million Americans, 29 percent of the population.

Some states, such as Iowa and Nebraska, experiencing declining populations, were actively recruiting immigrants before the 2008 recession, including Mexicans, to bolster their economically active populations. One might expect the Mexican influence on political values to be substantial, based on its presence in certain regions. But in the first available comparative research on Mexicans, Mexican-Americans, and non-Mexican Americans, which has not been replicated since 2000, the findings demonstrate that on attitudes related to politics generally Mexicans begin to take on the beliefs of other Americans, rather than altering American beliefs. This evolutionary pattern can clearly be seen among the three groups' views on the meaning of democracy (see Table 9-4). There is no reason to expect the direction of the change to alter in the future. However, if American definitions of democracy change, then views by recent Mexican immigrants to the United States are likely to follow.

The data in Table 9-4 illustrate the transformation in political beliefs among Mexicans residing in the United States. They demonstrate, for example, that once Mexicans moved to the United States, they quickly began to conceive of democracy as liberty, as did their American peers. Unlike

Table 9-4 Meaning of Democracy among Mexicans, Mexican-Americans, and Americans

Meaning of Democracy	Group (Percentages)		
	Mexicans	Mexican-Americans	Other Americans
Liberty	25	42	64
Equality	26	15	8
Voting/elections	11	5	4
Type of government	9	7	2
Respect/lawfulness	8	3	4
Well-being/progress	7	8	1
Other	14	19	12
Don't know/No response	0	0	5

Source: "Democracy through U.S. and Mexican Lenses," Grant, Hewlett Foundation, September 2000. Figures in some columns do not add up to 100% due to rounding.
The question asked: "In one word, could you tell me what democracy means for you?"

their Mexican counterparts, they no longer gave equal weight to equality and liberty and, instead, equality dropped dramatically as an important concept. Finally, while voting and elections were important to Mexicans' definition of democracy, they dropped significantly in importance among Mexican-Americans, who selected them as their definition about as frequently as other Americans.

ECONOMIC LINKAGES

One of the most sensitive issues in the United States–Mexican relationship, because of its prominence as a cause of the Mexican Revolution, is foreign investment. Even as late as the early twentieth century, some American diplomatic representatives maintained personal economic interests in Mexico that influenced their recommendations. By the beginning of the revolution, United States investment alone in Mexico had reached staggering figures. Roger D. Hansen remarks that under Díaz, foreign capital (38 percent from the United States) in percentage terms, exceeded that of European investment in the United States.[59]

The ideology of Mexicanization, which grew out of the revolutionary struggle, traces its strongest roots to United States economic influence and the presence of American businessmen, managers, professionals, and landowners, especially in the north.[60] In formulating its economic development policies, while protecting the sovereignty of its decision-making, Mexico has had to consider its economic relationship with the United States. President Salinas set in motion a revolutionary economic relationship between Mexico and the United States, encompassed in NAFTA. To accomplish this goal as part of his foreign and domestic policy agendas, he and his cabinet worked assiduously to persuade Mexicans that a formal economic linkage with the United States was beneficial financially and did not violate Mexican sovereignty. By the end of the 1990s, the majority of Mexicans had become convinced of NAFTA's benefits, viewing it positively from a variety of perspectives.[61] A decade after it went into effect, however, Mexicans expressed less positive views about NAFTA. Both Americans and Mexicans viewed its results as being more positive for their neighbor than for themselves.[62]

The North American Free Trade Agreement is a complex document with implications for member countries' social policies. Management-labor relations provide a useful example of how a foreign economic policy agreement can have broader political implications domestically. In Mexico, many of the export-oriented companies employ unionized workers. The structural and legal pattern of labor-business relations enables a government official to provide the decisive vote in arbitrated disputes. One of the most controversial side agreements in NAFTA required Mexico to conform to U.S. laws in protecting labor rights. The U.S. labor movement, though it opposed NAFTA, succeeded in obtaining certain agreements, which, if enforced, would strengthen workers' rights in Mexico. In April 1995, U.S. labor unions and human rights groups persuaded Robert Reich, the secretary of labor, to discuss with his Mexican counterpart the specific issue of workers in a Sony factory in Nuevo Laredo that had been prevented from establishing an independent union, thereby violating Mexico's own labor code.[63] The reverse is also true. In May 1998, four Mexican unions, with the support of the American teamsters union, filed a complaint against the Washington state apple industry for violating migrant worker rights, including safety and pay issues. The significance of this and other NAFTA side agreements is that they provide an important legal vehicle for American groups to become involved in numerous Mexican domestic issues, among them labor and environmental concerns, and for Mexicans to do the same in the United States. On the Mexican side, however, these legal changes have produced few successes in favor of labor rights some years later.

The broader issue that economic and commercial agreements emphasize for both countries, but especially Mexico, is nationalism. Some analysts have gone as far as to argue that not only has NAFTA shrunk Mexican national sovereignty, but a decline in state sovereignty, engineered through international agreements, limits the country's ability to protect ordinary citizens' interests.[64] This interpretation can be disputed, but NAFTA and the increasing economic dependency of the two countries definitely have determined other major policy decisions. The most striking example of such a consequence is the Clinton administration's financial rescue package offered in early 1995 shortly after NAFTA's implementation, after the devaluation of the peso led to extensive capital flight. Indeed, the size of the United States and international agency aid, some $49 billion, was in part based on Mexico's membership in NAFTA.[65] The package itself, because it required Mexico to guarantee repayment of its loans to the United States ($20 billion of the total), generated additional concern in Mexico, because numerous Mexicans viewed the aid as further evidence of the United States' infringement on their sovereignty. Mexico actually repaid the loan early.[66] Another way of understanding its impact on Mexican sovereignty is legally. As one scholar argues, Mexico has undergone a transformation from "national sovereignty" to "constitutional sovereignty" in the sense that it has begun to alter its "standards of legitimacy and to increase the importance of international standards."[67] An illustration of this to date is the extensive reform in its legal system, brought about by the broader economic linkages, and more recently the pressing weaknesses in Mexico's legal system in prosecuting drug traffickers and other criminals. The central component of this reform is creating a justice system involving oral trials and forensic evidence, imitating the American system.[68] These alterations continue to be implemented on a state-by-state basis since 2008. A comprehensive survey of judges and public prosecutors reports general satisfaction with the reforms to date in 2011, but they have yet to be completed.[69]

The implementation of NAFTA produced a dramatic increase in trade between the United States and Mexico. Trade tripled with the United States between 1990 and 2008, significantly influenced by NAFTA. In 2010, Mexico purchased $153 billion in goods from its neighbor.[70] "Mexico is now the United States' third largest trading partner and the second destination of exports, accounting for roughly an eighth of all U.S. exports. Twenty-two U.S. states depend on Mexico as their first or second destination for exports, and such exports are especially important for Texas, Arizona, Nebraska, California, and Iowa. The United States accounts for roughly two-thirds of Mexican trade and is the destination of 82% of its exports."[71] By 2012, Mexico accounted for 12 percent of the total trade figures with the United States after Canada and China.[72] Building on this level of economic integration, President Obama and Calderón agreed to expand efforts to improve and develop a border management program to address multiple facets of the relationship, including facilitating two-way commerce in goods and people across the borders and addressing numerous environmental health problems.[73]

Whereas NAFTA helped to expand and to globalize the Mexican economy through accelerated exports, evaluations of its impact on the alleviation of poverty and improving the standard of living of most Mexicans suggest much less success. Mexico has failed to implement many structural economic changes, including fiscal, educational, and labor policies, so the blame should not be attributed to NAFTA alone.[74] As the Mexico Institute of the Woodrow Wilson Center recommended, "A key goal of a post-NAFTA agenda should be to reduce income disparities and raise living standards."[75] This goal is critical, indeed, fundamental to Mexico's economic development and to the two other central issues in the bilateral agenda, drugs and immigration. The health of the Mexican economy, and the ability of the economy to create new jobs to meet the demands of an economically active population, directly impact on the attractiveness of drug cartels as employers for unemployed Mexicans, particularly young males, and on the decision of many Mexicans to migrate to the United States. The agreement was sold to citizens of both countries as a policy to improve their standard of living.[76] In Mexico, such improvements were linked to reducing immigration. Instead, many small businesses, especially in the Mexican agricultural sector, did not survive the competition from United States subsidized imports.[77] The level of integration between the two economies, and their interdependence, produced a devastating impact on Mexico after the global recession, an effect not felt to the same degree by any other Latin American economy.

Although it is difficult to link NAFTA to continued political reforms after 1994, several scholars have argued convincingly that president Zedillo introduced political reforms that complemented and accelerated the democratic transition. For example, Mark Williams notes that Zedillo "supported constitutional amendments that revamped the federal judiciary, helped professionalize the Supreme Court, and provided it greater political independence. The impact of judicial reform stretched well beyond economic matters. Citizens and opposition elements now had another avenue to contest the ruling party's power, and the revamped Court ventured quickly into a political realm it had long eschewed."[78] Furthermore, Pamela Starr has suggested that after the peso crisis in the first weeks of his administration, Zedillo was in a weakened political condition, and therefore was motivated to negotiate the significant 1996 electoral reforms, which as noted earlier, were critical to leveling the playing field among the political parties and to making the Federal Electoral Institute autonomous. The 2000 and 2006 opposition presidential victories benefitted from and were achieved under this legislation, which was not significantly altered until 2007.[79]

The economically related issue generating the most controversy on the bilateral agenda, especially in the eyes of ordinary Americans and Mexicans, is immigration. It is revealing because its consequences invoke cultural, economic, and political issues, which appear prominently on domestic agendas. Immigration has a long history throughout the twentieth century, and only in recent years has the United States attempted comprehensively and formally to prevent the flow of Mexican immigrants. Mexicans crossed the border to work for decades after the mid-nineteenth century without controls.

Labor tends to follow capital, especially when unemployment and underemployment reach significant levels. Thus Mexicans went northward during difficult times in search of work. In the past some eventually became U.S. citizens, but most returned to their homeland after short stays. What are the economic consequences of this relationship? For Mexico, it has meant increased economic opportunities for its people, in some cases the potential for learning new skills. Also, their wages in large part have been remitted to their places of origin, thereby creating local sources of capital.[80]

It has been estimated that just before the 2008 recession emigrants sent as much as $26 billion dollars back to Mexico, and those figures have remained above $21 billion from 2005 through 2012. Mexico ranks second in the world in terms of income earned in foreign currencies. By 2010, three out of ten families in Mexico were receiving half or more of their monthly income from remittances (see Table 9-1). For the United States, the economic benefits have been substantial. Historically, most of the migrants have worked in agriculture, providing cheaper foodstuffs than would have been otherwise available. In recent years, Mexicans have contributed millions of workers to the service sector.

The political consequences of the relationship are numerous. Those consequences, on both sides of the border, will multiply as the population increases dramatically. In Mexico, studies of local communities suggest that the volume of residents leaving poor rural communities, specifically indigenous communities, are unable to staff positions, thus forcing changes in the persistence of traditional social and political institutions.[81] In the United States, from 2000 to 2010, the U.S. Census reveals that the American population grew 9.7 percent, the Hispanic population 43 percent, and the Mexican population 54.1 percent. If the Hispanic population were removed from the figures for the total growth during this decade, it would only be 4.9 percent, half as much. The dramatic increase in the Mexican-origin population, originating both from legal and undocumented Mexicans, reveals the inability of the Mexican economy to provide adequate economic opportunities. California, Texas, Arizona, Illinois, and Colorado share in the highest Mexican-origin populations.

Recent surveys document the fact that economic opportunities are not the only motivation for leaving Mexico or Latin America. In fact, lack of personal security, strongly linked to the level of criminal violence in Mexico, is a strong causal factor, as well as having family members already living abroad.[82] Indeed, some scholars believe that "narco-refugees" are likely to become a serious challenge for United States national security.[83] In 2012, 37 percent of Mexicans said they would move to the United States, half of them without authorization, if given the opportunity.[84] Fourteen other countries in Latin America registered a higher response than did Mexico. Indirectly, the United States in the past aided Mexican domestic stability by channeling discontent northward. Yet Mexican nationalism—given the historical relationship discussed previously—forces Mexico to express concern over the migration. But as the data in Table 9-1 reveal, only a third of Mexicans believe the United States should legalize undocumented Mexicans and only 23 percent believe their government should negotiate a temporary workers program with the United States.

The terrorist attacks in September 2001 added a new political perspective to the immigration issue, discussed earlier, of border security. Fox and his first secretary of foreign relations made immigration reform the leading issue on the bilateral agenda. It was never removed from the agenda, but the Bush administration essentially ignored that issue after 2001. After continued pressure from the Mexican side, President Bush finally put forward his own concept of a temporary workers' program in his 2004 State of the Union address, but it was never approved by Congress.[85] When President Obama took office, some observers thought that his administration might be able to pass new immigration legislation. However, the damaging economic impact of the recession, and the efforts of states like Arizona to address undocumented immigration on its own (SB1070), resulted in the federal government enforcing existing laws more aggressively while opposing even more restrictive local legislation. To date, there is no progress on immigration reform between the two countries.

Another political consequence affecting both sides of the border relates to the political activity of this population. In 1998, the Mexican Congress granted dual nationality to Mexicans living abroad. Since 99 percent of all Mexicans living abroad reside in the United States, the implications of this legislation essentially are confined to the bilateral relationship. Politically, dual nationality opens up the door to Mexicans abroad being able to vote in Mexican elections. The Mexican government estimated that in 2000, 7.1 million adult Mexicans living abroad, and 2.8 million Americans of Mexican parentage, would take advantage of Mexican nationality.[86] In 2005, the Chamber of Deputies overwhelmingly passed a bill giving the right to vote in presidential elections to Mexicans abroad, just in time for the 2006 presidential contest. Those eligible were restricted to Mexicans who had obtained a voting credential before mid-February 2006 and applied for a mail-in ballot. This group was much smaller than their potential numbers originally suggested.[87] In 2012, the numbers of absentee voters did not increase significantly, with only 4,938 more requests being made than previously.[88]

Immigrants are politically active in both countries. In the United States, they have organized hundreds of groups, and their leaders have met with presidential advisers to push for immigration reform. On the Mexican side, they have formed political action committees and have sent delegations of campaign workers to help favored candidates. Some of these residents in the United States returned to Mexico to compete for political office and won a mayoralty race as well as a seat in the 2003–2006 Congress.

For the United States, the economic implications of immigration are obvious. The demand for unskilled workers now extends into a variety of occupational categories, but critics charge that American workers go unemployed. Some groups in the United States resent what they see as their displacement by immigrant labor from Mexico. Moreover, employers are accused of hiring Mexican workers in order to avoid paying certain benefits and taxes. Finally, middle-class taxpayers have begun to view immigrants as a tremendous drain on welfare resources and public education, which led to the passage of California's Proposition 187 in 1994. In reality, Mexican immigrants are net tax contributors to the federal government, but at the state level, depending on services available to them, their contributions vary. In New Jersey, they are net contributors; in California, they are net beneficiaries. Given the economic conditions of most states since the 2008 recession, these figures became serious economic and political issues.

Proposition 187 is essentially anti-immigrant legislation designed to exclude Hispanics from California's social services, specifically to remove children from public school classrooms and to prevent their parents seeking health care and unemployment benefits from the state. More than half of all Mexicans view this legislation as racist, and nine out of ten Mexicans strongly oppose similar legislation elsewhere in the United States.[89] The 2010 Arizona bill (SB1070) focuses instead on removing undocumented Mexicans from the state so that they would be unable to avail themselves of such benefits, to seek employment, and to commit crimes. It relies on enforcement by local authorities, specifically police officers.[90]

Culturally, immigration spills over into many of the issues affecting U.S.-Mexican relations. The English First movement came about largely through the rapid expansion of the U.S. Hispanic population and the visible immigration of Mexicans and Central Americans into the Southwest. Immigration is a perceived cultural threat, which translates into local and state policy debates, often placed before voters.[91] In Mexico, on the other hand, whole villages are literally ghost towns, as younger men and women leave for the United States. Children are often left in the hands of the mother alone or grandparents, breaking down the traditional family structure. Discouraged by the violence of U.S. cities, many migrant Mexicans who have children in the United States send them back to their home communities. But these children bring American values with them, threatening the integrity of the local culture.[92]

Immigration, trade, and investment have many more ramifications, both subtle and obvious. The point is that their proximity makes both countries prisoners, to some extent, of each other's problems. For example, Fox's ambitious policy agenda was adversely affected in 2001 and 2002 by the sharp downturn in Mexico's economy, heavily tied to the U.S. recession, similar to Calderón's efforts in increasing the pace of economic growth and employment since 2008 under similar and more long-lasting conditions.

And although Mexico labors under a much greater dependency and subordination, its economic situation affects the United States. For example, the United States experienced an unexpected and immediate increase in its trade deficit in the months immediately following the devaluation of the Mexican peso in 1994 as United States exports became excessively expensive and Mexican imports relatively cheap. Mexico's political system must consider carefully the domestic issues and associated policies that bear on this relationship. The United States has no direct veto power over Mexican politics, but its presence casts a permanent shadow that the Mexican political leadership cannot ignore.

CONCLUSION

As this chapter makes clear, it is obvious that the United States exercises a significant role in Mexico, not only in its dominance over the focus of Mexican foreign policy, but in numerous other facets, social, cultural, and economic. The North American Free Trade Agreement only has reinforced a level of influence long apparent, implicitly and explicitly, in the relationship between Mexico and the United States. While it is true that Mexico's strong sense of nationalism was a natural response to its historical experience with the United States, Mexico has found it necessary, for important economic and social reasons, to modify its traditional posture in return for identifying its future development more closely with the fortunes of the United States.

Numerous issues affect the bilateral relationship between these two neighbors. This chapter touches only on those that are most prominent, particularly in the 2000s and 2010s. The national security agenda between the two countries increasingly has taken precedence over other traditional issues such as immigration, but the scope of national security concerns, because of increased linkages practically and formally, has broadened and deepened.[93] Issues such as combating drug trafficking have gone well beyond social agendas typically associated with such problems to become inextricably intertwined with the very legitimacy of Mexican political institutions and the stability of its political system.

In other words, the anti-drug strategy pursued by Mexico and the United States is having a significant impact on democratic institutions, and on the ability of those institutions to function adequately to meet the needs of their citizens, specifically as relates to personal security. Local, state and national leaders have been compromised by drug traffickers. It has been suggested that military intelligence sources in Mexico allege that "between

55 and 65 percent of the political campaigns in Mexico have been infiltrated by criminal groups that are pumping money into the campaign process."[94] Other politicians, including gubernatorial and congressional candidates, have been assassinated by cartels in an effort to prevent them from holding or winning office. Mexican political institutions are being sorely tested in the confrontation with drug trafficking organizations, making it more difficult to achieve conditions that typically are identified with democratic consolidation. The media in Mexico cannot perform its investigative responsibilities, thereby broadening and deepening accountability of government officials, if their research and coverage involves drug trafficking linkages and corruption. Thus the intertwining of a bilateral issue and strategy with multiple domestic policy issues is also interwoven into Mexico's future democratic political development.

The intensity and breadth of the bilateral agenda, often involving issues affecting the domestic policy perspectives and postures of the two countries' voters and politicians, complicate their foreign relations. Some of these issues, such as corruption and illegal immigration, evoke heated, emotional responses on both sides of the border. A strong temptation exists, particularly in the United States, for national legislators to impose moral and philosophical judgments on Mexico's political model, specifically on the extent of corruption and on human rights issues. The increased involvement in Mexican domestic affairs by the U.S. media, and civic organizations such as human rights groups, ensures the U.S. government's continued and heightened involvement in Mexican matters.[95] At the same time, the expanding pluralization of Mexico's political process and the contentiousness of its differing political actors, nationally and regionally, further complicate relations between both countries. As individual states are linked more directly to Mexico, and as Mexicans have come to reside throughout the United States, state legislatures and governors have become significant actors. California, for example, has its own agency and legislative committee devoted to Mexican foreign relations.[96] Arizona's efforts to establish its own immigration standards different from the federal government created serious difficulties for the federal government's bilateral relationship.[97]

Foreign policy experts have raised a number of concerns about future issues on the bilateral agenda and about the inadequacies of the process through which they are dealt with by both countries. Many of these criticisms focus on security issues involving policing the border, drug enforcement corruption, and American officials' lack of concern toward Mexico's domestic economic failures, which can be linked to the drug cartels and immigration. A Council on Foreign Relations special report recommended increased cooperation at all levels of government in the border management process, rethinking U.S. drug policy, and increasing economic and educational assistance to Mexico.[98]

The PRI victory in the 2012 presidential election will introduce changes in the U.S.-Mexican relationship, most significantly with some alteration in the focus of the federal government's anti-drug strategy. Enrique Peña Nieto suggested during the campaign that as president he would focus on strengthening local and state police; that while continuing to rely on the armed forces, the government would borrow local strategies from other countries, including Colombia and the United States, using a collaborative approach among officials, police and community members, with an eye toward stemming the drug-related violence rather than capturing drug-cartel leadership; and that Mexico must focus on attacking the underlying poverty and lack of economic development which allows cartels to attract unemployed, young males.[99] The President's view is confirmed by the government's own national victimization survey in 2012 in which six out of ten Mexicans believe insecurity is the country's number one problem, while at the same time it believes poverty and unemployment are the principle causes.[100]

Under the Fox and Calderón administrations, despite the ups and downs in the bilateral relationship, cooperation between the two governments increased. Under Calderón, the relationship reached its low point after the WikiLeaks scandal, which made public dozens of communications between Ambassador Carlos Pascual and the U.S. State Department, in which the ambassador raised numerous criticisms including implementation of Mexico's anti-drug strategy. Pascual later resigned his post. Calderón publicly criticized the Obama administration in Mexico and the United States, including before the U.S. Congress, for its failure to produce immigration reform and to address the transfer of illegal weapons to Mexico.[101] Despite the critical rhetoric, the concrete results of the collaboration out of the public eye can be best seen in their anti-drug strategy, where numerous agencies, including their respective defense agencies, have established a closer relationship in sharing intelligence resulting in successful missions against the drug trafficking organizations. More members of Congress have been briefed on Mexico and have traveled in person to visit their counterparts. During the Calderón administration, members of the Mexican Congress and of executive agencies, as well as representatives of the Mexican armed forces, have visited Northern Command and have taken short courses at the Center for Hemispheric Defense Studies at the National Defense University in Washington, DC. Despite their closer collaboration on drug trafficking efforts, with the exception of cocaine, used by only 0.6 percent of the U.S. population over age twelve, all other drug use in America remains consistent or has increased from 2002 through 2010, with all illicit drug usage up 0.6 percent to 9 percent of the population over twelve, marijuana up 0.7 percent to 7 percent of the population over twelve, and psychotherapeutics, the same at 2.7 percent of the population over twelve.[102]

The closer relationship that gradually has emerged between the two countries in the last decade has not eliminated domestic issues involving nationalist concerns that impinge on the relationship. Under Calderón, President Obama was able to improve the United States' image through his general foreign policy posture and the withdrawal of troops from Iraq. As a result of those changes, Mexicans' positive views of the United States reached 62 percent in 2010. But when the governor of Arizona signed the anti-immigration bill in April of that year, a survey showed a dramatic drop in their positive image of the United States, to only 44 percent, while negative views increased even more significantly from 27 to 48 percent, comparable to survey data results during the earlier Iraq War. In 2011, their positive views were again on the rise, reaching 52 percent, and in 2012, they rose to 56 percent.[103] Future decisions made by the American government, and increasingly by state and local governments, could unexpectedly alter this evaluation. Thus, nationalism continues to affect support for and suspicion of the United States, and remains an essential ingredient in the two countries' relationship.

NOTES

1. Javier Santismo, "Mexico's Economic Ties with Europe: Business as Usual?" in *Mexico's Democracy at Work: Political and Economic Dynamics*, ed. Russell Crandall, Guadalupe Paz, and Riordan Roett (Boulder, CO: Lynne Rienner, 2005), 185.

2. "Prologue," *Unequal Partners: The United States and Mexico* (Pittsburgh, PA: University of Pittsburgh Press, 2010), 34.

3. Christopher Wilson, *Working Together: Economic Ties between the United States and Mexico* (Washington, DC: Woodrow Wilson Center for International Scholars, 2012), 11.

4. Tim Weiner, "Mexico's Influence in Security Council Decision May Help Its Ties with U.S.," *New York Times*, November 9, 2002.

5. Luz María de la Mora Sánchez, "Building a Global Presence: Institutional Challenges in Strengthening Mexico's Role in International Cooperation," Mexico Institute, Woodrow Wilson International Center for Scholars, March 8, 2010, 3.

6. It also organized the first Mexico-Caribbean Community Summit Meeting in Cancún in 2010. Emily Godoy, "Mexico Dusts off Leadership Role," Inter Press Service News Agency, February 25, 2010.

7. Dolia Estevez's interview with former ambassador John Gavin, in *U.S. Ambassadors to Mexico, the Relationship in Their Eyes* (Washington, DC: Woodrow Wilson Center, 2012), 41–56.

8. Guadalupe González González, et al., *México: Las Américas y el mundo 2010*, "Política exterior: Opinión pública y líderes" (Mexico: CIDE, 2011), 28.

9. David Thelen, "Rethinking History and the Nation-State: Mexico and the United States," *The Journal of American History* 86, no. 2 (September 1999): 439–55.

10. Raúl Benítez Manaut, "The Mérida Initiative: An Assessment," Mexico Institute, Woodrow Wilson Center, Washington, DC, 2009.

11. David G. Gutiérrez, "Migration, Emergent Ethnicity, and the 'Third Space': The Shifting Politics of Nationalism in Greater Mexico," *The Journal of American History* 86, no. 2 (September 1999): 512–13.

12. *The United States and Mexico: Towards a Strategic Partnership; A Report of Four Working Groups on U.S.-Mexico Relations* (Washington, DC: Mexico Institute, Woodrow Wilson International Center for Scholars, 2009), 4.

13. Embassy of Mexico, "Mexico-US Bilateral Action Plan, Inaugural Meeting of the Bilateral Executive Steering Committee on Twenty-First Century Border Management," May 19, 2010.

14. See "The Fight Against Drugs," Mexico, Office of the President, September 1997; *US/Mexico Bi-National Drug Strategy*, High Level Contact Group for Drug Control, U.S.-Mexico, February, 1998; and Executive Office of the President, Office of National Drug Control Policy, *Report to Congress* (Washington, DC: September 1997).

15. John Walsh, "Lowering Expectations, Supply Control and the Resilient Cocaine Market," Washington Office on Latin America, April 14, 2009.

16. United Nations Office on Drugs and Crime, *World Drug Report 2011* (New York: United Nations, 2011), offers the most comprehensive and up to date data on drug production and consumption patterns worldwide, 133.

17. Peter H. Reuter, "How Can Domestic U.S. Drug Policy Help Mexico?," in *Shared Responsibility: U.S.- Mexico Policy Options for Confronting Organized Crime*, eds. Eric H. Olson, Andrew Selee, and David Shirk (Washington, DC: Woodrow Wilson Center, 2010), 133.

18. Peter H. Reuter, *Quantity Illusions and Paradoxes of Drug Interdiction: Federal Intervention into Vice Policy* (Santa Monica, CA: RAND Corporation, 1989).

19. C. Peter Rydell and Susan Everingham, *Controlling Cocaine: Supply Versus Demand Programs* (Santa Monica, CA: RAND Corporation, 1994).

20. "U.S. Drug Czar Gil Kerlikowske Addresses Hemispheric Concerns at CHDS Conference," May 21, 2010. In President Obama's 2011 budget request, 36 percent was designated for treatment and prevention. Traditionally, U.S. drug budgets have devoted less than 10 percent to these approaches.

21. Sistemas de Inteligencia en Mercado y Opinión, June–August, 2009, "Encuesta Seguridad Nacional," 1,250 interviews nationally, +/− 1.9% margin of error, July 24–27, 2009.

22. Eric L. Olson, "Considering New Strategies for Confronting Organized Crime in Mexico," Mexico Institute, Woodrow Wilson International Center for Scholars, March 2012, 3.

23. "Mexico: City Police Force Disbanded," *The New York Times*, December 21, 2011.

24. "Police Reform," *Justice in Mexico News Monitor*, September 2012, 4.

25. Scott Stewart, "Corruption: Why Texas is Not Mexico," Stratfor Global Intelligence, May 27, 2011.

26. "Narcocorridos," 400 respondents, +/−4.9% margin of error, February 12–16, 2011, www.parametria.com.mx.

27. Four hundred respondents nationally, +/−4.9% margin of error, March 28–31, 2009, www.parametria.com.mx from Roderic Ai Camp, "Armed Forces and Drugs: Public Perceptions and Institutional Challenges," in Eric H. Olson, et al., eds., *Shared Responsibility*, Table 12, 319.

28. Pew Global Attitudes Project, "Most Mexicans See Better Life in U.S.—One in Three Would Migrate," September 23, 2009, one thousand interviews nationally, +/−3.0% margin of error, conducted May 26–June 2, 2009.

29. Colonel Julián Leyzaola Pérez, a retired army officer, battled the drug cartels' control over Tijuana, but used abusive techniques on his own police officers, see William Finnegan, "Letter from Tijuana, In the Name of the Law," *The New Yorker*, October 18, 2010.

30. Viridiana Rios, "Why Did Mexico Become So Violent? A Self-Reinforcing Violent Equilibrium Caused by Competition and Enforcement," *Trends in Organized Crime* (forthcoming, 2013).

31. Eduardo Rodríguez-Oreggia and Miguel Flores, "Structural Factors and the War on Drugs' Effects on the Upsurge in Homicides in Mexico," Unpublished paper, 2011.

32. Luis Astorga and David A. Shirk, "Drug Trafficking Organizations and Counter-Drug Strategies in the U.S.-Mexican Context," in Olson et al., eds., *Shared Responsibility*, 31–62.

33. Juan Carlos Garzón, *Mafia & Co.: The Criminal Networks in Mexico, Brazil, and Colombia* (Washington, DC: Woodrow Wilson Center, 2008).

34. See Steven S. Dudley, "Drug Trafficking Organizations in Central America: Transportistas, Mexican Cartels, and Maras," in Olson et al., eds., *Shared Responsibility*, 63–94.

35. John Bailey explores this issue extensively in his "Drug Traffickers as Political Actors in Mexico's Nascent Democracy," in *The Oxford Handbook of Mexican Politics*, ed. Roderic Ai Camp (New York: Oxford University Press, 2012), 466–96.

36. Roderic Ai Camp, "Armed Forces and Drugs: Public Perceptions and Institutional Challenges," in Olson et al., eds., *Shared Responsibility*, 317; and Pew Research Center, "Crime and Drug Cartels Top Concerns in Mexico: Fewer Than Half See Progress in Drug War," August 31, 2011, www.pewglobal.org, and "Mexicans Back Military Campaign Against Cartels," June 20, 2012, www.pewglobal.org.

37. "Rápido y furioso y la opinión pública," www.parametria.com.mx, 2010.

38. Alejandro Moreno and María Antonia Mancillas, "Ven fines distintos en guerra al narco," *Reforma*, April 1, 2011.

39. Ginger Thompson and Mark Mazzetti, "U.S. Drones Fight Mexican Drug Trade," *New York Times*, March 15, 2011.

40. Mark Mazzetti and Ginger Thompson, "U.S. Widens Role in Mexican Fight," *New York Times*, August 25, 2011.

41. John Bailey and Sergio Aguayo Quezada, eds., *Strategy and Security in U.S.-Mexican Relations Beyond the Cold War* (La Jolla, CA: Center for U.S.-Mexican Studies, UCSD, 1996), 3.

42. "Mexico, U.S. to Share Weapons Information," *Agora* 3, no. 2 (2010): 74–75.

43. Hal Brands, *Mexico's Narco-Insurgency and U.S. Counterdrug Policy* (Carlisle, PA: Strategic Studies Institute, U.S. Army War College, 2009), 44–45.

44. Clare Ribando Seelke and Kristin M. Finklea, "U.S.-Mexican Security Cooperation: The Mérida Initiative and Beyond," Congressional Research Service Report for Congress, July 29, 2010, 7.

45. Pamela Starr, "U.S.-Mexico Relations," *Hemisphere Focus* 12, no. 2 (January 2004): 6.

46. *Global Views 2004: Comparing Mexican and American Public Opinion and Foreign Policy* (Chicago: Chicago Council on Foreign Relations, 2004), adapted from Figure 1-4, 16.

47. *U.S.-Mexico Border Security and the Evolving Security Relationship: Recommendations for Policymakers* (Washington, DC: CSIS, 2004).

48. Agnes Gereben Schaefer, Benjamin Bahney, K. Jack Riley, "Security in Mexico: Implications for U.S. Policy Options," (Santa Monica, CA: Rand Corporation, 2009), xvii. See Deroy Murdock, "U.S.-Mexican Border is Terrorists' Moving Sidewalk," Offnews.info, June 28, 2010.

49. Ronald Inglehart, Miguel Basáñez, and Neil Nevitte, *Convergencia en Norte América: Comercio, política y cultura* (Mexico City: Siglo XXI, 1994), 190–91.

50. Michael Topmiller, Frederick J. Conway, and James Gerber, "US Migration to Mexico: Numbers, Issues, and Scenarios," *Mexican Studies* 27, no. 1 (Winter 2011): 45–71. The number of Americans who actually live in Mexico is unknown, either by Mexico or the United States.

51. Organización Mundial de Turismo (ONT), *Barómetro del turismo mundial* 8, no. 1 (June 2011).

52. "Como miramos al vecino," Encuesta CIDAC-ZOGBY México y Estados Unidos, 2,010 respondents, +/–3.2% margin of error, February 3–7, 2006.

53. www.pewhispanic.org, September 3, 2011.

54. "Encuesta: Las lenguas extranjeras en México," www.consulta.com.mx, June 11, 2007.

55. For excellent background on these issues, see Jaime Rodríguez and Kathryn Vincent, eds., *Common Border, Uncommon Paths: Race and Culture in U.S.-Mexican Relations* (Wilmington, DE: Scholarly Resources, 1997).

56. Oscar Martínez, *Troublesome Border* (Tucson: University of Arizona Press, 1988), 97.

57. Jorge G. Castañeda, "The Choices Facing Mexico," in *Mexico in Transition: Implications for U.S. Policy*, ed. Susan K. Purcell (New York: Council on Foreign Relations, 1988), 26.

58. Jorge I. Domínguez and Rafael Fernández de Castro, *The United States and Mexico: Between Partnership and Conflict* (New York: Routledge, 2001), 153.

59. Roger D. Hansen, *The Politics of Mexican Development* (Baltimore, MD: Johns Hopkins University Press, 1971), 15–17.

60. For its evolution, see Robert Freeman Smith, "The United States and the Mexican Revolution, 1921–1950," in *Myths, Misdeeds, and Misunderstandings: The Roots of Conflict in U.S.-Mexican Relations*, eds. Jaime Rodríguez and Kathryn Vincent (Wilmington, DE: Scholarly Resources, 1997), 181–98.

61. *Wall Street Journal*, April 16, 1998, poll of 13,000 adults in Latin America and the United States. +/−1% margin of error in Latin America.

62. *Global Views 2004: Comparing Mexican and American Public Opinion and Foreign Policy*, the Chicago Council on Global Affairs, 1,195 respondents, +/−3.2% margin of error, July 6–12, 2004.

63. Robert Bryce, "Gripe on Mexican Labor to Get NAFTA Hearing," *Christian Science Monitor* 87, no. 105, April 26, 1995, 6.

64. Julie A. Erfani, *The Paradox of the Mexican State: Rereading Sovereignty from Independence to NAFTA* (Boulder, CO: Lynne Rienner, 1995), 178–79.

65. Sidney Weintraub, "Prospects for Hemispheric Trade and Economic Integration," CSIS Policy Paper on the Americas, 1995, 5. Also see Weintraub's "Mexico's Devaluation: Why and What Next?," CSIS, January 4, 1994.

66. Precise details of the agreement are provided in "Statement of Treasury Secretary Robert E. Rubin, Mexico Agreement Signing Ceremony," *Treasury News*, February 21, 1995.

67. James Robinson, "NAFTA and Sovereignty," in *NAFTA's Impact on North America: The First Decade*, ed. Sidney Weintraub (Washington, DC: CSIS, 2004), 362.

68. For extensive analysis of these changes, see David Shirk, "Justice Reform in Mexico: Change & Challenges in the Judicial Sector," in Olson et al., eds., *Shared Responsibility*, 205–46.

69. Matthew C. Ingram, Octavio Rodríguez Ferreira, and David A. Shirk, "Justiciabarómetro: Survey of Judges, Prosecutors, and Public Defenders in Nine Mexican States," Justice in Mexico Project, University of San Diego, June 2011.

70. Presidencia de la República, *Quinto informe de gobierno: Anexo estadístico* (Mexico: Presidencia de la República, 2011), 204.

71. *The United States and Mexico: Towards a Strategic Partnership*, 25.

72. Andrew Selee, Christopher Wilson, and Katie Putnam, "The United States and Mexico: More Than Neighbors," Woodrow Wilson Center for Scholars, Washington, DC, May 2010.

73. "Environmental Issues," US-Mexico Border 2012 Program, www.epa.gov/usmexicoborder, 2011.

74. Sidney Weintraub, "Dealing with Neighbors," *Issues in International Political Economy*, No. 99 (March 2008): 1–2; Jeffrey Puryear, Lucrecia Santibañez, and Alexandra Solano, "Education in Mexico," in *A New Vision for Mexico in 2042: Achieving Prosperity for All*, eds. Claudio Loser and Harinder Kohli (Washington, DC: Emerging Markets Forum, 2012), 87–108.

75. *The United States and Mexico: Towards a Strategic Partnership*, 26.

76. One way in which NAFTA did have a positive impact on the cost of living of ordinary Mexicans was to reduce the costs of fruits, vegetables and other basic goods, including many household goods. Shannan O'Neil, "Two Nations

Indivisible: Modern Mexico and the Future of U.S.-Mexico Relations," Unpublished manuscript, 2012, 157.

77. See Carol Wise, "Unfulfilled Promise: Economic Convergence under NAFTA," in *Requiem or Revival: The Promise of North American Integration*, eds. Isabel Studer and Carol Wise (Washington, DC: Brookings Institute, 2007), 27–52. One of the most objective surveys of the analyses of NAFTA's failures and achievements can be found in M. Angeles Villarreal, "NAFTA and the Mexican Economy," Congressional Research Service, Washington, DC, June 3, 2010.

78. "The Path of Economic Liberalism," in Camp, ed., *The Oxford Handbook of Mexican Politics*, 759.

79. Pamela K. Starr, "Monetary Mismanagement and Inadvertent Democratization in Technocratic Mexico," *Studies in Comparative International Development* 33, no. 4 (Winter 1999): 35–65.

80. For evidence of their impact on municipal services, see Claire L. Adida and Desha M. Girod, "Do Migrants Improve Their Hometowns? Remittances and Access to Public Services in Mexico, 1995–2000," *Comparative Political Studies* 44, no. 1 (January 2011): 3–27.

81. James Robson and Fikret Berkes, "How Does Out-Migration Affect Community Institutions? A Study of Two Indigenous Municipalities in Oaxaca, Mexico," *Human Ecology* 39, no. 2 (April 2011): 189.

82. Alex Arnold, Paul Hamilton, and Jimmy Moore, "Who Seeks to Exit? Security, Connections, and Happiness as Predictors of Migration Intentions in the Americas," *AmericasBarometer Insights: 2011*, Latin American Public Opinion Project, 5–6.

83. Paul Rexton Kan, *Mexico's "Narco-Refugees": The Looming Challenge for U.S. National Security* (Carlisle, PA: Strategic Studies Institute, U.S. Army War College, 2011), 29–33.

84. Pew Research Center, "Crime and Drug Cartels Top Concerns in Mexico," 2011, and "Mexicans Back Military Campaign Against Cartels," June 20, 2012, www.pewglobal.org.

85. U.S.-Mexico Bi-national Council, "Managing Mexican Migration to the United States, Recommendations for Policymakers," (Washington, DC: CSIS, 2004), 11.

86. "The Issue of Voting by Residents Abroad," *Review of the Economic Situation of Mexico* 74 (November 1998), 429–32.

87. For detailed speculations about why the turnout was limited, see Jean-Michel Lafleur and Leticia Calderón Chelius, "Assessing Emigrant Participation in Home Country Elections: The Case of Mexico's 2006 Presidential Election," *International Migration* 49, no. 3 (June 2011): 99–124.

88. For detailed comparative information between 2006 and 2012, see www.migrationinformation.org, June 2012.

89. MORI de México weekly poll for *Este País*, November 9 and November 23, 1994.

90. Joseph M. Hayes and Laura E. Hill, "Immigrant Pathways to Legal Permanent Residence: Now and under a Merit-Based System," *California Counts: Population Trends and Profiles* 9, no. 4 (June 2008): 1–26.

91. Such a controversial argument was offered by Samuel P. Huntington, with little empirical research, in *Who Are We? The Challenges to American National Identity* (New York: Simon and Schuster, 2005).

92. A vast literature exists on this topic. Some of the best work is discussed and analyzed objectively in David Fitzgerald, *A Nation of Immigrants: How Mexico Manages Its Migration* (Berkeley: University of California Press, 2008).

93. Peter Hakim, "Is Washington Losing Latin America?," *Foreign Affairs* 85, no. 1 (January/February, 2006): 51.

94. "Justice in Mexico," Trans-Border Institute, University of San Diego, January 2011, 9.

95. Judith Adler Hellman, "Continuity and Change in the Mexican Political System: New Ways of Knowing a New Reality," *European Review of Latin American and Caribbean Studies* 63 (December 1997), 96.

96. The Select Committee on California-Mexico Bi-National Affairs, http://assembly.ca.gov/calmexico, 2011.

97. Clare R. Seelke, "U.S.-Mexico Relations: Issues for Congress," Congressional Reference Service, Washington, DC, September 2, 2010.

98. David A. Shirk, *The Drug War in Mexico: Confronting a Shared Threat*, Council Special Report, Council on Foreign Relations, New York, March 2011.

99. See Pamela K. Starr, "What Mexico's Election Means for the Drug War," *Foreign Affairs*, June 28, 2012, www.foreignaffairs.com.

100. Instituto Nacional de Estadística y Geografía, "Presenta INEGI Resultados de la ENVIPE 2012," Boletón de Prensa, no. 339, September 27, 2012.

101. See William Booth, "Preparing the New U.S. Envoy to Mexico," *The Washington Post*, September 10, 2011, A8.

102. Methamphetamine usage (part of the psychotherapeutics category) is down significantly from 2002, but remained the same from 2007 to 2010 at 0.1 percent. Many different and often out-of-date data are given for drug consumption in the United States. The most comparable data over time are from the United States Department of Health and Human Services, *2010 National Survey on Drug Use and Health: Summary of National Findings*, 2011.

103. Pew Research Center, "Crime and Drug Cartels Top Concerns in Mexico," 2011, and "Mexicans Back Military Campaign Against Cartels," 2012.

10

Political and Economic Modernization: A Revolution?

> It should be borne in mind that democracy is a social project as much as a set of constitutional guarantees about structures and processes of political representation. It will flower only when there are strong connections between the governors and the governed in a social contract that ties citizens to each other and to the state in a common framework for social order, political representation, and political action. For such a situation to materialize, citizens and the state must accept a single rule of law with predictable results and mechanism or structures of representation and accountability. But both the law and these mechanisms remain strangely elusive in Mexico today.
>
> DIANE E. DAVIS, *"Undermining the Rule of Law"*

BASES FOR ECONOMIC MODERNIZATION

For the average Mexican, the most important economic issues are employment and level of income. In 2001, Mexicans considered more sources of employment and better wages to be the most significant pending economic problems.[1] From 2001 through 2012, there has been little variation in what Mexicans perceive to be the country's most significant issues.[2] Basically, the economic crisis has been the most significant issue in seven out of ten years, lack of personal security four years out of ten, and unemployment one year out of ten. Combined responses to economic problems (economic crises, unemployment, poverty, low salaries, and inflation) over the entire period of Mexico's democratic consolidation account for 43 percent of the leading issues. In 2012, they considered these same economic issues to be equally significant.[3] Mexico, like many other Third World nations, faces numerous challenges in stimulating economic growth, regardless of its economic strategy. Equally important is the fact that for those Mexicans who have personally been victims of unemployment, the economic crisis or insecurity, they produced direct effects on their voting preferences in 2012. Depending on which of these experiences apply, Alejandro Moreno discovered that 13 to 38 percent shared in one of these experiences. Of those citizens, 73 compared to 47 percent expressed much greater dissatisfaction with democracy; 75 to 38 percent with the government's economic path; and 63 to 36 percent with personal security.[4]

Mexico's economy has changed significantly since the 1980s in both size and the composition of its workforce. In the past three decades, most of the new jobs in Mexico were in the manufacturing, commerce, construction, and transportation sectors. In volume, the service industry provided the most new jobs from 1950 to 2000, 8.1 million, equal to the total population then employed in agriculture. Today, services alone account for the largest single sector of the economy, employing 42.3 percent of Mexicans in 2011 compared to just 23 percent in 1999. In 2011, Mexico classifies its economically active population into three broad economic sectors: primary (agriculture, forestry and fishing), 13.2 percent; secondary (manufacturing, mining and extractive), 24.0 percent; and tertiary (retail, tourism, communications, transportation and services), 62.2.[5]

At the beginning of the second decade of the twenty-first century, Mexico could boast being the twelfth largest economy (value of its goods and services) in the world. Its Gross Domestic Product (GDP) per capita stood at $9,243. Based on its purchasing power parity with other nations, the per capita figure was $14,265. While these figures may seem impressive, they hide the fact that Mexico only ranks sixtieth in per capita GDP. In other words, Mexico has one of the world's largest economies, but its economically active population is not producing goods whose value is similar to other comparable economies, such as Spain, which ranked ninth globally but twenty-sixth in per capita GDP.[6] Economists point to other variables that reflect badly on its economic potential, including its lack of competitiveness (sixtieth out of 133 in 2009), as ranked by the World Economic Forum Global Competitiveness Index, as well as perceived levels of corruption in Transparency International surveys, where it ranks generally in the bottom half of all countries.

Mexico's macro-economic policies are critical to its strategies to increase the size and productivity of its economy, to reduce poverty and increase employment, and to expand its middle class. Each of these economic goals has significant linkages to its political goals, and is essential to achieving a consolidated democracy. As suggested in the introduction, Latin American specialists who examine democratic theory often incorporate social justice in their conceptualization of a consolidated democracy. Claudio Holzner, in a major work on the relationship between poverty and democratic participation, discovered numerous, complex relationships between poor Mexicans and the political system. Keeping in mind the importance of other variables he identifies, the elimination of poverty would likely produce changes that would alter the level of citizen interest and involvement in politics and elections.[7]

In the 1980s, Mexican administrations introduced a major shift in economic philosophy, and therefore in the economic strategies they encouraged to address the issues of growth, inequality, and poverty. Their strategy, which became popular elsewhere in the region, was labeled economic liberalization, and it involved significant alterations in Mexico's domestic economic structure and its global economic relationships, especially with the United States.

THE RISE OF ECONOMIC LIBERALIZATION

Whether the source of economic change in Mexico is international or domestic or both, there is no question that the administration of Carlos Salinas de Gortari instituted major economic reforms indicative of an altered government economic philosophy. A major basis for the economic liberalization program is the generation of capital for the Mexican economy, especially foreign investment. The data in Table 10-1 demonstrate the growing importance of this variable in Mexico's economic development strategy. From 1988 to 1994, foreign investment increased fourfold. Not surprisingly it increased after NAFTA was implemented in 1994, but it witnessed the slowest growth during the economic crisis in the early years of Zedillo's administration. The pace of foreign investment recovered under President Fox,

Table 10-1 Foreign Investment in Mexico

Administration	Totals (U.S. $ millions)	% Change
1970–1976	1,601.4	
1976–1982	5,470.6	241.7
1982–1988	13,455.4	146.0
1988–1994	60,565.5[a]	350.1
1994–2000	74,100.9	22.3
2000–2006	139,067.4	87.8
2006–2012[a]	102,842.3	

Source: Crónica del gobierno de Carlos Salinas de Gortari, 1988–1994: Síntesis e indíce temático (Mexico: Presidencia de la República, 1994), 441; and Mexico, Presidencia de la República, *Sexto informe de gobierno: Anexo estadístico,* September 1, 2000, 132; www.inegi .gob.mx, June 2005; *Quinto informe de gobierno: Anexo estadístico*, September 1, 2011, 211.
[a]Data are through the second quarter 2011.

reaching an all-time high. Calderón's government also attracted high levels of direct investment, but the 2008 global recession reduced those levels compared to his predecessor. The United States alone accounted for 26 percent of the investment from 2007 to 2011, followed by several European countries and Canada. It should also be pointed out that the monies earned by Mexicans in the United States, and remitted to their families in Mexico, accounts for an extraordinary form of "foreign" investment, much of which is spent on capital goods and housing in poorer, rural communities, among individuals most in need, and typically exceeds American direct foreign investment. More than a million households are beneficiaries of this economic assistance.[8]

Salinas saw capital as essential to Mexico's economic recovery in the short term and international competition in the long term. When he realized that European governments and lenders were preoccupied with Eastern Europe, he turned to a free-trade agreement with the United States and Canada. Bush, who had close personal ties to Salinas, committed himself and the United States to approve such an agreement and encouraged Salinas to move ahead on it. In anticipation, Salinas and his economic team, most of whose members had studied in the United States, began to put many government-owned firms up for sale and to cut tariffs dramatically—many dropped from as high as 200 percent to an average of only 9 percent in 1992. The initiatives led to the return of some domestic capital and to new foreign investment—more than $60 billion by 1994 (see Table 10-1).

The U.S. financial community responded favorably to these dramatic changes from a state-led to a free-market economy. Editorials in business-oriented publications like the *Wall Street Journal* praised Salinas and his collaborators. Other periodicals, such as *Business Week*, predicted a boom period for Mexico, making it attractive to investors. The Mexican government repeatedly cited its positive press as evidence supportive of its policies. Yet critics charged that the state-controlled sector remained bloated. They argued that twelve of the twenty largest firms in terms of employees were still under state control. Indeed, state-owned firms employed 79 percent of all workers, and the amount of all government workers was not much reduced from what it had been in 1987—from 4.4 to 4.1 million, largely the result of the sale of banks and government-owned companies.[9]

Parallel to his commitment to privatize and open up the economy to international competition, Salinas in 1992 startlingly proposed to overhaul the *ejido* land structure, a system of small-property holding controlled by each village. After the revolution, successive governments gave lands to individually operated *ejidos*, whose owners received use-right titles but not actual ownership from their local villages. Critics of the post-revolutionary agrarian reform charge that insufficient credit stems from an *ejidatarios's* lack of collateral. Salinas's new legislation granted actual ownership and contract rights to these farmers. To keep farmers on the land and to assist in the transition to a more competitive market with U.S. imports, the government introduced Procampo, a program designed to eliminate its price supports for food by giving stipends (which would begin to drop after ten years and end in fifteen) directly to producers.[10]

Regardless of the weaknesses and strengths of Salinas's economic policies, he pursued a consistent economic strategy, composed primarily of privatization, internationalization, and foreign investment. It is also important to note that de la Madrid, Salinas, and Zedillo significantly altered the distribution of funds assigned to federal social expenditures, compared to administrative and economic categories. In their three successive administrations, they increased social expenditures by 24, 22, and 12 percent, to over half of all government funding. As part of his overall strategy to modernize Mexico, Salinas was personally much more committed to economic than political liberalization. In fact, as he made clear, he intended to pursue modernization and, implicitly, the interrelationship of the two components.[11]

When Zedillo became the PRI candidate, he promised a ten-point program as his strategy for building on and continuing his predecessor's program. While praising the achievements of the preceding administration, Zedillo identified a number of problems that economic liberalization had not eliminated: insufficient jobs (with a 3 percent annual growth rate in the workforce, an average of 1 million new jobs were needed), a flat rate of productivity (only one-third of the population was economically active), and regional and sectoral inequities. Zedillo proposed boosting investment—public, private, and foreign—to increase money for education, altering the fiscal system to promote investment, encouraging saving, hastening deregulation, expanding new technological applications, broadening foreign competition, strengthening Procampo, and protecting the environment.[12]

But instead of having an opportunity to build on the economic structure left by his predecessor, Zedillo was confronted with a major economic crisis in the first month of his administration, the magnitude of which Mexico had not experienced even in the difficult days of the 1980s. Zedillo's economic team decided to devalue the Mexican peso against the dollar—a serious problem ignored by his predecessor—allowing it to float free (private market demand for pesos internationally).[13] Rather than the peso's stabilizing at a new exchange rate, there was a run on the peso. The New York financial community also shares the responsibility for Mexico's crisis, having pressured the Mexicans—with the threat of withdrawing their investments—into issuing billions of dollars worth of dollar-denominated, short-term bonds, *tesebonos*. The Mexican government issued so many of the devaluation-proof *tesebonos* that ten billion became due between the end of December 1994 and March 1995.[14] It was only able to meet its short-term obligations with the help of public, international financing.[15]

The result of the crises caused by the devaluation of the peso is that Mexico faced negative economic growth in 1995, a loss of somewhere between 250,000 and 1 million jobs before the end of the year, a reversal of foreign investment and capital flight, a dramatic rise in inflation exceeding 50 percent yearly, an extraordinary rise in private-bank interest for mortgages and loans far above the inflation rate, and numerous business closures and bankruptcies, including the threat of important state governments declaring financial insolvency. After pursuing a severe austerity program for two years, Zedillo introduced his own social programs, Progresa and Salud 2000, committed to increased spending in social development and health care. The federal budget's largest average outlay during his administration, 56 percent, was for social programs.[16] Through 2011, Calderón has maintained social expenditures at 57 percent. In spite of Zedillo's increased outlays on social expenditures, as measured by their real income, many Mexicans joined the ranks of the poor.[17]

An overview of economic statistics since the introduction of a neoliberal economic strategy in the 1980s, despite the significant ups and downs in the economy, confirms a long-term increase in economic growth, GDP, and foreign capital. However, the fundamental economic question facing Mexico during the democratic transition, and the period of democratic consolidation since 2000, is the economic model's success in producing upward social mobility and increasing the size of the middle class, while reducing the percentage of Mexicans who are living in poverty.

The data in Table 10-2 illustrate several features of the Mexican class structure. Most important, the middle class has witnessed stable growth and, from the 1950s to the 1990s, doubled.[18] The percentage of working-class Mexicans continues to fall, but the decline has been slow, particularly in the 1970s and early 1980s. The most dramatic change has been among Mexico's upper classes, which tripled in size from 1950 to 1990. These longer-term patterns, however, are dramatically reversed since 1990, and can be explained by the 1994–1996 economic crisis and the global recession since 2008.

What these figures do not reveal are two significant patterns. First, the rapid growth of the Mexican population, especially since the 1950s, created a working class and a marginal population, which in absolute numbers are far larger today than they were during the first half of the century. For

Table 10-2 Mexico's Class Structure from 1895 to 2010

Year	Upper	Change	Middle	Change	Lower	Change
			Class (%)			
1895	1.5	—	7.8	—	90.7	—
1940	2.9	93.3	12.6	61.5	84.5	−6.8
1950	1.7	−41.4	18.0	42.9	80.3	−5.0
1960	3.8	123.5	21.0	16.7	75.2	−6.4
1970	5.7	50.0	27.9	32.9	66.4	−11.7
1980	5.3	−7.0	33.0	18.3	61.8	−6.9
1990	6.8	28.3	38.2	15.8	55.0	−11.0
2010	3.0	—[a]	32.0	—	65.0	—

Source: Howard F. Cline, *Mexico: Revolution to Evolution, 1940–1960* (New York: Oxford University Press, 1963), 124; Stephanie Granato and Aida Mostkoff Linares, "The Class Structure of Mexico, 1895–1980," *Society and Economy in Mexico*, ed. James W. Wilkie (Los Angeles: UCLA Latin American Center, 1990); David Lorey and Aida Mostkoff Linares, "Mexico's Lost Decade," *Statistical Abstract of Latin America*, vol. 30, pt. 2 (Los Angeles: UCLA Latin American Center, 1994): 1339–60; Mund, "The Social Base of Hope and Fear in Mexico," Opinion and Policy Report, Series 10, no. 1, January 18, 2010; "Ingreso Corriente Total Promedio Trimestral," www.inegi.org.mx, 2011.
[a]The 2010 figures are not completely comparable to those used previously and therefore the level of change is not recorded from 1990–2010.

example, of Mexico's current population, 109 million, 46 percent, or 52 million, are classified as poor ($978 urban and $684 rural income yearly), a figure larger than Mexico's entire population in 1960. Moreover, the Mexican government classified 10.4 percent of the population as living in extreme poverty, 35.8 percent in moderate poverty, 5.8 percent at risk for income poverty, and 28.7 percent at risk for social poverty in 2011. In other words, only 22 million (19.3 percent) Mexicans are not poor or at risk of becoming poor.[19] During the recession from 2008 to 2011, 3.2 million Mexicans returned to living in poverty, raising the level back to 46 percent of the population.[20] What these figures also fail to show is the increasing concentration of wealth, as is true in the United States, among upper-income Mexicans. It is difficult to identify comparable statistical information on social class categories chronologically in Mexico, but measures of poverty have been relatively consistent over time, offering a clearer picture of the trends (see Table 10-3).

The measurements of poverty cited in Table 10-3 point to the difficulty in significantly altering such statistics over time. For example, although nutritional poverty levels fluctuated between 17 and 37 percent of the population, they have essentially declined only 2.6 percentage points in two decades, affecting a fifth of the population. It is also apparent that significant downturns in the economic growth quickly affect all three measurements of poverty, indicated by the dramatic increases in poverty under Zedillo, the significant declines in poverty under Fox, and a significant increase in

Table 10-3 Mexicans Living in Poverty Using Capacities Measurements

Year	Percentage		
	Nutrition[a]	Health/Education	Housing/Transportation
1992	21.4	29.7	53.1
1994	21.2	30.0	52.4
1996	37.4	46.9	69.0
1998	33.3	41.7	63.7
2000	24.1	31.8	53.6
2002	20.0	26.9	50.0
2004	17.4	24.7	47.2
2005	18.2	24.7	47.0
2006	13.8	20.7	42.7
2008	18.4	25.3	47.7
2010	18.8	26.7	51.3

Source: 2010 Census Data from INEGI and Coneval. www.coneval.gob.mx, 2011.
[a]*Definitions:* Food poverty = inadequate per capital income to purchase a basic basket of food; capabilities poverty = inadequate income to achieve acceptable levels of health and education while meeting the food poverty tests; asset poverty = inadequate income to provide minimum levels of shelter, clothing and transportation while meeting the other two tests.

poverty levels under Calderón. Indeed, it took thirteen years to increase the average household income in Mexico by 1 percent from 1994 to 2007. During the early years of economic liberalism, in spite of increased social expenditures, reductions in poverty remain flat. In all three categories, the percentages of Mexicans living in poverty do not decline to their pre-1994 levels until mid-way under the Fox administration.[21]

To what extent has economic liberalism, as pursued by each administration since 1982, improved the standard of living for most Mexicans? Expenditures increased dramatically from 1982 to the end of the century (see Table 10-4). Under Fox and Calderón, these expenditures increased modestly from 2000. One of the most important achievements of these two presidents was the "Seguro Popular" health care insurance begun in 2004, and expanded under Calderón.[22] Despite some improvement from 2000 to 2010, the distribution of income continues to favor wealthy Mexicans (see Table 10-5).[23] Sixty-two percent of all income is distributed to 30 percent of the population. (In the United States, the top 20 percent of the population receives 55 percent of the national income.) The lowest 30 percent of the population, measured by income, receives only 9 percent.[24] What is equally discouraging is that this pattern has remained unchanged since 1984. Per capita income in 2011 was $9,330 compared to $47,140 in the United States; Mexico ranked at 89th among two-hundred-plus countries.[25]

Internationally, economists use a measurement, the Gini coefficient, to describe a country's overall inequality. Compared to other countries in the middle-income category (which is where Mexico is currently placed), it

Table 10-4 The Evolution of Federal Social Expenditures

Presidential Administration		Expenditure Category (Percent of Total)		
		Economic	Social	Administrative
Calderón	2006–2011	33	57	10
Fox	2000–2006	31	59	10
Zedillo	1994–2000	32	56	12
Salinas	1988–1994	33	50	17
De la Madrid	1982–1988	39	41	20
López Portillo	1976–1982	41	33	26
Echeverría	1970–1976	62	29	9
Díaz Ordaz	1964–1970	55	32	13
López Mateos	1958–1964	39	19	42
Ruiz Cortines	1952–1958	53	14	33
Alemán	1946–1952	52	13	35

Source: Este País, (December 1999), 16; México, Presidencia de la República, *Quinto informe de gobierno, anexo estadístico,* September 1, 2011, 127–28.

Table 10-5 Distribution of Income in Mexico, 1984–2010 (in percentages)

Family Income by Deciles, Lowest to Highest	1984	1989	1992	1998	2000	2005	2010
1	1.72	1.58	1.56	1.50	1.52	1.1	1.8
2	3.11	2.81	2.75	2.70	2.64	2.5	3.1
3	4.21	3.74	3.70	3.60	3.60	3.6	4.2
4	5.32	4.73	4.70	4.70	4.59	4.7	5.2
5	6.40	5.90	5.70	5.80	5.70	5.9	6.4
6	7.86	7.29	7.11	7.20	7.08	7.2	7.7
7	9.72	8.98	8.92	8.90	8.84	9.0	9.5
8	12.16	11.42	11.57	11.50	11.24	11.7	12.0
9	16.73	15.62	16.02	16.00	16.09	16.1	16.3
10	32.77	37.93	38.16	38.10	38.70	38.2	33.9

Source: Fernando Pérez Correa, "Modernización y mercado del trabajo," *Este País,* February 1995, 27; "Mexico: Income Distribution," *Review of the Economic Situation of Mexico,* October 2000, 416–418, August 2001, 358.

ranks among the most unequal in income distribution, on par with Russia. The United States also is comparable to Mexico in its distribution of income as measured by the Gini coefficient. What is unusual about the Mexican case is the dramatically increased concentration of wealth in the hands of the rich between 1984 and 2000. An insightful comparative analysis of Taiwan and Mexico, which shared comparable economic statistics in their early stages of development, is suggestive of what happened in Mexico. Taiwan's success compared with that of Mexico was achieved through several strategies, including land reform, labor-intensive exports, domestic saving, small- and medium-sized enterprises, and basic education. The role of human capital, and specifically education, was crucial in explaining Taiwan's success. Mexico's educational efforts did not produce similar results as those found in Taiwan because of higher population growth rates, a slower gross domestic product, and a higher proportion of families in the extreme poverty category. The study concluded that market-oriented growth does not automatically reduce inequality or poverty, but policies that redistribute land, improve skills, facilitate small enterprises, and increase savings were instrumental in Taiwan's success.[26] A more recent comparative study of Korea and Mexico concluded that while Mexico actually devoted more resources to education than Korea, it did not allocate those resources efficiently, neglecting to carefully accelerate the growth in secondary and tertiary levels of education.[27]

Human capital is affected by the interrelationship between income and education. Mexico has a low rate of matriculation in upper secondary education. For example, in 2009, according to the Organization for Economic Cooperation and Development, 45 percent of Mexicans ages twenty-five to thirty-four had obtained a secondary education compared to an average of 85 percent among all member countries. Twenty-two percent of Mexicans in the same age group obtained a tertiary education (thirteen grade levels or higher).[28] Mexican expenditures on public education as a percentage of GDP has increase significantly in the last decade, and ranks one of the highest among all OECD countries. However, these educational attainment figures obscure the fact that the "quality of educational outcomes in Mexico, as indicated by both national and international achievement tests, is very poor. Averages are low, percentages of students below minimally-acceptable levels are very large, and those with top marks remain extremely small."[29]

Not surprisingly, the higher an individual's family income, the more likely he or she is to complete higher education. At the end of the twentieth century, the poorest 30 percent of the population in Mexico averaged only three years of education, while the wealthiest 10 percent achieved slightly more than twelve years.[30] What is potentially more devastating about the distribution of educational achievement in Mexico is the decline in upward social mobility, even through public institutions. National figures for 2006 suggest that intergenerational mobility from the lowest to the highest schools remains limited, with only one-fifth of children born to parents with six or fewer years of education completing high school. Only 11 percent of Mexicans whose parents did not complete elementary school managed to graduate from high school. Seven out of ten Mexicans whose parents were college graduates completed college, compared to one out of five who completed elementary school only.[31]

As analysts have argued, and economic statistics demonstrate, Mexico's chronological economic growth has been weak for the last three decades. Real growth in GDP has average only approximately 2.5 percent. In the last twenty years, each presidential administration has faced a major economic crisis (1994–1996, 2001–2003, 2008–2010). Despite the efforts of Presidents Fox and Calderón to increase their emphasis on social spending, and to implement antipoverty programs such as Oportunidades, which have been credited with reducing poverty and increasing educational levels among the poor, many of the structural problems related to income distribution, poverty, and marginalization remain relatively static.[32] Poverty programs, combined with income received from remittances abroad, accounted for nearly 11 percent of the total monetary income available to Mexican families. Among the poorest ten percent of Mexican families, the figure is 40 percent of their monetary income, and 69 percent of those families receive one or both sources of income.[33] It should be pointed out that migration produces a negative effect on one of the most important long-term goals of antipoverty programs, increasing educational levels, removing young males from school, and increasing household responsibilities of young females who drop out.[34]

Economists have identified conditions beyond improving the quality of human capital limiting Mexico's ability to achieve faster rates of economic growth and fairer distribution of income among all groups.[35] In one of the most widely cited articles on the causes of the country's slow growth, the author suggests that "Mexico's underperformance is overdetermined. The faulty provision of credit, persistence of informality, control of key input markets by elites, continued ineffectiveness of public education, and vulnerability to adverse external shocks each may have a role in explaining Mexico's development trajectory over the last three decades."[36] For example, Mexico is not viewed as highly competitive. In 2010, it ranked 60 out of 133 countries. When Calderón was elected president in 2006, members of the Senate identified monopolies, especially in communications, as detrimental to economic competition and growth.[37] A recent study confirms that family members still control a considerable percentage of stock issued by thirty-four of Mexico's fifty largest domestically-owned firms, a pattern which has continued for decades.[38] Ironically, a third of Mexicans actually favor fewer rather than more enterprises, and in the specific case of the production and sales of beer, half agree with this preference.[39] Efforts to increase competition in the least competitive economic sectors during the Calderón administration did not succeed, even though Congress passed a bill in 2011 that significantly increased fines and jail time for monopolies and their responsible officers, and strengthened the Federal Competition Commission.[40]

Another measure of a country's ability to modernize its economy and compete internationally is its access to technology. Mexico's access to the Internet in homes, and the use of computers, as is true of many countries, increased dramatically in the last decade. Despite the percentage increase, it ranks last in the OECD Broadband Portal survey of 2011, with 13 percent of households (nearly 21 million individuals) having access, compared to 51 percent in Spain and 67 percent in the United States.[41] To stay competitive globally, an essential component of Mexico's economic strategy, it needs also to remain competitive in its technological skills. One of the economic conditions where it ranks near the top, and where it demonstrated improvement during the Calderón administration, is its ranking as a country that facilitates business, comparable to Taiwan.[42]

A third issue that economists have identified is low worker productivity. In the 2000s, Mexico output per worker was 20 percent of a comparable worker in Chile, and one eighth of a Chinese employee. "Mexican economic growth depends largely on higher inputs of labor instead of increases in labor productivity thanks to greater efficiency."[43] Low levels of productivity in Mexico are attributed to inadequate domestic competition, to poor infrastructure, to human capital and education, and to continued corporatist legacies, especially those that produce inflexible labor conditions.

Finally, although many other economic variables deserve analysis, one special consideration raised previously in the analysis on national security is the economic impact of drug trafficking organizations.[44] The government's own survey in 2011 concluded that all of the costs combined represent 1.53 percent of the gross domestic product. Perhaps more significant than the direct economic costs to victims is the serious consequences on human behavior. More than six out of ten Mexicans do not feel safe in their larger communities, prompting half or more to feel unsafe in a grocery store or market, on the street, in a bank, on a highway, or on public transportation. One in four Mexicans report not going out to dinner, attending a movie, going for a walk, or visiting friends; half will not go out at night or allow their younger children to leave home.[45] The president of one of Mexico's most influential business organizations announced in 2012 that 160,000 businesses have left Mexico in search of security since 2006.[46] Mexico's leading criminologist estimates that organized crime involved in drugs, human trafficking, child prostitution, or the black market has infiltrated three-quarters of the economic sector, including supermarkets, the auto industry, and construction. He argued that by 2010, through their influence in local governments, they controlled 73 percent of Mexico's national territory.[47]

A comprehensive survey of American businesses in Mexico concluded that two-thirds of the respondents felt less secure in 2011 than in 2010.

Businessmen believed that extortion by organized crime, corruption, and impunity in the judicial process are the leading threats against their security. A third of the companies reduced travel to Mexico because of the security situation and eight percent have considered relocating their firm because of security concerns. One in four also has reconsidered their investment plans because of this situation.[48] In fact, a recent study of illicit financial flows from multiple forms of criminal activity, which does not fully capture drug cartel earnings, concluded that from 1970 to 2010, $872 billion dollars left Mexico. The average yearly outflow since 2000 has been $50 billion, accounting for over 6 percent of the country's Gross Domestic Product.[49]

DEMOCRATIZATION

In Mexico, as elsewhere in the world, political liberalization has meant democratization. Mexicans had long expressed an interest in democratization, which flared up during and after independence, in the 1860s and 1870s, at the time of the revolution, and then again in the 1960s and 1970s.[50] Scholars also have made the argument that plenty of evidence can be found to illustrate the desire of numerous Mexicans, at the local level, to use grassroots support to establish democratic institutions for two centuries.[51]

An examination of the democratic transition in Mexico, regardless of when we date the beginning of that transition, suggests five major themes. Many other important changes are part of the transition, identified elsewhere in the book, but these particular developments are most significant. Furthermore, a careful reflection of each of these explanations suggests their complex interactions with each other. They include: the decline in the legitimacy of political institutions, the increasing importance of federalism, the reliance on the electoral process to achieve a democratic model, the decline in economic revenues and the frequency of economic crises, and the increased activity of nonpolitical or nontraditional actors in the political process.

The initial catalyst for the decline in the legitimacy of political institutions is not a contested presidential election, but rather the 1968 student movement. The 1968 student movement would have become a minor footnote in Mexico's political history, and would not have played any role in the democratization process if the government had not challenged and then suppressed the movement with extraordinary levels of violence, turning it into an international incident. We raised a number of significant consequences produced by this event in an earlier chapter, but it can be credited with creating serious doubts about the semiauthoritarian government and about the excessive power of the Mexican presidency. It not only raised troubling questions among ordinary citizens about the legitimacy of the model on which Mexico modernized its economic development, but introduced those doubts among many members of the political elite. In the early 1970s, a number of guerrilla movements, representing diverse ideological and political goals, emerged. What unifies these movements is their use of violent channels of protest against what were clearly perceived as illegitimate political institutions and processes. From 1968 to 1989, the power and the legitimacy of the presidency were marked by a downward trajectory. Salinas contributed to its further decline in the fraudulent 1988 presidential election, but revived the influence of the presidency. But on January 1, 1994, the rebellion of a small group of Chiapas guerrillas calling itself the Zapatista Army of National Liberation (EZLN), dispelled the notion that all was well in Mexico, and that Salinas had been able to restore political legitimacy to governmental institutions. The rebellion, timed precisely with the date for implementing the NAFTA agreement, challenged the centerpiece of Salinas's neoliberal economic strategy, attracting, as was the case of the 1968 student movement, international and national media attention. The final blow to political legitimacy before 2000 was the assassination of Salinas's choice for the PRI presidential candidate during the campaign in March, 1994.

A second pattern that becomes increasingly visible at various stages in the democratic transition is the increasing importance of local politics and its impact on the transition. Political historians have identified the significance of contested local elections both on maintaining interest in political participation and achieving greater autonomy from authoritarian national control, but the example of the EZLN cited above also can accurately be viewed as a local and regional movement. Many of the themes cited in the EZLN's own literature involve grassroots issues centered on ethnic preferences characteristic of rural Chiapas (and elsewhere in Mexico). But the federalism issue extends far beyond the importance of local elections and local, discontented populations or ethnic groups. In my own recent research, made possible by Mexico's Chamber of Deputies putting online all of the recorded sessions of Congress since 1917, I discovered a fascinating pattern in the background of Mexico's longest-lived opposition party during the PRI hegemony, the PAN. In searching for the fathers of contemporary PAN politicians to determine their political involvement, if any, I found that dozens of them had been members of the PAN in the 1940s and 1950s, and had run for Congress.[52] Naturally, rarely were they declared the winner, but these and other races for mayors and for state legislatures—regardless of the actual influence such officeholders might have exercised—established a first generation of democratically-inclined politicians who encouraged their children to follow in their footsteps. They include President Calderón himself. These prior experiences legitimized local and regional political offices, and established them as the initial locus for opposition victories among both the PRD and PAN, which definitely can be traced to cities and states that disproportionately have voted for opposition parties since the 1940s.

Most analysts are in agreement that Mexicans fundamentally relied on the electoral process to bring about a transition to democracy. As noted previously, various administrations introduced changes in the electoral laws that intentionally or unintentionally produced incremental openings for opposition politicians to increase their representation in the political process. However, access to influential posts in the national government was essentially confined to the legislative branch until 2000. This branch, as was true of the judiciary, had little impact on policymaking. At the national level, legislative representation as a vehicle for democratization only became significant during the Salinas and Zedillo administrations, when during two separate sessions of Congress the PRI did not have a two-thirds majority required for constitutional changes. The use of electoral channels accelerated much more rapidly from 1988 to 2000, when the opposition parties combined achieved control over municipalities or state executive offices responsible for governing more than half the population. The ability of parties to win these elections without—or in spite of—electoral fraud legitimized elections as a peaceful path to democracy. It also enhanced the importance of federalism by stressing local and then state offices as alternatives to the presidency or the national Congress.

The fourth theme explaining the democratic transition is the increasing scarcity of revenues available to a semiauthoritarian government to maintain its preeminence over all other competing groups and parties. Sophisticated, empirical evidence demonstrates the linkage between PRI-controlled expenditures and the decline of its fortunes as a hegemonic party.[53] Thus, the economic strategies each administration pursued during the height of the transition to democracy became a critical ingredient in determining the pace of democratic change leading up to the 2000 presidential race. The downturns in the real purchasing power of working class Mexicans during the early 1980s, and again in the mid 1990s, affected the federal government's abilities to reward loyalty in the electoral arena.

The rise of nontraditional or nonpolitical actors during a transition from semiauthoritarian to participatory democratic politics is common to other transitions in Latin America, Eastern Europe, and Asia. In Mexico, two groups already have been mentioned, students as leaders of the 1968 movement, and indigenous peasants and mestizos in the EZLN.[54] As previously, other groups contributed importantly to the democratization movement. The armed forces, given the degree of autonomy they exercised prior to 2000, were viewed by political leaders and citizens alike as supportive of the state, which believed it would intervene in presidential elections if the officer corps did not agree with the outcome. I personally witnessed some members of the Federal Electoral Institute adopt this view at a private gathering, shortly before the election of Ernesto Zedillo in 1994, attempting to anticipate the position they would take if the PRI candidate lost the election. Despite the fact that there exists no evidence whatsoever to support such a desire on the part of the military, the lack of transparency led to this belief and to similar rumors in prior elections. Understanding the democratic changes taking place in Mexico, the military after 1994 invited leading opposition political candidates to lecture to its officers at the Higher War College, including Vicente Fox.[55] They definitively removed themselves as an obstacle to electoral democracy by publicly stating that they would support the outcome of the 2000 election regardless of which candidate won, as long as it was certified as a fair process.

President Ernesto Zedillo played a critical role in the democratic transition culminating in the 2000 opposition victory. He differed strongly from his predecessor in his political philosophy. He made it clear from the initial months of his administration that he would move away from a centralized, authoritarian executive with mega-constitutional powers.[56] There is no question that he paved the way for Fox's electoral victory by changing the Mexican presidency's substance and tone.[57] He set in motion four fundamental patterns that altered the Mexican political context, all of which contributed to advances in democratization. First, he decentralized presidential decision-making, rarely intervening in political disputes. He symbolized this philosophy most notably and publicly in his decision to implement a PRI primary, ignoring the traditional presidential prerogative of designating his own successor. Second, he granted governors increased autonomy, thereby strengthening their political resources and encouraging the democratic theme of federalism.[58] The growth of federalism at the state and local level may well have been the most influential characteristic of Mexican democratization in 2000.[59] Third, he separated the party from the state, and by encouraging public campaign financing, eliminated the government party's financial advantages. Fourth, and finally, he strengthened other governmental institutions. Most importantly, he laid the groundwork for an independent judiciary and a stronger legislative branch, essential for structural democracy at the national level.[60] Electorally, he encouraged voter participation by guaranteeing the autonomy of the Federal Electoral Institute to oversee the election process.

As has been asserted repeatedly in this book, the 2000 presidential election serves as a demarcation in the process of Mexican democracy, indicating the beginning of the development of a consolidating democracy to replace the electoral democracy achieved by the democratic transition. The 2000 contest took Mexico's political development, in terms of democratization, to a higher plane, opening the door to structural, as distinct from just electoral, democracy. Structural democracy implies that Mexicans have the opportunity to alter governmental institutions and to make their processes participatory and accountable. The PAN's electoral victory legitimized the electoral process, demonstrating to the average voter that the will of the electorate could be achieved at the ballot box.

MEXICO'S DEMOCRATIC CONSOLIDATION AND THE FUTURE

How has Mexico fared since 2000 in achieving the characteristics associated with a consolidated democracy? As suggested in the introduction, democracy, according to most analysts, goes well beyond the electoral process and includes the following features: policy debates and political competition, citizen participation, accountability for upholding the rule of law and representative mechanisms, civilian control over the military, and respect for the views and rights of others.[61] An analysis of Mexico's track record in achieving democratic consolidation under Presidents Fox and Calderón reveals the obstacles and pitfalls that characterize the road to a functioning, as distinct from an electoral, democracy.[62]

One of the most serious deficiencies in Mexico's democratic consolidation since 2000 is its record on human rights. Major national and international human rights organizations have repeatedly documented and criticized Mexico's record on human rights. Amnesty International releases frequent reports on a regular basis on its websites. In a letter addressed to the U.S. Secretary of State, it identified numerous human rights failures, including that "only a **single** human rights violation perpetrated since 2007 by a member of the military has resulted in a trial and upheld conviction in a military court. Despite clear mandates under international law and human rights requirements of the Mérida Initiative, **none** of the numerous human rights violations perpetrated by the military during President Calderón's administration have been tried by civilian prosecutors and judicial authorities"; that "recent reforms and public security policies fail to incorporate effective mechanisms for citizen participation and accountability"; and that the "use of torture to force confessions or other testimony continues to be a widespread practice."[63] The most significant recommendation accomplished by either administration in addressing the dramatic increase in human rights abuses by the armed forces is the Supreme Court decision in favor of removing alleged human rights violations from military jurisdiction. The executive branch's proposals in this regard only removed certain egregious crimes from military jurisdiction, not all crimes, and remains stuck in the legislative process.[64] Indeed, Human Rights Watch issued a scathing, detailed report at the end of 2011, calling for these changes to be implemented, and providing evidence that strongly suggests soldiers and police have carried out disappearances and extrajudicial executions.[65] Human rights allegations against the armed forces have increased 1,963 percent for the navy and 931 percent for the army from 2006 through 2011.[66] The Secretariat of Defense, in response to critics, noted in February 2012 that the National Human Rights Commission has received 6,065 complaints against the armed forces since Calderón took office, 86 percent of which have been processed, resulting in only 98 recommendations, all of which the defense ministry has accepted.[67]

According to the National Council to Prevent Discrimination, the first federal agency of its kind in Mexico, four years into the Calderón administration most Mexicans believe little respect for the rights of others exists in their country. Not surprisingly, Mexicans assert that homosexuals, immigrants (largely from Central America), and the indigenous receive the least respect from fellow citizens. More surprising is the fact that Mexicans who are elderly or handicapped rank a close second to the other categories in the perceived treatment among all citizens. Women and non-Catholics also are viewed as common recipients of mistreatment.[68] Recent analysis of governmental efforts toward reducing discrimination among certain groups does reflect some progress. For example, a combination of NGOs, international agencies, and Mexico's own agency devoted to the prevention and control of HIV has achieved some positive outcomes since 2003.[69]

Equally important to explaining, in part, why citizen rights are abused or not respected in Mexico is every citizen's tolerance toward fellow Mexicans, regardless of the source of their intolerance. Survey researchers have generated a question that they have used successfully to test respondents' attitudes toward other people, regardless of their particular bias, asking them if they would allow such an individual to live in their home. What is insightful about Mexican responses to this question is that some of their answers correspond to their own perceptions of individuals whose rights are most abused, including homosexuals and someone from a different race. If one compares Mexican views with others in the hemisphere on a more controversial issue involving homosexuals, same-sex marriage, Mexican attitudes are more positive than that of the average Latin American, comparable to Brazilians and Chileans. Canadians, Argentines, and Uruguayans express the most favorable views, followed by Americans.[70] Recent surveys in Mexico suggest the population was equally divided for and against such marriages.[71] It is important to mention, however, that Mexicans, like many other societies, including the United States, have altered their attitudes significantly in recent years toward minority groups. The World Values Survey documents these altered views from 1990 through 2006, asking respondents if they would not want a particular individual as a neighbor. Mexican responses to rejecting a homosexual as a neighbor declined from 60 to 30 percent during that period. For someone with AIDS, it went from 57 to 21 percent.[72]

What is even more interesting and significant about other responses is that they reflect on the difficulties Mexicans are likely to face in achieving a consolidated democracy (see Table 10-6). If six out of ten Mexicans are intolerant toward individuals from a different culture or a different religion, it suggests the difficulties Mexicans may face in developing a consensus about their society's goals and the beneficiaries of those goals.[73] Even more striking is the fact that six out of ten Mexicans would not want an individual with different political ideas living in their home. That response demonstrates a level of intolerance for different political values or attitudes, which would make it extremely difficult to achieve a compromise in a democratic political model in the policymaking arena, and may explain to some degree why Congress has often failed to pass definitive, innovative legislation affecting economic and fiscal strategies and political and security reforms under Fox and Calderón. This lack of political tolerance also can be linked to support for the suppression of minority rights in Mexico specifically and Latin America generally, measuring

Table 10-6 Tolerance Toward Others, 2010

Willingness to Let Someone Live in Your Home	Percent
Handicapped	75
Different religion	65
Different race	64
Different culture	60
Foreigner	58
Different political ideas	58
With HIV/AIDS	49
Homosexual	43
Lesbian	42

Source: "Encuesta Nacional sobre Discriminación en México: Resultados Generales," (Mexico: Consejo Nacional para Prevenir la Discriminación, 2010).

citizen responses to the question, "Once the people decide what is right, we must prevent opposition from a minority. How much do you agree or disagree with that view?" Mexico ranked in the top half of countries giving strong support for that statement.[74]

The third important issue that remains unaddressed by the success of electoral democracy is the public's cynicism about governmental and party institutions because of pervasive corruption in public life. As we have seen, the Mexican public believes that political corruption is the central explanation for the continuation of drug-related violence in their country. The extent of political corruption is linked to accountability and to the rule of law.[75] According to a global scorecard kept by Transparency International, Mexico ranked ninety-eighth out of 178 countries, its lowest score (the lower the ranking the higher the corruption) in the ten years the index has existed. In contrast, Chile ranked twenty-first, the best record in Latin America. The perceived level of corruption among public officials can lead to citizens believing that paying a bribe is justified. Mexicans ranked highest among all major Latin American countries in believing this to be the case.[76] The index also provides some evidence that corruption has not declined under two democratic administrations, but rather has increased.[77] The major legal reforms introduced by the Calderón administration to implement the rule of law in the judicial process, confront public skepticism expressed by the views of three in ten Mexicans that it is foolish to follow the law when there are no consequences for not doing so, or because the majority do not do so.[78] In fact, 43 percent of Mexicans indicated in 2011 that they would violate the law if they believed they were correct.[79] In fact, the justice system receives little support from ordinary citizens because more than a third of Mexicans report being badly treated by public prosecutors.[80]

The most comprehensive empirical evaluation of accountability, corruption, and rule of law are incorporated into the World Bank Governance Indicators, based on numerous variables for each category. The data suggest several significant patterns in these interrelated variables that impact on democratic consolidation (see Table 10-7). In the first place, during the last years of the democratic transition from 1996 through 2000, with the exception of regulatory quality, Mexico improved in all of these categories, and witnessed a dramatic improvement in political stability as it achieved electoral democracy. However, during the next six years, its ranking globally declined or remained the same, with the exception of control of corruption, which improved slightly. Mexico witnessed a dramatic decline in political stability from 43 to 29 percent. In the first three years of the Calderón administration, it declined or remained static in four of the categories, while

Table 10-7 Governance Indicators for Mexico

Indicator	Year			
	1996	2000	2006	2009
Voice & Accountability	44.0	54.8	51.0	53.6
Political stability	17.8	43.8	29.3	22.2
Government effectiveness	55.3	63.1	58.7	60.5
Regulatory quality	70.7	64.4	63.9	61.0
Rule of law	35.2	43.3	42.9	34.0
Control of corruption	41.7	47.1	49.5	49.0

Source: World Bank Governance Indicators, www/info.worldbank.org/governance, 2011.
Key: Percentages refer to the percentage of countries globally that Mexico scored above. The higher the percentage, the better the ranking. The governance indicators presented here aggregate the views on the quality of governance provided by a large number of enterprise, citizen, and expert survey respondents in industrial and developing countries. These data are gathered from a number of survey institutes, think tanks, nongovernmental organizations, and international organizations.

improving slightly in accountability and government effectiveness. There was a significant decline in political stability and the rule of law, almost to the predemocratic level of 1996. The presence of an electoral democracy has not produced the desired consequences in achieving the rule of law.[81] For example, the actual or perceived level of crime and corruption affects the degree to which citizens would justify a military coup against the government. Fifty-eight and fifty-four percent of Mexicans justified such actions in the face of high levels of crime or corruption.[82] The fact that half of all Mexicans in 2011 perceive the authorities in Mexico as arbitrary suggests a serious disconnect between electoral democracy and a functioning, consolidated democracy.[83]

A decade ago, Steve Morris argued that levels of corruption at the state level are not affected by voting patterns, level of competitiveness, the party in power, or the power of incumbency.[84] Other studies suggested at the beginning of the consolidation era that organized crime's involvement in the political system at various levels significantly threatened public security and democratic government in Mexico.[85] Studies of Latin America have established a clear relationship between insecurity created by crime, and as suggested above, support for those who seek to remove governments by force. Mexicans rank near the very top of Latin Americans who would support a military coup under conditions of high crime levels.[86] As Morris argues in his most recent book, "At the structural and institutional level, early democratization in Mexico has had a mixed effect on corruption. By redistributing and fragmenting power, it has opened up some new opportunities for corruption (state capturing, conflict of interest, new clientelism, campaign finance) and even facilitated the continuation of certain authoritarian enclaves (by removing the informal controls that once existed on state and local governments, leaving unions virtually unaccountable). At the same time, by strengthening competition and official mechanisms of accountability, democratization has heightened the exposure (and accusations) of corruption, greatly "politicized" the issue, and triggered real institutional reforms that seem to be playing a role in limiting the ability of officials to hide grand corruption, that guarantee transparency, and that seem to be slowly depoliticizing the administration, thereby limiting older forms of petty, bureaucratic corruption."[87]

It is not just obvious forms of corruption that detract from the integrity of the institutions and the leadership, but also corruption's detrimental effects on the sense of community interest and trust. Pervasive corruption complements the belief that public life provides opportunities to benefit family and friends rather than to serve the interests of all Mexicans.[88] This is not to say that all public officials in Mexico are dishonest, but to suggest that an ambience favorable to self-interest, dishonesty, and favoritism prevails in many areas and at numerous levels of the public and private sector, accentuated by the active involvement of drug trafficking organizations. It explains why, since 2000, Mexican "citizens view corruption as the main obstacle to a democratic consolidation."[89]

An appraisal of Mexico's economic and political future suggests two immediate and long-term challenges, both of which have delayed and complicated Mexico's path to democratic consolidation. The economic issue of greatest importance is consistent economic growth characterized by increased efforts to reduce poverty and redistribute the wealth.[90] The overwhelming majority of Mexicans currently hold the federal government, more than individuals, responsible for ensuring their well-being.[91] Half of all Mexicans believe that addressing poverty and unemployment is the best way to solve drug-related criminal activity and violence.[92] An equal number believe the battle against drug-traffickers is impeding Mexico's democratic consolidation.[93] The central political issue is how to confront drug trafficking organizations while reducing widespread levels of violence and the influence of criminal organizations in public life and the private sector.[94] Two-thirds of Mexicans believe that half or more of their national territory is controlled by drug-traffickers, thus Mexico faces serious issues about governmental sovereignty.[95] To be clear, however, Mexico is not on the verge of being a failed state.[96]

A unique survey by CIDE captures Mexican expectations, but breaks them down by elite versus ordinary citizen responses (Table 10-8). The responses evaluating satisfaction with three goals two hundred years after independence reflect two important considerations in assessing Mexico's future and the two central issues identified above. First, approximately only

Table 10-8 Elite and Citizen Satisfaction with Mexican Achievements since Independence in 1810

| | Very or Somewhat Satisfied | |
| | Percentage | |
Goal	Leaders	All Mexicans
Social Equality	20	57
Economic Development	31	54
Internal Peace and Security	28	42

Source: Guadalupe González Gónzalez, et al., *México: Las Américas y el Mundo 2010, Política exterior: Opinión pública y líderes* (Mexico: CIDE, 2011), Table 1.4, 31.

half the population is satisfied with social equality and economic development, and only two-fifths with peace and security, an issue central to political stability.[97] In a survey of national values, all citizens listed violence, corruption, and poverty as the three major failures of their country since 1810. Surprisingly, however, more than half of all Mexicans with families believe their children will achieve a higher social position.[98] Second, and extremely important for understanding political behavior in the future, is the significant disjuncture in the level of satisfaction between leaders from all sectors versus ordinary Mexicans for each of these goals, but especially the social equality goal (20 percent of leaders) which affects human rights and respect for others, and the economic development goal (31 percent), particularly economic development for all Mexicans regardless of income or ethnicity.[99]

The administrations from 2000 to 2012 have introduced legislation and reforms that have strengthened electoral democracy in Mexico, an essential component of a consolidated democracy. Further, Mexicans believe their country's major achievement since independence is its culture and arts, democracy, and order and stability.[100] Yet, Mexicans remain seriously unsatisfied with democracy's performance. Indeed, in the 2011 Latinobarómetro survey, Mexico boasted the highest level of dissatisfaction (73 percent) with democracy of any country in the region. Moreover, more than a third expressed no preference for democracy over an authoritarian government, and 14 percent actually preferred the latter.[101] A year later, two-fifths believed other forms of government were as good as democracy.[102] Only if Mexico can effectively address both income inequality and political corruption and the rule of law in the next decade, improving its performance in both areas, will it strengthen the path to consolidation. If it fails to address these issues adequately, the achievement of a functioning democracy will be difficult if not impossible to attain.

NOTES

1. "Public Opinion: Balance and Expectations," *Review of the Economic Situation of Mexico*, (October 2001): 436.

2. Consulta Mitofsky, "Felipe Calderón, Evaluación de 19 Trimestres de Gobierno," August 2011, www.consulta.mx.

3. Consulta Mitofsky, "Felipe Calderón, Evaluación de 19 Trimestres de Gobierno," August 2011, and "Décima Encuesta Nacional sobre Percepción de Inseguridad Ciudanana en México," March 2012, www.consulta.mx.

4. Alejandro Moreno, "Radiografía de los indignados," *Enfoque, Reforma,* August 7, 2011.

5. www.observatoriopoliticasocial.org, 2011.

6. Roderic Ai Camp, *Mexico: What Everyone Needs to Know* (New York: Oxford University Press, 2011), 24–25.

7. *Poverty of Democracy: The Institutional Roots of Political Participation in Mexico* (Pittsburgh, PA: University of Pittsburgh Press, 2010).

8. Ernesto López-Córdova, "Globalization, Migration and Development: The Role of Mexican Migrant Remittances," Inter-American Development Bank, Working Paper 20, August 2006.

9. *Mexico Report*, February 10, 1992.

10. Sidney Weintraub, *NAFTA: What Comes Next?* (Washington, DC: CSIS, 1994), 53–54.

11. "A New Hope for the Hemisphere?," *New Perspective Quarterly* 8 (Winter 1991): 128.

12. Ernesto Zedillo, "A Strategy for Mexico's Economic Growth," June 6, 1994.

13. Nora Lustig, *Mexico in Crisis: The U.S. to the Rescue; The Financial Assistance Packages of 1982 and 1995* (Washington, DC: Brookings Institution, 1996).

14. Douglas W. Payne, "Wall Street Blues," *The New Republic* (March 13, 1995), 20, 22.

15. Claire Poole, "Beast of Burden," *Mexico Business* (December 1996): 30.

16. Ernesto Zedillo, "Social Policy, a Commitment to Mexicans," Mexican Embassy of Canada, September 1997.

17. "Zedillo Will Leave Behind More Poverty," *El Financiero Internacional* (September 13, 1999): 11.

18. Two highly respected economists, Luis de la Calle and Luis Rubio, argue according to their calculations that Mexico's middle-class through 2009 is much larger than government figures would indicate. Using a much broader set of variables examining economic behavior and consumption, as well as focusing on unreported income transfers and other economic and social behaviors that can be identified with "middle-class behavior," that the middle-class is actually at least 53 percent, and poor Mexicans account for 25 percent. I would argue that so many of those 53 percent are on the margin, that it makes their middle-class status less convincing. *Mexico: A Middle-Class Society; Poor No More, Developed Not Yet* (Washington, DC: Woodrow Wilson International Center for Scholars, 2012).

19. www.coneval.gob.mx (informes tab), 2011.

20. www.coneval.gob.mx, February 10, 2012.

21. Miguel Székley, "Pobreza y desigualdad en México entre 1950 y el 2004," *El Trimestre Económico* 72, no. 4 (July 2005): 913–31.

22. Pamela K. Starr, "Mexico's Big, Inherited Challenges," *Current History* 111, no. 742 (February 2012): 45–46.

23. James Cypher, "Mexico Since NAFTA: Elite Delusions and the Reality of Decline," *New Labor Forum* 20, no. 3 (Fall 2011): 61–69, 118.

24. For a discussion, see John Sheahan's insightful "Effects of Liberalization Programs on Poverty and Inequality: Chile, Mexico, and Peru," *Latin American Research Review* 37, no. 3 (1997): 7–37.

25. World Development Indicators database, World Bank, July 1, 2011, 1, www.siteresources.worldbank.org/datastatistics/resources, 2011.

26. H. Li, "Political Economy of Income Distribution: A Comparative Study of Taiwan and Mexico," unpublished paper, Merrimack College, 1999.

27. Chong-Sup Kim and Min-Kyung Hong, "Education Policy and Industrial Development: The Cases of Korea and Mexico," *Journal of International and Area Studies* 17, no. 2 (December 2010): 141–82.

28. *Education at a Glance 2011: OECD Indicators*, www.oecd.org, September 2011.

29. Blanca Heredia, "Mexico's Education Problem: Low Returns to Merit," Mexico Under Calderón Task Force, Center for Hemispheric Policy, University of Miami, August 3, 2010, 6.

30. "Indicators of Income Distribution," *Latin American Economic Policies*, no. 5 (Fourth Quarter 1998), 8.

31. Florencia Torche and Seymour Spilerman, "Intergenerational Influences of Wealth in Mexico," *Latin American Research Review* 44, no. 3 (2009): 75–101.

32. Nora Lustig discovered that "social democratic governments have reduced poverty and inequality faster than non-left governments. This is significant because redistributive policies in social democratic regimes have not been associated with unsustainable fiscal policies." However, recent leftist/populist regimes have been more successful than their predecessors, but not as successful as social democratic governments. "Poverty, Inequality and the New Left in Latin America," Democratic Governance and the "New Left," Woodrow Wilson Center Update on the Americas, No. 5, October 2009, 13.

33. See the fascinating analysis, Guillermina Rodríguez and Sergio Luna, "Household Income is Finally Above the 1994 Threshold," *Review of the Economic Situation of Mexico* (August 2007): 225–26.

34. See the revealing study by David MacKenzie and Hillel Rapoport, "Can Migration Reduce Educational Attainment? Evidence from Mexico," World Bank Policy Research Paper, June 2006. www.worldbank.org (publications tab, 2006), 2011.

35. Erik Lee and Christopher E. Wilson, "The State of Trade, Competiveness and Economic Well-being in the U.S.-Mexico Border Region," Working Paper, Woodrow Wilson Center, June 2012; Eduardo Zepeda, Timothy Wise and Kevin P. Gallaher,

"Rethinking Trade Policy for Development: Lessons from Mexico under NAFTA," Policy Outlook, Carnegie Endowment for International Peace, Washington, DC, 2009.

36. Gordon H. Hanson, "Why isn't Mexico Rich?," University of California, San Diego and the National Bureau of Economic Research, September 2010, 23.

37. Carlos Salas and Anselmo dos Santos, "Diverging Paths in Development, Brazil and Mexico," *International Journal of Labour Research* 3, no. 1 (2011): 128–29.

38. Taeko Hoshino, "Propiedad y control en las grandes empresas mexicanas," *Este País*, No. 193, April 18, 2007: 18–29.

39. "Disfrutando en el país monopolios," April 2010, www.parametría.com.

40. Gerardo Esquivel and Fausto Hernández-Trillo, "How Can Reforms Help Deliver Growth in Mexico?" in *Growing Pains in Latin America*, ed. Liliana Rojas (Washington, DC: Center for Global Development, 2009), 192–235

41. www.oecd.org, 2011.

42. México, Presidencia de la República, *Sexto informe de gobierno: Anexo estadístico,* September 1, 2011, 671.

43. Joydeep Mukherji, "Mexico's Challenge: Moving from Stability to Dynamism," Mexico Under Calderón Task Force, Center for Hemispheric Policy, University of Miami, August 11, 2008, 6.

44. Instituto Ciudadano de Estudios Sobre la Inseguridad, *Encuestas nacionales sobre inseguridad, El costo de la inseguridad en México*, November 2009, and their extensive victimization study: Encuesta nacional sobre inseguridad, Primera Parte, 2010. www.icesi.org.mx, 2011.

45. Instituto Nacional de Estadística y Geografía, *Encuesta Nacional de Victimización y Percepción sobre Seguridad Pública*, September 20, 2011.

46. "160 mil empresas dejan México a causa de la violencia," *Voz de América*, April 4, 2012, www.voanoticias.com.

47. Julie Ray and Steve Crabtree, "Many See Drug Trafficking Widespread, Rising in Latin America," www.gallup.com, 2010. "Justice in Mexico News Report," Trans-Border Institute, University of San Diego, January 2010, 6.

48. American Chamber of Commerce in Mexico, "The Impact of Security in Mexico on the Private Sector," Kroll, 2011.

49. See Dev Kar, *Mexico: Illicit Financial Flows, Macroeconomic Imbalances, and the Underground Economy*, Global Financial Integrity, January 2012, i.

50. See Jaime E. Rodríguez O., "Democracy from Independence to Revolution," in *The Oxford Handbook of Mexican Politics*, ed. Roderic Ai Camp (New York: Oxford University Press, 2012), 31–52.

51. Paul Gillingham, "Mexican Elections, 1910–1940: Voters, Violence, and Veto Power," in Camp, ed., *The Oxford Handbook of Mexican Politics*, 53–76.

52. See my chapter, "All Politics Is Local: Mexico's Local Path to Democracy?," *The Metamorphosis of Leadership in a Democratic Mexico* (New York: Oxford University Press, 2010), 22–45.

53. Kenneth Greene, "Dominance Defeated," in *Why Dominant Parties Lose: Mexico's Democratization in Comparative Perspective* (Cambridge, UK: Cambridge University Press, 2007), 210–54.

54. Dolores Trevizo's *Rural Protest and the Making of Democracy in Mexico, 1968–2000* (University Park: Pennsylvania State University, 2011).

55. For some of these changes in the 1990s and early 2000s, see my *Mexico's Military on the Democratic Stage* (Westport, CT: Praeger, 2005).

56. Mara Steffan, "The Political Impact of NAFTA on the Mexican Transition to Democracy, 1988–2000," *Bologna Center Journal of International Affairs* 10 (Spring 2010), www.bcjournal.org.

57. Pamela K. Starr, "Monetary Mismanagement and Inadvertent Democratization in Technocratic Mexico," *Studies in Comparative International Development* 33, no. 4 (Winter 1999): 35–65.

58. David Merchant and Paul Rich, "Prospects for Mexican Federalism: Roots of the Policy Issues," *Policy Studies Journal* 31, no. 4 (November 2003): 661–67.

59. Support for this argument can be found in Andrew Selee, *Decentralization, Democratization, and Informal Power in Mexico* (University Park: Pennsylvania State University Press, 2011).

60. Silvia I. Oseguera, "Judicial Reform in Mexico: Political Insurance or the Search for Political Legitimacy?," *Political Research Quarterly* 62, no. 4 (December 2009): 753–66.

61. Terry Lynn Karl, "Dilemmas of Democratization in Latin America," *Comparative Politics* 23, no. 1 (October 1990): 2–3.

62. Pamela K. Starr, "Mexico and the United States: A Window of Opportunity?," Special Report, Pacific Council on International Policy, April 2009, 6ff.

63. "Human Rights Concerns to Inform the U.S. Department of State's Mérida Initiative Reporting on Mexico," Amnesty International, May 26, 2010.

64. Amnesty International, "An Historic Step for Justice in Mexico," July 14, 2011.

65. *Neither Rights Nor Security: Killings, Torture, and Disappearances in Mexico's "War on Drugs,"* (New York: Human Rights Watch, 2011). It can be downloaded in its entirety from www.hrw.org, 2011. For an update, see Catherine Daly, et. al., *Armed with Impunity, Curbing Military Human Rights Abuses in Mexico*, Special Report, Trans-Border Institute, University of San Diego, July 2012.

66. Consulta Mitofsky, "Décima encuesta nacional sobre percepción de inseguridad ciudadana en México," March 2012, 4.

67. Grupo Fórmula, "En el combate al crimen organizado se respetan derechos humanos: Sedena," January 23, 2012, www.radioformula.com.mx.

68. "Encuesta Nacional sobre Discriminación en México: Resultados Generales," (Mexico: Consejo Nacional para Prevenir la Discriminación, 2010).

69. Antonio Torres-Ruíz, "HIV/AIDS and Sexual Minorities in Mexico: A Globalized Struggle for the Protection of Human Rights," *Latin American Research Review* 46, no. 1 (2011): 48–49.

70. Germán Lodola and Margarita Corral, "Support for Same-Sex Marriage in Latin America," *AmericasBarometer Insights: 2010*, No. 44, 2.

71. See Parametría's summary of other surveys, "Bodas Gay," www.parametria.com.mx, 2011.

72. Ronald Inglehart and Miguel Basáñez, *Changing Human Beliefs and Values, 1981–2007: A Cross-Cultural Sourcebook Based on the World Values*

Surveys and European Values Studies (Mexico: Siglo XXI, 2010). Table based on 2006 data.

73. Edward Telles and Liza Steele, "Pigmentocracy in the Americas: How is Educational Attainment Related to Skin Color?," *AmericasBarometer Insights: 2012*, No. 73, 4; Mollie J. Cohen, "Explaining Support for Interethnic Marriage in Four Countries," *AmericasBarometer Insights: 2012*, No. 77, 2.

74. Diana Orces, "Popular Support for Suppression of Minority Rights," *AmericasBarometer Insights: 2010*, No. 34, 1. This question appeared in the 2008 survey.

75. Enrique Krauze, "Furthering Democracy in Mexico: A Return to Oligarchy?," *Foreign Affairs*, 85, no. 1 (January/February, 2006): 58.

76. Juan Camilo Plata, "To Bribe or Not to Bribe," *AmericasBarometer Insights: 2011*, No. 72, 5.

77. "Justice in Mexico News Report," Trans-Border Institute, University of San Diego, November 2010, 7–8.

78. The Fletcher School and CIDAC, *Encuesta valores: Diagnóstico axiológico México*, February 2, 2011, 7.

79. Raúl Benitez Manaut, et al., *Encuesta ciudadanía: Democracia y narcoviolencia* (Mexico: Cidena, 2011), 174.

80. Instituto Nacional de Estadística y Geografía, *Encuesta nacional de victimización y percepción sobre seguridad pública*.

81. Diane E. Davis, "Undermining the Rule of Law: Democratization and the Dark Side of Police Reform in Mexico," *Latin American Politics and Society* 48, no. 1 (Spring 2006): 80–81; Pamela K. Starr, "Authoritarian Inheritances and Mexico's Incomplete Democratic Transition," Mexico Under Calderón Task Force, Center for Hemispheric Policy, University of Miami, June 24, 2010.

82. 2010 Latin American Public Opinion Project Survey, Mexico, raw data, frequency tables, courtesy of Pablo Páras, October, 2011; Brandon Bell, "When Do High Levels of Corruption Justify a Military Coup?," *AmericasBarometer Insights: 2012*, No. 79, 1.

83. Ibid., 6.

84. Stephen D. Morris, "Political Corruption in Mexico: A Comparative State-Level Analysis," paper presented as the Latin American Studies Association Meeting, Dallas, Texas, March 2003, 13–14.

85. John Bailey and Roy Godson, *Organized Crime & Democratic Governability: Mexico and the U.S.-Mexican Borderlands* (Pittsburgh, PA: University of Pittsburgh Press, 2000), 222.

86. Arturo Maldonado, "Insecurities Intensify Support for Those Who Seek to Remove Government by Force," *AmericasBarometer Insights: 2010*, No. 48, 1–10. For the Mexican ranking, see Orlando J. Pérez, "Crime and Support for Coups in Latin America," *AmericasBarometer Insights: 2009*, No. 32, 2; José Miguel Cruz, "Public Insecurity in Central America and Mexico," *AmericasBarometer Insights: 2009*, No. 28, 1–7; and Cornelia Buchanan, et al., "*Mano Dura* in the Americas: Who Supports Iron Fist Rule?," *AmericasBarometer Insights: 2012*, No. 80, 1–8.

87. *Political Corruption in Mexico: The Impact of Democratization* (Boulder, CO: Lynne Rienner, 2009), 231; Kate Doyle, "Investigative Journalism and Access

to Information in Mexico," Working Paper 29, Center for Latin American Studies, University of California, Berkeley, April 2011.

88. Ricardo R. Gómez-Vilchis, "Democratic Transition and Presidential Approval in Mexico," *Mexican Studies* 28, no. 1 (Winter 2012): 64.

89. "Justice in Mexico News Report," Trans-Border Institute, University of San Diego, April 2010, 7.

90. Francisco González, "Drug Violence Isn't Mexico's Only Problem," *Current History* 110, no. 733 (February 2011): 68–74.

91. Margarita Corral, "To What Extent Should Government Ensure Citizen Well-Being?," *AmericasBarometer Insights: 2009*, No. 16, 1–5.

92. It is acceptable and justified for a peasant who receives assistance from the government but barely produces at a subsistence level to grow marijuana (11 percent); unacceptable but justified (44 percent); and unacceptable and not justified (44 percent). Raúl Benitez Manaut, et al., *Encuesta ciudadanía: Democracia y Narcoviolencia* (Mexico City: Cidena, 2011), 92.

93. Ibid., 83, 89.

94. Mark Kleiman, "Surgical Strikes in the Drug Wars: Smarter Policies for Both Sides of the Border," *Foreign Affairs* 90, no. 5 (September–October, 2011): 89–101; Eric L. Olson, "Considering New Strategies for Confronting Organized Crime in Mexico," Mexico Institute, Woodrow Wilson Center, March 2012. Viridiana Rios, "Why Did Mexico Become So Violent? A Self-reinforcing Violent Equilibrium Caused by Competition and Enforcement," *Trends in Organized Crime* (August 2012).

95. "Colombianización de México," 500 respondents, +/−4.4% margin of error, August 2010, www.parametría.com.mx; "Crece tolerancia al narco por miedo a la violencia," 1,200 respondents, +/−2.8% margin of error, December 17–21, 2009, www.parametría.com.mx.

96. Brian Michael Jenkins, "Could Mexico Fail,?" *Homeland Security Today*, February 13, 2009; Adam David Morton, "Failed-State Status and the War on Drugs in Mexico," *Global Dialogue* 13, no. 1 (Winter–Spring 2011): 94–107; and Phil Williams and Vanda Felbab-Brown, *Drug Trafficking, Violence, and Instability* (Carlisle: Strategic Studies Institute, U.S. Army War College, 2012), 16.

97. Raúl Benitez Manaut, et al., *Encuesta ciudadanía: Democracia y narcoviolencia*, 95.

98. Banamex, *Encuesta nacional de valores: Lo que une y lo que divide Mexicanos* (Mexico, 2010), 5, 21.

99. Isabel Guerrero, Luis Felipe López Calva, and Michael Walton, "The Inequality Trap and its Links to Low Growth in Mexico," Working Paper, Stanford Center for International Development, November, 2006, www.stanford.edu/group/siepr/cgi-bin/siepr/?q=system/files/, 2011.

100. Banamex, *Encuesta nacional de valores: Lo que une y lo que divide Mexicanos*, 3.

101. Alejandro Moreno, "La democracia mexicana en crisis," *Enfoque, Reforma*, October 30, 2011.

102. Carta Paramétrica, "Pierde aprecio la democracia en México," 1,000 respondents, +/−3.1% margin of error, April 18–22, 2012, www.parametria.com.mx.

Bibliographic Essay

For the student initially exploring Mexican politics, a voluminous literature exists in both Spanish and English. The purpose of this essay, however, is only to list sources that can lead to more detailed analyses for the general reader. Most of these sources are those readily available, generally in English, and published in the last two decades, covering the democratic transition and consolidation periods. I will also make reference to numerous Internet sources that provide archived data sets and statistics for all aspects of Mexican politics.

The most useful reference source is the Library of Congress website for the *Handbook of Latin American Studies*. You can search all of the previous volumes by author, title, subject, and so on. Each entry, including books, scholarly articles, and chapters, includes a fifty-word annotation on the entry's content: http://lcweb2.loc.gov/hlas. For unpublished, recent scholarly papers, readers should use the Social Science Research Network, at http://papers.ssrn.com/sol3/displayabstractsearch.cfm, a collaborative project that again can be searched for papers on Mexico.

There also exist some excellent broad surveys of various facets of Mexican politics, but most predate Calderón's victory. For the period from 2000 to 2012, the most useful, broad interpretation is that of David A. Shirk and Emily Edmonds-Poli, *Contemporary Mexican Politics*, 2nd ed. (Lanham, MD: Rowman & Littlefield, 2011), and Nora Hamilton, *Mexico: Political, Social and Economic Evolution* (New York: Oxford University Press, 2010). For Calderón's government, see Andrew Selee and Jacqueline Peschard, *Mexico's Democratic Challenges: Politics, Government, and Society* (Washington, DC: Woodrow Wilson Center Press, 2010). For the Fox administration, see Luis Rubio and Susan Kaufman Purcell, eds., *Mexico under Fox* (Boulder, CO: Lynne Rienner Publishers, 2004).

Several additional edited collections also provide more focused interpretations of political developments and the democratic consolidation since

2000. They include: Joseph Tulchin and Andrew D. Selee, eds., *Mexico's Politics and Society in Transition* (Boulder, CO: Lynne Rienner, 2003); Kevin Middlebrook, ed., *Dilemmas of Political Change in Mexico* (La Jolla, CA: Center for U.S.-Mexican Studies, UC–SD, 2004); Russell Crandall, Guadalupe Paz, and Riordan Roett, eds., *Mexico's Democracy at Work* (Boulder, CO: Lynne Rienner, 2004); and Armand B. Peschard-Sverdrup and Sara R. Rioff, eds., *Mexican Governance, From Single-Party Rule to Divided Government* (Washington, DC: CSIS, 2005). These works contain some of the best interpretative essays on recent Mexico by North American and Mexican scholars.

The most extensive, recent broad comparative analysis of Mexico and another country is that of Chile and Mexico, in Francisco E. González's revealing *Dual Transitions from Authoritarian Rule: Institutionalized Regimes in Chile and Mexico, 1970–2000* (Baltimore, MD: Johns Hopkins University Press, 2008). Equally interesting is He Li, *From Revolution to Reform: A Comparative Study of China and Mexico* (Lanham, MD: University Press of America, 2004). Of course, numerous edited collections include Mexico as part of a larger regional approach to understanding consolidating democracies. Among the best are Alberto J. Olvera Rivera, "Social Accountability in Mexico: The Civic Alliance Experience," in *Enforcing the Rule of Law: Social Accountability in the New Latin American Democracies*, ed. Enrique Peruzzotti and Catalina Smulovitz (Pittsburgh, PA: University of Pittsburgh Press, 2006), 178–212; Denise Dresser, "Mexico: Dysfunctional Democracy," in *Constructing Democratic Governance in Latin America*, 3rd ed., ed. Jorge Domínguez and Michael Shifter (Baltimore, MD: Johns Hopkins University Press, 2008), 321–350; and Claudio A. Holzner, "Mexico: Weak State, Weak Democracy," *The Quality of Democracy in Latin America*, ed. Daniel H. Levine and José E. Molina (Boulder, CO: Lynne Rienner, 2011): 83–110.

The historical literature on Mexico is extensive and detailed, although there are gaps for many topics and periods. The best comprehensive survey of Mexican history remains Michael Meyer, William L. Sherman, and Susan M. Deeds, *The Course of Mexican History*, 9th ed. (New York: Oxford University Press, 2010). The most recent collection by leading historians is Michael C. Meyer and William H. Beezley, eds., *The Oxford History of Mexico* (New York: Oxford University Press, 2010), and William Beezley, ed., *A Companion to Mexican History and Culture* (New York: Wiley-Blackwell, 2011). A Mexican perspective can be found in Alicia Hernández Chávez, *Mexico: A Brief History* (Berkeley: University of California Press, 2006) and Enrique Krauze, *Mexico: Biography of Power; A History of Modern Mexico, 1810–1996* (New York: HarperCollins, 1997).

For a historical survey focusing on popular culture and the perspective of the masses, see Colin M. MacLachlan and William H. Beezley, *El Gran Pueblo: A History of Greater Mexico*, 3rd. ed. (Englewood Cliffs, NJ: Prentice-Hall, 2003). Colin M. MacLachlan provides a broad overview of political characteristics stemming from the colonial system in *Spain's Empire in the New World* (Berkeley: University of California Press, 1988. For the late-nineteenth-century political heritage, Charles A. Hale, *The Transformation of Liberalism in Late Nineteenth-Century Mexico* (Princeton, NJ: Princeton University Press, 1989), and Jaime E. Rodríguez O., *The Divine Charter: Constitutionalism and Liberalism in Nineteenth-Century Mexico* (Lanham, MD: Rowman & Littlefield, 2005) offer helpful and provocative interpretations.

The subject of contemporary Mexican political culture has received more attention from Mexican than from U.S. analysts. The most recent comparative study is Matthew Cleary and Susan Stokes, *Democracy and the Culture of Skepticism: Political Trust in Argentina and Mexico* (New York: Russell Sage Foundation, 2006), and Roderic Ai Camp, ed., *Citizen Views of Democracy in Latin America* (Pittsburgh, PA: University of Pittsburgh Press, 2001), comparing democratic values in Chile, Costa Rica, and Mexico. The extraordinary, extensive surveys directed by Mitchell Seligson at Vanderbilt University, however, have produced dozens of short reports by his students, most of which are cited in the text. There also are book-length reports of which the most recent is *The Political Culture of Democracy, 2010; Democratic Consolidation in the Americas in Hard Times*. All of these can be found online at the Latin American Public Opinion Project website: http://www.vanderbilt.edu/lapop/. One may use the raw data from any of the survey projects (online data analysis tab) or download past published reports. It is a gold mine of attitudinal studies of the region, comparing Mexico, Latin American, and American and Canadian views through 2012.

On the relationship between cultural values and democracy, a good place to begin is Ronald Inglehart, "The Renaissance of Political Culture," *American Political Science Review* 82, no. 4 (November 1988): 1203–30. For some useful comparisons with Mexico, see Mitchell Seligson and Amy Erica Smith, eds., *The Political Culture of Democracy, 2010: Democratic Consolidation in the Americas in Hard Times*, cited above; Ronald Inglehart et al., *Changing Human Beliefs and Values: A Cross-Cultural Sourcebook Based on the World Values Surveys and European Values Studies* (Mexico: Siglo XXI, 2010), which provides extensive comparisons from the World Values Surveys through 2006; and Alejandro Moreno and Patricia Méndez, "Attitudes Toward Democracy: Mexico in Comparative Perspective,"

International Journal of Comparative Sociology 43, no. 3–5 (2002), 350–67. For comparisons between leaders and ordinary citizens, see Lucía Miranda, "The State of Democracy in Latin America: A Comparative Analysis of the Attitudes of Elites and Citizens," *Boletin PNUD & Instituto de Iberoamérica*, January 2011, available on the Vanderbilt LAPOP website.

In regard to the more specific issue of how values affect partisanship, alienation, and tolerance, little literature on Mexico exists. The most important analyses are Timothy J. Power and Mary A. Clark, "Does Trust Matter? Interpersonal Trust and Democratic Values in Chile, Costa Rica, and Mexico," in *Citizen Views of Democracy in Latin America*, 51–70; Joseph L. Klesner, "Legacies of Authoritarianism," in *Citizen Views of Democracy in Latin America*, 118–138; and Alejandro Moreno's "Citizens' Values and Beliefs toward Politics: Is Democracy Growing Attitudinal Roots?," in *Mexico's Democratic Challenges: Politics, Government, and Society*, ed. Andrew Selee and Jacqueline Peschard (Washington, DC: Woodrow Wilson Center Press, 2010): 29–49.

Excellent interpretations of key elections and the impact of specific variables during the democratic transition are available in Jorge I. Domínguez and James A. McCann, *Democratizing Mexico: Public Opinion and Electoral Choices* (Baltimore, MD: Johns Hopkins University Press, 1996); and Joseph Klesner, "The 1994 Elections: Manifestation of a Divided Society?" *Mexican Studies* 11 (Winter 1995): 137–49. The two fundamental elections for the democratic consolidation have been examined extensively in two outstanding collections. For many variables which played a role in 2000, see various essays in Jorge Domínguez and Chappell Lawson, eds., *Mexico's Pivotal 2000 Election* (Stanford, CA: Stanford University Press, 2004). For the 2006 election, see Jorge Domínguez, Chappell Lawson, and Alejandro Moreno, eds., *Consolidating Mexico's Democracy: The 2006 Presidential Campaign in Comparative Perspective* (Baltimore, MD: Johns Hopkins University Press, 2009). Also see Joseph Klesner, "Who Participates Politically in Mexico? Socioeconomic Resources, Political Attitudes, and Social Capital as Determinants of Political Participation," *Latin American Politics and Society* 51, No. 2 (2009): 59–90. For the impact of religion, see my "Exercising Political Influence: Religion, Democracy, and the Mexican 2006 Presidential Race," *Journal of Church and State* 50, no. 1 (Winter, 2008): 101–122. On the subject of gender, the only recent analysis specifically on this topic is that of Victoria Rodríguez, "Women, Politics, and Democratic Consolidation in Mexico: Two Steps Forward, One Step Back," in the *The Oxford Handbook of Mexican Politics*, ed. Roderic Ai Camp (New York: Oxford University Press, 2012), 446–65, and Roderic Ai Camp and Keith Yanner, "Democracy

Across Cultures: Does Gender Make a Difference?" in *Citizenship in Latin America*, ed. Joseph S. Tulchin and Meg Ruthenburg (Boulder, CO: Lynne Rienner, 2006), 149–170.

The most comprehensive work on Mexican political recruitment is my own, *The Metamorphosis of Leadership in a Democratic Mexico* (New York: Oxford University Press, 2010), which examines Mexican leadership over three time periods, contrasting the predemocratic with the democratic transition and consolidation eras. For a broad work covering all elites from 1970 to 2000, see Roderic Ai Camp, *Mexico's Mandarins: Crafting a Power Elite for the Twenty-First Century* (Berkeley: University of California Press, 2002). For work on specific types of political leaders during the democratic consolidation, see Joy Langston's, "The Dinosaur that Evolved: Changes to the PRI's Gubernatorial Candidate Selection, 1980 to 2009," in the *The Oxford Handbook of Mexican Politics*, ed. Roderic Ai Camp (New York: Oxford University Press, 2012), 143–66. For women, these sources provide additional insights: Lisa Baldez, "Elected Bodies: The Gender Quota Law For Legislative Candidates in Mexico," *Legislative Studies Quarterly* 29, no. 2 (May 2004): 231–58; and Kathleen Bruhn, "Whores and Lesbians: Political Activism, Party Strategies, and Gender Quotas in Mexico," *Electoral Studies* 22, no. 1 (March 2003): 101–19. For technocrats during and after the transition, see Roderic Ai Camp, "The Time of the Technocrats and Deconstruction of the Revolution," in *The Oxford History of Mexico*, eds. William H. Beezley and Michael C. Meyer (New York: Oxford University Press, 2010), 569–97.

The relationship between the government and newly important interest groups or actors are analyzed in Shannan Mattiace, "Social and Indigenous Movements in Mexico's Transition to Democracy," in *The Oxford Handbook of Mexican Politics*, ed. Roderic Ai Camp (New York: Oxford University Press, 2012), 398–422; John Bailey, "Drug Traffickers as Political Actors in Mexico's Nascent Democracy," in *The Oxford Handbook of Mexican Politics*, ed. Roderic Ai Camp (New York: Oxford University Press, 2012), 466–95; Todd A. Eisenstadt, *Politics, Identity, and Mexico's Indigenous Rights Movements* (New York: Cambridge University Press, 2011); and Mariclaire Acosta, "NGO's and Human Rights," in *The Oxford Handbook of Mexican Politics*, ed. Roderic Ai Camp (New York: Oxford University Press, 2011), 423–45.

To understand policymaking since 2000, the best sources include José L. Velasco, *Insurgency, Authoritarianism, and Drug Trafficking in Mexico's Democratization* (London: Routledge, 2005); Jeffrey A. Weldon, "State Reform in Mexico: Progress and Prospects," in *Mexican Governance, From Single-Party Rule to Divided Government*, ed. Armand B. Peschard-Sverdrup and

Sara R. Rioff (Washington, DC: CSIS Press, 2005), 27–107; "Part III: The Changing Nature of State-Society Relations," in *Mexico's Democratic Challenges: Politics, Government, and Society*, ed. Andrew Selee and Jacqueline Peschard (Washington, DC: Woodrow Wilson Center Press, 2010), 231–306. For a local perspective, see Caroline Beer, "Invigorating Federalism: The Emergence of Governors and State Legislatures as Powerbrokers and Policy Innovators," in *The Oxford Handbook of Mexican Politics,* ed. Roderic Ai Camp (New York: Oxford University Press, 2012), 119–42.

For institutional groups and their relationship to the state, several studies are available on the military: Jordi Diez, "Civil-Military Relations in Mexico: the Unfinished Transition," in *The Oxford Handbook of Mexican Politics,* ed. Roderic Ai Camp (New York: Oxford University Press, 2012), 265–85; Inigo Guevara Moyano, *Adapting, Transforming, and Modernizing Under Fire: The Mexican Military 2006–11* (Carlisle, PA: Strategic Studies Institute, 2011); Sigrid Arzt, "Democracia, Militares, y Seguridad en México," Ph.D. dissertation, University of Miami, April, 2011, and Roderic Ai Camp, *Mexico's Military on the Democratic Stage* (Washington, DC: CSIS and Praeger, 2005).

Works on the private sector that examines the relationship in comparative context include William T. Barndt, "Managing Democracy, the Ascendance of Business Entrepreneurs in Latin American Party Politics," paper presented at the American Political Science Association, Seattle, Washington, September, 2011. The evolution of the relationship before and during the democratic consolidation is presented clearly in Mark Williams, "The Path of Economic Liberalism," in *The Oxford Handbook of Mexican Politics*, ed. Roderic Ai Camp (New York: Oxford University Press, 2012), 744–76. For business and politics, the best works on industrial groups are Strom C. Thacker, *Big Business, the State, and Free Trade: Constructing Coalitions in Mexico* (Cambridge, UK: Cambridge University Press, 2000), and his "Big Business, Democracy, and the Politics of Competition," in *The Oxford Handbook of Mexican Politics*, ed. Roderic Ai Camp (New York: Oxford University Press, 2011), 313–34. For a small business perspective, see Kenneth C. Shadlen, *Democratization without Representation: The Politics of Small Industry in Mexico* (University Park: Pennsylvania State University Press, 2004). For an examination of the drug trafficking organizations as an influential economic actor, see William P. Glade's imaginative analysis: "Economy as Grand-Guignol: The Postreform Era in Mexico," in *The Oxford Handbook of Mexican Politics*, ed. Roderic Ai Camp (New York: Oxford University Press, 2012), 722–43. Steven T. Wuhs focuses on business's relationship to political parties in "From the Boardroom to the Chamber: Business Interests and Party Politics in Mexico," *Journal of Politics in Latin America* 2, no. 1 (2010): 121.

The most neglected link in the relationship to the government is that between church and state. The most comprehensive work remains Roderic Ai Camp, *Crossing Swords: Politics and Religion in Mexico* (New York: Oxford University Press, 1997). For a Mexican view, Roberto Blancarte, "Churches, Believers, and Democracy," in *Mexico's Democratic Challenges: Politics, Government and Society*, eds. Andrew Selee and Jacqueline Peschard (Washington, DC: Woodrow Wilson Center Press, 2010), 281–95. Raúl González Schmal provides an excellent analysis since the consolidation began in "The Evolving Relationship Between Church and State," in *Mexican Governance: From a Single-Party Rule to Divided Government*, ed. Armand Peschard-Sverdrup and Sara Rioff (Washington, DC: CSIS Press, 2005), 230–70.

Labor's relationship to the Mexican government has received more attention than the church or the military. Graciela Bensusán and Kevin T. Middlebrook, "Organized Labor and Politics in Mexico," in *The Oxford Handbook of Mexican Politics*, ed. Roderic Ai Camp (New York: Oxford University Press, 2012), 335–66, provides the most recent overview. For numerous changes in the 2000s in a democratic context, see Katrina Burgess, "Mexican Labor at a Crossroads," in *Mexico's Politics and Society in Transition*, ed. Joseph S. Tulchin and Andrew D. Selee (Boulder, CO: Lynne Rienner, 2003), 73–108; and Mark Eric Williams, "Learning the Limits of Power: Privatization and State-Labor Interactions in Mexico," *Latin American Politics and Society* 43, no. 4 (Winter 2001): 91–126. Michal Kohout, "The New Labor Culture and Labor Law Reform in Mexico," *Latin American Perspectives* 35, no. 1 (January 2008): 135–50; and Tina Hilgers, "Mexican Organized Labour at a Critical Juncture," *Innovations: A Journal of Politics* 5 (2004–2005): 17–32, explore the relationship midway through the consolidation era.

The other group whose relationship is analyzed is intellectuals, a more amorphous sector institutionally. Various studies explore the development and contributions of individual intellectual groups, especially writers, but the literature is sparse on the issue of broad intellectual-state relationships. For recent trends under Fox and Calderón, Yvon Grenier's "Octavio Paz and the Changing Role of Intellectuals in Mexico," *Discourse* 23, no. 2 (Spring 2001): 124–43; and Ignacio M. Sánchez Prado, "Claiming Liberalism: Enrique Krauze, *Vuelta*, *Letras Libres*, and the Reconfiguration of the Mexican Intellectual Class," 26, no. 1 (Winter 2010): 47–78, provide helpful insights.

Dissenting groups, in the form of nongovernmental organizations and popular organizations during the democratic transition, are discussed in Paul Lawrence Haber, *Power from Experience, Urban Popular Movements in Late Twentieth-Century Mexico* (University Park: Pennsylvania State University Press, 2006), who provides numerous case studies. A revealing account of urban movements in comparative context is found in Kathleen Bruhn, *Urban Protest in Mexico and Brazil* (Cambridge, UK: Cambridge University Press, 2008). For the democratic consolidation, the best overview can be found in Jonathan Fox, *Accountability Politics: Power and Voice in Rural Mexico* (New York: Oxford University Press, 2007); Mariclaire Acosta, "NGOs and Human Rights," in *The Oxford Handbook of Mexican Politics*; and Cristina Puga, "Associations and Governance in Mexico," a paper presented at the Latin American Studies Association, Las Vegas, Nevada, October 2004. Other valuable scholarship includes: Alberto J. Olvera's excellent "Social Accountability in Mexico: The Civic Alliance Experience," *Enforcing the Rule of Law: Social Accountability in the New Latin American Democracies*, ed. Enrique Peruzzotti and Catalina Smulovitz (Pittsburgh, PA: University of Pittsburgh Press, 2006): 178–212.

Probably no topic on Mexican politics has generated more literature, but few serious, objective analyses, than armed movements. For the EZLN, the most useful historical works include Thomas Benjamin, *A Rich Land, a Poor People: Politics and Society in Modern Chiapas* (Albuquerque: University of New Mexico Press, 1989); Tom Barry, *Zapata's Revenge: Free Trade and the Farm Crisis in Mexico* (Boston: South End Press, 1999); George A. Collier, "The New Politics of Exclusion: Antecedents to the Rebellion in Mexico," *Dialectical Anthropology* 19, no. 1 (May 1994): 1–44. For its impact during the democratic transition, see Richard Stahler-Sholk, "Globalization and Social Movement Resistance: The Zapatista Rebellion in Chiapas, Mexico," *New Political Science* 23, no. 4 (2001): 493–516; and for the democratic consolidation, Niels Barmeyer, *Developing Zapatista Autonomy, Conflict and NGO Involvement in Rebel Chiapas* (Albuquerque: University of New Mexico Press, 2009), is a helpful source.

The EZLN and indigenous movements are analyzed among social movements generally in Shannan Mattiace, "Social and Indigenous Movements in Mexico's Transition to Democracy," in *The Oxford Handbook of Mexican Politics*, cited above. For an insightful and thoughtful view historically through the democratic transition, but focused on rural protests and the 1968 student movement, consult Dolores Trevizo's *Rural Protest and the Making of Democracy in Mexico, 1968–2000* (University Park: Pennsylvania State University, 2011). Two works explore indigenous participation exclusively: Todd A. Eisenstadt's outstanding book, *Politics, Identity, and Mexico's Indigenous Rights Movements*, cited previously, and Martha Singer Sochet, ed., *México: Democracia y participación política indígena* (Mexico: Ediciones Gernika, 2007).

A group that demands increasing analysis during the consolidation of democracy, both at the elite and the mass level, is that of women. The most comprehensive books available to date are Victoria E. Rodríguez's *Women in Contemporary Mexican Politics* (Austin: University of Texas Press, 2003) and her edited volume, *Women's Participation in Mexican Political Life* (Boulder, CO: Lynne Rienner, 1998). For potential political consequences since the democratic consolidation, Rodríguez's "Women, Politics, and Democratic Consolidation in Mexico: Two Steps Forward, One Step Back," in *The Oxford Handbook of Mexican Politics*, is the most recent overview. For the impact of democratization on female leadership, see Roderic Ai Camp, "Has Democracy Favored Women Politicians?," in *The Metamorphosis of Leadership in a Democratic Mexico* (New York: Oxford University Press, 2010), 103–125. For political participation broadly as voters, citizens, or as politicians, see Paul Haber, *Power from Experience: Urban Popular Movements in Late Twentieth-Century Mexico* (University Park: Pennsylvania State University Press, 2007); Roderic Ai Camp and Keith Yanner, "Democracy Across Cultures: Does Gender Make a Difference?" In *Citizenship in Latin America*, ed. Joseph S. Tulchin and Meg Ruthenburg (Boulder, CO: Lynne Rienner, 2006); and Lisa Baldez, "Elected Bodies: The Gender Quota Law for Legislative Candidates in Mexico," *Legislative Studies Quarterly* 29, no. 2 (May 2004): 231–58.

To understand all aspects of the impact of drug trafficking organizations and the government's attempts to reduce their influence, the most complete discussion appears in *Shared Responsibility: U.S.-Mexico Policy Options for Confronting Organized Crime*, ed. Eric L. Olson, David A. Shirk, and Andrew Selee (Washington, DC: Woodrow Wilson International Center for Scholars, 2010). The most comprehensive monograph in English is George Grayson, *Mexico: Narco-Violence and a Failed State?* (New Brunswick, NJ: Transaction Publishers, 2009). For the argument that they have become major political and economic actors respectively, see John Bailey, "Drug Traffickers as Political Actors in Mexico's Nascent Democracy," and William P. Glade, "Economy as Grand-Guignol: The Post-reform Era in Mexico," in *The Oxford Handbook of Mexican Politics*, cited above.

The branches of government and their relationship to the policymaking process have been seriously neglected in the literature on Mexican politics. The most comprehensive studies are Luis Carlos Ugalde, *The Mexican Congress: Old Player, New Power* (Washington, DC: CSIS, 2000); and Alonso Lujambio, *El poder compartido: Un ensayo sobre la democratización mexicana (Con una cierta mirada)* (Mexico: Oceano, 2000). Some of the best work on its inner workings are Jeffrey A. Weldon,

"State Reform in Mexico: Progress and Prospects," in *Mexican Governance, From Single-Party Rule to Divided Government*, ed. Armand B. Peschard-Sverdrup and Sara R. Rioff (Washington, DC: CSIS Press, 2005), 27–107; and the work of Benito Nacif, "The Fall of the Dominant Presidency: Lawmaking under Divided Government in Mexico," in *The Oxford Handbook of Mexican Politics*, ed. Roderic Ai Camp (New York: Oxford University Press, 2012), 234–64. For another assessment of the relationship in the Calderón administration, see María Amparo Casar, "Executive-Legislative Relations: Continuity or Change?," in *Mexico's Democratic Challenges: Politics, Government, and Society*, eds. Andrew Selee and Jacqueline Peschard (Washington, DC: Woodrow Wilson Center Press, 2010): 117–34. The best work on the policymaking process generally is Fabrice Lehoucq et al., *Political Institutions, Policymaking Processes, and Policy Outcomes in Mexico*, (Mexico: CIDE, 2005).

Much new work has appeared on the judicial branch, specifically the Supreme Court. For the democratic transition and early consolidation era, see Pilar Domingo, "Judicial Independence: The Politics of the Supreme Court of Mexico," *Journal of Latin American Studies* 32, no. 3 (October 2000): 705–35; Jodi Finkel, "Supreme Court Decisions on Electoral Rules After Mexico's Judicial Reform: An Empowered Court," *Journal of Latin American Studies* 35, no. 4 (November 2003): 777–99, and Julio Ríos-Figueroa, "Fragmentation of Power and the Emergence of an Effective Judiciary in Mexico, 1994–2002," *Latin American Politics and Society* 49, no. 1 (April 2007): 49. For an evaluation of state-level judicial behavior, see Caroline C. Beer, "Judicial Performance and the Rule of Law in the Mexican States," *Latin American Politics and Society* 48, no. 3 (Fall 2006): 33–50; as well as Lourna M. Márquez-Carrasquillo and David A. Shirk, "State Level Justice Reform Initiatives in Mexico," Trans-Border Institute, University of San Diego, February 25, 2008. For the most up-to-date and original evaluations of the impact of Calderón's legal reforms, see Matthew Ingram and David A. Shirk, *Judicial Reform in Mexico: Toward a New Criminal Justice System*, Special Report, Transborder Institute, University of San Diego, May 2010. For police reform specifically, Daniel M. Sabet, *Police Reform in Mexico: Informal Politics and the Challenge of Institutional Change* (Stanford, CA: Stanford University Press, 2012) is the most comprehensive account.

Political parties continue to attract attention in the literature, but usually in an electoral context. Several outstanding works on the PAN analyze different perspectives on its evolution during the competitive 1990s and 2000s. They include two major studies: Yemile Mizrahi, *From Martyrdom to Power: The Partido Acción Nacional in Mexico* (Notre Dame, IN: University of Notre Dame Press, 2003); and David A. Shirk, *Mexico's New Politics: The PAN and Democratic Change* (Boulder, CO: Lynne Rienner, 2005). The most recent work is Steven T. Wuhs, *Savage Democracy: Institutional Change and Party Development in Mexico* (University Park: Pennsylvania State University Press, 2008), and his "Holding Power: The PAN as Mexico's Incumbent Party," in *The Oxford Handbook of Mexican Politics*, ed. Roderic Ai Camp (New York: Oxford University Press, 2012), 167–86, which brings his book up to the present. The PRD has not received adequate treatment because of its recent origins. The best analytical work remains Kathleen Bruhn, *Taking on Goliath: The Emergence of a New Left Party and the Struggle for Democracy in Mexico* (University Park, PA: Pennsylvania State University Press, 1997). The PRI has not been the subject of a serious analysis since the 1980s. Todd A. Eisenstadt's superb insights into all the parties' political behavior since the consolidation can be found in *Courting Democracy in Mexico: Party Strategies and Electoral Institutions* (Cambridge, UK: Cambridge University Press, 2004).

Analyses of elections, election data, and the 1988, 1994, 2000, and 2006 elections abound. Some of the better work in English can be found in Edgar W. Butler and Jorge A. Bustamante, *Sucesión Presidencial: The 1988 Mexican Presidential Election* (Boulder, CO: Westview Press, 1991), the most detailed examination in English of this benchmark election. For the 1991 elections and comparisons between 1988 and 1991, Jorge Domínguez and James McCann, *Democratizing Mexico: Public Opinion and Electoral Choices* (Baltimore, MD: The Johns Hopkins University Press, 1996). For 1994, see Joseph Klesner, "The 1994 Elections: Manifestation of a Divided Society?," and John Bailey, *The 1994 Mexican Presidential Election Post-Election Report*, Election Studies Series (Washington, DC: CSIS, 1994). The 2000 election is best described in Joseph Klesner, *The 2000 Mexican Presidential and Congressional Elections: Pre-Election Report* (Washington, DC: CSIS, 2000), and the comprehensive analysis of why Fox won is provided in Jorge Domínguez and Chappell Lawson, eds., *Mexico's Pivotal 2000 Elections* (Stanford, CA: Stanford University Press, 2003). The 2006 election has been best analyzed in Jorge I. Domínguez, Chappell Lawson, and Alejandro Moreno, eds., *Consolidating Mexico's Democracy: The 2006 Presidential Campaign in Comparative Perspective* (Baltimore, MD: John Hopkins University Press, 2009). For the consequences of the 2006 elections, see Matthew R. Cleary, "Electoral Competition, Participation, and Government Responsiveness in Mexico," *American Journal of Political Science* 51, no. 2 (April 2007): 283–99; and Chappell Lawson, "How Did We Get Here? Mexican Democracy after the 2006 Elections," *PS: Political Science and Politics* 40, no. 1

(January 2007): 45–48, as well as other contributions to a special series of essays in this issue on the 2006 presidential election.

Political and economic liberalization have received considerable attention since 1988, especially after Salinas's first year in office. A broad, theoretical context can be found in Terry Lynn Karl, "Dilemmas of Democratization in Latin America," *Comparative Politics* 23, no. 1 (October 1990): 1–21. For the early transition see John Bailey and Leopoldo Gómez, "The PRI and Liberalization in Mexico," *Journal of International Affairs* 43 (Winter 1990): 291–312. For the post-2000 period under Fox and Calderón, see the previously cited collections by Tulchin and Selee, *Mexico's Politics and Society in Transition*; Crandall, Paz, and Roett, *Mexico's Democracy at Work*; Rubio and Purcell, *Mexico Under Fox*; Peschard-Sverdrup and Rioff, *Mexican Governance*; Selee and Peschard, *Mexico's Democratic Challenges*; and Claudio A. Holzner, "Mexico: Weak State, Weak Democracy," *The Quality of Democracy in Latin America*.

The economic side, specifically the potential impact of NAFTA, is analyzed by Mark Williams, "The Path of Economic Liberalism," in *The Oxford Handbook of Mexican Politics*; Sidney Weintraub, *Unequal Partners: The United States and Mexico* (Pittsburgh, PA: University of Pittsburgh Press, 2010); M. Angeles Villarreal, "NAFTA and the Mexican Economy," Congressional Research Service, Washington, DC, June 3, 2010; Carol Wise, "Unfulfilled Promise: Economic Convergence under NAFTA," in *Requiem or Revival: the Promise of North American Integration*, eds. Isabel Studer and Carol Wise (Washington, DC: Brookings Institute, 2007), 27–52; Sidney Weintraub, ed., *NAFTA's Impact on North America: The First Decade* (Washington, DC: CSIS Press, 2004); and Ricardo Grinspun and Maxwell Cameron, eds., *The Political Economy of North American Free Trade* (New York: St. Martin's Press, 1993).

For the implications of recent changes in U.S.-Mexican relations as they relate to Mexican domestic political and policy issues, insightful recommendations for the Calderón and Fox eras are provided in: Clare R. Seelke, "U.S.-Mexico Relations: Issues for Congress," Congressional Reference Service, Washington, DC, September 2, 2010; *The United States and Mexico: Towards a Strategic Partnership; A Report of Four Working Groups on U.S.-Mexico Relations* (Washington, DC: Mexico Institute, Woodrow Wilson International Center for Scholars, 2009); Jorge I. Domínguez and Rafael Fernández de Castro, *The United States and Mexico: Between Partnership and Conflict* (New York: Routledge, 2009); Pamela Starr, "U.S.-Mexico Relations," *Hemisphere Focus* 12, no. 2 (January, 2004); *New Horizons in U.S.–Mexico Relations: Recommendations for Policymakers* (Washington, DC: CSIS, 2001). For the Zedillo era, see Jacqueline Mazza,

Don't Disturb the Neighbors: The United States and Democracy in Mexico, 1980–1995 (New York: Routledge, 2001). For Mexican views of the relationship, comparing leaders and ordinary citizens, see Guadalupe González González et. al., *México, las Américas y el mundo 2010: Política exterior; Opinión pública y líderes* (Mexico: CIDE, 2011).

To understand the economic context of the relationship, see Christopher E. Wilson, *Working Together: Economic Ties Between the United States and Mexico* (Washington, DC, Woodrow Wilson Center, 2011); Sidney Weintraub, *Unequal Partners: The United States and Mexico*; Carol Wise, "Unfulfilled Promise: Economic Convergence under NAFTA," in *Requiem or Revival: the Promise of North American Integration*, 27–52; Sidney Weintraub, ed., *NAFTA's Impact on North America: The First Decade* (Washington, DC: CSIS Press, 2004); George Grayson, *The North American Free Trade Agreement: Regional Community and the New World Order* (Lanham, MD: University Press of America, 1995); and Sidney Weintraub's classic, *A Marriage of Convenience: Relations Between Mexico and the United States* (Oxford, UK: Oxford University Press, 1990). To explore the impact of globalization on ordinary Mexicans, a vivid portrait, in their own words, is offered by Judith Hellman, *Mexican Lives*, 2nd ed. (New York: New Press, 1999), and similarly for immigrants, *The World of Mexican Migrants: The Rock and the Hard Place* (New York: New Press, 2008).

For the U.S. views of Mexico and mutual views, CIDAC's study "Como miramos al vecino," Encuesta CODAC-ZOGBY México y Estados Unidos, 2010, is outstanding; as well as *Global Views 2004: Comparing Mexican and American Public Opinion and Foreign Policy* (Chicago: Chicago Council on Foreign Relations, 2004). For Mexican perceptions of the United States, Stephen D. Morris's fascinating book, *Gringolandia: Mexican Identity and Perceptions of the United States* (Lanham, MD: Rowman & Littlefield, 2005), provides numerous insights.

For security concerns related to drugs, see David A. Shirk, "The Drug War in Mexico: Confronting a Shared Threat," Council Special Report, Council on Foreign Relations, New York, March 2011; Agnes Gereben Schaefer, Benjamin Bahney, K. Jack Riley, *Security in Mexico: Implications for U.S. Policy Options* (Santa Monica, CA: Rand Corporation, 2009); Clare Ribando Seelke and Kristin M. Finklea, "U.S.–Mexican Security Cooperation: The Mérida Initiative and Beyond," Congressional Research Service Report for Congress, July 29, 2010. To understand all aspects of the influence of drugs, the best place to begin is Eric H. Olson, Andrew Selee, and David Shirk. eds., *Shared Responsibility: U.S.-Mexico Policy Options for Confronting Organized Crime* (Washington, DC: Woodrow Wilson Center, 2010); and Juan Carlos Garzón's broader insights into regional criminal organizations, *Mafia & Co.: The Criminal Networks in Mexico, Brazil, and Colombia* (Washington, DC: Woodrow Wilson Center, 2008). For other security issues, see Peter Andreas, *Border Games: Policing the U.S.-Mexico Divide* (Ithaca, NY: Cornell University Press, 2000); John Bailey and Roy Goodson, eds., *Organized Crime and Democratic Governability, Mexico and the U.S.-Mexican Borderlands* (Pittsburgh, PA: University of Pittsburgh Press, 2000); and *U.S.-Mexico Border Security and the Evolving Security Relationship: Recommendations for Policymakers* (Washington, DC: CSIS, 2004).

On the issue of corruption, Stephen D. Morris, *Political Corruption in Mexico: The Impact of Democratization* (Boulder, CO: Lynne Rienner, 2009), and his *Corruption and Politics in Contemporary Mexico* (Tuscaloosa: University of Alabama Press, 1991), are the only book-length works to wrestle with this difficult and influential topic in Mexican politics. For a comparative exploration, see Roderic Ai Camp, Charles Davis, and Kenneth Coleman, "The Influence of Party Systems on Citizens' Perceptions of Corruption and Electoral Response in Latin America," *Comparative Political Studies* 37, no. 6 (August 2004): 677–703.

Human rights continue to be neglected from an analytical point of view, but the recent publications of international and national human rights organizations provide some first-hand data on the Mexican situation. Among the most useful are the Amnesty International and Human Rights Watch Americas reports, especially *Human Rights Concerns to Inform the U.S. Department of State's Mérida Initiative Reporting on Mexico*, Amnesty International, May 26, 2010; and the Human Rights Watch reports: *Uniform Impunity: Mexico's Misuse of Military Justice to Prosecute Abuses in Counternarcotics and Public Security Operations* (April 2009); *Lost in Transition: Bold Ambitions, Limited Results for Human Rights under Fox* (2006); and *Systemic Injustice: Torture, "Disappearance," and Extrajudicial Execution in Mexico* (January 1999). The best surveys of Mexican attitudes toward human rights can be found in: "Encuesta nacional sobre discriminación en México: Resultados generales," (Mexico: Consejo Nacional para Prevenir la Discriminación, 2010); Bimsa, "Derechos Humanos: Encuesta nacional trimestral de opinión pública" (November 2004), 1,000 interviews, November 5–10, 2004, +/–3.5 percent margin of error; and the comparative data from the World Values Surveys through 2010, most of which are available online at: www.worldvaluessurvey.org. The most helpful analytical writings are: Mariclaire Acosta, "NGOs and Human Rights," in *The Oxford Handbook of Mexican Politics*; Antonio Torres-Ruíz, "HIV/AIDS and Sexual Minorities in Mexico: A Globalized Struggle for the Protection of Human Rights," *Latin American Research Review* 46, no. 1 (2011): 48–49;

and Jordi Diez, "The Importance of Policy Frames in Contentious Politics: Mexico's 2005 Anti-Homophobia Campaign," *Latin American Research Review* 45, no. 1 (February 2010): 33–54.

The Internet has become an increasingly useful tool for Mexican research, primarily for documentary and bibliographic searches, but also for articles in the media and leading magazines. Many published reports and scholarly articles are now available for downloading in PDF format. For online addresses to important Mexican magazines and newspapers, and to all other sources organized by category, see www.lanic.utexas.edu/la/mexico. For relevant material in the United States media, as well as related articles, see the *New York Times*, specifically the "Americas" tab under "World": http://www.nytimes.com/pages/world/americas/index.html. The most comprehensive Internet source, which can be a useful starting place, are the Spanish language and English Wikipedia websites, which include articles on nearly every nongovernmental organization, governmental agency, and branch of government. For electoral results and parties, see the Federal Electoral Institute, www.ife.org.mx, which directs you to individual party websites. The two best sources for up-to-date articles from the Mexican media are *El Universal*, www.eluniversal.com.mx, the influential, independent Mexico City daily, which can be searched for free for archived materials, and *Reforma*, at www.reforma.com.mx, which cannot be searched without a paid subscription. Many regional newspapers are now archived and can be readily searched on the Internet. *Proceso*, a muckraking political weekly, at www.proceso.com.mx, is a highly useful, critical source. Census statistics are available through www.inegi.gob.mx. Other important economic statistics can be found at the World Bank website. Valuable survey research is available from multiple sources, dozens of which are cited in tables and notes throughout the text. Among the most useful for Mexico specifically, because of their efforts to research similar topics over time, are: www.parametria.com.mx, and www.mitofsky.com.mx. For crime statistics in Mexico, go to www.inegi.org.mx, for extensive data by state from the Instituto Ciudadano de Estudios Sobre la Inseguridad.

Index

Note: page numbers followed by t and m refer to tables and maps respectively.

A

Abortion, as issue, 154–55
Accountability
  and democratization, 19, 311, 314–16
  Fox reforms and, 11
  impediments to in Mexican system, 257–58
  media intimidation by drug cartels and, 286
  public opinion on, 314–15, 315t
Accused, rights of, 204
Acosta, Mariclaire, 169
Advertising, political
  negative, 166, 238–39, 240
  regulation of, 227, 240
Affirmative action. *See* Quota system
African Americans
  in New Spain, 26
  voting rights, 32
Age
  political attitudes and, 103–5
  and voting behavior, 104, 231, 237t, 241t
Aguayo, Sergio, 168
Aguilar Camín, Héctor, 47, 163
AIDS, public opinion on, 313, 313t
Alamo, 49
Alemán, Miguel, 118–19, 120t, 303t
Alianza Cívica. See Civic Alliance
Alliance for Change, 232
Almond, Gabriel, 59, 91
Amalistas faction of PRD, 251
AmericasBarometer, 68
Amigos de Fox. *See* Friends of Fox
AMIS. *See* Mexican Insurance Association
Amnesty International, 311–12
Amparo writ, 207
Anahuac University, 133
Anti-foreignism, 266
Anti-Reelectionist Party, 45
Argentina
  and civilian control of military, 17
  crime in, 64
  political tolerance in, 106
  religious intolerance in, 91
  women's education in, 125
Arizona
  immigration laws, 267, 283, 284, 286, 288
  Mexican-descent residents of, 282
  trade with Mexico, 280
Armendáriz, Antonio, 118
Art, and renaissance of 1920s, 46
Aspe, Pedro, 214n8
Assassinations
  of Colosio, 64–65, 173, 226, 308

  by drug cartels, 286
  of journalists, 164–65, 166
  of Madero, 50
  of Obregón, 48
  of Ochoa, 169
Atheism, and political attitudes, 94
Atlacomulco, and political recruitment, 117–18
Attorney General of the Republic
  as cabinet agency, 191, 192
  under Fox, 148–49
  legal reforms and, 207
Audiencia, 32
Authentic Party of the Mexican Revolution (PARM), 225t
Authoritarianism
  age-related attitudes toward, 103
  in Chinese system, 3, 7
  under Díaz, 40
  dinosaurs (los dinos) and, 135
  and law, lack of respect for, 205
  in Mexican political tradition, 1–2, 10, 42–43
  of military culture, as danger, 150
  ongoing influence of, 11, 14–15, 20
  ongoing support for, 78, 78t
  and politics of 19th century, 35, 36
  regional attitudes toward, 78, 78t
  Spanish colonialism and, 32, 52
Autonomous Technological Institute of Mexico (ITAM), 120, 133, 133t, 134, 162
Avila Camacho, Manuel, 120t
Ayuntamientos, 25, 32
Aztec empire, 27

B

Baja California
  and presidential election of 2000, 228
  PRI in, 228
  U.S. designs on, 50
Bajío, political attitudes in, 92, 92t
Baldez, Lisa, 99
Banco Unión, 206
Bankers Club, 157
Bank of Mexico, 119, 137, 192
Banks, nationalization of, 194
Baptist religion, 94
Barracca, Steven, 20
Barreda, Gabino, 37
Basáñez, Miguel, 103
Beer, Caroline, 195
Belize, corruption in, 76
Birthplace, political recruitment and, 122, 124
Boidi, María Fernanda, 107

341